CALIFORNIA

Central Coast

- **Santa Barbara County**
- **San Luis Obispo County**
- **Ventura County**

Automobile Club of Southern California

Although information presented in this publication has been carefully researched and was as accurate as possible at press time, the Automobile Club of Southern California is not responsible for any changes or errors which may occur. The Automobile Club of Southern California is not responsible for the performance of any agency or service mentioned in this publication. It is wise to verify information immediately prior to your visit.

Only attractions or establishments that are approved by an Automobile Club of Southern California field representative may advertise. The purchase of advertising, however, has no effect on inspections and evaluations. Advertisements provide the reader with additional information which may be useful in selecting what to see and where to stay.

Additional advertisements (excluding attractions and establishments) for travel-related services may also be included in ACSC publications. Acceptance of these advertisements does not imply endorsement by ACSC.

For-sale edition distributed by authorized distributors only.

ISBN: 1-56413-309-5
Printed in the United States of America

Contents

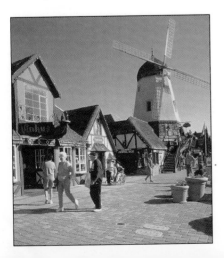

CENTRAL COAST

It's California's Central Coast, so of course there are beaches, and waves breaking against rocky cliffs. There are towns that date back a couple of hundred years, so you're sure to find antique shops and historic buildings. The climate is just right for growing things, so naturally there are wineries and citrus groves. There also happens to be a national park completely surrounded by water, an archaeological dig in the middle of a town, and a fantastic castle on a hill. There are trout in mountain streams and sea lions on offshore rocks; tigers in cages and butterflies in trees; fragile wildflowers and sturdy oak trees.

In addition to these intriguing attributes, the beauty of the land, the relaxed pace and the friendly people have combined to make the Central Coast one of the state's most popular areas to visit. In keeping with that popularity, this book has been compiled as a visitors' reference guide. It contains a wealth of information about points of interest, annual events, recreational activities and accommodations, as well as county maps and detailed maps of popular destinations.

Traveling south to north, **Ventura County** has first geographical place. With hills and mountains as a backdrop and facing the Santa Barbara Channel to the south, Ventura County's coastal plain supports farmland, communities, naval bases and light industry. Offshore lies Channel Islands National Park. Inland are wonderfully scenic areas such as Lake Casitas and the charming communities of Ojai and Santa Paula. The county's Conejo and Simi valleys lie on inland plateaus, where in any direction there are views of rolling hills or mountain peaks.

West of Ventura County is **Santa Barbara County.** Civilization is mostly clustered along a 60-mile portion of the coastline that faces south. Separating this coastal strip from inland portions of the county are the rugged Santa Ynez Mountains, which are within Los Padres National Forest. The coastal portion facing west is occupied largely by Vandenberg Air Force Base.

A craggy coastline is part of Montaña de Oro State Park.

Completed in 1894, this mansion near Santa Paula was the culmination of George Washington Faulkner's dream of "a beautiful home."

Charming little towns abound: Arroyo Grande, Pismo Beach, Cambria, Paso Robles, Atascadero. The city of San Luis Obispo began as a mission village and is now home to a major university. The county's spectacular shoreline offers popular dunes, beaches, landmarks and rugged scenery. The northeast portion of the county is known for its horse ranches, farms and wineries.

There are many roads in the backcountry that lead to **Los Padres National Forest.** Covering nearly half of Ventura County and vast areas of Santa Barbara and San Luis Obispo counties, Los Padres not only delights with wonderful mountain and valley views, but offers hiking, camping, fishing and—when the weather cooperates—skiing.

Northwest of Santa Barbara, bordered by the Santa Ynez and San Rafael mountains, the Santa Ynez Valley encompasses gently rolling green or golden hills; side roads lead to cattle ranches, horse farms, wineries, and citrus groves and croplands. Solvang, a Danish-style village famous for shops and pastries, also lies in this valley. Lompoc Valley, lying between the Santa Ynez Mountains and the Purísima Hills, has two extremes: a military facility for space launches and an old Spanish mission. Flat, fertile Santa Maria Valley extends from the foothills of the Sierra Madre Mountains to the sand dunes bordering the Pacific Ocean.

Towns, missions, lakes, a university, a zoo, military bases and a castle comprise **San Luis Obispo County**.

Local residents bill Carpinteria State Beach as "The World's Safest Beach."

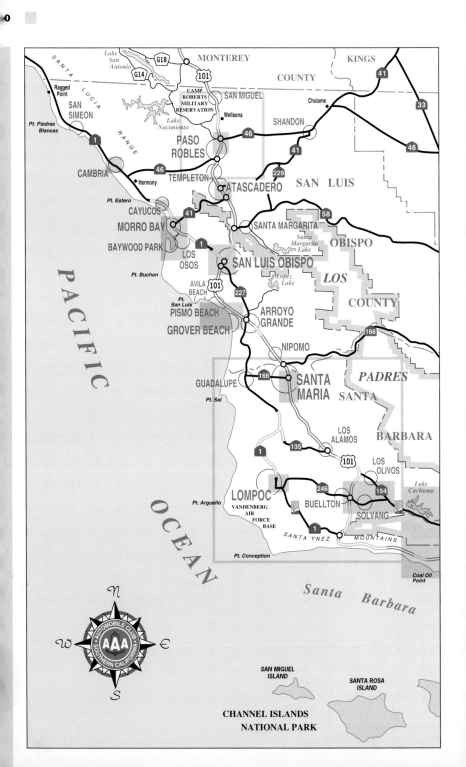

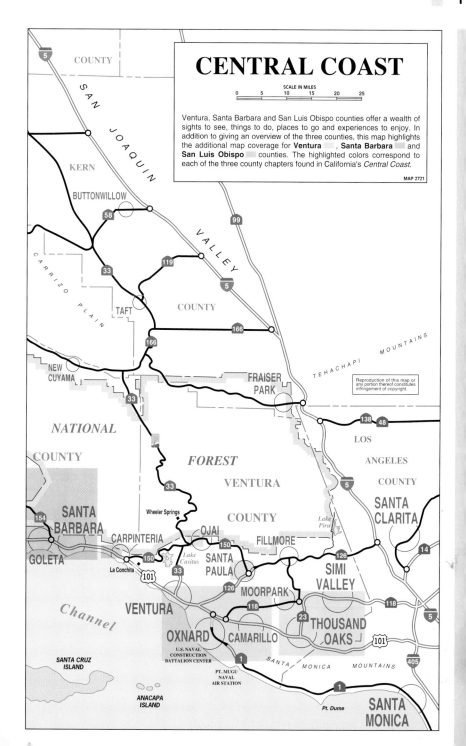

CENTRAL COAST

SCALE IN MILES

0   5   10   15   20   25

Ventura, Santa Barbara and San Luis Obispo counties offer a wealth of sights to see, things to do, places to go and experiences to enjoy. In addition to giving an overview of the three counties, this map highlights the additional map coverage for **Ventura** , **Santa Barbara** and **San Luis Obispo** counties. The highlighted colors correspond to each of the three county chapters found in California's *Central Coast*.

MAP 2721

COUNTY

SAN JOAQUIN

KERN

BUTTONWILLOW

58

99

VALLEY

CARRIZO PLAIN

33

119

5

TAFT

COUNTY

166

166

NEW CUYAMA

TEHACHAPI MOUNTAINS

FRAISER PARK

33

138 48

LOS

NATIONAL

COUNTY

FOREST

ANGELES

COUNTY

VENTURA

33

5

SANTA CLARITA

154

SANTA BARBARA

Wheeler Springs

COUNTY

Lake Piru

GOLETA

CARPINTERIA

OJAI

150

FILLMORE

126

14

150

Lake Casitas

SANTA PAULA

126

SIMI VALLEY

118

La Conchita

101

33

MOORPARK

118

5

Channel

VENTURA

126

23

THOUSAND OAKS

101

OXNARD

118

CAMARILLO

U.S. NAVAL CONSTRUCTION BATTALION CENTER

1

SANTA MONICA MOUNTAINS

405

SANTA CRUZ ISLAND

PT. MUGU NAVAL AIR STATION

ANACAPA ISLAND

Pt. Dume

1

SANTA MONICA

▼ *Showing The Way*

To help you find your way around the Central Coast, the Automobile Club of Southern California publishes a number of comprehensive maps, guides and books covering the area. For a statewide overview, there's the *California* map. Each county—Ventura, Santa Barbara and San Luis Obispo, has its own *Explore!* map, which includes brief descriptions of points of interest and extensive recreational information. Detailed street maps can be found on *Cities of Ventura County*, *Cities of Santa Barbara County* and *Cities of San Luis Obispo County*. Three other Auto Club publications that include locations in the Central Coast are *Bed & Breakfast-Southern California*, *California Winery Tours* and *Central and Southern California Golf Courses*. All of these handy reference guides are available in selected bookstores throughout Southern California, and are also available to Auto Club members at district offices.

Geography

Ventura and Santa Barbara counties have much the same geographical look, in that land features in the two counties range from sky-high mountain peaks to dramatically eroded canyons to flat grasslands to rocky and sandy seashores. Cutting west to east through both counties, the Transverse Ranges began more than 500,000 years ago as a great accumulation of marine sediment, then underwent enormous pressures and upheavals, folding and fracturing. Most of the mountains and valleys were formed in this way; the Santa Ynez Mountains and Santa Ynez Valley, Topatopa Mountains and the Ojai Valley come to mind. Valley floors and floodplains long ago cut by rivers are, in many places, covered with rich alluvial soil; the Oxnard Plain and the Santa Maria Valley are good examples.

San Luis Obispo County is likewise a land of widely varying terrain. From US 101 and SR 1 a portion of the county's diverse geologic history can be seen in the forms of volcanic rock or sand dunes. Some of the most obvious geological formations, seven volcanic peaks, stretch from San Luis Obispo to Morro Bay, culminating at Morro Rock. These peaks, formed about 50 million years ago, served as vents for eruptions of volcanoes that have long since eroded away.

In the eastern portion of the county along the Carrizo Plain, clear evidence exists of the San Andreas Fault, the world's best-known and most-studied earthquake fault. This 700-mile-long fracture, which has played a major role in shaping all of California, marks the point in the earth's crust where two land masses or plates meet. (Because the western plate moves northwest about two inches each year, the town of San Luis Obispo once sat about 250 miles southeast of its present location.)

Climate

Ventura and Santa Barbara coastal areas enjoy a temperate climate year round, with sunshine nearly 75

Sunset spangles the waters of Morro Bay.

percent of the year. The towns of Ventura and Santa Barbara have a summer temperature range of about 55 to 75 degrees and in winter 45 to 65 degrees. Santa Maria, while a little cooler in winter, averages about the same temperatures in summer.

Inland valleys generally range from a winter low of 40 degrees to a 75-degree high in the summer, with the Ojai and Santa Paula areas experiencing temperatures into the high 80s on some summer days. Happily for vacationers, but worrisome for growers and ranchers, is a low incidence of rain throughout these two counties. Humidity is low, and winter rainfall is seldom more than 18 inches.

San Luis Obispo County is roughly bisected from north to south by the Santa Lucia Range, which forms a barrier between relatively wet coastal and dry inland regions. The coastline is noted for its year-round mild weather and dense seasonal fog. The northern inland region, however, fosters extremes of climate found nowhere else in the county: temperatures in Atascadero can range from a chilly 20 degrees on the coldest winter mornings to a sizzling 115 degrees on summer's warmest afternoons.

The southern half of the county, including the town of San Luis Obispo, features sunshine about 75 percent of the year, especially from late April through October. Daytime temperatures average 60 to 70 degrees the year round. Rainfall in the county averages 22 inches, most of which occurs during the winter.

Los Padres National Forest varies in altitude from well under 1000 feet near the coast to inland mountain peaks that sometimes rise to over 8000 feet, and the weather varies accordingly.

Oso Flaco Lake, plant life and, of course, sand dunes are all part of Pismo Dunes Preserve.

Getting back into the heavily forested areas or higher elevations generally means that temperatures will be at least a few degrees cooler year round than the surrounding terrain. In the winter, higher elevations can experience snow and freezing temperatures, while a summer high near the coast can be in the 80s.

In spring the Central Coast is sprinkled with magenta ice plant, golden poppies and blue lupine.

Plants And Animals

Among the most noticeable growing things in the valleys and on the hillsides of the Central Coast are graceful oak trees, gathered in small groves or standing majestically alone. Their branches and leaves often furnish shade for cattle and horses, and their acorns provide food for birds and squirrels. The three most common oaks are the valley, coast live and scrub. A deciduous valley oak is generally 40 to 75 feet high, with a dark brown or ash-gray bark. The coast live oak, an evergreen, attains a height just under 70 feet, and has bark resembling birch, while the evergreen scrub oak, with its gray-brown bark, rarely reaches over eight feet.

While the oak is native to the Central Coast and was around thousands of years ago, a highly visible newcomer to the Central Coast is the eucalyptus tree, sometimes reaching as high as 75 feet and often clad in a smooth, cream-colored bark. Imported from Australia in the 19th century, there are now upwards of 30 varieties of eucalyptus in Southern California serving as windbreaks or ornamental and shade trees.

Pods of some eucalyptus species have a pungent aroma reminiscent of certain mentholated ointments.

As ubiquitous as oak and eucalyptus in valleys and on hillsides is the chaparral in the foothills and mountains. "Chaparral" is something of a catch-all term for a plant community of shrubs and dwarf trees, some of which are adorned with tiny blossoms in spring. Then too, the Indian pink exhibits a bright red flower on a slender stem, while the ceanothus puts out tiny flowers on a large shrub. With its varying shades of blue and lavender, ceanothus is often referred to as "wild lilac."

Spring also is the time that California's state flower, the golden poppy, makes its bright orange appearance in the Central Coast valleys; four petals form a flower from one to three inches broad. In the coastal foothills and inland valleys, the yucca tree's cream-colored, lily-like flowers appear on stalks that sometimes attain five or six feet in height. The coast sand dunes dress themselves in blue sand verbena or the reddish-purple beach sand verbena.

The plateaus and cliffs of the Channel Islands are host to such native plant life as wild grasses, Catherine's lace, coreopsis, mallow and goldfield. A scuba dive in island waters reveals a colorful array of aquatic plants and beautiful fish.

Turning from flora to fauna, it may be safe to say that among the more interesting birds and mammals along the Central Coast are those found in and around the coastal waters. Gray whales migrate through California seas from December through March; take a whale-watching trip for a close-up view. Sea lions and harbor seals like to haul out on offshore rocks, particularly off San Luis Obispo County, with the waters around Morro Bay also playing host to the playful sea otter. Channel Islands National Park harbors myriad seals and sea lions (pinnipeds) and various ocean birds that include the brown pelican and cormorant. Sea gulls, particularly the imposing western gull, seem to think they own the piers up and down the coast. Marshy areas are stopovers for a variety of migrating water fowl, and the Morro Bay estuary is tops in the Audubon Society's Christmas bird count.

Inland, Los Padres National Forest is the best place for observing wildlife. Falcons and hawks soar high overhead, and quail scurry along the forest floor.

Elephant seals like to haul out on rocky shores.

Near dawn or sunset deer often feed in meadows, and throughout the day squirrels and rabbits dash about in almost any part of the forest. Forest residents that appear much less often are mountain lions and black bears.

There are even interesting insects along the Central Coast! From November through February vivid orange and black monarch butterflies cluster in the pine and eucalyptus groves around Pismo Beach.

Economy

Throughout the Central Coast there's plenty of urban growth; at the same time farmland remains, contributing to both a peaceful landscape and a vibrant economy. Along the coast, ocean breezes and occasional fog combine with rich soil to create an abundance of agricultural and horticultural products. It's a good place for growing vegetables, strawberries, avocados, citrus fruit and flowers; there's even a banana plantation.

In Santa Barbara and San Luis Obispo counties the interior valleys garner some ocean winds, but more importantly, the warm afternoon sunshine and cool evening breezes account for the growth of grapes and the subsequent emergence of these regions as major California wine producers.

Much of Ventura County's interior valleys is devoted to citrus fruit, particularly in the Ojai and Santa Paula areas. Lemons are the most important crop, with almost half the lemons grown in the United States coming from Ventura County.

There are other riches in the soil of the Central Coast. Beneath the surface of Ventura and Santa Barbara counties,

Agriculture and oil: two important components of Ventura County's economy.

particularly Ventura, lie great pools of "black gold," and oil pumpers have risen in the valleys, along the coast and offshore.

Aside from farms, orchards, vineyards and oil wells, grass-covered hills support horse ranches and herds of cattle. Other boosts to the Central Coast economy include tourism, light industry, military installations, state institutions and universities.

Activities For Children

Throughout the Central Coast there are plenty of sights and activities that appeal to children, as well as their adult companions. A boat trip out to Channel Islands National Park from the Ventura harbor will delight children of all ages, and chances are that everyone will enjoy a cruise of Ventura Harbor from Ventura Harbor Village. Farther up the coast, there's a shipboard tour of Morro Bay on *Tiger's Folly* or a cruise along the coast on a Central Coastal Cruises' ship. Many boating establishments offer whale-watching trips, usually from December through February.

The Sea Center on Stearns Wharf in Santa Barbara has a touch tank where visitors can get personally acquainted with sea life native to the Santa Barbara Channel. An entirely different type of aquatic life can be observed at the Fillmore Fish Hatchery, east of Fillmore. Over two million rainbow trout are raised here from eggs to catchable size, and a vending machine allows visitors to feed these finny friends.

If the kids want to catch fish, they can try their luck at two Santa Barbara County fishing ponds. One is located at River Park in Lompoc and the other at Waller County Park in Santa Maria. (The latter also offers pony rides.) In Simi Valley a lake at Rancho Simi Community Park also gives children a chance to try their fishing skills. Let the whole family take a hike along trails in scenic areas like Los Padres National Forest, Montaña de Oro State Beach or Lopez Lake.

For the budding naturalists, a trip to Pismo Beach is in order anytime from late November through March. That's when thousands of migrating monarch butterflies cluster on eucalyptus and Monterey pines that are found just south of the North Beach campground.

If the small fry prefer animals in zoos, visit the nearly 500 animals from around the world at the Santa Barbara Zoological Gardens in Santa Barbara. The zoo also has picnic grounds, a small carousel and a miniature train that gives riders glimpses of the adjacent coast and bird refuge. Another good bet is the smaller Charles Paddock Zoo in Atascadero, home to bears, monkeys, meerkats, exotic birds and a pair of Bengal tigers. The zoo is located in a park that also boasts a lake and picnic areas.

There are plenty of outdoor family activities available along the Central Coast: bicycling, hiking, fishing and

Inhabitants of the lake at Rancho Simi Park enjoy handouts.

swimming, to name a few. During warm weather, beaches and inland lakes are popular destinations for camping or day use. Daily lifeguard service is provided at most beaches during the summer months and on weekends the rest of the year. Mustang Water Slide and Hot Springs at Lake Lopez is open late April to early June and mid-September to early October.

Just hanging out at the Charles Paddock Zoo, waiting for feeding time.

All year round there are two children's museums that give the kids plenty to do. At the Gull Wings Children's Museum in Oxnard they can go from putting on a puppet show to making giant bubbles to learning about fossils and minerals. The Children's Museum in San Luis Obispo has lots of lively hands-on exhibits and "I can do it myself" activities.

The colorful history of the Central Coast comes alive at several "grown-up" museums and historic sites that kids also enjoy. The Parks-Janeway Carriage House in Santa Ynez showcases one of the West's finest collections of horse-drawn vehicles, and kids will learn what transportation was like before the automobile. On the eastern edge of Arroyo Grande at Santa Manuela School kids can see what a school looked like in their great-grandparents' day, ink wells and all.

El Paso de Robles Area Pioneer Museum in Paso Robles, San Luis Obispo County Historical Museum in San Luis Obispo and Ventura County Museum of

History & Art in Ventura have all sorts of interesting things that go back to the early days of the Central Coast and provide an introduction to a very different way of life.

Elementary school-age children who live in California learn about the Spanish missions in school, and the two missions which provide perhaps the best depictions of 18th-century mission life are Mission Santa Barbara in Santa Barbara and La Purísima Mission just outside Lompoc.

Three unique, child-friendly places are worth a visit. The Seaside Banana Garden, north of Ventura, will prove to the kids that bananas don't grow in supermarkets. The Santa Claus area near Carpinteria is the place where a letter can be mailed and postmarked "Santa Claus"— especially timely when mailed in December. The Apple Farm Millhouse is located near downtown San Luis Obispo. It's a working replica of a water-powered mill, with all the requisite gears, shafts, pulleys and belts.

At various times of the year there are parades and festivals that kids will enjoy, including exciting Fourth of July celebrations and special Christmas festivities.

Performing Arts

Diverse entertainment can be found throughout the Central Coast as drama, music and dance occupy the stages of large and small theaters. Names and telephone numbers are listed under the appropriate city in the county chapters. For additional information, consult local newspapers.

The Ventura County Symphony offers an annual season of classical music at the Oxnard Civic Auditorium and the Thousand Oaks Civic Arts Plaza. Summertime in Ojai is drama and music time, with Libbey Park the scene of two well-attended annual events: a Shakespeare festival and a contemporary classical music series. Summer is also the season for outdoor concerts in Camarillo's Constitution Park and Conejo Community Park in Thousand Oaks.

The Civic Arts Plaza, an attractive theater complex in Thousand Oaks, presents dance, drama and music throughout the year. Music Academy of the West, Santa Barbara City College, Westmont College and the University of California at Santa Barbara all present high-caliber music and drama programs on their campuses.

Rock music devotees can enjoy Ventura Concert Theatre in the city of Ventura, and Santa Barbara County Bowl is an outdoor venue that presents pop music groups April through November.

In addition to San Luis Obispo County's annual Mozart Festival, a major classical music offering, there is also the San Luis Obispo County Symphony Orchestra. Musical and dramatic programs are offered throughout

The theater begun in 1873 by José Lobero is still going strong in Santa Barbara.

the year at Cal Poly San Luis Obispo and Cuesta College.

Live dramatic performance venues in Ventura County include the Plaza Players at the Livery Arts Center in Ventura. The Conejo Players Theatre in Thousand Oaks presents good calibre community theater entertainment, while the Santa Paula Theatre Center offers classic drama, modern comedy and children's theater. Presentations at the Magnificent Moorpark Melodrama & Vaudeville Company combine both amateur and professional talent.

In Santa Barbara, the Alhecama and Granada theatres host dramas and musicals respectively. Live entertainment is also presented in Santa Barbara's Lobero Theatre and Arlington Center for the Performing Arts.

The Pacific Conservatory of the Performing Arts (PCPA) presents a year-round series of music and drama in repertory at the Marian Performing Arts Center on the campus of Allan Hancock College in Santa Maria and in Solvang at the outdoor Solvang Festival Theater.

Among community theater groups in San Luis Obispo County are the San Luis Obispo Little Theatre in San Luis Obispo, The Great American Melodrama and Vaudeville in Oceano, the Pewter Plough Playhouse in Cambria and the Pioneer Players in Paso Robles.

For those who enjoy meals with their entertainment, the Santa Barbara area has two dinner theaters: Circle Bar B and Starlight Entertainment.

Shopping

Throughout the Central Coast it's easy to shop 'til you drop, whether your taste runs to cavernous shopping malls or cozy antique shops or something in

between. There are 10 major shopping complexes featuring large department stores and numerous retail outlets. Thousand Oaks has **The Oaks Mall** on Hillcrest Drive east of Moorpark Road, while Simi Valley enjoys **Simi Valley Shopping Center** at Sycamore Drive and Cochran Street. Ventura offers **Buenaventura Plaza** at Main Street and Mills Road. **The Esplanade** in Oxnard stands at Vineyard Street and Esplanade Drive. Santa Barbara has **La Cumbre Plaza** at State Street and La Cumbre Road, and **Paseo Nuevo**, downtown on State Street, between Ortega and Canon Perdido streets. In Santa Maria there's **Santa Maria Town Center** at Broadway and Main Street, as well as **Santa Maria Shopping Center** at Broadway and Stowell Road. Two adjacent shopping malls, open-air **Madonna Shopping Plaza** and the enclosed **Central Coast Plaza**, lie south of downtown San Luis Obispo at Madonna Road, just west of US 101.

Factory outlet malls are springing up all along the highways. As this book goes to press there are at least three in the Central Coast, and more may be opening even as you read this. In Oxnard off Gonzales Road near Rice Avenue, the **Oxnard Factory Outlet** has dozens of shops with an architectural theme that reflects the town's citrus-growing, packing-shed history. Pismo Beach offers a long row of shops in the **Pismo Beach Factory Outlet Mall**, along Five Cities Drive on the south side of US 101 just west of 4th Street. The Spanish-mission themed **Atascadero Factory Outlets** is located in Atascadero at El Camino Real and Del Rio Road.

Antique collectors and browsers can spend hours going in and out of all the shops along **Ventura's Main Street**, west of Seaward Avenue; charming antique and collectible shops can also be found in the much smaller town of **Santa Paula**. The little town of **Los Alamos** and shops along **Brinkerhoff Avenue** in Santa Barbara are noted for antiques, while **Arroyo Grande Village** and Templeton's **Vineyard Antique Mall** also offer an intriguing assortment of elderly items.

Two picturesque shopping arcades enliven State Street in downtown Santa Barbara: **El Arcada** at Figueroa Street and **El Paseo** near De La Guerra Street. **East and West villages** in Cambria feature specialty and one-of-a-kind shops. In the Danish-American town of **Solvang** you'll find a wide assortment of merchandise with an emphasis on imported Danish handicrafts and baked goods, and factory outlet stores can be found here and there. Harbor and marine areas offer tourist-oriented shopping with a nautical theme. **Ventura Harbor Village** in Ventura includes 40 shops, restaurants and a carousel, and Oxnard's **Fisherman's Wharf** offers specialty shops, restaurants and a maritime museum. Merchandise in the shops on Santa Barbara's **Stearns Wharf** range from post cards to art works.

Art fanciers rejoice in the large selection of locally produced works sold at several galleries in Santa Barbara and in Ojai. The city of Santa Barbara hosts the **Arts and Crafts Show** every Sunday, weather permitting, along Cabrillo Boulevard east from State Street. The small town of **Los Olivos** is a haven for western-style artists, and several art galleries in the town sell their works.

In Ojai the shops along **The Arcade** are known for their one-of-a-kind jewelry and other works of art, much of which is locally handcrafted. It's often possible to visit the studios of some of the Ojai area artists, watch them work and purchase original paintings, sketches or sculpture.

Art galleries, restaurants and a variety of specialty shops await visitors to the pleasant San Luis Obispo County community of Cambria.

Santa Barbara's State Street provides a pleasant atmosphere for strolling, shopping and dining.

After all that, if you're still looking for a special something, don't forget that virtually every museum along the way— historic, art or special interest—has a shop with attractive, unique merchandise just right for keeping or giving.

CAMINO REAL
SION SANTA BARBARA
FOUNDED DECEMBER 3 1786
SION SAN BUENA VENTURA 30
SION SANTA INEZ 48
AUTO CLUB OF SO. CAL.

History

Native American Period

The history of California's Central Coast begins with an indigenous people whose story can be read only in fragmented artifacts, foreign explorers' narratives and painted symbols on hidden rocks and cave walls. Yet these were a sturdy, vibrant people who established villages near the coast, in the foothills and valleys, and lived in harmony with the sea and land for nearly 10,000 years.

Evidence from the archaeological sites in San Luis Obispo County indicates that people inhabited some canyons and beaches there as early as 7000 B.C. (or 4000 years before the Egyptian pyramids were built). Not much is known about this group, called the Oak Grove people, except that they had a diet of nuts, seeds and berries, and left behind *metates* (meh-tah´-tehs) or grinding holes used in preparing their food.

Much more is known about the Chumash, who came to the Central Coast about 6000 B.C. (*Chumash* is an English term based most likely on the Indian name *Mi-tcu´-mac*.) Archaeologists have discovered that as the final stages of prehistory evolved, numerous Chumash villages appeared along the coast, in the inland valleys and on the Santa Barbara Channel islands. By the 16th century, about 25,000 Chumash lived along the coast between what became Malibu and Cambria, according to accounts by European explorers who visited California.

Chumash houses, probably from 12 to 20 feet in diameter, were made of willow poles lashed together at the center to form a dome shape. Tule (too´ le) (reeds growing wild in marshy areas) covered the willow structures, with a hole left at the top for smoke to escape from a circular fire pit. Food sources from the nearby hills and valleys were provided by acorns and grasses and small mammals, such as rabbits.

Throughout the Central Coast, tribes were organized into several villages, many of them clusters of huts on level, sheltered sites close to fresh water. (The obvious advantages of this kind of site also appealed to the European settlers who came later.) Village sites that were established near the ocean provided a livelihood based on fishing and using shells for ornamental and trading purposes. Beyond day-to-day demands, the life of the Chumash included music, dancing and games. Their daily rituals and special ceremonies often reflected a caste system that placed shamans and astronomers in the upper class.

The Chumash were particularly skilled in basketry and woodworking; the latter included canoes which they fashioned of planks. The craft, made to withstand the rough waters of the open sea, were worked with tools of shell and flint and caulked with the tar (asphaltum) that came from seashore and inland deposits. The tar or *pismu* used to seal the canoe seams eventually lent its name to Pismo Beach.

Relics of early Chumash handicrafts, such as baskets, wooden tools and stone vessels, have been unearthed

---

Father Serra stands beside a symbolic mission bell and sign marking "The Royal Highway."

throughout the Central Coast. More than a thousand known archaeological sites exist, with perhaps a few thousand more still to be discovered. (Anyone who finds artifacts is asked to leave them as they are and report their location to a local historical museum.)

Almost every Central Coast museum displays some Chumash relics—Albinger Archaeological Museum in Ventura and Santa Barbara Museum of Natural History are among the most notable. Paintings on the rock walls of several mountain caves reflect Chumash culture and religion; some pictographs on Painted Rock in the Carrizo Plain date back a thousand years.

It is worth noting that since the beginning of the 20th century, the Chumash population—albeit of mixed blood—has rebounded, and there are now approximately 3000 people of Chumash ancestry living throughout the United States; the 126-acre Santa Ynez Chumash Indian Reservation, 33 miles northwest of Santa Barbara, supports a population of about 300.

The various peoples who first occupied California's Central Coast believed that the bounty of land and sea was part of a communal birthright, not to be individually owned, but carefully used and preserved. Ultimately there came a race with completely different concepts of rights and property, and the forceful persuasion to back up their ideas. Force was not really necessary—time and lack of immunity to the white man's diseases took their toll, drastically diminishing the native population.

In the 16th century, Spain, already a power in Mexico and looking northward to increase her empire, commissioned the Portuguese explorer Juan Rodríguez Cabrillo to find the fabled waterway connecting the Atlantic and Pacific oceans. Therefore, the first Europeans to see California's Central Coast sailed with Cabrillo in two small ships along the California coast in the winter of 1542-43, mapping the shoreline and claiming the land for Spain.

In October 1542 they reached Catalina Island and continued northwest, traveling along the Santa Barbara Channel. It is possible that they may have come ashore near what is now the city of Ventura. In any case, Cabrillo made note of the friendly natives in their well-crafted canoes caulked with tar, then continued northward. This was to be Cabrillo's last voyage, for in January 1543 he died of complications from a broken bone. Although his successor sailed as far as Oregon, no east-west passage was sighted, nor did they find a large, safe port along the West Coast.

During the following 50 years Spain turned its attention to other national interests and ignored California. But as other countries became eager for exploration and settlement, it became necessary to protect naval and trade interests in Mexico and Central America (New Spain). To that end, Spain sent a seafaring merchant, Sebastián Vizcaíno, to the California coast to search out suitable ports and claim them for Spain.

In May 5, 1602, Vizcaíno headed a Spanish expedition that left Acapulco, Mexico, with three ships, a crew of 200, an expert cartographer and three Carmelite friars. Within seven months they reached the Central Coast, and on December 4, 1602, Vizcaíno gave the Santa Barbara Channel its name, for that was the feast day of the legendary third-century martyr Saint Barbara. Although the expedition's discoveries and descriptions reached as far as Northern California, Spain's politics and ambitions soon changed, and none of the data was utilized. Then lengthy, expensive wars ensued, and it was more than 150 years before Spain once more turned her attention to Alta (Upper) California.

Mission Period

By 1768 Charles III of Spain had decided that the time was ripe to colonize Alta California and protect the crown's interests from the incursion of other nations. Plans drawn up in Mexico decreed that the native peoples in California should become Christians and colonists through the establishment of missions. At the same time *presidios* (fortresses) would enforce Spain's authority and provide protection for the missions' inhabitants.

Between January and May 1769, three ships and two land contingents, all under the command of Capitán Gaspar de Portolá, left Mexico bound for Alta California. The company included two Franciscan friars: Father Junípero Serra, who was to lay the groundwork for the missions, and Father Juan Crespí, appointed as diarist for the journeys.

In July 1769 Portolá arrived in San Diego, in command of 63 men and nearly 200 horses and cattle. From there the expedition set out overland to establish a land route northward along the coast. An important goal was to find the natural harbor which had been described in reports from earlier ocean expeditions. The group averaged 8 to 10 miles a day, clearing a trail for future travelers and bestowing place names, many still in use.

Meanwhile in San Diego, Father Serra had a small, crude chapel built and raised a cross to mark a site for the first mission in Alta California. The Mission

San Diego de Alcalá originally stood on Presidio Hill overlooking San Diego Bay and five years later was moved to its present location, about six miles east, near the San Diego River.

In August 1769, Portolá and his men reached what is now Ventura County. For three successive nights they camped close to Indian villages that lay near what became Fillmore, Santa Paula and Saticoy. On August 14, the party stopped near the site of the city of Ventura; Crespí named the village La Asunsión de Nuestra Señora (The Ascension of our Lady), expressing hope that it would become the site of a good mission. Unfortunately, supply problems, then political and military considerations, delayed for years the founding of a mission at this location.

On September 2, the party reached what is now San Luis Obispo County and camped at a lake surrounded by sand dunes. Along with numerous snakes, they found grizzly bears, one of which they shot and ate for dinner. The expedition named the place El Oso Flaco (the lean bear). Oso Flaco lives on as the name of the southernmost of several small lakes near the Pismo State Beach dunes.

Traveling on, Portolá and his men made a rest stop in a Chumash settlement (now Pismo Beach), then continued northward, passing through hills and good pasture lands. After three days they came to a large village with many lagoons, which they named Cañada de los Osos (Valley of the Bears) for the roaming "troops of bears." Inhabitants of a nearby Chumash village at the mouth of Chorro Creek, near what became Morro Bay State Park, welcomed the explorers. Father Crespí entered the following in his diary:

"To the south an estuary of immense size enters this valley, so large that it looked like a harbor to us; its mouth opens to the southwest, and we noticed that it is covered by reefs which cause a furious surf. At a short distance from it, to the north we saw a great rock in the form of a *morro* [crown-shaped rock or hill], which, at high tide, is isolated and separated from the coast by little less than a gunshot."

Realizing that this was not the large, sheltered harbor for which he searched, Portolá's group continued north, reaching "a mountain range covered with pines" and a deep valley. Friendly natives visited them at this place, now known as Cambria. The expedition passed San Simeon and went inland near Ragged Point before entering Monterey County on September 17, 1769. Continuing on, Portolá finally found at San Francisco Bay the safe harbor for which he had been searching.

The party began the return trip almost immediately and, during December, journeyed a second time through San Luis Obispo County. They were again welcomed by the Chumash; gifts of food from the natives were reciprocated with gifts of beads. Portolá's group spent Christmas Day in Cambria before continuing southward, reaching San Diego on January 24, 1770.

After a time of rest and re-supplying, Portolá, Crespí and company began a second, north-bound land march on April 16, 1770, with Father Serra sailing aboard a ship that roughly paralleled the land route. The land contingent reached Monterey in May; Father Serra arrived in June, and California's second mission, San Carlos Borromeo, was established on June 3, 1770. (A year later the mission was relocated to the Carmel Valley.)

This was Father Serra's headquarters as he served as Father-President of the missions between Monterey and San Diego; by the end of his life in 1784, nine missions had been founded. These and others that came later were connected by a road called *El Camino Real* (The Royal Highway). In time El Camino Real became a stagecoach road, and today US 101 closely follows that historic highway through the Central Coast.

In 1771, a party traveling from Monterey to pick up supplies in San Diego included Father Serra, who intended to establish a mission en route. Serra chose a site in San Luis Obispo County, a few miles inland from Los Osos Valley, with a large native population, fertile land and "a stream of the finest water" (San Luis Obispo Creek). The mission was established on September 1, 1772, and named San Luis Obispo de Tolosa in honor of the 14th-century Saint Louis, Bishop of Toulouse. The following day the group continued south, leaving behind Father José Cavaller to administer the mission with eight assistants and only meager supplies. More than a year later, when Father Francisco Palóu finally brought much-needed aid to San Luis Obispo, he reported that it had survived its first winter only because of the generosity of the Chumash, who "would frequently visit the Mission, bringing little presents of venison and wild seeds." Palóu believed the Chumash were grateful to the Spaniards for ridding the area of many troublesome bears. By 1776, when Captain Juan Bautista de Anza stopped briefly on his trip north to San Francisco with settlers, Mission San Luis Obispo was prospering with nearly 200 resident native converts.

▼ *Una Leccion de Español Muy Pequeña**

Did you hear the one about the fellow from Nebraska who came to California and told his host that he wanted to visit San Josie and San Jewon Capistrano? "Those are Spanish names," he was told. "In Spanish, *J* is pronounced as *H; San Jose* is San Hoezay and *San Juan Capistrano* is San Huahn Capistrano." The Nebraskan took the lesson to heart, conscientiously practiced changing j's to h's during his two-week vacation, and upon his departure promised to return "next Hoon or Hoolie."

No wonder the poor guy was confused. Thanks to Spain's nearly 250 years of influence, California has towns, streets, rivers, mountains—all sorts of places with names that reflect early Spanish visitors and settlers. Notice those places beginning with *San* or *Santa*; both terms mean "saint" or "holy." *Santa* is the feminine form (as in Santa Maria, Santa Barbara), and *San* is the masculine (as in San Miguel [Michael], San Marcos [Mark]). Then there's *los*—it's the masculine plural for "the", and *las* is the feminine plural. *El* is the masculine singular for "the", while *la* is the feminine singular form. So now you have such names as *Los Padres*, meaning "the fathers," and *La Purísima*, "the most holy one."

This seems as good as place as any for a quick, and by no means comprehensive, introduction to Spanish.

Spanish vowels are **a**, **e**, **i**, **o,u** and occasionally **y**. (Except for references to other languages, Spanish has no **w**.) Pronounce **a** as in far; **e** somewhere between long a in mate and short e in met; **i** as in police; **o** as in note; **u** is like oo, as in moon, but is silent in the syllables que, qui, gue or gui. It's interesting to note that no Spanish vowel is ever silent, except for **u** as noted.

Some consonants in Spanish are pronounced the same as in English. Differences in pronunciation mean **b** is softer than in English; **c** before a, o, u or another consonant has a k sound; **c** before e or i sounds like s; **ch** is soft as in cheese; **d** is softer than in English; **g** before a, o, u or a consonant sounds as in go, but **g** before e or i sounds like the Spanish j; **h** is always silent; **j** is like the English h; **ll** sounds as y; **ñ** is like ny in canyon; **n** without a tilde (that little squiggly line) sounds as it does in English; **t** is softer than in English; **x** is like ks or gs; **y** as a consonant sounds as in year; **y** standing alone (meaning "and") or at the end of a word is pronounced like the Spanish i; **z** is like s.

Just one more thing: In Spanish words, the stress falls on the next to last syllable unless indicated by an accent, as in Purísima.

¿Sí, amigos?

A very brief Spanish lesson

Twelve years later the mission had 580 resident converts who harvested thousands of pounds of wheat, corn and beans for the mission community. Cattle and sheep numbered 3000 head each; goats, hogs and horses numbered about 200 each. Mission farming extended almost to Avila Beach, and adjoining land was used for livestock.

Mission San Luis Obispo continued to prosper, and some of its bounty was sent to Mission San Miguel Arcángel, founded in 1797 by Father Lasuén. This mission, located near the junction of the Salinas and Estrella rivers, was successful in the number of natives it attracted and in agricultural production, once irrigation dams and canals were built.

Although Portolá's first expedition had reached Ventura County in 1769, founding a mission there was delayed for 13 years. On March 31, 1782, Father Serra established Mission San Buenaventura, a few hundred yards south of its present site in the city of Ventura. (San Buenaventura, Saint Good Fortune, was named for a 13th-century Italian saint.) This, the last mission that Father Serra would found, began with a chapel, then living quarters for the priests and guards, and a surrounding stockade. Immediately back of the mission, on La Loma de la Cruz (the Hill of the Cross), a cross was erected, as was the custom. This served not only as a religious symbol but as a beacon for travelers in search of the mission; the cross that stands today replicates the original.

While Spain planned to maintain only a mission in San Buenaventura, it was felt that a site about a day's journey northwest should have both a mission and presidio. Three weeks later Father Serra and a contingent of soldiers under the command of Lt. José Francisco de Ortega set out, and in mid-April made camp on what was then the shore of a large lagoon. On April 21, 1782, a shelter with an altar and cross was erected, Father Serra celebrated mass, and the land was formally claimed for Spain. Thus the Royal Presidio of Santa Barbara was founded, its site cutting at an angle through what is now the intersection of Santa Barbara and Canon Perdido streets.

Father Serra had expected that the founding of the mission would soon follow; however, at Spain's insistence, work on the presidio began first. A wall, approximately eight feet high and more than three feet thick, was built to enclose barracks, a chapel, officers' quarters and storerooms bordering a large open area. It is believed that work was completed in the 1790s; the presidio chapel was dedicated on December 12, 1797.

The San Buenaventura Mission as it appeared around the turn of the 20th century.

San Buenaventura was the last mission which Father Junipero Serra established in California, for he died on August 28, 1784, in the mission which he had founded in Carmel. At his request, he was buried in the chapel of San Carlos Borromeo de Carmelo. Today, because of his considerable influence in the settlement of California, a likeness of Father Serra stands in Statuary Hall in the United States Capitol Building.

The Santa Barbara Mission was founded two years after the death of Father Serra. An elevated site was chosen, with views of the valley, presidio and ocean; nearby ran a stream of clear water. On December 16, 1786, Father Lasuén conducted the official dedication of the site, and work on the first mission buildings began the following spring. During the years that followed, the mission's growth exceeded that of the presidio, as large numbers of Chumash came into the mission community.

By the early 1800s, thanks to the mission system, Spain's Catholic Church owned vast acreages throughout the Central Coast. In addition, grants from the governor enabled favored individuals to hold huge parcels of land. The missions and many of the land grants ultimately formed the nucleus of settlements which became the towns of the Central Coast. The land was used primarily for cattle raising, and the resulting hides were used for everything from jackets to beds (rawhides stretched between four posts).

Rancho Period

By the end of the 1700s, Spain had become embroiled in war with France and revolutions in Latin America, leaving Spain's rulers with little thought, time or money for the Alta California settlements. Mexico seized this time to seek its independence from Spain, and following a series of skirmishes, obtained just that. California was now under Mexico's rule, and in April 1822, Mexico's independence from Spain was proclaimed.

The Mexican government decreed that the Catholic Church must release control of its land, which was thereupon divided into ranchos. Then beginning in 1833, the missions were to be secularized and the mission buildings used as parish churches. The mission lands were typically given to former military officers or others who had served Mexico, with the average land grant covering 50,000 acres. The processing of land grants sometimes included interesting rituals. In some cases after the land was marked off, the *ranchero* (ranch owner) pulled up grass clumps, broke off tree branches and threw a rock in each compass direction, demonstrating that he might do anything he wished with his land.

The economic base of the ranchos expanded from primarily cattle raising to include other livestock, grain, and citrus and nut trees. Socially, the ranchos were much like self-sufficient small towns, with a work force of Chumash, who received shelter, food and clothing for their labor. The *Californio* (Mexican or Spanish resident of California) ranch owners became famous for a hospitality that included rodeos, feasting and music.

While the ranchos prospered, settlements near the presidios and missions were growing. Santa Barbara, for example, changed from a fort to a town as the port attracted commerce, and seafarers made it their home. Early settlers throughout the Central Coast were often military personnel or civil servants living near the presidios and missions. By the 1840s adobe or frame houses and businesses marked the beginnings of such towns as San Luis Obispo, Ventura and Santa Barbara.

Since the 1820s American commercial interests and pioneer settlers had been establishing themselves in California. This expansion was coupled with a desire to keep England from getting a foothold on the West Coast, and by 1846 the United States under President James K. Polk had become increasingly interested in acquiring California. On June 14 of that year the "Bear Flag Revolt" occurred. Explorer and soldier Captain John C. Frémont led a motley troop of Americans in raising the new banner of the California Republic over the village of Sonoma, about 40 miles northeast of San Francisco. The banner's likeness of a grizzly bear and the words "California Republic" remain on California's state flag.

This was the beginning of the end of Mexican rule in California, as a number of skirmishes between American and Californio troops ranged up and down the length of California. Frémont, by now a colonel, often figured prominently in these maneuvers, and on January 13, 1847, at Cahuenga Pass in the Los Angeles area, organized resistance to American occupation ended as General Andres Pico surrendered to Colonel Frémont. On February 2, 1848, the Treaty of Guadalupe Hidalgo ceded California to the United States.

One month before that treaty, gold had been discovered in California, adding an exciting impetus toward statehood. In September 1849 a constitutional convention was convened in Monterey to decide whether to admit California as free or slave state, and to draw up a constitution for the 31st state. On September 9, 1850, California was admitted to the Union as a free state, with a constitution written in both English and Spanish.

American Period

Drawn not just by gold but by other riches to be taken from the earth, more and more Americans began trekking to California, many of them choosing the Central Coast. Throughout the 1850s and 1860s the area grew and prospered as more Americans acquired title to land, and settlements began to rise along the coast and in the inland valleys. A combination of hard work, beneficent climate and good soil produced grain, vegetables and fruit; dairy farms and horse ranches became part of the landscape. Because dairy and agricultural products had to be shipped by sea to outlying markets, steamships called regularly at ports between San Francisco and Los Angeles, including Santa Barbara, Port San Luis and Port Hueneme.

While steamships plied the waters, the Coast Line Stage Company had a route in 1861 between Los Angeles and San Francisco, carrying passengers and small freight. By the following year, stagecoaches were making daily runs in 3½ days. Then came a behemoth to challenge both the steamship and stagecoach. From the ambitions and fortunes of the "Big Four"— Charles Crocker, Collis P. Huntington, Mark Hopkins and Leland Stanford—and the labor of countless workers, mostly Chinese, came the Southern Pacific Railroad. As track was laid through the Central Coast area, townsites were planned around railroad stops.

If "Gold!" was the magic cry in the 1840s, "Oil!" replaced it in the 1860s. In the area which was to become Ventura County, interest began to center around

In 1906, reaching the summit of Casitas Pass was a real motoring adventure.

that heavy, black substance seeping up from under the ground. Early prospectors in the Ojai/Santa Paula area managed, after painstaking drilling through rock and shale, to reach oil.

For the next two decades the burgeoning oil industry went through boom and bust times; in the 1880s it became and remains an important part of the economy in Ventura and Santa Barbara counties.

There was more to be taken from the ground than oil: the Central Coast continued to offer rich farming land. Following passage of the Homestead Act in 1868, Civil War veterans came to California to take advantage of free arable land. A year before that, 17,000 acres of fertile land—once part of a rancho—were offered for $10 an acre,

payable over 10 years. Such bargains as these were irresistible to venturesome farmers both in California and those coming from other states and territories, as well as other countries. Then the railroad came through, bringing tourists and settlers, and taking produce to far-away markets.

Today, the 16-wheelers on Interstate 5 have taken over most of the freight once moved by railway. Time has brought other dramatic changes: military bases, public universities, extensive freeways, housing developments, small industries and oil exploration— all these play a part in the look of California's Central Coast. Still, beautiful and varied scenery remains, and a multilayered history is reflected in landmarks, street names and annual events all along the way.

VENTURA COUNTY

Going north along State Route 1 through Los Angeles County, Ventura County begins at the northern border of Leo Carrillo State Beach. Skirting the seaward edge of the Santa Monica Mountains, the **Ventura Coast** includes Point Mugu State Park and continues as a coastal plain through Oxnard, where SR 1 joins US 101. As it reaches the city of Ventura, the highway provides dramatic vistas as it becomes a narrow strip between steep hills and the sea. In addition to Ventura, coastal area communities include Port Hueneme, with its Seabee base; Oxnard, combining agricultural and maritime pursuits; and Camarillo, an important residential and business center. Also along the county's coastline lie Oxnard, a major agricultural center, and Port Hueneme, important to the U.S. Navy since 1941. Offshore lies Channel Islands National Park.

These golden globes are part of the Central Coast citrus crop.

Southwest of Ventura, in the area between US 101 and SR 118, **Conejo and Simi valleys** lie on inland plateaus, and in any direction there is a view of rolling hills or mountain peaks. The largest communities here, Thousand Oaks in the

Pleasure boats abound in Ventura Harbor.

Conejo Valley and the town of Simi Valley, are attractive centers of residence and commerce. From US 101 south of the city of Ventura, SR 126 leads east past citrus groves and oil fields to the small towns of Santa Paula and Fillmore, both of which are historically and agriculturally important.

This 1890 building in Santa Paula now houses the Santa Paula Union Oil Museum.

Go inland northeast of the town of Ventura, and you can enjoy the wonderfully scenic **Ojai and Santa Paula areas**. Along the way is Lake Casitas, a great place for camping and fishing. The town of Ojai, with its artistic reputation and dramatic valley setting, and Santa Paula, a town of Victorian houses and colorful history, are both within a half-hour's drive of US 101.

Scenic SR 33 winds through a portion of Los Padres National Forest, where mountain ranges look down on deep valleys cut by creek beds (see *Los Padres National Forest* chapter).

Oak trees dot the hills and valleys along State Route 126.

Ventura Coast

Backed by seemingly endless ranges of hills, and facing the Santa Barbara Channel to the south, Ventura County's coastal plain supports communities, farmland, orchards, naval bases and light industry. Camarillo, Oxnard, Port Hueneme and Ventura enjoy this coastal locale, while offshore lies Channel Islands National Park. While this region's economic basis is provided by agricultural, military and small industries, groves of tall, steel pumpers, resembling gigantic grasshoppers, attest to Ventura County's very important oil industry.

The U.S. Navy has found Ventura's coast an ideal location for the construction center and air station that bracket Port Hueneme. Southeast of Port Hueneme, and beyond Point Mugu Naval Air Station, lies Point Mugu State Park. The park embraces sandy beaches and the rugged Santa Monica Mountains.

Birthplace of the county and site of the historically important San Buenaventura Mission are claimed by the city of Ventura. The city also boasts important cultural resources: a symphony orchestra as well as museums displaying Central Coast archaeology, art and history. As attractive and important as the city of Ventura is in its own right, it is also the gateway to the Ojai and Santa Paula valleys, Lake Casitas and Los Padres National Forest.

Camarillo

Although it is about eight miles from the coast, Camarillo is included in this book's coastal section because it lies on the Oxnard Plain, an area with a mild coastal climate comfortable for people and conducive to agriculture. Camarillo is a city of approximately 55,800 people who enjoy living within an area of planned residential developments and light industrial growth.

Originally called Pleasant Valley, Camarillo began as part of the Rancho Calleguas in the 1890s, and was named for the Juan Camarillo family, owners of the ranch. The townsite was laid out in 1910, with much of the land, houses and stores located around the Southern Pacific train depot. As elsewhere in the county, most of the economy depended upon ranching and farming. All was not work, however, as Juan Camarillo's descendants upheld the tradition of hosting fiestas and rodeos for the townspeople.

Throughout the first half of the 20th century Camarillo remained a small farming community, but the 1950s and '60s brought the freeway, and though many farmers took the opportunity to sell their acres to developers, a good portion of the land is still devoted to crops.

Boats and sea gulls find a haven in Ventura Marina.

CHANNEL ISLANDS AVIATION *At Camarillo Airport, 305 Durley Ave. (805) 987-1301. Scenic flights daily, weather and visibility permitting, 8 a.m. to 5 p.m.; closed Dec. 25. Basic fare $30 per person; reservations suggested.* Scenic flights go along the Ventura coast, to the Channel Islands, over the Ojai Valley or south to Malibu. Passengers may decide upon the route and the time spent.

Santa Rosa Island Day Trip *Year round; call for departure days and reservations, (805) 987-1301. Fare $85; ages 2-12, $60 (lunch not provided). Plane departs at 9 a.m., returns at 3 p.m.* Channel Islands Aviation takes passengers on a scenic flight over Anacapa and Santa Cruz islands to Santa Rosa Island. Passengers are met by a park ranger and given a narrated combination hiking and four-wheel-drive tour of the island. On the itinerary are a century-old cattle ranch that is still operating, indigenous birds, plants, sea mammals and stories of the intriguing history of this island. Sturdy shoes are a must, and because the island is often cold and windy, layered clothing is recommended.

CONCERTS IN THE PARK *Constitution Park, Camarillo and Carmen drs. (805) 987-7847. Every other Sat. at 7 p.m., beginning the first part of June and run-*

ning through Labor Day weekend, weather permitting. Free. From blue grass groups to armed forces' concert bands—everyone is sure to find music they like in this summertime outdoor series of live performances. Audience members need to bring a blanket to sit on, and picnicking is welcome.

FARMERS MARKET *2220 Ventura Blvd.; (805) 482-0089. Sat. 8:30 a.m. to noon.* A variety of fruits, vegetables and nuts is offered, and sometimes there are crafts, prepared food and entertainment.

Channel Islands National Park

Less than 15 miles off the Santa Barbara and Ventura coastline, in the Santa Barbara Channel, lie six islands. On a day when coastal visibility is clear, people new to the Central Coast and traveling along US 101 between Oxnard and Gaviota, may be rather mystified by seeing land "out there." What they are looking at are Anacapa, San Miguel, Santa Barbara, Santa Cruz and Santa Rosa islands, all of which make up Channel Islands National Park. The sixth island, San Nicolas, is under the jurisdiction of the U.S. Navy.

These islands provide an unparalleled introduction to the flora and fauna of the Central Coast marine environment. Nature, unspoiled and beautiful, is the main attraction, indeed the *only* attraction.

Accommodations are sparse and primitive; where you can stay overnight, you must bring your own gear; there are no refreshment stands; and the only thing that comes close to a "thrill ride" is being in a small skiff in Santa Cruz Island's Painted Cave when the waves are boisterous.

Anacapa Island, actually three small islets with a total land area of about one square mile, is only 11 miles from the mainland. Brown and dull much of the time, winter rains clothe Anacapa in green, and the bright yellow coreopsis flower soon follows. All through the year, Western gulls, black oystercatchers, cormorants and brown pelicans make their home here. West Anacapa serves as a research area and is closed to the public, so most visitors go to East Anacapa, where picnicking is permitted (pack out your trash).

Among San Miguel Island's claims to fame are that it shelters the islands' largest land mammal, the island fox, and that a great number and variety of

An island fox is represented at the Channel Islands Visitor Center.

other mammals—seals and sea lions—love to haul out on its shores. Humans have enjoyed this place too: More than 500 archeological sites date back thousands of years, and it is thought that a few hundred years ago (1543, to be precise) Juan Rodriquez Cabrillo died and may have been buried here. (See *History*.)

Santa Barbara Island is the southernmost and smallest of the park's islands, comprising only 640 acres. The island's checkered history includes serving as a rest stop for Chumash traveling to the other islands hundreds of years ago and, during the World War II years, as a U.S. Navy early warning outpost. In spring the island blooms with the tiny yellow flowers called goldfields, and bird watchers enjoy the American kestrels, horned larks and meadowlarks.

The largest island in the park is Santa Cruz—24 miles long, with a land area of 96 square miles. While the other islands have hills, Santa Cruz boasts a mountain 2400 feet high. Here is an island with a huge sea cave, coves, sandy beaches and steep cliffs. An under-

▼ *Natural Beauty*

What is approximately 24 miles long, from two to seven miles wide and as high as 2400 feet? If you answered, "Santa Cruz Island," you're absolutely right. Largest of the five islands comprising Channel Islands National Park, Santa Cruz stands about 23 miles from the mainland and encompasses 96 square miles. This beautiful island supports woodland, grassland, beaches, dunes, freshwater streams, a great sea cave and two mountain ranges.

Not only that, but there's also quite a range of flora and fauna. Among the 600 species of plants on the island, eight occur only on Santa Cruz, including the Santa Cruz Island ironwood and the Island Oak. The land mammals include the red island fox. Seals and sea lions by the hundreds enjoy the island's protected coves, and sea birds abound on cliffs and offshore rocks.

As pristine as the island appears, its history is one of settlement and exploitation. In 1542, explorer Juan Cabrillo estimated the Chumash Indian population at between 2000 and 3000. By 1839 the last of the Chumash had been removed to missions, and the island became a land grant. Following a series of owners, a colony of French and Italian immigrants was established on the island in 1880. The colony became a ranching endeavor that produced cattle, sheep, walnuts, olives, honey and a reputedly good wine bearing the Santa Cruz Island label.

In 1937, nine-tenths of the island was acquired by Edwin L. Stanton, who concentrated on cattle ranching. In 1975 Stanton's son, Dr. Carey Stanton, formed a partnership with the Nature Conservancy to ensure preservation of the island. Cattle ranching continues, but beyond that, Santa Cruz Island stands as a unique, protected, island environment.

ground fresh water supply helps support more than 600 different plants and 140 land bird species. It is believed that the Chumash occupied Santa Cruz Island for more than 6000 years, and scattered archeological evidence of their habitations remain. While Santa Cruz Island is within park boundaries, technically speaking it is owned almost entirely by the Nature Conservancy, not the National Park Service, and special restrictions apply to landing permits.

Santa Rosa Island is the park's second-largest island, with high mountains, canyons, hills and terraces within its 53,000 acres. Great expanses of kelp beds surround the island and support the sea life which serves as food for marine mammals and sea birds on Santa Rosa's shores and offshore rocks.

Channel Islands National Park is obviously a unique place, and its offshore waters are just as special. That being the case, the ocean for six nautical miles around the islands is designated Channel Islands National Marine Sanctuary. The waters here are in a zone that lies between tropical warm waters and cold waters from the arctic seas, and this makes for a breeding ground of great diversity. Seals, sea lions, sharks and dolphins live here,

Animals and artifacts found on the Channel Islands are displayed in the park's Visitor Center.

and whales pass through on their annual migration. Closer to the sea floor are smaller sea creatures in myriad shapes and colors.

Because the park and marine sanctuary support such a fragile balance of nature, strict regulations govern visitors' activities. The limited number of visitors who are allowed must take their own food and water. Primitive camping is permitted on all the islands but Santa Cruz, and guided hikes are conducted by rangers on San Miguel and Santa Rosa islands. Camping and hiking must be arranged in advance through park headquarters; call (805) 658-5700. Private boats going to the islands must have landing permits; call (805) 964-7839.

There are no hourly ferry boats and, of course, no bridges to any of the islands; transportation is limited to private boats, chartered craft and scheduled tour boats. The best place to learn everything you want to know about the islands and how to get there is at the Channel Islands National Park Visitor Center (see description below). The Nature Conservancy and Sea Center on Stearns Wharf in Santa Barbara also offer displays and information on aspects of the Channel Islands (see Stearns Wharf listing under *Santa Barbara County*, Santa Barbara).

Trips to the islands or offshore waters are offered by the following establishments; write or telephone for schedules, prices and reservations. (It is advisable to make reservations at least two weeks in advance.)

Channel Islands Aviation *At Camarillo Airport, 305 Durley Ave., Camarillo 93010. (805) 987-1301. (To Santa Rosa Island exclusively.)*

Island Packers Company *1867 Spinnaker Dr., Ventura 93001; (805) 642-1393. (This is the only company authorized by the Park Service to land paying boat passengers on any of the islands.)*

Sea Landing Sportfishing *301 Cabrillo Blvd., Santa Barbara 93010; (805) 963-3564.*

CHANNEL ISLANDS NATIONAL PARK VISITOR CENTER *1901 Spinnaker Dr., Ventura 93001. (805) 658-5730. Open daily; from Memorial Day through Labor Day 8 a.m. to 5:30 p.m.; the rest of the year, Mon. through Fri. 8:30 a.m. to 4:30 p.m., Sat. and Sun. 8 a.m. to 5 p.m.; closed Thanksgiving and Dec. 25. Special live programs are offered on Sat. and Sun.* Within this harbor-side structure are exhibits that graphically describe the park, including stuffed and mounted mammals and birds, and an indoor tidepool. Books and pamphlets about this and other national parks are available, and there are a video and movie about the islands. On an outdoor deck are large, detailed models of the park's islands. A stairway and elevator lead up to the observation tower that affords a 360° view of the harbor and, on a clear day, the islands.

La Conchita

With a population around 1100, La Conchita is among the smallest towns in Ventura County. Situated on the coast, on the north side of US 101, about 10 miles north of Ventura, the tiny community's claim to fame is the Seaside Banana Garden, at the west end of Santa Barbara Avenue.

SEASIDE BANANA GARDEN *La Conchita exit, off US 101 at 6823 Santa Barbara Ave., 93001. (805) 643-4061. Sales hut open daily 9 a.m. to 5 p.m.; closed major holidays.* This plantation

Oxnard

In the late 1890s a sugar beet process-ing factory owned by the Oxnard brothers—Henry, Robert, Benjamin and James—and the homes of the factory workers were the beginnings of any serious growth of the town which became Oxnard. The railroad came to Oxnard in 1898, and soon other businesses, homes, churches and schools were established, leading to incorporation of the city in 1903.

The sugar beet factory has passed into history, but Oxnard continued to grow and prosper, and is now the largest of Ventura County towns, with a popula-tion of nearly 147,000. In addition to residential areas from the ocean to the foothills, Oxnard has rich agricultural land, well-designed business parks and a coastline offering sandy beaches and full-service marinas.

Bananas in their natural state delight visitors to Seaside Banana Garden.

of banana trees is situated on a narrow shelf of land between the ocean and 300-foot-high bluffs; the resultant blanket of relatively warm air that cov-ers the trees comes close to approxi-mating tropical temperatures. More than 50 varieties of bananas are grown here, and visitors are welcome to walk through the groves of trees.

Much of the unusual and tasty fruit is for sale on the premises. Among the exotic bananas are the ice cream banana, lady finger, Hawaiian apple (Brazilian) and the Polynesian Haa-Haa. The fruit ripens at various times throughout the year, but the pickings are somewhat sparse in January and February. Also for sale are other types of fruit, as well as honey, dates and tropical plants.

Oxnard has not forgotten its history, as can be seen by a visit to Heritage Square, while another of the city's cul-tural advantages is the Ventura County Symphony.

CARNEGIE ART MUSEUM *424 S. C St., 93030. (805) 385-8157. Open Thur. through Sat. 10 a.m. to 5 p.m., Sun. 1 to 5 p.m.; closed Jan. 1, Thanksgiving, Dec. 25 and periodically between exhibits. Admission $2; seniors and ages 6-12, $1.50.* Art works are displayed in an imposing, two-story, Greco-Roman-style structure that was built as a library in 1906. The museum's permanent collection focuses on 20th-century California painters. Changing exhibits that include oil paintings, sketches, photographs and sculpture range from the sublime to the hilarious.

FARMERS MARKETS *Corner of B and 5th sts.; (805) 483-7960. Thur. 10 a.m. to*

1 p.m. The citrus fruit and avocados for which the county is known are usually much in evidence at this market.

2800 block, S. Harbor Blvd. in Channel Islands Harbor; (805) 985-8954. Sun. 10 a.m. to 2 p.m. Fresh produce, flowers and seafood are offered here. Once each month there are demonstrations of recipes and cooking techniques using market produce.

GULL WINGS CHILDREN'S MUSEUM
418 W. 4th St., 93030. (805) 483-3005. Open Wed. through Fri. and Sun. 1 to 5 p.m.; Sat. 10 a.m. to 5 p.m. Admission $3; $2, ages 2-12. Children will find plenty to do here, for a variety of

hands-on exhibits and activities include puppets and a stage, costumes and uniforms for acting out adult occupations, and a make-believe campground with a tent and "fishing pond." There are also a medical room with cutaway anatomical models and medical equipment, apparatus for making giant soap bubbles, and a rock and mineral display that includes fossil remains.

HERITAGE SQUARE *715 S. A St.; 93030. (805) 483-7960. Open daily during daylight hours. Free.* A visitor to Oxnard might feel transported by a time machine when confronted by

Reproduction of this map or any portion thereof constitutes infringement of copyright.

VENTURA-OXNARD AREA

- FREEWAY & ACCESS RAMPS
- POINT OF INTEREST
- GOLF COURSE
- PARK
- CAMPGROUND
- BOATING FACILITY
- SURFING AREA
- SPORTFISHING FACILITY

SCALE IN MILES
0   0.5   1   1.5   2   2.5

MAP 2691

Heritage Square preserves a number of Oxnard's imposing Victorian-era structures.

what seems to be a well-kept, intact, 100-year-old neighborhood. Constructed in the late 1800s and early 1900s, the church, water tower, pump house and houses here reflect such architectural styles as Queen Anne, Italianate and Craftsman. The buildings were moved from various parts of the Oxnard area to a single block, carefully restored and enhanced by landscaping and walkways. These charming houses are now occupied by offices and shops. For guided tours and special events, call the above number.

OXNARD CIVIC AUDITORIUM *In Community Center Park, Hobson Way between 7th and 9th sts.* This is the home of the Ventura County Symphony, a fine ensemble with an annual performance schedule that runs from October through the first week in May. Concerts are given here and at the Civic Arts Plaza in Thousand Oaks (see listing). For symphony ticket and schedule information call (805) 643-8646.

SANTA CLARA ESTUARY NATURAL PRESERVE *McGrath State Beach, off Harbor Blvd. about ½ mile south of Olivas Park Dr. Trail open daily 8 a.m. to sunset. (805) 654-4744.* This preserve protects two endangered bird species, and fresh- and saltwater plants. A ½-mile self-guided trail winds among some of the preserve's trees and plants and leads to an estuary where the fresh water of the Santa Clara River meets the salt water of the ocean, and great flocks of shore birds gather. Printed trail guides are available at the state beach entrance station.

VENTURA COUNTY MARITIME MUSEUM *Just past Channel Islands Blvd. at 2731 S. Victoria Ave., 93035. (805) 984-6260. Open Thur. through Mon. 11 a.m. to 5 p.m.; closed Jan. 1, Thanksgiving and Dec. 25. Free.* This museum harbors a collection of ship models built around the Marple Fleet of nine beautifully crafted vessels. Included are 56 models that illustrate the evolution of ocean-going vessels from 4000 B.C. to the present. The museum walls are graced by fine marine paintings, prints and engravings, some of which date to 1750.

Point Mugu State Park

Approximately 7 miles south of Oxnard off Interstate 1 at 9000 Pacific Coast Hwy., Malibu 90265. (800) 533-7275. Open daily. Day-use admission fee is $6 per vehicle; camping fees vary.

Point Mugu State Park is a place of dramatic contrasts: rugged mountains and sandy beaches; ferns growing by inland springs and chaparral-covered hillsides. Within the park's 15,000 acres are a five-mile shoreline just right for swimming, fishing or strolling. The backcountry offers hiking, camping and horseback riding. (See *Recreation* and *Campgrounds & Trailer Parks*.)

Point Mugu's wildlife includes deer and rabbits, foxes and coyotes, and marine life such as seals and sea lions. In the early autumn hundreds of migrating monarch butterflies cluster here within sheltered groves of trees.

Port Hueneme

In 1840, eight valorous and loyal Mexican soldiers were awarded a land grant of 44,883 acres called Rancho el Rio de Santa Clara o la Colonia. The land, used largely for cattle-raising, included the western edge of the Oxnard Plain, with a point of land reaching into the Pacific. Twenty-four years later over 32,000 acres of the rancho were acquired by a Pennsylvania speculator, who in turn sold the land to a group of farmers and ranchers.

The town was plotted in 1869 and took its name from the Chumash settlement, Weneme or Wenemu, which had once occupied that area. Within two years the town included warehouses and a deepwater wharf, thus making Port Hueneme (wi-nee´-me) the focal point for the transportation of grain and livestock. The town continued to grow through the remainder of the 19th century, but eventually was overshadowed by neighboring Oxnard.

Port Hueneme, however, boasted the only deep-water port between Los Angeles and San Francisco, and in 1941 the U.S. Navy took advantage of this to build a construction battalion (Seabee) training and shipping base. The center is the site of a museum to which civilian visitors are welcomed (see below).

In 1946, about four miles south of the Seabee base, the Navy launched a missile from Pt. Mugu and then went on to build facilities for the development and testing of many more missiles. From these beginnings grew the Naval Air Weapons Station. The base is used for research, testing, and engineering for air warfare's weapons systems and all their technical ramifications. Visitors, except on official business, are not permitted on the weapons station.

The military presence aside, Port Hueneme, with a population of more than 20,000, is an area of farmland and residential neighborhoods, and the site of a number of beaches and sportfishing landings (see *Recreation*).

U.S. NAVAL CONSTRUCTION BATTALION CENTER *Off 23rd Ave. just west of Ventura Rd. (mailing address: 621 Pleasant Valley Rd., 93043-4300). Tour information (805) 982-5611.* Built in the early days of World War II, this is the Pacific center for the Navy Seabees, skilled construction experts. Seabees have actively fought in military engagements from World War II through Operation Desert Storm and built camps, roads, airstrips and bridges in these war zones. CBC serves as home port, training, and logistical support for Seabees serving around the world. Visitors are allowed on base to visit the Seabee Museum (see below) or as members of group tours.

CEC/Seabee Museum *(805) 982-5163. Open Mon. through Fri. 8 a.m. to 4:30 p.m.; Sat. 9 a.m.; Sun. 12:30 to 4:30 p.m.; closed holidays; phone to confirm hours. Free.* Models of equipment and battle scenes, weapons, uniforms, and arts and crafts by and about the Civil Engineer Corps and the Navy Seabees are housed here. Obtain a visitor pass at the Ventura Gate; those under age 16 must be accompanied by an adult.

Ventura

Following the secularization of San Buenaventura Mission's lands in 1834,

Spanish and Mexican settlers built adobe homes near the mission and took their places as tradespeople, government workers and officials. In the 1860s American and European settlers began coming into the area, and by the 1870s, because of economics and government regulations, most of the ranch lands had passed into American hands. Added to these were "Yankee" merchants and oil speculators, so that by the time the railroad arrived in 1887, San Buenaventura—now called Ventura—had become a thriving town of two- and three-story frame houses, stores with plate glass windows, mills and brickyards, school and churches.

Today Ventura, with a population of about 94,000, is considered a major agricultural center and oil producer, with the added advantage of miles of beaches and a warm, sunny climate

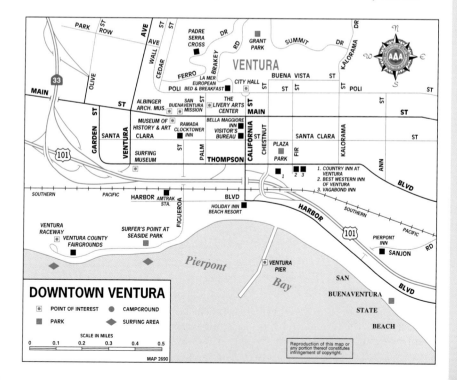

DOWNTOWN VENTURA

□ POINT OF INTEREST   ● CAMPGROUND
■ PARK   ◆ SURFING AREA

SCALE IN MILES
0   0.1   0.2   0.3   0.4   0.5

MAP 2690

Reproduction of this map or any portion thereof constitutes infringement of copyright.

▼ *A Quick Guide to Ventura Information*

Population: 96,100

Elevation: 35 ft.

*Telephone numbers are in the **805 area code**, unless noted otherwise.*

Emergency 911

Police (non-emergency) 339-4400

Emergency Road Service for AAA Members (800) 400-4222

Highway Conditions (800) 427-7623

Hospitals

St. John's Regional Medical Center
1600 N. Rose Ave.
Oxnard 93030
988-2500

Ventura County Medical Center
3291 Loma Vista Rd.
Ventura 93003
652-6000

Time 486-9311

Weather 988-6610 (included in Santa Barbara forecast)

Radio and TV

Radio station KTRO (1250 AM) or KELF (96 FM) in Ventura offer news and traffic reports. KCRU (89.1 FM) is a member of National Public Radio. Ventura's Spanish language station is KOXR (910 AM).

Network television channels are 2 (CBS), 3 or 7 (ABC), and 4 (NBC). The PBS channel is 10. For a complete list of radio and television programs, consult the daily newspapers.

Automobile Club of Southern California

Ventura County District Office
1501 S. Victoria Ave.
Mailing address: P.O. Box 3618
Ventura 93306-3618
Phone: 644-7171
Office hours: Mon. through Fri. 9 a.m. to 5 p.m.

Visitor Services

Ventura Chamber of Commerce
6824 Seaward Ave.
Ventura 93001
Phone: 648-2875
Office hours: Mon. through Fri. 8:30 a.m. to 5 p.m.

Ventura Visitors & Convention Bureau
89-C S. California St.
Ventura 93001
Phone: 648-2075
Office hours: Mon. through Fri. 8:30 a.m. to 5 p.m.; Sat. 9 a.m. to 4 p.m.; Sun. 10 a.m. to 4 p.m.

Newspapers

The major daily newspapers in the Ventura area are the *Star-Free Press* and the Ventura County edition of the *Los Angeles Times*; both contain local events and entertainment information.

Public Transportation & Taxis

South Coast Area Transit (SCAT) operates buses throughout Ventura County; for schedule and route information, call 487-4222, 643-3158 or 647-4241. Yellow Cab provides service in the Ventura area; call 643-2221. Other taxi companies are listed in the yellow pages of the local telephone directory.

The 1847 Olivas Adobe was once the home of the Raymundo Olivas family.

averaging 74 degrees year round. Ventura Harbor shelters a number of marinas and is the gateway to Channel Islands National Park. The city's ties to its past are beautifully displayed in the Albinger Archaeological Museum, the County Art and History Museum and the Olivas Adobe. The contemporary crowd responds to rock concerts presented year round at the Ventura Concert Theatre; (805) 648-1936.

ALBINGER ARCHAEOLOGICAL MUSEUM *113 E. Main St. (805) 648-5823 (mailing address: P.O. Box 99, 93002). Open Memorial Day weekend through Labor Day, Wed. through Sun. 10 a.m. to 4 p.m.; rest of the year, Wed. to Fri. 10 a.m. 2 p.m., Sat. through Sun. 10 a.m. to 4 p.m.; closed Jan. 1, Easter, Thanksgiving and Dec. 25. Free.* Artifacts spanning 3,500 years are displayed here; all were excavated from a single site next to San Buenaventura Mission. Evidence of an early native culture dating from 1600 B.C. and the later Chumash dating from A.D. 1500 is exhibited, along with objects dating from the mission's founding to the early 1900s. The original mission foundation and an earthen oven lie outside in the dig area. Two audiovisual programs are presented to visitors on request.

FARMERS MARKETS *Corner of Santa Clara and California sts.; (805) 529-6266. Sat. 8:30 a.m. to noon.* Citrus fruits and a variety of vegetables are displayed.

Montgomery Wards' parking lot, Main St. and Mills Rd.; (805) 529-6266. Wed. 10 a.m. to 1 p.m. A good variety of Ventura County produce is offered here.

FIRST SUNDAY IN THE PARK *Northwest corner of Plaza Park at Chestnut and Santa Clara sts. Held the first Sun. of Oct. through Dec. from 10 a.m. to 4 p.m. Also, every Sun. mid-July through Labor Day on the Promanade near Ventura Pier. (805) 658-4742.* Like Santa Barbara, the city of Ventura boasts a Moreton Bay fig tree. It stands in Plaza Park and is 73½ feet high, with a branch spread of 139 feet. Beneath that tree, and throughout the park, a Sunday celebration of creativity is held.

California arts and crafts people are represented by paintings, jewelry, needlework, handmade clothing and other handcrafted wares; food booths are also set up.

THE LIVERY ARTS CENTER *Just north of Main St. on N. Palm St.* Colorful murals mark the place where a handful

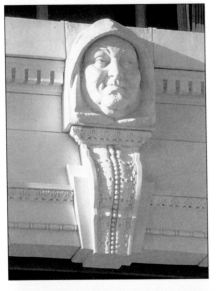

of whimsical shops and outdoor eating places are centered around a plaza. This is also home to the Plaza Players, a community theater group whose presentations range from children's theater to adult drama to Broadway musicals.

Plaza Players *(mailing address: 34 N. Palm St., 93001-2635.) (805) 643-9460. Performances Wed., Friday and Saturday 8 p.m. Tickets $8-10.* This community theatrical group performs throughout the year in a 135-seat theater. Since the theater is dark between each six-week run of a production, it is best to call ahead.

OLIVAS ADOBE HISTORICAL PARK *4200 Olivas Park Dr. (mailing address: P.O. Box 99, 93002). (805) 644-4346. Grounds open Tues. through Fri. 10 a.m. to 4 p.m.; house and exhibit building open Sat. and Sun. 10 a.m. to 4 p.m.; closed major holidays. Free.* A two-story adobe house was built in the Monterey style in 1847 by Raymundo Olivas, and its displays of period furnishings and handi-

From the city hall, a Spanish padre continues to oversee life in San Buenaventura.

Completed in 1809, Mission San Buenaventura marked the beginning of the town of Ventura.

crafts help to make early California history come alive. An exhibit building contains artifacts from the adobe and rancho eras in Ventura County. The grounds include a small adobe, an adobe pit, and rose and herb gardens. A 12-minute audio-visual program and self-guided tours are available.

SAN BUENAVENTURA CITY HALL *501 Poli St., north end of California St. (mailing address: P.O. Box 99, 93002). (805) 654-7850. Open Mon. through Fri. 9 a.m. to 5 p.m.; closed legal holidays. Tours available upon request (fee); call (805) 658-4756.* This imposing city landmark was built in 1913 and served originally as the county courthouse. Set on a hillside and beautifully land-scaped, the building is noted for its terra cotta exterior, copper-covered dome, marble foyer, rooms and hall-ways with paneled walls and coffered ceilings. A bronze statue of Junípero Serra stands in its own small plaza south of the city hall across the street.

SAN BUENAVENTURA MISSION *225 E. Main St., 93001. Entrance is through a gift shop just east of the mission. (805) 648-4496. Open Mon. through Sat. 10 a.m. to 5 p.m., Sun. 10 a.m. to 4 p.m.; closed major holidays. Admission $1; under age 16, 50¢.* Founded in 1782 and completed in 1809, the present mission includes a small museum, and its restored church still serves an active congregation. Within the museum are Chumash artifacts and vestments, books and other items from the mission's early days. The courtyard is centered by a tiled fountain and contains an antique olive press.

SURFING MUSEUM *In the Ventura Surf Shop, 88 E. Thompson Blvd., 92001. (805) 643-1062. Open Mon. through Sat. 10 a.m. to 5 p.m.; Sun. until 4 p.m. Free.* This small museum contains surf-boards—both historically significant and modern. Additionally there are photographs and memorabilia pertain-ing to surfing.

Ventura Pier: a fine place for fishing or strolling.

VENTURA COUNTY MUSEUM OF HISTORY & ART *100 E. Main St., 93001. (805) 653-0323. Open Tues. through Sun. 10 a.m. to 5 p.m.; closed Jan. 1, Thanksgiving and Dec. 25. Admission $2; ages 6 through 12, free when accompanied by an adult.* American Indian, Spanish and pioneer influences in Ventura County are all reflected in the exhibits in this attractive museum. In addition to historical artifacts, space is devoted to visual art. The museum includes displays of agricultural equipment, the George Stuart Historical Figures, changing exhibits and a research library.

VENTURA HARBOR VILLAGE *1559 Spinnaker Dr., about 1 mile west of Harbor Blvd. (805) 642-6746. Most shops open 10 a.m. to 6 p.m.; restaurant hours vary.* This shopping and entertainment center is situated beside a marina and offers specialty shops, restaurants and a carousel. Harbor tours and other watery delights are available here.

VENTURA PIER *Just east of the south end of California St.; parking area through entrance to San Buenaventura State Beach off Harbor Blvd.* The first pier at this location was completed in 1872 and served as a harbor for steamships. Today this 1958-foot-long pier, reputedly the longest wooden pier in California, boasts a sturdy Douglas fir deck on which are a bait shop, fish-cleaning facilities, snack bar and rest rooms.

A copper kinetic sculpture, *Wavespout*, acts as a small blow hole when the tidal action is right. The pier is a good place from which to enjoy ocean and city views while fishing or strolling. There are benches along the way, and plaques on the railings explain the area's marine life and the pier's history.

VENTURA RACEWAY *At Ventura County Fairgrounds, 10 W. Harbor Blvd.; 93001. (805) 656-1122. Races held Apr. through Nov. most Fri. and Sat.; call for* *exact dates. Gates open Fri. 5:30 p.m.; racing starts 7:30 p.m.; Sat. gates open 5 p.m.; racing starts 7 p.m. Admission $8-$12; under age 12, free.* This seaside, ⅕-mile dirt oval racetrack hosts stock cars, midgets, sprints and just about everything else that comes under the category of open-wheel and stock-car racing vehicle.

WINERY *Hours are subject to change; please call ahead. More complete descriptions of wineries offering tours appear in the Auto Club's* California Winery Tours *book.*

Leeward Winery *2784 Johnson Dr., near southeast corner of Capri Ave. and Johnson Dr. (805) 656-5054. Open daily 10 a.m. to 4 p.m.; closed Thanksgiving and Dec. 25.* This small winery purchases grapes from California vineyards to produce Cabernet Sauvignon, Chardonnay, Pinot Noir and Merlot.

Simi and Conejo Valleys

The Conejo and Simi valleys lie on plateaus approximately 800 feet in elevation, and in any direction there is a view of rolling hills or mountain peaks. The largest communities here, Thousand Oaks in the Conejo Valley and the city of Simi Valley, are centers of residence and commerce that nevertheless retain something of a feeling of country living, in marked contrast to the urban sprawl just across the Los Angeles County line. This area is also home to a private four-year school, California Lutheran University.

From the mid-1800s to the early 1900s, ranching and agriculture were important economic factors in this area, and horse ranches and orchards continue to border residential neighborhoods. In the 1920s and '30s movie-making came to the valleys; the Santa Monica Mountains were irresistible backgrounds, and a lake was named Sherwood following the filming of *Robin Hood*. Once Hollywood discovered the Simi Hills, they became a believable locale for dozens of television and feature-film Westerns.

Simi Valley

In 1795 Rancho Simi became the first land grant in present Ventura County and, with its more than 113,000 acres, one of California's largest. Following several changes of hands, the land was ultimately acquired by American settlers. In 1888 a colony called Simiopolis was established as a health resort that included an imposing hotel. After three years, the colony died out, and only a few farm families remained in the area. They established a school, built stores and shortened the town's name to Simi. ("Simi" is apparently derived from the name of the original Chumash village that stood here: Shimiyi or Shimii.)

As the Southern Pacific Railroad tunneled through the Santa Susana Mountains on the way to Los Angeles from 1900 to 1904, Simi began to grow. Farmers, attracted to a land in which fruit and walnut orchards prospered, enjoyed the presence of a packing house near the railroad in the vicinity of what is now the town of Simi Valley.

The valley remained a small farming community until the real estate boom of the early 20th century brought more settlers to the area. The proliferation of the automobile and the construction in the 1970s of SR 118, the Simi/San Fernando Freeway (now the Ronald Reagan Freeway), brought even more people into the area. Simi Valley, population now over 100,800, has grown as a town in its own right and as a bedroom community for people working in Los Angeles or the San Fernando Valley.

A whole-access interpretive trail in Thousand Oaks offers dappled sunlight through oak trees.

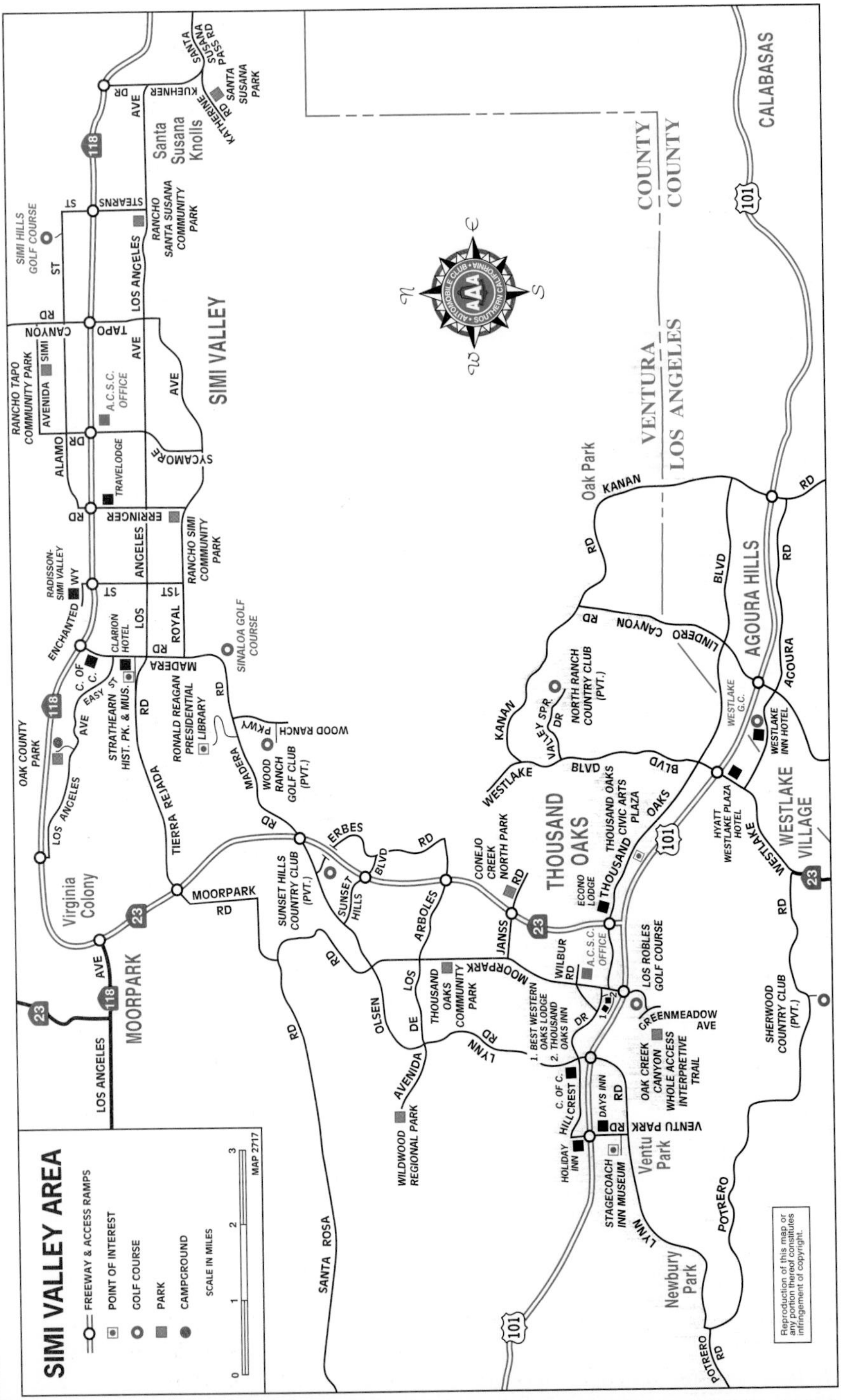
SIMI VALLEY AREA
FREEWAY & ACCESS RAMPS
POINT OF INTEREST
GOLF COURSE
PARK
CAMPGROUND
SCALE IN MILES
0 1 2 3
MAP 2717
Reproduction of this map or any portion thereof constitutes infringement of copyright.
SIMI VALLEY
THOUSAND OAKS
MOORPARK
AGOURA HILLS
WESTLAKE VILLAGE
CALABASAS
Oak Park
Newbury Park
Ventu Park
Virginia Colony
Santa Susana Knolls
VENTURA COUNTY
LOS ANGELES COUNTY
RONALD REAGAN PRESIDENTIAL LIBRARY
STRATHEARN HIST. PK. & MUS.
RANCHO SIMI COMMUNITY PARK
RANCHO TAPO COMMUNITY PARK
RANCHO SANTA SUSANA COMMUNITY PARK
SANTA SUSANA PARK
OAK COUNTY PARK
SIMI HILLS GOLF COURSE
SINALOA GOLF COURSE
WOOD RANCH GOLF CLUB (PVT.)
SUNSET HILLS COUNTRY CLUB (PVT.)
NORTH RANCH COUNTRY CLUB (PVT.)
LOS ROBLES GOLF COURSE
SHERWOOD COUNTRY CLUB (PVT.)
CONEJO CREEK NORTH PARK
THOUSAND OAKS COMMUNITY PARK
THOUSAND OAKS CIVIC ARTS PLAZA
WILDWOOD REGIONAL PARK
OAK CREEK CANYON WHOLE ACCESS INTERPRETIVE TRAIL
STAGECOACH INN MUSEUM
WESTLAKE G.C.
A.C.S.C. OFFICE
RADISSON-SIMI VALLEY
CLARION HOTEL
TRAVELODGE
ECONO LODGE
1. BEST WESTERN OAKS LODGE
2. THOUSAND OAKS INN
DAYS INN
HOLIDAY INN
HYATT WESTLAKE PLAZA HOTEL
WESTLAKE INN HOTEL
C. OF C.
101
118
23

A section of the infamous Berlin Wall stands on the grounds of the Ronald Reagan Presidential Library.

was originally part of a Spanish land grant given to Santiago Pico in 1795, then purchased by Jose de la Guerra in 1842. The Robert P. Strathearn family acquired a portion of the land and built a two-story house there in 1892-93, incorporating two rooms of the original 1840s adobe.

A docent-led tour includes the Strathearn house and its period furnishings, as well as structures which have been relocated to the site. These include a Simi Colony house, the original Simi Library and two barns. A visitor center, through photos, maps, paintings and artifacts, evokes Simi Valley's history from the 1800s to the mid-1900s. A film shown before the tour includes information on Chumash culture, Spanish rancho days and turn-of-the-century American farm life.

RONALD REAGAN PRESIDENTIAL LIBRARY *40 Presidential Dr., 93065. (805) 522-8444. Open daily 10 a.m. to 5 p.m.; closed Jan. 1, Thanksgiving and Dec. 25. Admission $4; over age 62, $2; under age 16, free.* This significant library and museum is housed in a Spanish Mission-style structure built around a courtyard. The complex is set upon a hilltop that affords a view of the surrounding countryside, including the Simi Hills. Included in the library's collection are photographs and memorabilia of President Reagan's life, gifts of state received during his administration, a full-size replica of the Oval Office and a large section of the Berlin Wall.

STRATHEARN HISTORICAL PARK AND MUSEUM *137 Strathearn Pl., 93062. (805) 526-6453. Tours Sat. and Sun. 1 to 4 p.m.; one tour Wed. 1 p.m.; closed during rainy weather, Jan. 1, Mother's Day and Dec. 25.* Today's park

Thousand Oaks

Thousand Oaks, with a population of approximately 104,000, was once an extensive land grant called Rancho El Conejo (*Conejo* is Spanish for rabbit). When the three families which had come to own the land in the 1840s began selling off acreage to other ranchers, they in turn began farming and raising cattle and horses. Ranching and agriculture thrived for decades, then in the 1920s and '30s moviemaking became an added industry in the Conejo Valley. Tourists were attracted to a large menagerie of animals used for motion pictures, and as businesses grew to serve the visitors, the town of Thousand Oaks began to develop. It remained a very small town, however, until the construction of the US 101 freeway in the 1950s, followed by a master plan which led to incorporation in 1964.

In the latter part of the 20th century, Thousand Oaks is a pleasant and attractive community of wide streets, well-kept houses and carefully tended parks and business areas. Parenthetically, it is doubtful that anyone has ever counted the oak trees in Thousand Oaks; the name was determined by the winner of a contest sponsored by land developers in the 1920s.

In the western portion of Thousand Oaks lies Newbury Park, named for the Newbury family, one of the three families originally holding title to Rancho El Conejo. Today Newbury Park, in addition to being a pleasantly sited bedroom community, boasts what was originally the imposing two-story Grand Hotel. Constructed in 1876, the structure was rebuilt following a move and a disastrous fire. Now it is the Stage Coach Inn Museum, an important repository of Conejo Valley history and memorabilia.

Performing arts are well represented in Thousand Oaks. Free concerts ranging from jazz to country to salsa and more are presented at Conejo Community Park; (805) 495-6471. The Conejo Players Theatre is a community acting group; (805) 495-3715. Presentations at the Magnificent Moorpark Melodrama & Vaudeville Company combine both amateur and professional talent; (805) 529-1212.

FARMERS MARKET *Janss Mall at Moorpark Rd. and Hillcrest Dr.; (805) 529-6266. Thur. from 4 to 7 p.m.* Crafts and entertainment are sometimes included.

OAK CREEK CANYON WHOLE ACCESS INTERPRETIVE TRAIL *Green Meadow Dr., ½ mile north of Moorpark Rd. (805) 495-6471.* Part of the Los Robles Open Space, this ¼-mile trail follows a portion of Oak Creek Canyon and is designed for those with special mobility and communication challenges. A wide, specially surfaced trail winds past oak and sycamore trees, following a sturdy wooden fence, with a bridle path on the opposite side of the fence. Along the way are blind-guide cables, Braille interpretive posts and picnic tables.

STAGECOACH INN MUSEUM *51 S. Ventu Park Rd., Newbury Park (mailing address: P.O. Box 1025, Thousand Oaks 91358). (805) 498-9441. Open Wed. through Sun. 1 to 4 p.m.; closed holidays. Admission $2, over age 62 and ages 5-12, $1.* The original structure, now faithfully reproduced, first opened in 1876 as a stopping place for travelers journeying between Los Angeles and Santa Barbara. The reconstructed Monterey-style building houses changing exhibits, Victorian furnishings and artifacts from Conejo Valley's early days. A restored carriage house, pioneer house, adobe and displays of Chumash artifacts are open on Sunday only.

THOUSAND OAKS CIVIC ARTS PLAZA *2100 E. Thousand Oaks Blvd., 91362. (805) 449-2787.* This complex, which sits on 210,000 square feet of land, comprises an 1800-seat auditorium, a 400-seat theater, a city government center and a seven-acre park. Architect Antoine Predock's creation follows the curves of the landscape, with its peaks, canyons, valleys and mesas. Inside, meticulous attention has been paid to sight-lines and acoustics.

Performance art in all its forms—dance, drama, music—take place on the stages here. This is the second home of the Ventura County Symphony; for symphony program information, call (805) 643-8646.

WILDWOOD REGIONAL PARK *Parking area at Avenida Los Arboles and Big Sky Dr. (805) 495-6471. The gate into*

the parking area opens every day at 8:30 a.m.; closed May through Sep. 15 at 8 p.m.; rest of the year, at 5 p.m. Free.
At the northwest edge of carefully planned and tended residential neighborhoods are over a thousand acres of wild and open space called Wildwood Regional Park. Within the park is a wide range of plant and animal life, unusual geologic forms and archaeological sites. Among the vegetation are spring wildflower displays and, all year, oak, chaparral and sage. Wildlife includes mule deer, ground squirrels, rabbits and coyotes. Within the bird community are hummingbirds, kestrels, scrub jays and meadowlarks. Running through the park from east to west is a dramatic volcanic outcropping named Mountclef Ridge. The north fork of the Arroyo Conejo flows through one of the park's two canyons, and following a rainy season, waterfalls are evident. Artifacts such as stone tools, shell beads and arrowheads have been found here. Believed to date back many thousands of years, the artifacts indicate seasonal and permanent Indian tribal settlements.

The park is not open to motor vehicles except for park department vehicles. From the parking area at Avenida Los Arboles and Big Sky Drive, people can hike, bicycle or horseback ride on designated trails. Primitive camping is allowed twice a year by reservation only; a fee is charged. From February through May free naturalist-guided hikes are given on Saturdays from 9 to 11 a.m. Call (805) 494-8301 for information on camping and hiking.

Ojai and Santa Paula Areas

With the founding in 1874 of the town of Nordhoff (later to be called Ojai), people started coming into the Ojai Valley to enjoy the mild, invigorating climate, to sightsee among the hills and valleys or to establish farms and orchards. When the railroad began running from Ventura in 1898, even more people ventured into the valley, including wealthy Easterners such as millionaire John D. Rockefeller Sr., Charles Pratt (secretary of Standard Oil) and glass manufacturer Edward D. Libbey. It was Libbey who ultimately had a deciding influence on the distinctive architecture of downtown Ojai.

In the meantime, the fledgling citrus industry in the Santa Paula and Fillmore area was given a boast in 1887 when a branch of the Southern Pacific Railroad reached the area and began providing transportation for the growers' oranges and lemons. A second important industry, begun in the 1860s, made a spectacular comeback 20 years later, when one oil company began producing 6000 barrels a day. In 1890 this and two other companies met in Santa Paula to incorporate as the Union Oil Company.

Fillmore

Named for a Southern Pacific Railroad Official, J.P. Fillmore, this attractive valley town was laid out in 1887 by the Sespe Land and Water Company and grew up around the railroad depot. Only 150 residents occupied the town by 1900, and the remaining land was divided into parcels on which ranchers built homes and planted citrus orchards. In the early 1860s oil had been discovered around Fillmore and Santa Paula, but the biggest boom came to Fillmore after 1915. Soon many of the citrus orchards were subdivided and houses built for the oil workers and others who began pouring into the area. The town continued to expand, as citrus orchards, and walnut and apricot groves kept pace with the oil industry.

Surrounded by orchards, vegetable farms and oil fields, and with a population near 13,000, Fillmore today is a pleasant town of tree-shaded streets. Many houses, business structures and churches remain from the late 1800s, and visitors to the town are welcome to view these buildings. The town is also home to Shortline Enterprises, which includes an old steam train, diesel locomotives and 45 railroad cars. Information on when and where to admire the Victorian buildings and visit the train is available from the Chamber of Commerce at 460 Main Street; (805) 524-0351.

Built in the early 1900s, an arcade and post office are Ojai landmarks.

FILLMORE FISH HATCHERY *1 mile east of Fillmore off SR 126. Visiting hours daily 8 a.m. to 3:30 p.m. Free.* Over a million rainbow trout are on view here. Raised from eggs to catchable size, the fish are then transported in specially equipped trucks to over 40 lakes and streams in Los Angeles, Ventura, Santa Barbara and San Luis Obispo counties. A nickel in a machine buys a handful of special food for these finny friends. California Department of Fish and Game personnel are on hand to answer questions.

Lake Casitas

Off SR 150, approximately 3 miles west of junction with SR 33.

Lake Casitas Recreation Officer, *1131 Santa Ana Rd., Ventura 93001. (805) 649-2233. Open year round for day use; during standard time from 5:30 a.m. to 6 p.m.; Pacific Daylight Time from 6 a.m. to 7:30 p.m.; campers admitted at any time, space permitting. Day-use admis-sion, $5 per vehicle; $4 extra per boat; camping fees vary.*

Lake Casitas is set in a valley surrounded by rolling hills and graced with oak, fir and sycamore trees, while the Santa Ynez Mountains serve as dramatic background. The main entrance to the recreation area is off SR 150, approximately 3 miles west of its junction with SR 33.

With its 35-mile-long, irregularly shaped shoreline, Lake Casitas is actually a man-made reservoir which provides water for the daily use of more than 50,000 Ventura County residents. There is also recreation here for both local residents and visitors: Fishermen can haul in trout, bass, crappie, catfish and red-ear sunfish; over-nighters and day-users are lured by more than 700 picnicking and camping sites (see *Campgrounds & Trailer Parks* and *Recreation*). In March, Lake Casitas is the site of the Ojai Renaissance Festival (see *Annual Events*). From mid-April

A variety of recreational opportunities is offered at scenic Lake Casitas.

through mid-September a small store is open at the lake, and a snack bar is open all year.

Ojai

A gentleman named Charles Nordhoff wrote a book in the 1870s called *California for Health, Pleasure and Residence* and consequently in 1874 had a California town named for him. His fame was short-lived, however, for in 1917 the town of Nordhoff became Ojai (O´-hi), a Spanish-style word derived from the Chumash word *Awhai*, meaning either "nest" or "moon," depending upon the translator.

From its earliest days, the town had assumed the role of vacation destination, particularly for Edward D. Libbey, glass manufacturing millionaire. Under Libbey's direction, architect Richard Requa designed the arched arcade fronting two blocks of the downtown shops. The arcade remains today, and just across the street is Requa's inviting entrance to Libbey Park, while his Spanish-style tower rises above Ojai's post office.

With a population of approximately 7600 and boasting only three traffic signals, Ojai sits in an especially beautiful valley, sheltered by rugged mountains

Horse ranches are part of the landscape near Ojai.

and gentle hills, and bordered with horse ranches and citrus orchards. Ojai is perhaps best known for its artists, musicians and philosophers, and many of the artists periodically open their studios to visitors (contact the Ojai Chamber of Commerce, 338 East Ojai Avenue, telephone (805) 646-8126, for details). June is the month for the decades-old Ojai Festival, when classical music is presented outdoors in Libbey Park. The Ojai Valley Tennis Tournament, held annually since 1899, is an April event (see *Annual Events*).

THE ARCADE *North side of Ojai Ave. between Signal and Montgomery sts.* This Mission Revival-style shopping arcade,

built in 1917, has shops that offer such tempting merchandise as handcrafted jewelry, sculpted figures and vessels, "wearable art," clothing and objects from Central America and Mexico, and American Indian jewelry and clothing. There's even an English tea room. A medium-sized, traditional department store is also located here. An air of relaxed independence prevails among the store owners, so most stores open about 10 a.m., and a few close at 4 p.m., more at 5 p.m., with some staying open until 6 p.m. on weekends.

FARMERS MARKET *Parking area between Signal, Aliso, Montgomery and Matilija sts; (805) 646-4444. Sun. 10 a.m. to 2 p.m.* In addition to fresh fruits and vegetables, there are herbs, flowers, baked goods and fresh seafood.

THE OJAI CENTER FOR THE ARTS *113 Montgomery St., Ojai 93024. (805) 646-0117. Open Tues. through Sun. noon to 4 p.m. Free.* Displayed here are the works of California artists: paintings, sketches and sculpture that in a diversity of media capture a diversity of people and moods. Since these are changing exhibits, and the gallery is closed during changeovers, visitors are advised to call ahead. A vital cultural asset to Ojai, the center also offers arts classes, workshops and seminars.

A 100-seat community theater presents live performances of musical comedy and drama on weekends throughout the year; call (805) 646-0117 for schedule. Tickets for theater performances range from $5 to $10 each.

OJAI STUDIO ARTISTS TOUR *Various locations, Ojai. (805) 646-8126. One weekend 11 a.m. to 4 p.m. in mid-Oct. $12 per person for tickets in advance; $15 day of tour.* Once a year nearly 30 artists in the Ojai area open their studios, homes and gardens to the public. This is an opportunity to view the artistic process in media that include oil, watercolors, sculpture and neon art. Ticket prices include a champagne and dessert reception. Proceeds from ticket sales benefit art scholarships and art instruction in elementary schools.

THE OJAI TROLLEY COMPANY *Daily except major holidays. 25¢ fare; under age 5 and over age 75, free.* A bus that's made to look like an old fashioned trolley car, inside and out, takes passengers all over Ojai for just a quarter. The route runs along Ojai Avenue to La Luna Avenue and Maricopa Highway on the west; Grand Avenue and Gridley Road on the east. Stops are clearly marked with trolley signs. A central boarding point is in front of the Chamber of Commerce office on the north side of Ojai Avenue near Montgomery Street.

OJAI VALLEY HISTORICAL MUSEUM *109 S. Montgomery St., 93024. (805) 646-2290. Open Wed. through Mon. 1 to 4 p.m. Admission $3; under age 12, free.* In what was once a fire station, the local historical society has assembled attractive displays of the natural and human history of the Ojai Valley. Among the exhibits are flora, fauna, shells and rocks found in the area; a representative array of Chumash artifacts; and tools, furniture, household items and photographs that reflect the early settlement of Nordhoff/Ojai.

WINERY *Hours are subject to change; please call ahead. More complete descriptions of wineries offering tours appear in the Auto Club's* California Winery Tours *book.*

Old Creek Ranch Winery *1½ miles south of Oak View at the end of Old Creek Rd. (805) 649-4132. Open for tasting Fri.*

through Sun. 10 a.m. to 4:30 p.m.; tours by appointment. Grapes from the Santa Maria Valley and Ventura County are used in six varietal wines produced here.

Santa Paula

When in 1875 Santa Paula was established as a townsite in the Santa Clara River Valley, the surrounding land already had hundreds of acres devoted to fruit trees. Through the decades, orchards, particularly lemon and orange, have continued to prosper, and the oil industry has kept pace with the citrus industry. During the 1880s three oil companies, Hardison and Stewart, Sespe Oil, and Torrey Cañon Oil, made significant strikes in Ventura County. In October 1890, in the Santa Paula building now housing the Santa Paula Union Oil Museum, the principal stockholders of these companies signed incorporation papers to become the Union Oil Company. Three years later a group of businessmen and growers formed the Limoneira Company in Santa Paula, a partnership that eventually became one of the largest lemon producers in the world.

Santa Paula was incorporated in 1902, and today its population of nearly 26,000 enjoys a small town ambience, along with such modern amenities as shopping centers and a general aviation airport. Visitors can find good examples of Victorian architecture throughout the town and in the countryside. One of the finest examples is the 1894 Faulkner House at 4292 Telegraph Road, just west of Briggs Road. While this beautifully restored three-story mansion is not open to the public, it can be seen from the road. The bright red barn on the grounds houses the Ayers Pumpkin Patch; pumpkins are sold to the public in

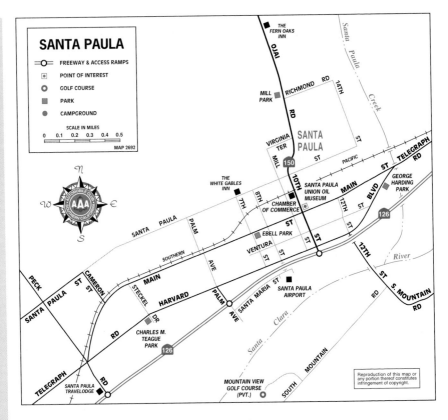

October, and from the day after Thanksgiving until December 22, Christmas trees are offered for sale. A brochure outlining scenic areas and historic buildings is available free of charge from the Santa Paula Chamber of Commerce, located in the train depot at 10th and Santa Barbara streets; telephone (805) 525-5561.

Along SR 126 east of Santa Paula citrus groves and ranches nestle against rolling hills, and roadside stands offer such local produce as avocados, strawberries, lemons, grapefruit and oranges. A little over four miles east of Santa Paula on the south side of SR 126 stands Santa Clara Elementary School, a genuine "Little Red Schoolhouse," built in 1896. With its bell tower and white Colonial Revival trim, this historic landmark still functions as a county elementary school.

Performing arts take shape in classic drama, modern comedy and children's theater at the Santa Paula Theatre Center; (805) 525-4645.

SANTA PAULA AIRPORT *Entrance is off Santa Maria St., just east of 8th St. (mailing address: P.O. Box 308, 93061); (805) 933-1155. Antique and classic aircraft on public display first Sun. of each month 10 a.m. to 3 p.m. Free.* This well-maintained general aviation airport was founded in 1930, and today is probably best known for its extensive collection of privately owned antique, classic, home-built and modern small planes.

The nearly century-old Little Red Schoolhouse is still in use.

Santa Paula Flight Center-Scenic Rides *Santa Paula Airport; P.O. Box 857; 93061. (805) 525-3561. Scenic rides given daily, weather and visibility permitting, 8 a.m. to 5 p.m.; closed Dec. 25. 20-minute basic flight, $40; additional time for coastal flights or viewing Channel Islands, additional $1 per minute. Reservations are suggested.* For an exhilarating high-in-the-sky view of the Santa Clara River Valley, these scenic flights take you over farmlands, suburbs, orchards, hills and canyons to the Ventura coast and back. The aircraft is a Cessna 172, which has room for three passengers.

SANTA PAULA UNION OIL MUSEUM *1001 E. Main St., 93060. (805) 933-0076. Open Thur. through Sun. 10 a.m. to 4 p.m.; closed major holidays. Donation.* The 1890 landmark building in which the Union Oil Company was founded is today devoted to showing the history and science of oil exploration in California through memorabilia, photographs, murals and interactive videos. One room in the museum houses changing exhibits on various subjects, from Santa Paula's airport to works by local artists. Visitors may take a guided tour of the building's second floor, where the oil company's 19th-century offices and a 1930s apartment have been recreated, including original woodwork, 10 fireplaces with original tiles, and journals and ledgers dating back to the late 1800s.

In a separate building stands an impressive, 100-year-old, steam-powered Cable-Tool drilling rig. A small, pleasant grassy area with wooden benches adjoins the museum, just right for resting and picnicking.

SANTA BARBARA COUNTY

Santa Barbara County is made up of a series of coastal plains and interior valleys, with geographical features ranging from sky-high mountain peaks to dramatically eroded canyons to flat grasslands to rocky and sandy seashores.

The **Santa Barbara Coast**, beginning at the Ventura County line, first runs east and west for about 60 miles, facing the Santa Barbara Channel to the south. Along here, off highway US 101, lie the cities of Santa Barbara, Carpinteria, Goleta and the smaller towns of Summerland, Montecito and Isla Vista. About 35 miles east of Santa Barbara at Gaviota State Beach, US 101 takes a turn north, but the coastline continues to Point Conception, then it too turns north.

A seahorse and rider watch over Santa Barbara Harbor.

Those objects in the Santa Barbara Channel are offshore oil rigs.

Northwest of Santa Barbara, bordered by the Santa Ynez and San Rafael mountains, the **Santa Ynez Valley** encompasses gently rolling green or golden hills dotted with oak and eucalyptus trees. Side roads lead to cattle ranches, horse farms, wineries, and citrus groves

Drum Canyon Road out of Los Alamos passes lush ranchland sprinkled with graceful oak trees.

from the foothills of the Sierra Madre Mountains to the sand dunes bordering the Pacific Ocean.

To the north, as a backdrop to it all, stand the rugged Santa Ynez Mountains within Los Padres National Forest (see *Los Padres National Forest* chapter). San Marcos Pass Road is a scenic highway that leads from the Santa Ynez Valley past Lake Cachuma and into Los Padres National Forest.

and croplands. Solvang lies in this valley. A favorite destination for tourists, it's a Danish-style village famous for shops and pastries.

West of the Santa Ynez Valley, the **Lompoc Valley** lies between the Santa Ynez Mountains on the south and the Purísima Hills on the north. Traversed by SR 246, you can also get there by taking SR 1, two miles north of Gaviota State Park. Reflecting the valley's diversity is the fact that it's home to Vandenberg Air Force Base, the western base or military space launches, and about five miles from this modern facility stands La Purísima Mission, founded by Spanish missionaries in 1787.

The last sizable town in the northern part of Santa Barbara County lies just off US 101: Santa Maria in the **Santa Maria Valley**. This flat, fertile valley extends

Tranquil scenery is found along Paradise Road in Santa Barbara County's backcountry.

Santa Barbara Coast

Nestled between the rugged Santa Ynez Mountains on the north and Pacific beaches on the south, this long, east-west plain is never more than 10 miles wide. The area's south-facing configuration and protective mountains guarantee a mild, Riviera-style climate throughout the year.

The region possesses a varied economy that reflects its ties with the past and its expectations for the future. Agricultural production (particularly lemons, avocados and vegetables) and flower cultivation flourish in the favorable climate and fertile soil. Oil exploration, and research and development in electronics and space technology also contribute significantly. As in other portions of the Central Coast, tourism makes a major contribution to the local economy.

The principal and most populous city along the coast, Santa Barbara serves as both the county seat and a magnet for tourists, thanks to its mild climate, charm and attractive Spanish architecture. East of Santa Barbara lies Carpinteria, which pardonably boasts of its broad state beach, while Goleta on the west serves as home to the University of California at Santa Barbara.

Carpinteria

Carpinteria, a city of nearly 14,000 people, is located 12 miles east of Santa Barbara in a small valley between the Santa Ynez Mountains and the coast. It apparently acquired its name in 1769 when Spanish soldiers in Gaspar de Portolá's explora-

tory expedition, intrigued with the Chumash canoe-building, called the area Carpinteria, roughly translated as "carpenter shop."

The valley's agricultural production, still vital to the local economy, was originally slow to develop. Land division didn't begin until the mid-1800s because the entire Carpinteria Valley was considered a prize location for large Spanish, and later, Mexican land grants. In 1858 the first American rancher began acquiring land for orchards and over time developed what was reputedly the world's largest walnut grove. Then, about 30 years later, lima beans were introduced as a commercial crop.

Not only a producer of edible crops, the Carpinteria Valley is a major flower-growing region. It is recognized as one of the world's orchid capitals and the largest producer of cymbidium orchids in the nation. Other flowers grown here include carnations, azaleas, roses and tulips.

Historically, there was one other highly prized segment of the Carpinteria Valley economy: Tar, which the Chumash had used to caulk their canoes, became an object of strip mining along the coast from 1875 to the

---

Figures adorning the Santa Barbara County Courthouse reflect the city's marine aspects.

early 1920s. The tar was so pure that it was not only used for paving and roofing but for producing printers' ink and artists' colors, as well.

Despite its early successes in farming and mining, the Carpinteria Valley was slow in drawing tourists into the area because the slopes of adjacent Rincon Mountain drop directly to the sea, severely limiting access by land. A roadbed along the shore for stagecoaches was almost impossible to maintain because of constant landslides. In order to get through, stages had to wait for low tide. Finally in 1887, the Southern Pacific Railroad carved a right-of-way and built a mile-long ledge for track out of the side of the mountain, thus opening the Carpinteria Valley to visitors. In 1912 the Rincon Causeway, with its 6100-foot viaduct of wood planks over eucalyptus pilings spanning the water, opened to allow automobile traffic into Carpinteria. A paved highway was

completed 10 years later, replacing the causeway.

Today Carpinteria's residents proudly proclaim their shore to be the "world's safest beach," because of its natural reef breakwater and absence of riptides. One of California's largest public beach camping units is at Carpinteria State Beach (see *Campgrounds & Trailer Parks*), and Rincon Point is considered one of the best surfing spots in Southern California.

CARPINTERIA VALLEY MUSEUM OF HISTORY *956 Maple Ave., 93013. (805) 684-3112. Open Tues. through Fri. and Sun. 1:30 to 4 p.m.; Sat. 11 a.m. to 4 p.m.; closed major holidays. Free.* Exhibits in this attractively arranged museum depict a typical turn-of-the-century lifestyle by means of household furnishings and clothing contributed by descendants of Carpinteria's pioneer families. One wing contains agricultural and oil-boom artifacts and a very early 20th-century schoolroom. A

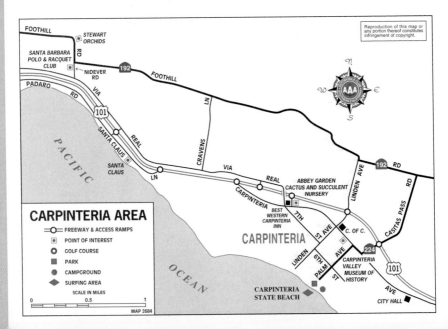

Yes, there is a Santa Claus; he has his own town just ½ mile west of Carpinteria.

number of Chumash artifacts, including ornaments and utensils, are also on display.

FARMERS MARKET *800 block of Linden Ave.; (805) 962-5354. Thu., in spring and summer 4 to 7 p.m.; rest of year 3 to 6:30 p.m.* Local farmers set up shop each week at this popular market featuring fresh fruit, vegetables and flowers.

SANTA BARBARA POLO & RACQUET CLUB *1 mile west of Carpinteria at 3375 Foothill Rd., 93013. (805) 684-8667 (recording), 684-6683. Polo games, Apr. through Oct., each Sun. at 1 p.m., feature match at 3 p.m. Free.* Visitors are welcome to view these exciting games. For information about matches and schedules, telephone either of the above numbers.

SANTA CLAUS *Santa Claus Ln., off US 101, ½ mile west of Carpinteria. Most shops open summer months daily 10 a.m. to 8 p.m.; rest of the year, Mon. through Thur. 9 a.m. to 6 p.m., Fri. and Sat. until 8 p.m.* Much of the merchandise and

decor of this tourist attraction is based on Christmas themes. In addition to a bakery, restaurants and candy kitchen, shops feature toys, dates and gifts. Many visitors enjoy sending mail from Santa Claus, especially in December, because of the postmark.

STEWART ORCHIDS *1 mile west of Carpinteria at 3376 Foothill Rd., 93014. (805) 684-5448. Open Mon. through Fri. from 8 a.m. to 4 p.m. and Sat. 10 a.m. to 4 p.m.; closed Sun. and major holidays.* This large nursery is devoted solely to the growing and selling of orchids. More than 80,000 square feet of greenhouse space encloses plants of contrasting shape, size and color.

Goleta

Lying just west of Santa Barbara between the Santa Ynez Mountains and the ocean, this area in the 1840s was the Dos Pueblos land grant, and extensive herds of cattle grazed here. Over time the land changed hands, and by the late 1800s, citrus, walnut

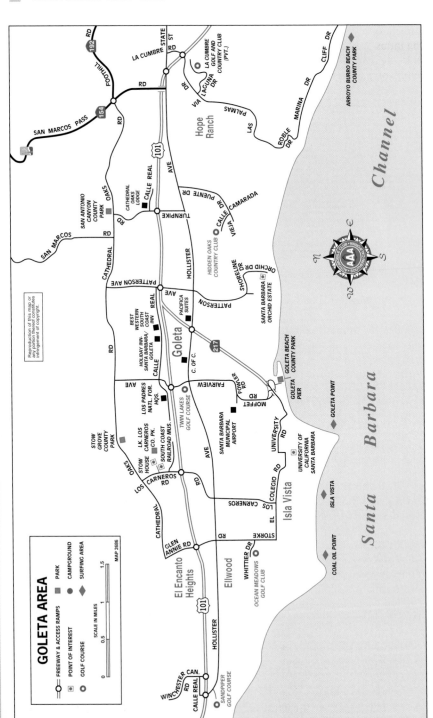

and almond orchards became the leading industry of the valley, thanks largely to the pioneering efforts of the Stow family on La Patera Ranch.

Today Goleta, from the Spanish word for schooner, is a busy, unincorporated community of more than 72,000 people. Like Carpinteria, agriculture and flower-growing play a part in Goleta's economy. More importantly, however, Goleta houses approximately 80 research and development firms in the fields of electronics and space technology. Also located here is the Santa Barbara Municipal Airport, and nearby Isla Vista is the home of the University of California at Santa Barbara.

FARMERS MARKET *5700 block of Calle Real Shopping Center (805) 962-5354. Thurs., in spring and summer, 3 to 7 p.m.; rest of year 3 to 6:30 p.m.* Flowers, local honey and live entertainment are featured at this market.

SANTA BARBARA ORCHID ESTATE
1250 Orchid Dr., Santa Barbara 93111. (805) 967-1284. Open Mon. through Sat., 8 a.m. to 4:30 p.m.; Sun. 11 a.m. to 4 p.m.; closed major holidays. Two acres, one under glass and one outdoors, are used to display a multitude of orchids. At any one time, many varieties are in bloom, with each month having its own specialty. Both cut flowers and plants, exclusively orchids, are available to retail buyers as well as wholesalers. Those who wish to simply stroll and enjoy the beauty of the plants are always welcome.

SOUTH COAST RAILROAD MUSEUM
300 N. Los Carneros Rd., 93117. (805) 964-3540. Open Wed. through Sun. 1 to 4 p.m. Free. This wooden building, with its distinctive "SP yellow" color, was constructed by the Southern Pacific Railroad Company in 1901, handling freight and passengers until the early 1970s. The station was relocated to its present site, and

Built in 1901, the Goleta Depot was moved in 1981 to its present location and now houses the South Coast Railroad Museum.

restoration began in 1981. Antique railroad artifacts, photographs and hands-on exhibits are located in the agency office and passenger waiting rooms. A 300-square-foot, HO-scale model railroad is also on display. An old Southern Pacific caboose sits on tracks in front of the museum. Rides aboard a miniature train are offered Saturdays 1 to 4 p.m., Wednesday, Friday and Sunday 2 to 3:30 p.m.

STOW HOUSE *304 N. Los Carneros Rd., 93117. (805) 964-4407. Open Sat. and Sun. 2 to 4 p.m.; closed on rainy days. Free. Group tours can be arranged.* This restored ranch house, built by the Stow family in the 1870s, is a rambling, two-story, Victorian-style structure with some "Carpenter's Gothic" touches. Its wide veranda is shaded by a great Australian primrose tree. Inside, rooms and hallways contain such beautiful period furnishings as chairs, tables, hand-hooked rugs, period clothing and toys. Some of the outbuildings have also been restored and contain the Goleta History Museum, the Maritime Interpretive Display and antique farm equipment. Special events are held here on July 4th, in October during Goleta Valley Days and during the Christmas season (see *Annual Events*).

UNIVERSITY OF CALIFORNIA AT SANTA BARBARA *2 miles south of*
US 101 via Clarence Ward Memorial Blvd. (SR 217) (mailing address: UCSB, Santa Barbara 93106). (805) 893-8000. Founded in 1891 as a trade school near downtown Santa Barbara, a greatly expanded curriculum brought it into the University of California system in 1944. In 1954 the campus was relocated to its present site—815 acres by the Pacific Ocean in Isla Vista near Goleta.

In addition to traditional programs, UCSB has an extensive Marine Sciences Institute, which uses a large adjacent lagoon as one of its research areas. The major architectural landmark on the campus is 175-foot-high Storke Tower, which houses a 61-bell carillon that is heard twice each hour. The Santa Barbara community is enriched by the university's cultural events presented both on and off campus throughout the year; the fields of music, drama, dance and visual arts are well represented.

Free guided tours of the campus can be arranged all year by contacting the Office of Relations with Schools, 1234 Cheadle Hall, Santa Barbara 93106; or by calling (805) 893-8175 (recording) or 893-2485. Parking is free during evening hours and on weekends and university holidays. On weekdays a $5 pass must be purchased at the entrance gate; the pass includes a map of the campus and visitor parking.

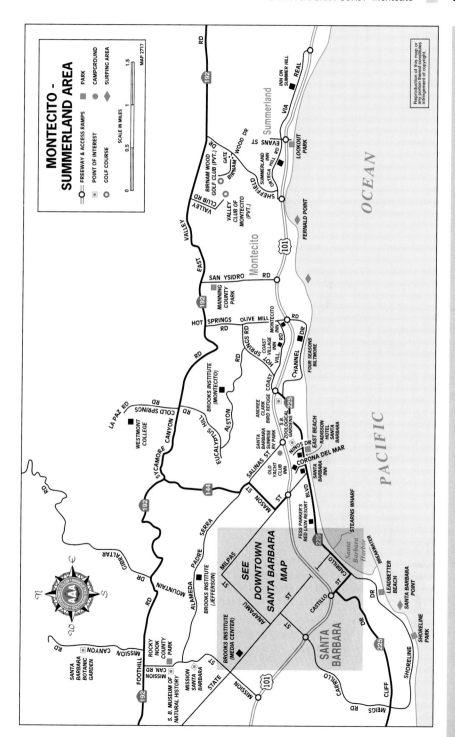

MONTECITO - SUMMERLAND AREA

- ◯ FREEWAY & ACCESS RAMPS
- ▣ POINT OF INTEREST
- ◎ GOLF COURSE
- ■ PARK
- ◆ CAMPGROUND
- ◆ SURFING AREA

SCALE IN MILES

0   0.5   1   1.5

MAP 2717

Montecito

Along the border of Santa Barbara's eastern limits lies Montecito, a community that grew from a resort area to which wealthy people flocked during the late 19th century. Most of them were from the East Coast, and having fallen in love with the mild climate, mineral hot springs, and mountain and ocean vistas, many decided to stay. By the early 20th century large, lush estates had been established. Names prominent in American business had Montecito addresses: Armstrong, Du Pont, Fleischmann, Pillsbury and Stetson.

During the 1920s and '30s Montecito continued to experience an influx of well-to-do people. These later arrivals, however, chose not to build such elaborate domiciles. Nevertheless, the community continues to enjoy a reputation for beautiful, lavishly landscaped homes, and some prominent entertainment industry figures have settled here. Unfortunately (for tourists), most of the impressive residences are screened from view by hedges, trees and walls, but the overall beauty of the community makes a sightseeing drive worthwhile.

In the hills above Sycamore Canyon Road in Montecito, Ganna Walska Lotusland embraces 37 acres of gardens that include a Japanese water garden, dozens of varieties of euphorbia, cactus, ferns, palms and an unparalleled area of cycads. Lotusland is open for guided tours, by reservation only, mid-February to mid-November. Call (805) 969-9990 at least two months in advance; there is an admission fee.

Santa Barbara

One of California's most attractive communities, Santa Barbara occupies a narrow plain that slopes southward from the rugged Santa Ynez Mountains to palm-fringed Pacific beaches. Benign weather supports a lush growth of subtropical and Mediterranean foliage that provides the city with vivid color and greenery year round, while an abundance of Spanish-Mediterranean architecture, with its red-tiled roofs and white walls, is found throughout the city.

Establishment of a mission and a presidio in the 18th century was the beginning of Santa Barbara's settlement. Following secularization of the missions, the United States developed an interest in acquiring California. By 1846, thanks in part to Captain John C. Frémont's California Battalion, America's authority had been established in Santa Barbara. As American occupation continued, soldiers mustered out of the service in Santa Barbara were absorbed into the community.

During the second half of the 19th century, Santa Barbara began to assume its present shape. Streets were laid out, and many were given names reflecting the town's Spanish heritage. Americans acquired title to land on which they established farms for raising crops and cattle. One- and two-story frame houses were built in town, often in New England architectural styles.

From the 1870s into the early 20th century, Santa Barbara's popularity was greatly increased by the discovery of mineral springs that were believed to have medicinal value. Inviting spas were built near the springs, and eager patrons traveled to Santa Barbara by ship or stagecoach. In 1901, however, steamer and stagecoach travel came to an end as rail lines were completed through Santa Barbara to San Francisco.

One glamorous aspect of Santa Barbara's history was the town's role in movie making. By 1910 the American Film Company had a studio in the center of town, and stars such as Wallace Reid, "Fatty" Arbuckle, Mabel Normand and director D.W. Griffith made celluloid history. For nearly a decade the area's mansions, streets and scenic foothills provided excellent backgrounds, while local residents found work as extras.

History and glamour aside, the early 1920s brought an awareness that many buildings in the downtown area were unattractive or in need of repair; the

timetable for rebuilding was dictated by an earthquake on June 29, 1925, that demolished much of central Santa Barbara. Structures were rebuilt, not only with fire and earthquake safety in mind, but also with architecturally harmonious exteriors in the Hispanic style.

The following decades brought growth and prosperity to Santa Barbara. Tourism continued to provide employment in a variety of fields. The University of California, begun in 1891 as Anna S.C. Blake Training School, created a number of jobs and became a catalyst for cultural stimulation. Light industry was brought into the area by several

UPPER STATE STREET

- ◉ POINT OF INTEREST
- ⬛ PARK
- ○ GOLF COURSE
- ● CAMPGROUND

SCALE IN MILES
0 0.1 0.2 0.3 0.4 0.5

MAP 2716

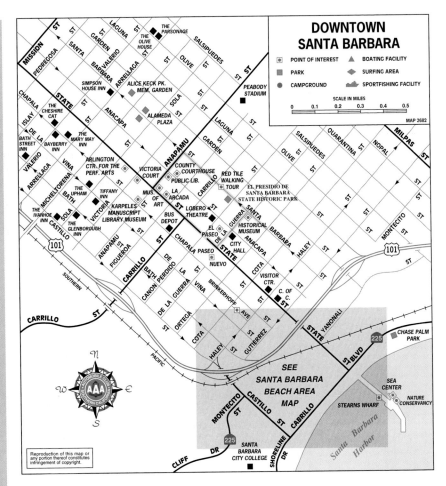

DOWNTOWN SANTA BARBARA

- POINT OF INTEREST
- PARK
- CAMPGROUND
- ▲ BOATING FACILITY
- SURFING AREA
- SPORTFISHING FACILITY

SCALE IN MILES
0   0.1   0.2   0.3   0.4   0.5

MAP 2682

electronic and computer firms. The public school system that began in the late 19th century continued to grow, while special schools like Brooks Institute added prestige to the community.

With the city's growth, cultural and recreational opportunities increased. A resident symphony orchestra was founded in 1953. The visual arts flourished, as small galleries sprang up to house them, and an attractive, comprehensive art museum became a midtown landmark. Theaters like the Arlington and Lobero were adapted to present motion pictures, as well as live entertainment. Stearns Wharf and the breakwater helped make Santa Barbara's harbor safe and convenient for commercial and pleasure boats. Outdoor recreational facilities expanded as people developed interests in everything from bird-watching to polo.

The Santa Barbara area has also become a center of activity for serious students in many fields, particularly the arts. The University of California at Santa Barbara, the Music Academy of the West, Santa Barbara City College and Brooks Institute of Photography in

Santa Barbara all contribute to the city's educational climate.

Performing arts in Santa Barbara offer just about anything anyone could want. Two dinner theaters are available: the Circle Bar B west of Goleta at 1800 Refugio Road, (805) 965-9652; and Starlight Entertainment At Villa Santa Barbara, downtown at 227 E. Anapamu Street, (805) 964-3688. Arlington Center hosts musical, theatrical and dance programs as well as motion pictures (see listing). The Lobero Theatre presents drama, music and dance (see listing). The Alhecama Theatre (914 Santa Barbara Street) hosts the Ensemble Theatre Company in new, revival and classical plays; (805) 962-8606. The Granada Theatre at 1216 State Street is home to Santa Barbara Civic Light Opera's Broadway musicals; (805) 966-2324 or (800) 549-7386. Music in the outdoors is enjoyed April through November at the Santa Barbara County Bowl on Milpas Street near Anapamu Street, where recording stars such as Sting or James Taylor are usually featured; seating is reserved; (805) 568-2695. Throughout the school year, and often in the summer, other academic institutions in the Santa Barbara area present high-caliber music and drama programs on their campuses. Contact the following for program information. In Santa Barbara: Music Academy of the West, (805) 969-4726; Santa Barbara City College, (805) 965-5935; Westmont College, (805) 565-6040; in Goleta, University of California at Santa Barbara, (805) 893-3535.

Within a short drive of downtown Santa Barbara are several smaller communities which, because of beauty or historical significance—or both—merit a visit.

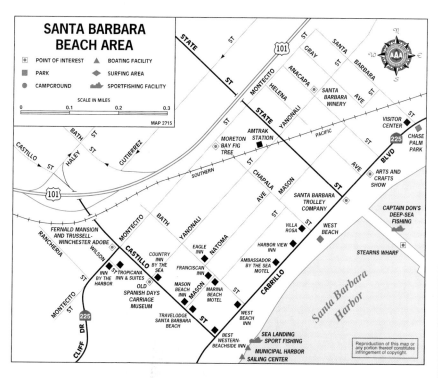

▼ A Quick Guide to Santa Barbara Information

Population: 88,900

Elevation: 33 ft.

Telephone numbers are in the 805 area code, unless noted otherwise.

Emergency 911

Police (non-emergency) 897-2300

Emergency Road Service for AAA Members (800) 400-4222

Hospitals

St. Francis Medical Center
601 E. Micheltorena St.
Santa Barbara 93103
962-7661

Goleta Valley Community Hospital
351 S. Patterson Ave.
Santa Barbara 93111
967-3411

Time 966-0611

Weather 988-6610

Highway Conditions (800) 427-7623

Radio and TV

Radio station KTMS (1250 AM) in Santa Barbara offers news, talk and traffic reports. KFAC (88.7 FM) is a member of National Public Radio. Santa Barbara's Spanish language station is KOXR (910 AM).

Network television channels are 2 (CBS), 3 (ABC), 4 (NBC). The PBS channel is 10. For a complete list of radio and television programs, consult the daily newspapers.

Automobile Club of Southern California

Santa Barbara District Office
3712 State St.

Mailing address: P.O. Drawer 3860
Santa Barbara 93130-3860
Phone: 682-5811
Office hours: Mon. through Fri.
9 a.m. to 5 p.m.

Visitor Services

Santa Barbara Chamber of Commerce
504 State St.
Santa Barbara 93102
Phone: 965-3023
Office hours: Mon. through Fri.
9 a.m. to 5 p.m.

Santa Barbara Visitors Information
  Center
Cabrillo Blvd. & Santa Barbara St.
Santa Barbara 93101
Phone: 965-3021
Office hours: Apr. through Labor Day, daily 9 a.m. to 6 p.m.; rest of year, daily 9 a.m. to 5 p.m.

Newspapers

The major daily newspapers in the Santa Barbara area are the *Santa Barbara News-Press* and the Santa Barbara County edition of the *Los Angeles Times*; both contain local events and entertainment information.

Public Transportation & Taxis

Santa Barbara Metropolitan Transit District (MTD) operates buses in Santa Barbara, Carpinteria and Goleta. For schedule and route information call 683-3702.

Yellow Cab provides service in the Santa Barbara area; call 965-5111. Other taxi companies are listed in the yellow pages of the local telephone directory.

Among them is Hope Ranch, an exclusive and beautiful residential area, lying just west of Santa Barbara, on the south side of US 101. This area was originally part of a Mexican land grant called Cañada de Calera. A patent on the land grant was issued to Thomas W. Hope in 1870, and the Spanish designation was changed to Hope Ranch by his heirs. During the early 1900s the land was subdivided and sold in large sections. Few of the fine homes later built on these estates are visible from the street; however, Las Palmas Drive winds through the area and provides a scenic trip leading past the beautiful lake and greens of La Cumbre Golf and Country Club.

ALAMEDA PLAZA *Bounded by Micheltorena, Garden, Sola and Anacapa sts.; bisected by Santa Barbara St.* In the square on the east side of Santa Barbara Street are over 70 species of trees, singly or in small groves, that provide an inviting midtown area for picnicking or relaxing. There are benches, picnic tables and children's play equipment, and the park area to the west has a large gazebo used for concerts and speeches.

ALICE KECK PARK MEMORIAL GARDEN *Bounded by Arrellaga, Garden, Micheltorena and Santa Barbara sts.* This inviting park in the midst of the city emphasizes the diverse plant life to be found in Santa Barbara. Plant environments range from marshy to arid, and colors throughout the gardens vary from section to section and season to season. Within the grounds are a pond that hosts a variety of marine plants, two meandering streams, winding pathways, benches and a gazebo.

ANDREE CLARK BIRD REFUGE *1400 E. Cabrillo Blvd.* This preserve of more than 40 acres includes a lagoon that is dotted with islands and enhanced by well-kept gardens. The refuge provides a sheltered home for many migratory and nonmigratory bird species, including a wide variety of waterfowl.

Waterfowl of all sorts find a permanent home or a migratory-path stopover at the Andree Clark Bird Refuge.

Walkways and bicycle paths border the refuge, and space is provided for free automobile parking off Los Patos Way.

ARLINGTON CENTER FOR THE PERFORMING ARTS *1317 State St. (805) 963-4408.* Live entertainment is presented here in an unusual setting. The entryway is in the style of a Spanish courtyard, the lobby ceiling has a mural depicting fiesta dancers, and the theater's interior walls are constructed to resemble a Spanish town with a starry sky. Home of the Santa Barbara Symphony, Arlington Center also presents visiting orchestras and ballet companies, dramatic and musical programs, and motion pictures.

ARTS AND CRAFTS SHOW *Along Cabrillo Blvd., east from State St. (805) 962-8956. Sun. and holidays 10 a.m. to dusk, weather permitting.* A stroll eastward from State Street along the beach side of Cabrillo Boulevard leads past an extensive arts and crafts show. Since 1966, artisans of Santa Barbara have been displaying their works here in an outdoor setting that often extends three-quarters of a mile. There is a wide range of artistic taste, style and ability expressed through various media; painting, ceramics, sculpture and photography among them. Everything is for sale, and conversations with the displaying artists are encouraged.

BRINKERHOFF AVENUE *Between Cota and Haley sts. Most shops open 11 a.m. to 5:30 p.m.; days closed vary.* Along both sides of this single block are charming old houses which have been converted to antique and gift shops. All sorts of collectible items, from buttons to bathtubs, can be found here; browsing is welcomed.

BROOKS INSTITUTE OF PHOTOGRA-PHY *801 Alston Rd., 93108. (805) 966-*

3888. This world-renowned private institute, established in 1945, occupies three campuses in the Santa Barbara area. Graduate and undergraduate degrees are offered in all phases of photography, from portraiture to scientific research. Photographs are on display at all three campuses, with the main hallway galleries on the Jefferson and Montecito campuses.

Jefferson Campus *1321 Alameda Padre Serra. Open Mon. through Fri. 8 a.m. to 5 p.m. Free.* This campus houses the institute's illustration/advertising, audio visual and industrial/scientific departments and an advanced electronic imaging lab. The campus is also home to one of the nation's finest photographic libraries.

Media Center *1722 State St. Open to visitors Mon. through Fri. 8 a.m. to 5 p.m. when school is in session. Free.* This facility contains the motion picture/video department for the institute.

Montecito Campus *801 Alston Rd. Free conducted tours given by request daily 3 p.m. when school is in session.* This campus contains the institute's portrait and color departments.

CHANNEL ISLANDS NATIONAL MARINE SANCTUARY TOUR *Departs Sea Landing, foot of Bath St. at Cabrillo Blvd. (mailing address: 301 W. Cabrillo Blvd., 93101). (805) 963-3564. Six or seven tours June through Oct.; call for schedule. Fare $65; under age 12, $35. Reservations are necessary.* All-day excursions aboard the 88-foot ship *Condor* go to the waters of the National Marine Sanctuary, with particular emphasis on the waters off Santa Cruz Island (see *Ventura County*, Channel Islands National Park). The cruise is narrated by naturalists, divers and other experts. Passengers watching a large video monitor can track divers from the ship as they go over the side to give a tour of kelp forests and underwater reefs. A good view of sharks is included, and smaller marine life is brought aboard and placed in a touch tank for close-up examination.

At Santa Cruz Island passengers can board manned skiffs and visit Painted Cave, one of the world's largest sea caves. Going to and from the island there are often sightings of marine birds, sea lions, harbor seals and dolphins.

Passengers can bring their own food or buy hot or cold food from the ship's galley during the cruise. Layered warm clothing and comfortable shoes are essential.

EL PASEO *East side of State St., near De la Guerra; access also off Anacapa St. Shops generally open Mon. through Sat. 10 a.m. to 5 p.m.; a few open Sun. 11 a.m. to 4 p.m.* Winding walkways, adobe walls and wrought iron railings contribute to this picturesque shopping arcade. Outdoor dining patios are open year round.

EL PRESIDIO DE SANTA BARBARA STATE HISTORIC PARK *123-126 E. Canon Perdido St. (mailing address: P.O. Box 388, 93102). (805) 966-9719. Open daily 10:30 a.m. to 4:30 p.m.; closed Jan. 1, Thanksgiving and Dec. 25. Free.* The presidio is often referred to as the birthplace of Santa Barbara. During the late 18th and early 19th centuries it was the seat of military and civil government for an area extending from Los Angeles to just south of San Luis Obispo. Today the business area around the intersection of Canon Perdido and Santa Barbara streets covers much of the site. Many of the presidio's foundations and walls are being uncovered and rebuilt during ongoing excavation and reconstruction.

Commandant's Quarters include the reconstructed office and a portion of the living room from the original

A hint of Old Spain is reflected in El Paseo.

commandant's residence. Historically accurate furnishings and decor illustrate the lifestyle of a frontier military and civil official in early California.

El Cuartel *122 East Canon Perdido St.* This is the oldest residence (1788) in Santa Barbara and is considered the second oldest building in California. El Cuartel (Soldier's Quarters) was originally one in a row of buildings that formed the west side of the presidio. It now houses furnishings representative of the lifestyle of a presidio soldier and his family.

Padre's Quarters features authentically reproduced architecture and furnishings. Especially noteworthy are roof tiles made by a 200-year-old method, the 22-inch-thick adobe walls, dirt floor and rawhide bed. In the room adjoining the Padre's Quarters, a 15-minute slide show on the history of the presidio is shown on request.

Presidio Chapel, reconstructed on its original foundations, contains authentically restored 18th-century decorative art. It serves as a museum and public hall for performances and limited religious services.

Presidio Northeast Corner, now under construction on original foundations, will include a *cocina* (kitchen), *despensa* (pantry), two-story *torreon* (tower), officers' quarters and soldiers' family quarters.

FARMERS MARKETS *976 Embarcadero del Mar in Isla Vista; (805) 962-5354. Wed. at 3 p.m., in spring and summer to 7 p.m.; rest of year to 6:30 p.m.* The town's student population and artistic locals make this an enjoyable shopping place.

Corner of Santa Barbara and Cota sts. in Santa Barbara; (805) 962-5354. Sat. 8:30 a.m. to noon. Over 100 farmers display fresh produce, specialty crops, flowers and tropical fruit. Live entertainment is presented.

500 to 600 block of State St. in Santa Barbara; (805) 962-5354. Tue., in spring and summer 4 to 7:30 p.m.; rest of year 3 to 6:30 p.m. Produce and flowers are combined with a Mediterranean flair.

FERNALD MANSION AND TRUSSELL-WINCHESTER ADOBE *414 W. Montecito St. (805) 966-1601. Both houses open Sun. 2 to 4 p.m. Free.* **Fernald Mansion,** with its many gables, was built in 1862 and is considered one of the finest remaining examples of Victorian architecture in Santa Barbara. This 14-room house features hand-carved ornamentation and wainscoting. Members of the Fernald family lived in the house continuously for more than 90 years, and many of the furnishings, paintings and personal effects now displayed belonged to Judge and Mrs. Fernald or one of their descendants. Of special interest is the nursery, filled with antique toys and dolls.

Trussell-Winchester Adobe provides a fine example of the transitional architecture that was prevalent between Santa Barbara's Spanish and American periods. The adobe house, constructed in 1854 by sea captain Horatio Trussell, is built of native adobe bricks, as well as salvaged timber and brass from a ship wrecked off Anacapa Island. Occupied for 15 years by the Trussell family, then sold to William Eddy, the house was purchased in 1882 by Sara Winchester. Today 100-year-old furnishings from the Trussell and Winchester families add to the visual interest and historical significance of this house.

HISTORIC ADOBES *Downtown.* In the midst of Santa Barbara's modern business district are a number of "adobes" dating back over one hundred years (buildings constructed of adobe are often designated by that name). Adobe, as a building material, refers to bricks made of wet, clay-like soil and straw, which are then dried in the sun.

Except as noted, these structures are closed to the public. The best way to see them is on the self-guided Red Tile Tour or the guided Walking Tours Through History (see separate listings). **Casa Covarrubias** (1817), 715 Santa Barbara Street, may have been used briefly as headquarters by the last Mexican governor of California, Pío Pico. **Casa de la Guerra** (1827), 15 East De la Guerra Street, was the home of Don José de la Guerra, a commandante of the Presidio. **Hill-Carrillo Adobe** (1826), 11 East Carrillo Street, was built by an American for his Spanish bride and contains the town's first wooden floor. **Historic** (Fremont) **Adobe**, adjoining Casa Covarrubias, was probably built in 1836, and is now standing on its second or third site. **Orena Adobes**, 27-29 East De la Guerra

Street, built between 1849 and 1858, are fine examples of homes built by the city's early wealthy Spanish families. **Rochin Adobe**, 820 Santa Barbara Street, was constructed of bricks from the abandoned presidio. It has since been covered by clapboard except for one square of original wall.

KARPELES MANUSCRIPT LIBRARY MUSEUM, *21 W. Anapamu St, 93101. (805) 962-5322. Open daily 10 a.m. to 4 p.m.; closed Thanksgiving and Dec. 25. Free.* Beautifully crafted wooden cases and pedestals are used to display an extensive collection of original and facsimile manuscripts that includes books, treaties, letters, maps, illustrations and music scores, with many items dating back several centuries. Peter the Great, Wolfgang Amadeus Mozart, Thomas Jefferson, Mark Twain and Leonard Bernstein are among the scores of significant persons whose works are displayed.

LA ARCADA *East side of State St., at Figueroa St. Shops generally open Mon. through Sat. 10 a.m. to 5 p.m., some open*

▼ *Lost: One Cannon*

One of the most noteworthy acts of rebellion during the 1847 American occupation of California occurred in Santa Barbara. A severe storm had wrecked the American brig Elizabeth off Santa Barbara, and one of its small cannons was salvaged and dragged to the fort. Under cover of night, California rebels stole the cannon, rolled it back down to the beach and buried it during low tide.

Fearing a full-blown rebellion, the American captain demanded that the townspeople return the cannon or pay a $500 fine. A per capita fee was collected to pay the fine, and that would have been that, except that another storm uncovered the cannon, and the Americans gleefully hauled it back to headquarters.

The money was eventually remitted, and the cannon became a hitching post on a street dubbed La Calle del Cañón Perdido (the street of the lost cannon). The street name exists today as Canon Perdido (Santa Barbara uses no accent marks on its street signs); another street bears the name Quinientos (five hundred).

Sun. 11 a.m. to 5 p.m.; restaurants have varying hours. This charming arcade has shops and art galleries enhanced by tile walkways, imaginative outdoor sculptures, hanging flower baskets and replicas of antique light fixtures. Indoor and outdoor dining is offered at four restaurants, all but one of which are open for breakfast.

LOBERO THEATRE *33 E. Canon Perdido St. (805) 963-0761.* This city- and state-designated historic landmark is among the oldest legitimate theaters in California. In 1873 an Italian gentleman known as José Lobero brought a new cultural dimension to Santa Barbara by enlarging a school building so that he would have a place in which to present concerts and other staged entertainments. The present theater was built in 1924 and currently hosts a year-round program of drama, music and dance.

MISSION SANTA BARBARA *Los Olivos and Laguna sts. (mailing address: Upper Laguna St., 93105). Open daily 9 a.m. to 5 p.m.; closed Easter, Thanksgiving and Dec. 25.* This beautiful structure of classic Roman and Spanish architecture is considered "Queen of the Missions." The mission was established December 1786, and construction began the following year. After a series of rebuildings, the mission church acquired its present appearance in 1820. A self-guided tour includes a museum, gardens, cemetery and the church interior, rich in Spanish Colonial art. The cemetery is the final resting place for some of Santa Barbara's ethnically diverse early settlers, including the Chumash "lone woman" of the book, *Island of the Blue Dolphins*. Mission rooms display historical items such as Chumash artifacts, illuminated manuscripts, antique furniture and musical

Mission Santa Barbara, known as "Queen of the Missions," features classic Roman and Spanish architecture.

instruments, embroidered vestments and journals.

A few hundred feet north of the mission across Los Olivos Street are the remains of tanning vats, a pottery kiln and parts of a water system. The latter, built in the early 1880s, was so well constructed that one of its reservoirs is still in use.

MORETON BAY FIG TREE *Chapala and Montecito sts.* Although not the only Moreton Bay fig tree in Santa Barbara, this is certainly the largest. In fact, it may be the largest in the northern hemisphere. The gnarled, venerable giant began as a seedling in 1876, having been transported from Australia's Moreton Bay in Queensland. In time the seedling grew into a tree with above-ground roots that cover half a city block and branches that provide over 21,000 square feet of shade. It is not a true fig tree, but a member of the rubber tree family.

More than a century ago, this huge Moreton Bay fig tree arrived in Santa Barbara as a seedling from Queensland, Australia.

OLD SPANISH DAYS CARRIAGE MUSEUM *129 Castillo St. Open Sun. 2 to 4 p.m. Special tours at other times may be arranged by calling (805) 962-2353 or 569-2077. Free.* This collection contains scores of carriages, some of which date back more than 200 years. Such transportation as buggies, stagecoaches and army wagons are arranged in rows, seeming to need only horses and drivers to bring them back to life. Once a year some of the carriages do roll down the streets of Santa Barbara during the Old Spanish Days Parade. Two of the more eye-catching vehicles are a bright red steam pumper for fire fighting and a black hearse complete with coffin. Also on display is a handsome frieze by cowboy artist Edward Borein, and one long wall of the museum is devoted to an extensive collection of saddles.

PASEO NUEVO *11 W. De la Guerra St., bounded by State, Chapala, Cannon Perdido and Ortega sts. Shops open Mon. through Fri. 10 a.m. to 9 p.m., Sat. 10 a.m. to 7 p.m., Sun. 11 a.m. to 6 p.m.; restaurants have varying hours.* Courtyards, fountains, pleasant winding walkways and staircases compose the setting for this attractive open-air complex. Two major department stores are located here, as well as 60 other shops and restaurants, a museum and a theater. Characterized by distinctive stylized Spanish architecture, the colorful two-square-block center fits comfortably into the heart of downtown Santa Barbara.

Center Stage Theater *The Arts Terrace, second level. (805) 963-0408. Call for schedule. Ticket prices vary.* Locally produced dance, music and dramatic programs, and touring professional groups are presented in an intimate studio theater.

Santa Barbara Contemporary Arts Forum *The Arts Terrace, second level. (805) 966-5373. Open Tues. through Sat. 10 a.m. to 5 p.m.; closed Jan. 1, Thanksgiving, Dec. 24 and 25 and during art installations. Free.* Within spacious galleries are contemporary paintings, sketches, sculpture and other works of local and internationally known artists.

RED TILE TOUR, a self-guided walking tour in the downtown area, covers a section roughly bordered by Victoria, Santa Barbara, De la Guerra and State streets. The tour includes historic and cultural landmarks, as well as tucked-away plazas and shopping arcades. Tour maps are available at the Visitor Centers (see *Tourist Information Sources*).

SANTA BARBARA BOTANIC GARDEN *1212 Mission Canyon Rd., 93105. (805) 682-4726. Open Mar. through Oct., Mon. through Fri. 9 a.m. to 5 p.m., Sat. and Sun. until 6 p.m.; rest of the year, Mon. through Fri. 9 a.m. to 4 p.m, Sat. and Sun. until* 5 *p.m. Admission $3; seniors, ages 13-17 and students with ID, $2; ages 5-12, $1.* Native California plant life, including golden poppies, redwoods and cacti, blanket 65 acres in the foothills of the Santa Ynez Mountains. More than five miles of inviting, self-guided trails wind through meadow, desert and manzanita sections, and along the stream that flows through Mission Canyon to the woodland, redwood, canyon and island areas. A year-round demonstration garden features drought-tolerant plants suitable for residential landscaping.

There are drink and snack vending machines and a picnic area. Plants are for sale in the Garden Grower's Nursery.

SANTA BARBARA COUNTY COURT-HOUSE *1100 Anacapa St., 93101. (805) 962-6464. Courthouse open Mon. through Fri. 8 a.m. to 4:45 p.m.; Sat., Sun. and holidays 9 a.m. to 4:45 p.m.; closed Dec. 25. Guided tours given Mon. through Sat. at 2 p.m.; additional tours Wed. and Fri. at 10:30 a.m. Appointments can be made for groups of at least six at times other than those shown. Free admission and*

A visit to the tower of the Santa Barbara County Courthouse provides a panoramic view of the city.

tours. More reminiscent of a palace than a courthouse, this beautiful Spanish-Moorish structure has many outstanding features. Specially designed windows, staircases, balconies, turrets and archways reflect the imaginative skill of architect William Mooser, as do the ornately carved doors and imported tiles. On the second floor, murals by Dan Sayre Groesbeck depict Santa Barbara's history. Visitors to the tower can enjoy a good view of the city and seacoast. Beautifully landscaped grounds include extensive lawns and graceful palms.

SANTA BARBARA HARBOR AND CHANNEL CRUISES Telephone for detailed information and reservations.

Sailing Center of Santa Barbara *(800) 350-9090, (805) 962-2826.* Harbor, coastal and dinner cruises; coastal island and whale-watch trips also available.

Sea Landing *(805) 963-3564.* Channel Islands, dinner and party cruises; whale-watch trips also available.

SANTA BARBARA HISTORICAL MUSEUM *136 E. De la Guerra St. (mailing address: P.O. Box 578, 93102-0578). (805) 966-1601. Open Tues. through Sat. 10 a.m. to 5 p.m., Sun. noon to 5 p.m.; closed major holidays. Guided tours Wed., Sat. and Sun. 1:30 p.m. Free. Research library open Tues. through Fri. 10 a.m. to 1 p.m., first Sat. of each month 10 a.m. to 1 p.m. Nominal library-use fee.* This handsome structure, which follows classic Spanish colonial lines, contains spacious rooms that house memorabilia from Santa Barbara's multi-national past. The bricks used in the museum's construction were made from the adobe soil on which it stands, and the floor tiles were handmade in Mexico. A quiet, shady courtyard, graced by a fountain, is located at the rear of the museum.

The museum's exhibits include documents, furniture, decorative and fine arts, and costumes from Santa Barbara's Spanish, Mexican and American periods. Works by famed Santa Barbara artist Edwin Deakin form the nucleus of an extensive collection of regional art. The research library specializes in Santa Barbara history.

SANTA BARBARA MUSEUM OF ART *1130 State St., 93101. (805) 963-4364; (805) 963-2240 (TDD) for the hearing impaired. Open Tues. through Sat. 11 a.m. to 5 p.m., Thur. until 9 p.m., Sun. noon to 5 p.m.; closed holidays. Guided tours Tues. through Sun. 1 p.m. Admission $4; seniors, $3; ages 6-17 and students, $1.50; free to all on Thur. and the first Sun. of each month.* This museum houses within its permanent collections Asian, American and European art (including French Impressionism), classical antiquities and photography. Displays include touring exhibits from other museums and loans from private collectors. Lectures, films and performance arts are also offered. For information on current programs, call the museum.

SANTA BARBARA MUSEUM OF NATURAL HISTORY *2559 Puesta del Sol Rd., 93105. (805) 682-4711. Open Mon. through Sat. 9 a.m. to 5 p.m., Sun. and holidays 10 a.m. to 5 p.m.; Space Lab open daily noon to 4 p.m.; closed Jan. 1, during Old Spanish Days Parade in Aug., Thanksgiving and Dec. 25. Admission $5; seniors and ages 13-17, $4; under age 13, $3.* This attractively designed complex is located in a peaceful, natural setting. Within its halls are exhibits on mammals, birds, geology, botany and marine life. The Insectary features a friendly biologist who shares his collection of live and pinned insects. In the Indian Hall, visitors will find an excellent introduction to the Chumash culture.

*The skeletal remains of a young blue whale greet visitors at the
Santa Barbara Museum of Natural History.*

The museum also has a planetarium which includes the E.L. Wiegand Space Lab, featuring exhibits of state-of-the-art interactive computer technology. Planetarium shows are presented on Saturday and Sunday each hour on the half hour from 12:30 to 3:30 p.m.; admission is 50¢, in addition to the museum entrance fee. Once each month, on a Friday evening, visitors may choose between a planetarium show and a telescope observation. Planetarium show admission is $3; observation, $1. Call (805) 682-3224 for planetarium program information.

SANTA BARBARA PUBLIC LIBRARY *40 E. Anapamu St. (mailing address: P.O. Box 1019, 93102). (805) 962-7653. Open Mon. through Thur. 10 a.m. to 9 p.m., Fri. and Sat. 10 a.m. to 5:30 p.m., Sun. 1 to 5 p.m.; closed major holidays. Free.* Casual visitors and frequent patrons alike enjoy this spacious and inviting library. Opposite colorful murals of the adventures of Don Quixote in the main lobby, the Faulkner Galleries display works by local artists. (If you forgot to bring a book for leisure-time reading, check out the shelves of used books for sale on the first floor.)

SANTA BARBARA TROLLEY COMPANY *36 State St. (805) 965-0353. Fare $4; ages 12 and under, $2.* This shuttle bus, designed to look like an old-fashioned trolley, runs daily on a regularly scheduled route throughout the city of Santa Barbara, connecting visitors with major hotels, shopping areas and local tourist and cultural attractions. The route begins and ends at Stearns Wharf at the foot of State Street.

SANTA BARBARA ZOOLOGICAL GARDENS *500 Niños Dr., 93101. (805) 962-6310 (recording), 962-5339. Open daily; summer months 9 a.m. to 6 p.m.; rest of the year, 10 a.m. to 5 p.m.; closed Thanksgiving and Dec. 25. Admission $5; seniors and ages 2-12, $3. Train rides $1; children, 50¢.* The zoo, with its charmingly landscaped grounds, is located on land that was once part of a palatial estate. Today a beautiful botanical collection and nearly 700 animals from around the world are on view.

Creatures great and small are on view at the Santa Barbara Zoological Gardens.

A ride on the zoo's miniature train provides views of the park's lush foliage, a portion of the seacoast and the neighboring bird refuge. Picnic grounds, restaurant, gift store and a playground add to visitors' enjoyment.

SCENIC DRIVE, designated by blue-and-white street signs featuring an arrow and ocean wave, is a do-it-yourself driving tour. The route goes from Montecito's Olive Mill Road to Las Palmas Drive in Hope Ranch, passing beach parks, bluff-top ocean views, Hope Ranch estates, downtown's historic and cultural buildings and Mission Santa Barbara. Scenic Drive maps are available at the visitor centers (see *Tourist Information Sources*).

STEARNS WHARF *Foot of State St. at the harbor. (805) 564-5518. Most shops generally open in summer daily 10 a.m. to 9 p.m.; in winter daily 10 a.m. to 6 p.m.;*

Marine exhibits, shops and restaurants make Stearn's Wharf a popular waterfront attraction.

restaurants have varying hours, at least one open for breakfast daily. Parking $2 per hour; two hours free with validation. Where State Street ends at Cabrillo Boulevard, Stearns Wharf begins. A Santa Barbara landmark, the wharf has a long and checkered history. Built in 1872 by John Peck Stearns, it was the site of cargo and passenger activity for many years. In the 1930s, visitors to gambling ships used the wharf as a departure point, and during World War II it served as a naval installation.

Today people can walk or drive onto the wharf to fish, enjoy the restaurants, visit the Sea Center and Nature Conservancy, browse in the specialty shops or purchase fresh fish. Stearns Wharf also provides a fine view of the small-craft harbor, as well as a panorama of Santa Barbara and its mountain backdrop.

Harbor Queen *219 Stearns Wharf, 93101. (805) 969-5217. Tours given Memorial Day through Labor Day, daily 11 a.m. to 6 p.m. on the hour; rest of the year, weekends and holidays 11 a.m. to 6 p.m. on the hour. Fare $7; ages 12 and under, $5.* Forty-minute harbor and coastal cruises are offered. Additionally, there are two-hour sunset buffet cruises, at a cost of $20 per person, which depart at 6:30 p.m.

Nature Conservancy *213 Stearns Wharf, 93101. (805) 962-9111. Open Mon. through Fri. noon to 4 p.m., Sat. and Sun. 11 a.m. to 5 p.m. Free.* Here visitors can obtain information on the Santa Cruz Island Preserve and other conservancy projects throughout the state. Inside the visitor center stands a scale model of Santa Cruz Island (largest of the Channel Islands), a habitat case with an island fox and a mounted peregrine falcon. Video programs on conservancy preserves throughout the nation are also shown.

Sea Center *211 Stearns Wharf, 93101. (805) 962-0885. Open daily noon to 5 p.m.; closed Jan. 1, Thanksgiving and Dec. 25. Admission $2; seniors, $1.50; ages 3-17, $1.* Managed by the Santa Barbara Museum of Natural History with support from the Channel Islands National Marine Sanctuary, this center features life-size models of a California gray whale and her calf, a gray whale

SANTA BARBARA WINERY

Experience the Wine Country in the Heart of Santa Barbara

Open Daily 10 - 5   Tours 11:30 & 3:30

202 Anacapa Street, Santa Barbara - 2 Blocks from the Beach

1-800-225-3633

skeleton, six aquariums housing many species native to the Santa Barbara Channel and marine photos. Other highlights include a sea bird display and exhibits on the marine archaeology in the Santa Barbara Channel. An outdoor touch tank affords visitors a truly hands-on experience with various marine invertebrates.

VICTORIA COURT *Victoria and State sts. Most shops open Mon. through Sat. 10 a.m. to 6 p.m., many open on Sun.; special hours during Dec. holiday season.* Walkways wind through this two-story complex, which has inviting shops around each turn. A wide range of goods and services is offered, including six restaurants and a post office.

WALKING TOURS THROUGH HISTORY *18 San Marcos Trout Club. (805) 967-9869. 2-hour tours for a minimum of four people. Reservation only. Fee, $10; seniors, $8; students, $5; under age 10, free. Group rates are available.* A local historian conducts guided walking tours of historic Santa Barbara. The tours, requiring a moderate amount of walking, depart the Santa Barbara Courthouse and include visits to El Paseo, the historic adobes, El Presidio de Santa Barbara State Historic Park and the grounds of the Santa Barbara Historical Museum.

WINERY *Hours are subject to change; please call ahead. More complete descriptions of wineries offering tours appear in the Auto Club's* California Winery Tours *book.*

Santa Barbara Winery *202 Anacapa St., 93101-1887. (800) 225-3633. Open daily 10 a.m. to 5 p.m. Guided tours daily 11:30 a.m. and 3:30 p.m.* Having opened in 1962, this is the oldest producing winery in Santa Barbara County. A variety of wines can be sampled in the tasting room.

Summerland

About five miles east of Santa Barbara, the small town of Summerland climbs steep hills north of US 101 and spills over onto the cliff tops south of the freeway. Traveling either east or west, exit the freeway at the sign directing you to Summerland. Along the street north of the freeway are several antique shops and little cafes that offer outdoor dining.

Historically, the town is best known as the site of the first offshore oil drilling in the Western Hemisphere. A plaque notes that "the Summerland Oilfield initially produced from onshore wells, but beginning in 1896, production was extended offshore." More recent history is reflected in a bar and restaurant, The Nugget, where President Bill Clinton took a chorus or two on the saxophone.

Evans Street (you can't miss it) goes south under the freeway overpass to Lookout Park, a pleasant grassy area with picnic tables, playground, volleyball court, rest rooms, a paved walkway down to the beach, and an unobstructed view of the ocean and the distant drilling platforms.

Santa Ynez Valley

Northwest of Santa Barbara, the Santa Ynez Valley, bordered by the Santa Ynez and San Rafael mountains, encompasses gently rolling green or golden hills sprinkled with oak trees and stands of eucalyptus. Three highways (US 101, SR 154 and SR 246) and many side roads lead to extensive cattle ranches, horse farms, wineries set amid vineyards, and carefully tended citrus groves and croplands.

Much of the valley's beauty and character remains undiscovered by the many travelers who simply exit US 101 at Buellton to dine at Pea Soup Andersen's Restaurant or take in the Danish village atmosphere of Solvang. Visitors with a bit more adventurous turn of mind leave the main highway and discover the valley's century-old "country towns." These were established to serve the area's farming and ranching families, and they still do just that. But visitors will be pleased to find art galleries and antique shops; former stagecoach stops that, in one case, house a restaurant and, in another, a restored hotel. Also tucked away in the valley is the smallest county branch library in California; a collection of old-fashioned wagons and carriages; an operating "little red schoolhouse" (circa 1883); one of Southern California's largest, man-made freshwater lakes; and wineries open for tours.

The Santa Ynez Valley has regained its reputation as a major California wine-producing region that it lost during the Prohibition and the years that followed. An ideal grape-growing climate—warm days and cool nights—contributes to the success of the award-winning wines bottled here since the early 1970s.

Acre after acre of lush green pastures, scored by white rail fences, indicate another valley specialty: horse breeding. American Paints, Andalusians, Arabians, Icelandics, Miniatures, Peruvian Pasos, Quarter Horses and Thoroughbreds are all bred here, and some of the ranches welcome visitors, when given advance notice. For the names and phone numbers of the ranches that welcome visitors, call the Solvang Visitor Information Center at (805) 688-3317.

Santa Ynez Valley was first scouted in 1798 when a military party was dispatched from Mission Santa Barbara to find a suitable spot for a mission between Santa Barbara and La Purísima Mission in Lompoc. The site chosen (in what is now Solvang) became Mission Santa Inés in 1804. The original church and surrounding buildings were rendered unsafe in an 1812 earthquake, and the present church was constructed in 1817. In 1834 mission lands were divided into land grants that, over decades, were further parceled into rural and town sites. As the century progressed,

Solvang offers Danish pastries and shops galore.

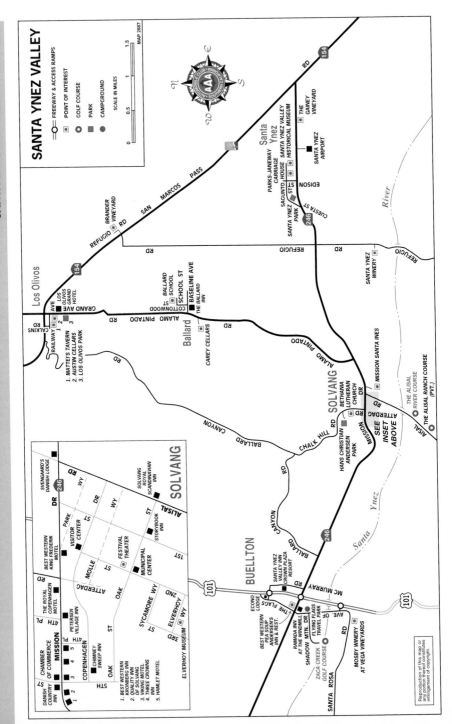

SANTA YNEZ VALLEY

- ⊖ FREEWAY & ACCESS RAMPS
- ▣ POINT OF INTEREST
- ◉ GOLF COURSE
- ▪ PARK
- ▪ CAMPGROUND

SCALE IN MILES

0   0.5   1   1.5

MAP 2687

Los Olivos

1. MATTEI'S TAVERN
2. AUSTIN CELLARS
3. LOS OLIVOS PARK

LOS OLIVOS GRAND HOTEL

BRANDER VINEYARD

SAN MARCOS PASS

Ballard

BALLARD SCHOOL
THE BALLARD INN
CAREY CELLARS

Santa Ynez

PARKS-JANEWAY CARRIAGE HOUSE
SANTA YNEZ VALLEY HISTORICAL MUSEUM
SAGUNTO HOUSE
THE GAINEY VINEYARD
SANTA YNEZ AIRPORT
SANTA YNEZ PARK
SANTA YNEZ WINERY

SOLVANG

MISSION SANTA INES
BETHANIA LUTHERAN CHURCH
HANS CHRISTIAN ANDERSEN PARK
SEE INSET ABOVE

THE ALISAL RIVER COURSE
THE ALISAL RANCH COURSE (PVT.)

BUELLTON

SANTA YNEZ VALLEY INN CROWN PLAZA RESORT
ECONO LODGE
BEST WESTERN ANDERSEN'S INN & REST.
RAMADA INN AT THE WINDMILL
THE FLAGS
FLYING FLAGS TRAVEL PARK
SHADOW MTN. DR.
ZACA CREEK GOLF COURSE
MOSBY WINERY AT VEGA VINEYARDS

SOLVANG

SVENGAARD'S DANISH LODGE
BEST WESTERN KING FREDERIK MOTEL
VISITOR CENTER
SOLVANG ROYAL SCANDINAVIAN INN
THE ROYAL COPENHAGEN MOTEL
PETERSEN VILLAGE INN
FESTIVAL THEATER
MUNICIPAL CENTER
STORYBOOK INN
CHAMBER OF COMMERCE
DANISH COUNTRY INN
CHIMNEY SWEEP INN
ELVERHOY MUSEUM

1. BEST WESTERN KRONBERG INN
2. QUALITY INN OF SOLVANG
3. VIKING MOTEL
4. THREE CROWNS INN
5. HAMLET MOTEL

Still in use today, the Ballard School has been open for more than 100 years.

train and stagecoach lines were routed through the Santa Ynez Valley, and towns became more firmly rooted.

Ballard

Ballard holds the distinction of being Santa Ynez Valley's oldest (1880) and smallest (250 residents) community. Pioneer George Lewis first built an adobe house on a large ranch in the valley, which was known then as El Alamo Pintado (the painted cottonwood). When Lewis traveled to Mexico, he left his holdings with his friend William Ballard, for whom the town was later named. The township's past can still be seen in two buildings from the town's earliest days: the 1883 Ballard School (see listing) and the Santa Ynez Valley Presbyterian Church, completed in 1889. The church is now Ballard Country Church and is located on Baseline Avenue, just east of Alamo Pintado Road.

BALLARD SCHOOL *Cottonwood and School sts.* Framed by two black walnut trees and topped with a steeple, this picturesque "little red schoolhouse" opened its doors in 1883 and has been in continuous use ever since. It currently houses kindergarten through second-grade classes. Grades three through eight are in an adjacent building.

Buellton

Located at the junction of US 101 and SR 246, Buellton's convenient location attracts travelers to the town's motels, restaurants, service facilities, trailer parks and gift shops. Buellton is best known as "the home of split pea soup," in reference to Pea Soup Andersen's Restaurant (see listing). It also boasts an expansive parkway with eight giant-sized American flags flying from 50-foot-high poles.

Buellton had its beginnings in 1867 when a portion of a Mexican land grant was deeded to Rufus Thompson Buell and his brother Alonzo. The brothers developed a highly successful cattle ranch until a drought in 1890 forced the sale of 10,000 acres of land to the Santa Ynez Land Development

*What began as a tiny cafe in 1924 has grown to the spacious
Pea Soup Andersen's Restaurant and adjoining inn in Buellton.*

Company. In 1920 part of that acreage became Buellton.

PEA SOUP ANDERSEN'S RESTAURANT *On SR 246, one block west of junction with US 101 (mailing address: P.O. Box 195, 93427). (805) 688-5581. Open daily 6:30 a.m. to 10 p.m.* The restaurant which began in 1924 as a very small cafe owned and operated by Anton and Juliette Andersen now encompasses several dining rooms, a coffee shop, wine cellar and gift shop.

WINERIES *Hours are subject to change; please call ahead. More complete descriptions of wineries offering tours appear in the Auto Club's* California Winery Tours *book.*

Mosby Winery at Vega Vineyards *9496 Santa Rosa Rd. (mailing address: P.O. Box 1849, 93427). (805) 688-2415. Tasting daily 10 a.m. to 4 p.m., $2.50 fee; guided tours by appointment only.* Once part of a 19th-century land grant, the winery was founded in 1979 in a restored carriage house. Today Chardonnay, Gewürz-

traminer, Pinot Noir and Italian-style varietals, including Nebbiolo and Pinot Grigio, are produced from estate-grown grapes. Picnic area.

Sanford Winery *4 miles west of Buellton at 7250 Santa Rosa Rd., Buellton 93427. (805) 688-3300. Open daily 11 a.m. to 4 p.m.* Open for tasting only.

Lake Cachuma County Park

Approximately 18 miles northwest of Santa Barbara off SR 154.

Chief Ranger *Star Route; Santa Barbara, CA 93105. (805) 688-4658. Open year round for day use from 7 a.m. to 10 p.m.; campers are admitted at any time, space permitting. Day-use admission, $5 per vehicle; $4 per boat.*

Nestled in the Santa Ynez Mountains, this man-made lake takes its name from a Chumash village, called either *Juichama* or *Juichuneas*, that once stood on the land now covered by the waters

Lake Cachuma is a practically perfect picnicking place.

of Cachuma (Ka-choo´-ma) Bay. The water serves two purposes: it is both a recreation site and Santa Barbara's water supply. Beginning in 1910, successively more ambitious projects were proposed to dam flood waters in the upper Santa Ynez Valley and carry the water to Santa Barbara via a tunnel through the Santa Ynez Mountains. In 1953, all the planning and construction culminated in the Bradbury Dam and the Cachuma Reservoir.

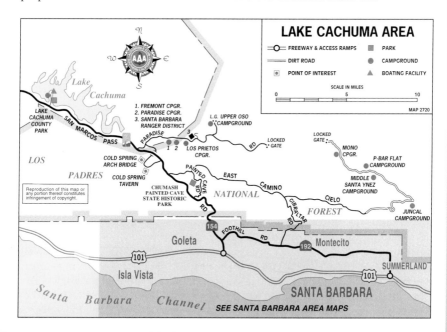

Fishermen are challenged by the lake's population of bass, crappie, catfish, bluegill and trout. Rental boats and motors are available, and fishing licenses can be purchased at a bait and tackle shop. In addition to fishing and boating, there are sites for picnicking and camping (see *Recreation* and *Campgrounds & Trailer Parks*). Although swimming in the lake is prohibited, two pools within the recreational area are open during the summer. The park also has a snack bar, general store, service station and rental bicycles.

Lake Cachuma Boat Cruises *(805) 568-2460. Departs park marina. Summer, Fri. through Sun.; Nov. to mid-Mar., Wed. through Sun. Call for exact times; reservations are recommended. Fare $10; under age 12, $5.* Two-hour cruises allow viewing of the lake's wildlife and bird populations. Passengers on winter cruises can observe the American bald eagle.

Los Alamos

Although not technically a part of the Santa Ynez Valley, Los Alamos shares historic and geographic traits with, and is easily reached from, the valley. What is now Los Alamos Valley, 13 miles north of Buellton off US 101, was originally two land grants—Rancho Los Alamos and Rancho La Laguna—following Mexico's independence from Spain in 1821. The acreage, used extensively for cattle grazing, was first subdivided in 1878 when two men from San Francisco bought 28,000 acres and established a town. Visitors began arriving in the valley by stagecoach following the opening of the Union Hotel in 1880 (see listing). When the Pacific Coast Railroad reached here in 1882, even more people came to discover the verdant scenery and peaceful countryside.

Today Los Alamos (population 950) maintains strong ties with its heritage and continues to serve the neighboring farming and ranching families. The town celebrates "Old Days" the last weekend of September with entertainment, a parade, barbecue and roping demonstrations. Old-time residents use this as an opportunity to reminisce. Throughout the year, visits to antique stores and art galleries are a popular pastime, as are picnics beneath oak and maple trees in Los Alamos County Park.

UNION HOTEL *362 Bell St. (mailing address: P.O. Box 616, 93440). (805) 344-2744, (800) 230-2744. Hotel and mansion open daily. Restaurant open for dinner Fri. through Sun. at 5 p.m. Dining is family style with a selection of 10 entrees. Restaurant reservations suggested for parties of more than six. Hotel reservations required.* Built in 1880 as a stagecoach stop, the Union Hotel has been restored in a manner as authentic as possible, even to the boardwalk which fronts the street. Architecture, interior design and furnishings all reflect the late 19th century. Adjacent is a restored 1864 Victorian house known as the "Victorian Mansion," with six thematically decorated guest rooms.

Los Olivos

Small-town charm exudes from this community set amid oak-studded rolling hills off SR 154, three miles east of US 101. From the flagpole at the center of town, erected in 1918 to honor America's World War I veterans, to the water tower beside the century-old stagecoach stop, Los Olivos (the olives) evokes a bygone era. Artists in various media have discovered the attraction of this hamlet of about 350, and more than a dozen galleries are now open.

The community traces its roots to the opening of Mattei's Tavern in 1886 (see listing). With the arrival of the stagecoach and later the narrow-gauge Pacific Coast Railroad, the town prospered. Besides Mattei's tavern and hotel, Los Olivos contained several stores, livery stables and blacksmith shops, a post office and a public school. At the turn of the century, however, decisions were made to route the first major north-south railroad (the Southern Pacific) and highway (now US 101) along the coast and west of town. This precluded major development in Los Olivos and helped preserve its rural atmosphere.

MATTEI'S TAVERN *Railway Ave., block west of SR 154 and Grand Ave. junction (mailing address: Highway 154, 93441). (805) 688-4820. Open daily for dinner, also open Fri. through Sun. for lunch (see Lodging & Restaurants listings). Reservations are advised.* In 1886 Felix Mattei, a Swiss immigrant, built a combination hotel and restaurant to accommodate the railroad and stagecoach passengers stopping in Los Olivos. Now more than 100 years later, the restaurant is still in operation. Among the charms of this rambling structure is that each dining area is decorated differently.

WINERIES *Hours are subject to change; please call ahead. More complete descriptions of wineries offering tours appear in the Auto Club's* California Winery Tours *book.*

Austin Cellars *2923 Grand Ave., 93441. (805) 688-9665. Open daily 11 a.m. to 6 p.m.* Open for tasting only.

Beckman Vineyards *Off US 101 via SR 154 at 2670 Ontiveros Rd. (mailing address: P.O. Box 542, Los Olivos 93441). (805) 688-8664. Open daily 10 a.m. to*

4 p.m. Sauvignon Blanc, Chardonnay, Cabernet Sauvignon and Rosé are produced here.

Brander Vineyard *2 miles southeast of Los Olivos off SR 154 at 2401 Refugio Rd., 93441. (805) 688-2455. Open daily 10 a.m. to 5 p.m. Tours by appointment only.* The 40-acre vineyard was planted in 1975, and the winery was built in 1980. Today 8000 cases of estate-bottled varietals are shipped annually, with emphasis on Sauvignon Blanc.

Fess Parker Winery *5 miles east of junction U.S. 101 and Zaca Station Rd. at 6200 Foxen Canyon Rd. (mailing address: P.O. Box 908, 93441). Open daily 10 a.m. to 5 p.m. Tours are given at 11 a.m., 1 and 3 p.m.* In 1989 former film and TV star Fess Parker began his career as a vintner. Among the wines available

Fess Parker Winery and its vines, off Foxen Canyon Road.

here are Chardonnay, Pinot Noir, Merlot and Johannisberg Riesling.

Firestone Vineyard *Near Los Olivos, 2 miles north of US 101 and Zaca Station Rd. junction (mailing address: P.O. Box 244, 93441). (805) 688-3940. Open daily 10 a.m. to 4 p.m.* The winery sits on a hill in the midst of its vineyards and is housed in a modern wooden structure that blends beautifully with the landscape. Firestone sells Gewürztraminer, Riesling, Sauvignon Blanc, Chardonnay, Merlot, Cabernet Sauvignon and a Rosé.

Zaca Mesa Winery *Foxen Canyon Rd., 8 miles north of US 101 and Zaca Station Rd. junction (mailing address: P.O. Box 899, 93441). (805) 688-3310. Open daily 10 a.m. to 4 p.m.* In 1973 Zaca Mesa Ranch converted 160 acres of grazing land to vineyard, and a new winery was completed in time for the 1978 harvest. Now Zaca Mesa offers a full line of estate-bottled varietal wines. Picnic area and nature trails.

Santa Ynez

Here is a town that's kept alive its pioneer flavor with some false-front, old-west-style buildings in the business district. Located about three miles east of Solvang off SR 246, Santa Ynez once served as a principal stagecoach stop between the Santa Ynez Valley and the town of Santa Barbara. At the time of its incorporation in 1882, Santa Ynez was the social and economic center of the valley, housing many stores, saloons, Chinese laundries, and even more important, the impressive two-story College Hotel. The hotel, built in 1891 for $30,000, was considered one of the finest accommodations in all of California until it was destroyed by a fire in 1935.

PARKS-JANEWAY CARRIAGE HOUSE *3596 Sagunto St. (mailing address: P.O. Box 181, 93460). (805) 688-7889. Open Tues. through Thur. 10 a.m. to 4 p.m; Fri. through Sun. 1 to 4 p.m.; closed major holidays. Free.* Opened in 1978, the carriage house contains one of the West's finest collections of horse-drawn vehicles and accessories. More than 35 vehicles range in age from a covered freight wagon built around 1860 to a 1940 jog cart. An overland mail stage (circa 1898) boasts a restored interior, and the original paint and gilt exterior; one of the largest in the country, it carried as many as 15 people. Besides the coaches, the collection also includes buggies and phaetons and a Sicilian donkey cart. In addition, the museum houses an extensive saddle exhibit, including work by famed silversmith Edward Bohlin.

SANTA YNEZ VALLEY HISTORICAL MUSEUM *3596 Sagunto St. (mailing address: P.O. Box 181, 93460). (805) 688-7889. Open Fri. through Sun. 1 to 4 p.m.; closed major holidays. Free.* Articles made or used by area residents and early settlers are housed in this seven-room museum. A gallery devoted to Chumash culture features a diorama, baskets and tools. Other galleries depict the lifestyle of valley residents in the late 19th century with clothing, furnishings and other items. A 1907 two-cylinder "car" plus old farm machinery and equipment are also on display.

On Sagunto Street near the museum stands the county's first public library, built in 1912. It happens also to be one of the state's smallest. It is open Friday from 2 to 5 p.m.

WINDHAVEN GLIDER RIDES *Santa Ynez Airport, Santa Ynez Airport Rd., off SR 246, just west of SR 154 and SR 246 junction (mailing address: P.O. Box 625, CA 93460. (805) 688-2517. Flights daily*

This museum holds treasured artifacts of Santa Ynez Valley's pioneer days.

10 a.m. to 5 p.m., weather permitting; closed Dec. 24 and 25. Fares $65 for the 15-20 minute Scenic Flight at 2500 feet; $110 for the 25-30 minute Mountain Adventure Flight at 4000 feet; $135 for the 35-40 minute Mile-High Flight at 5280 feet. Reservations suggested for week-end flights. Passengers soar high above the Santa Ynez Valley's hills, towns and vineyards in aircraft flown by FAA-certified commercial glider pilots.

WINERIES *Hours are subject to change; please call ahead. More complete descriptions of wineries offering tours appear in the Auto Club's* California Winery Tours *book.*

The Gainey Vineyard *1 mile east of Santa Ynez on SR 246 (mailing address: P.O. Box 910, 93460). (805) 688-0558. Open daily 10 a.m. to 5 p.m.; last tour at 3 p.m. Tasting fee $2.50, includes glass.* This modern winery features informative tours covering all phases of wine-making. The adjacent 65-acre vineyard produces much of the fruit for the win-ery's 15,000-case-per-year, five-varietal output. Picnic area.

Santa Ynez Winery *343 North Refugio Rd., 93460. (805) 688-8381. Tasting offered daily 10 a.m. to 5 p.m.; self-guided tours (groups should make advance reservations for tours).* In 1969 this family-owned winery began converting dairy land into vineyards and remodeled a barn to house its winemaking facilities. Today 18,000 cases are shipped annually, and the emphasis is on white varietals, including Sauvignon Blanc, Chardonnay and Riesling, all from the winery's 110-acre vineyard.

Solvang

Tourists from all parts of the world find their way to Solvang and take in the Danish-village atmosphere, complete with gas streetlights from Copenhagen, working windmills, a horse-drawn streetcar, and 19th-century timber and plaster architecture. Located 45 miles northwest of Santa Barbara

Horse-drawn carriages are among the many delights of Solvang.

on SR 246, Solvang has a permanent population of about 4800 people. A larger, impermanent number results from the visitors who partake of fresh Danish pastries and the wide assortment of merchandise in the many shops and galleries: imported Danish handicrafts, prints and original art works, jewelry, clocks and holiday decorations, and since the early 1990s, factory outlet stores have been springing up here and there in Solvang.

Every year during the third weekend in September, the city celebrates Danish Days with entertainment, dancing, special foods and a parade. Each December is highlighted by Winterfest, featuring a Christmas parade, as well as tree-lighting ceremonies, special shop window displays and caroling (see *Annual Events*).

Solvang was established in 1911 when a group of Danish educators chose the Santa Ynez Valley as the ideal place to build a college and establish a colony.

Soon they were joined by others from the midwest and Denmark, and by 1914, with the building of Atterdag College, Solvang became a cultural center and gathering place for Danes on the West Coast. The college is no longer in existence, but the Bit O'Denmark Restaurant on Alisal Road occupies the site of the original two-story school.

Originally, Solvang developed as an agricultural community serving the needs of the neighboring farmers. It wasn't until 1947, after an article appeared in the *Saturday Evening Post* describing the people of Solvang and the Danish-style structures, that tourism became a major economic factor. There is more to Solvang than its inviting shops: two nearby county parks provide recreation for the area's residents and visitors, Lake Cachuma and Nojoqui Falls (see listings).

BETHANIA LUTHERAN CHURCH *603 Atterdag Rd., 93463. (805) 688-4637.*

Open for visiting Mon. through Sat. 8 a.m. to 5 p.m. Built in 1928, this church is a fine example of 14th-century Danish architecture. The interior is noted for its hand-carved pulpit and carefully detailed miniature sailing ship that is suspended from the ceiling. The presence of the ship is a Danish tradition; it represents a soul on life's sea, guided by God.

ELVERHOY MUSEUM *624 Elverhoy Wy., 93463. (805) 686-1211. Open Wed. through Sun. 1 to 4 p.m. and by appointment. Free.* The museum, located on a residential street, is housed in a structure representative of a typical 18th-century Danish farm house. Danish artifacts and memorabilia, as well as various types of art, are housed in rooms devoted to Solvang's history, Danish heritage and an art gallery.

HANS CHRISTIAN ANDERSEN PARK *Off Atterdag Rd., 3 blocks north of Mission Dr. Open daily 8 a.m. to dusk.*

Free. Beautiful trees, including coast live oak and valley oak, grace this park. An Old World-style entrance leads to a 50-acre site offering barbecue and picnic facilities, tennis courts and a playground.

THE HONEN *Various locations. (805) 686-0022. Daily in summer 11:30 a.m. to 5 p.m.; rest of year, Fri. through Mon., holidays and during festivals, hours vary. Fare $3; seniors, $2.50; under age 12, $2.* These horse-drawn replicas of early 20th-century streetcars in Copenhagen, Denmark, offer guided tours of downtown Solvang. Excursions aboard the bright yellow and brown cars depart from the Conference & Visitors Bureau office on Copenhagen Drive and last about 15 to 20 minutes. Also, one car operates Wednesday through Sunday between the Visitors Bureau and the Elverhoy Museum.

MISSION SANTA INES *1760 Mission Dr. (805) 688-4815. Tours Mon. through*

In the Denmark-inspired town of Solvang, Mission Santa Inés is a reminder of Spain.

A lovely park is the setting of the legendary Nojoqui Falls.

Sat. 9:30 a.m. to 4:30 p.m., Sun. 1:30 to 4:30 p.m.; closed Jan. 1, Easter, Thanksgiving and Dec. 25. Donation $2; under age 16, free. This mission was founded in 1804, and the reconstructed *campanario* (bell tower) and authentically restored church sanctuary reflect its original beauty. The mission complex is currently being restored to its original configuration. Rooms open to the public contain mission furnishings and artifacts dating to the early 19th century. A side door of the church leads to a quiet, attractively landscaped garden.

NOJOQUI FALLS COUNTY PARK
7 miles southwest of Solvang on Alisal Rd. Open daily 8 a.m. to dusk. Free. This 82½-acre site offers barbecue and picnic areas, as well as softball diamonds, volleyball courts, horseshoe pits and children's play areas. The park is named for the 164-foot-high falls that, after a sufficient rainy season, cascades

▼ A Love Story

It was a dark and stormy night. While rain pelted down, wind howled, lightning flashed and thunder rolled, a band of Chumash sheltered in a cave to escape the tempest. As the storm passed, a young warrior from another village was found to be trapped by a great fallen tree limb. In spite of tribal animosity, the chief's beautiful daughter lifted the heavy branch and helped the young man into the cave.

As weeks passed, the recuperating handsome young man and the caring lovely young woman fell in love, a development that was unwelcome, to say the least, by many in her tribe. There was, in fact, a plan to kill the brave if he stayed. That being the case, one dark night the lovers ran away, taking the trail that followed Nojoqui Creek above the falls.

With warriors from her village in hot pursuit, the lovers lost their way in the darkness and suddenly found themselves on the edge of the crumbling cliffs over the falls. Was it an accident that sent them plunging to their deaths, or did they chose to die together rather than be separated?

Thus the legend goes.

over a moss-covered limestone cliff.
A pleasant, non-strenuous trail up to
the falls winds beside a creek and is
bordered by live oak, sycamore and
California bay trees.

THEATERFEST *At Solvang's Festival
Theater, 420 2nd St. (805) 922-8313.*
From June through October, the Pacific
Conservatory of the Performing Arts
(PCPA), based at Allan Hancock
College in Santa Maria, presents music
and drama in repertory. The productions, which range from musicals to
classic drama, are noted for their high
quality. (This is an outdoor theater;
patrons should dress accordingly.)
Call for information on schedules and
ticket prices.

WINERIES *Hours are subject to change;
please call ahead. More complete descriptions of wineries offering tours appear in
the Auto Club's* California Winery Tours
book.

Buttonwood Farm Winery *1½ miles
northeast of Solvang at 1500 Alamo
Pintado Rd., Solvang 93469. (805) 688-
3032. Open daily 11 a.m. to 5 p.m.*

Carey Cellars *3 miles north of Solvang
off SR 246 at 1711 Alamo Pintado Rd.
(805) 688-8554. Open daily 10 a.m. to
4 p.m.* The winery began operations
in 1978, and today vintage-dated
varietals, including Sauvignon Blanc,
Chardonnay, Merlot and Cabernet
Sauvignon, are produced in a renovated barn. Picnic area.

Lompoc Valley

Located between the Santa Ynez Mountains on the south and the Purísima Hills on the north, the Lompoc Valley lies about 55 miles northwest of Santa Barbara. Its diverse economy ranges from oil and space exploration to flower seed production.

Massive oil reserves below the valley floor yield several thousand barrels daily. Diatomaceous earth (fossilized remains of microscopic plants that grew beneath the prehistoric ocean floor) is mined just below the surface and then processed into a fine, powdery substance used as a filter for items such as swimming pools and pharmaceutical products. Vandenberg Air Force Base, the western base for all military space launches, hosts many divisions, and leading aerospace companies provide launch and support facilities. The area is also known as "The Valley of Flowers," with its rich soil contributing to the cultivation of more than a dozen varieties of flowers grown for seed. A colorful salute to this industry is held in Lompoc on the last full weekend in June (see *Annual Events*). Rounding out the valley's economy are prize Herefords, Black Angus and dairy cattle that roam the grassy rangelands.

Lompoc Valley's history can be traced to the Chumash people who settled in the valley hundreds of years before the first European settlers. In 1787, La Purísima Mission, number 11 of Spain's 21 Franciscan missions, was dedicated in a location called *Algascapi* by the natives. (American settlers later changed the name to Lompoc.) Completed in 1791, the mission attracted many converts and prospered until an earthquake in 1812 destroyed it. Following the earthquake, torrential rainstorms inundated the valley floor making it impossible for the padres to rebuild the mission on the same site. A location was selected four miles northeast of the original, and the new mission was built in record time using a then-innovative design to resist the threat of future earthquakes. The edifice was buttressed with stone, and its walls were built of adobe 4½ feet thick. The mission again flourished until 1822 when Mexico declared independence from Spain.

In 1824 a revolt by the American Indian population at nearby Mission Santa Inés in Solvang spread to La Purísima. Indians took command of La Purísima, and soldiers from the army garrison at Monterey were called in to reclaim it. Ten years later this mission was closed permanently, and the padres moved to Mission Santa Inés. The buildings fell into disrepair and were finally auctioned off in 1845. The land was used for sheep ranching and farming until the early 1900s, when the property was purchased by the Union Oil Company. In 1933, the mission's renovation began with property donations by the Union Oil Company, the Catholic Church, Santa Barbara County and the State of California. Work by the National Park Service and the Civilian Conservation

Mission life and architecture of the early 1800s are featured at La Purísima Mission.

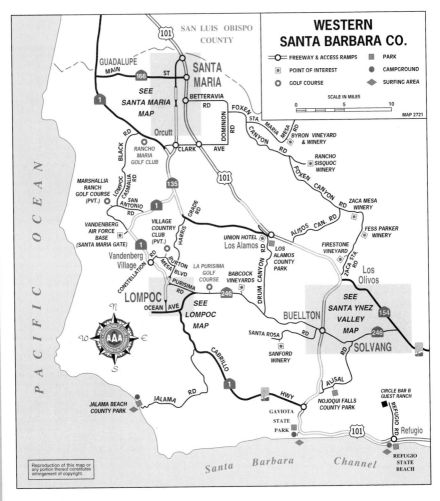

Corps restored the mission to its status of the early 1800s, and it opened to the public in 1941.

Jalama Beach County Park

20 miles southwest of Lompoc off SR 1 and Jalama Rd.

Santa Barbara County Director of Parks, *Star Route, Santa Barbara 93105. (805) 736-6316. Open year round for day use from sunrise to sunset; campers admitted at any time, space permitting. Day-use* *admission, $3.50 per vehicle; camping fees vary.*

This 28-acre park was originally a Chumash settlement; its name comes from the Spanish spelling of the Indian village, "Halam." The park lies on the ocean shore, just north of Point Conception, and offers surf fishing for perch, cabezon, kelp bass and halibut, as well as sailboarding, surfing at nearby Tarantula Point, picnicking, barbecues and camping (see *Recreation* and *Campgrounds & Trailer Parks*). A general store sells tackle, bait and camping supplies; other amenities include a snack bar, horseshoe pits and two play areas for children.

In February and March and from September through November, whales can be spotted offshore, while bird-watching and rockhounding can be enjoyed all year. Strong ocean winds can be expected at this park, and swimming is not recommended because of severe riptides.

Lompoc

Considered one of California's first successful land colonization projects, Lompoc got its start in 1874 when the California Immigrant Union purchased, then subdivided, Lompoc and Mission Vieja ranchos. Deeds of sale decreed that no liquor could be sold on the land, and thus Lompoc became a pioneer of prohibition in California—a stricture which obviously did not last.

Lompoc (lom´ poke) appears to have come from a Chumash name for the area, the meaning of which has not been established. In any case, comedic actor W.C. Fields found both the name and the town irresistible and some-times used the valley as a motion pic-ture locale in the 1930s.

Today, with a population of more than 38,800, Lompoc is the largest commu-nity in Lompoc Valley and the third largest city in Santa Barbara County. A mild climate and long summers are accompanied by a virtually constant coastal breeze that often escalates to flag-snapping winds.

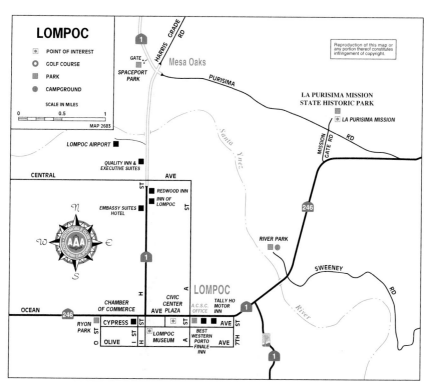

SANTA BARBARA COUNTY

FARMERS MARKET *Corner of Ocean Ave. (SR 246) and I St. (805) 343-2135. Fri. 2 p.m. to dusk.* A variety of seasonal fresh produce, flowers, honey and herbs are sold.

LA PURISIMA MISSION STATE HISTORIC PARK *3 miles northeast of Lompoc, off SR 246 (mailing address: 2295 Purisima Rd., 93436). (805) 733-3713. Open daily 9 a.m. to 5 p.m.; closed Jan. 1, Thanksgiving and Dec. 25. Admission $5 per car. Guided group tours can be arranged; call (805) 733-1303.* Extensive restoration work has been done on this handsome mission built in the early 1800s, and today La Purísima represents one of California's most complete and authentic examples of mission life and architecture. The imposing colonnade of the residence building is especially noteworthy, as is the simple beauty of the chapel. The primitive but effective water system has been restored, complete with picturesque fountain. The park area around the mission has gardens, riding and hiking trails and picnic facilities. For a schedule of special events at the park, call (805) 733-3713.

LOMPOC FLOWER FIELDS *SR 246; SR 1; Central Ave.; Sweeney Rd. Map of flower fields drive available at Lompoc Chamber of Commerce, 111 S. I St.; (805) 736-4567.* With its soil and climate ideal for raising flowers, the Lompoc area produces a prodigious amount of the flower seeds sold throughout the world. From early June through mid-July, 1000 acres bloom with more than 200 varieties of flowers. To aid in identifying the blossoms, a visit to the labeled display garden in Lompoc's Civic Center Plaza at the corner of Ocean Avenue and C Street is recommended. Among the flowers that grow in Lompoc's fields are marigolds, sweet peas, asters, larkspur, calendula, lavender, lobelia and cornflowers. The Lompoc Flower Festival is held each year in June (see *Annual Events*).

Chumash artifacts and Lompoc area historical exhibits are found in the Lompoc Museum.

LOMPOC MUSEUM *200 South H St., 93436. (805) 736-3888. Open Tues. through Fri. 1 to 5 p.m., Sat. and Sun. 1 to 4 p.m.; closed major holidays. Group tours can be arranged by telephone. Free admission and tours.* Converted from one of the nation's few remaining Carnegie library buildings, this attractive museum houses an extensive collection of American Indian artifacts. Emphasis is on the Chumash, and exhibits include basketry, weapons and the shells that were used for money and ornamentation.

The downstairs gallery contains models, photographs and displays that portray Lompoc's history from the founding of La Purísima Mission through the development of Vandenberg Air Force Base. A public research library includes volumes on local archaeology and history. The museum also hosts temporary exhibits and offers public lectures and film presentations.

VANDENBERG AIR FORCE BASE TOURS *Spaceport Park, 2999 Lompoc-Casmalia Rd., 93436. (805) 736-6381. 4½-hour tours Fri. 8 a.m., except during scheduled missile launches. Reservations required one week in advance. $14-$17 per person. Children under age 10 are not permitted.* This base, begun in 1941 as a training facility for infantry and armored divisions, was originally named Camp Cooke to commemorate a general in America's Civil War Union Army, Philip St. George Cooke. The area became Cooke Air Force Base in the late 1950s, and research, development and launching of ballistic missiles and space vehicles was begun. In 1958 the name was changed to honor Hoyt S. Vandenberg, the nation's second Air Force Chief of Staff, and since then the base has grown to encompass 98,400 acres. In addition to the acreage used for military activities, tens of thousands of acres comprise an ecological preserve.

Narrated tours in either a van or bus, depending upon the size of the group, leave from Spaceport Park and are conducted through a large portion of the base to view such buildings as dormitories, headquarters, the community center and schools. Highlights of the tour are visits to the Titan II and Thor Space Launch Complexes (SLC). (The control room of the Titan silo almost makes you feel like an extra on "Star Trek.") While neither SLC (known as "slick") is still in use, each—except for missiles—is completely intact. Air Force personnel are on hand to explain equipment and procedures from the Titan underground silo's control room to the Thor's warehouse-like housing that moves on tracks.

The tour also includes the coastal area, covered with such native plants as chaparral, sage, manzanita and coreopsis. There's a stop at Honda Point, near Point Pedernales, a dramatic seascape and site of historic shipwrecks. Before returning to Spaceport Park, the route leads past several of Lompoc's flower fields and diatomaceous earth mines.

Comfortable, low-heeled shoes are a must. While there's not a lot of walking, there's quite a bit of standing and a little ladder-climbing. You'll probably want to take a jacket, since the weather can change suddenly.

Santa Maria Valley

The flat, fertile Santa Maria Valley extends some 20 miles from the brush-covered foothills of the Sierra Madre Mountains to the sand dunes bordering the Pacific Ocean. The valley's early-morning fog and afternoon sunshine are instrumental in the growth of flowers and plants that give the area its second name, "Valley of Gardens."

Today's Santa Maria Valley looks completely different from when Gaspar de Portolá's expedition passed through in 1769 in pursuit of the elusive Monterey Bay. The Spanish explorers saw nothing more than a wind-swept desert with scant vegetation and a dry riverbed. Prior to the expedition's visit the only settlement, by the Chumash, had occurred along the slopes of the Sierra Madre Mountains where moisture could gather in the canyons permitting the growth of oak and sycamore trees. As Franciscan missionaries followed Portolá's party, missions were established both north and southwest of Santa Maria.

Following secularization of the missions in 1834, their lands came into the hands of individual citizens. William Benjamin Foxen and his family purchased Rancho Tinaquaic in 1837 and their descendants lived there for many generations. More extensive development didn't begin until after the Civil War, when veterans were given free land in the valley as a result of the Homestead Act. The first settlers planted grain and beans on land they found to be fertile and easy to plow. Dairymen and farmers from various European countries soon moved in, giving the valley a multi-national population. The first settlement was established in 1868 near present-day Orcutt, just south of Santa Maria.

Today agriculture, the dairy industry and cattle-raising continue to be the major economic forces in the valley, with oil exploration, business interests and the expanding wine industry lending strong support.

Santa Maria

Santa Maria got its start in 1874 when four land owners, whose property bordered the corner of present-day Broadway and Main Street, donated acreage where their properties adjoined. Originally called "Central City," the name was changed in 1882 to Santa Maria because so much mail intended for residents was being sent by mistake to Central City, Colorado. Also in 1882, the narrow-gauge Pacific Coast Railroad from San Luis Obispo County arrived to help move the valley's produce to markets outside the area. Nineteen years later the Southern Pacific Railroad from the north was built through the lower part of the valley en route to Los Angeles.

Diversity is the key to the present city of Santa Maria. In addition to being the

---

This appealing sculpture by Clement Renzi is titled **Mother and Son.**

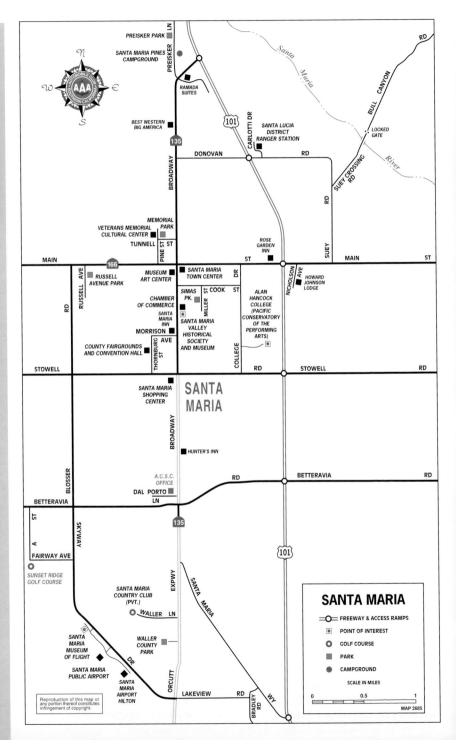

Santa Maria City Hall exemplifies the Spanish-Mediterranean architecture found throughout the county.

agricultural and business hub of the Santa Maria Valley, the city boasts a mild year-round climate that encourages participation in a number of outdoor events. Golf and tennis are popular, while nearby beaches, lakes and mountain recreation areas foster such activities as fishing, boating, swimming, bicycling, hiking and hunting.

Cultural activities within the community focus on the Marian Performing Arts Center at Allan Hancock College. Plays, musical programs, lectures and concerts are presented during the school year, and the theater hosts the Pacific Conservatory of Performing Arts (PCPA) programs (see listing).

Major annual events in Santa Maria include the Elks Rodeo and Parade in June and the Santa Barbara County Fair, which is held during the last week of July (see *Annual Events*).

FARMERS MARKETS *In Orcutt, Oak Knoll shopping area, Clark Ave. and Bradley Rd. (805) 343-2135. Tue. 10 a.m. to 1 p.m.* Growers display produce, nuts, honey and flowers.

In Santa Maria, Mervyn's parking lot, Westside Town Center, corner Broadway and Main St. (805) 343-2135. Wed. from 1 to 5 p.m. Fresh produce, flowers, honey and herbs are for sale.

MUSEUM ART CENTER *Near Cook and Pine sts (mailing address: 323-C Town Center West, 93454. (805) 346-1855. Open Tues. through Fri. 11 a.m. to 5 p.m.; closed New Year's Day, Thanksgiving, Dec. 25 and periodically between exhibits. Free.* The Art Center works closely with the Santa Barbara Museum of Art, and within a small space, makes up in quality what it lacks in size. Works of outstanding local artists are on view, and traveling exhibitions of award-winning paintings and sculpture are featured throughout the year.

PACIFIC CONSERVATORY OF THE PERFORMING ARTS (PCPA) *Allan Hancock College, 800 South College Dr., 93456. (805) 922-8313. Call for current schedule and ticket prices.* This professional-quality theater group presents high-caliber productions ranging from musicals to classic drama year-round in the Marian Performing Arts Center at Allan Hancock College and from June through October in Solvang at the Festival Theater (see Theaterfest under Solvang).

SANTA MARIA MUSEUM OF FLIGHT *3015 Airpark Dr., 93455. (805) 922-8758. Open Apr. through Nov., Fri. through Sun. 9 a.m. to 5 p.m.; rest of the year, 10 a.m. to 4 p.m.; closed Jan. 1 and Dec. 25. Free.* Within an aircraft hangar are displayed such airplanes as the World War II SNJ, a Great Lakes biplane and the gull-wing Stinson V77-Reliant. An extensive collection of model planes depicts aviation history from the Wright brothers' pioneering effort to the "flying wing" Stealth bomber. Also on view is the once-highly secret Norden bombsight and its accessories. Picnic tables are available.

SANTA MARIA-STYLE BARBECUE
Back in the 1800s, during the time of the vast valley ranchos, at round-up time ranchers would assist neighbors with the gathering and branding of new calves. Following this, the host ranch would provide a feast under the oak trees, where beef was barbecued over the coals of a red oak fire and then served with bread, beans and salad. The barbecue can be enjoyed today at many restaurants, public gatherings and annual events in the Santa Maria Valley. The menu has changed very little—the meat, the top block of choice grade sirloin known as tri-tip, is seasoned only with salt, pepper and garlic salt; chefs cut the beef into three-inch thick pieces of about 3 to 5 pounds each and prepare it the original way. Tri-tip is served with a Santa Maria Valley exclusive—the little, pink pinquito bean—sautéed with onion, garlic and chili sauce. A tossed green salad, salsa, macaroni and cheese and sweet French bread complete the menu.

SANTA MARIA VALLEY HISTORICAL SOCIETY AND MUSEUM *616 S. Broadway, 93454. (805) 922-3130. Open Tues. through Sat. noon to 5 p.m.; closed major holidays. Free.* Changing displays, which include artifacts from the Chumash, Spanish rancho and American pioneer eras, depict the early history of the Santa Maria Valley. The museum also has a replica of a portion of a turn-of-the-century schoolroom.

WALLER COUNTY PARK *Orcutt Expressway and Waller Ln. (805) 937-1302.* This 100-acre park, covered with Monterey and other pines, serves as home to numerous ducks and geese. It features vast expanses of lawn, a lake with fountains and waterfalls, a fishing area, several play areas, basketball courts, a softball field, group and family picnic areas with barbecue equipment, pony rides, and volleyball and horseshoe areas.

WINERIES *Hours are subject to change; please call ahead. More complete descriptions of wineries offering tours appear in the Auto Club's* California Winery Tours *book.*

Byron Vineyard & Winery *12 miles southeast of Santa Maria at 5230 Tepusquet Rd.; 93454. (805) 937-7288. Open daily 10 a.m. to 4 p.m.; groups of 10 or more should call for reservations.*

Since its first crush in 1984, the winery has emphasized the production of Chardonnay and Pinot Noir, while also turning out limited quantities of Pinot Blanc, Pinot Gris and Sauvignon Blanc. All of the grapes used by the winery are estate grown or purchased from vineyards in the Santa Maria and Santa Ynez valleys. Picnic area.

Cottonwood Canyon Vineyard & Winery *3940 Dominion Rd., Santa Maria 93454 (mailing address: P.O. Box 3459, San Luis Obispo 93403). (805) 937-9063. Open 10 a.m. to 5 p.m. for tasting.* Guided tours. This family-owned win-ery produces 4000 cases of Chardonnay and Pinot Noir annually. There are picnic facilities and a gift shop.

Rancho Sisquoc Winery *18 miles southeast of Santa Maria via US 101, Betteravia and Foxen Canyon rds. (mailing address: 6600 Foxen Canyon Rd., 93454). (805) 934-4332. Open daily 10 a.m. to 4 p.m.* The owners of Rancho Sisquoc, a large cattle ranch in the foothills of the San Rafael Mountains, turned over a small portion of land to grapes, with the first crush in 1972. Now the winery bottles more than 8000 cases of vari-etals yearly. Picnic area.

SAN LUIS OBISPO COUNTY

San Luis Obispo County residents envision their county as divided into quarters, based on the geography and character of each region, so this county's chapter is divided that way for easy reference.

Rocky inlets are a hallmark of the Central Coast.

US 101 goes through **South County**, an area that encompasses all the inland and coastal towns south of the town of San Luis Obispo. Among the inland communities is Arroyo Grande, with its charming, "old town" village, while along the coast lies Pismo Beach, famous for clams and sand dunes.

Above this region is the county seat: **San Luis Obispo**, with the mission that began the town, and Cal Poly, a state university that adds zest to the town. US 101 crosses SR 1 at the northern edge of town and angles inland to the northeast.

Cal Poly enjoys a picturesque valley setting.

SR 1 leads to and follows the narrow **North Coast** strip, with a spectacular shoreline that reaches to Monterey County. Among other attractions along the coast, you'll find the volcanic peak called Morro Rock that stands in Morro Bay, the must-stop-and-shop village of Cambria, and farther north, the majestic "Hearst Castle" looking down on San Simeon.

Meanwhile, in San Luis Obispo County's northeast section, US 101 cuts through **North County**, containing vast agricultural and grazing lands, Thoroughbred horse farms and wineries, extensive lakes and numerous streams. Paso Robles, home of the California Mid-State Fair, and Atascadero, boasting a lake and a zoo, are just two of the attractive towns in this area. North County also holds Lake Nacimiento, and nearby Lake San

Iceplant brightens the roadside along San Luis Obispo's coastline.

Antonio, although in Monterey County, merits a description.

Within San Luis Obispo County, Los Padres National Forest occupies far fewer acres than in other Central Coast regions. Nevertheless, majestic mountains, meandering creeks and challenging wilderness are part of the Forest here. (See *Los Padres National Forest*.)

Both inside and out, El Paso de Robles Area Pioneer Museum is filled with interesting things.

South County

The southernmost portion of San Luis Obispo County, known appropriately as South County, stretches northward from the Santa Barbara County line nearly to Point Buchon on the coast, skirts the city of San Luis Obispo and extends into the Los Padres National Forest north of Lopez Lake. The region's geography varies widely: rocky, sea-cut cliffs in the Shell Beach area contrast with the wide sandy beaches of Pismo State Beach and the dramatic coastal sand dunes of Oceano. Inland, topography varies from the flat, fertile Arroyo Grande Valley to the rugged mountain country of the Santa Lucia Wilderness.

A majority of the region's residents have settled in towns clustered between the coast and US 101 which are collectively known as "Five Cities." Numerous accommodations and services have developed here to support a thriving tourist and recreation industry. Nearby, farm and ranch lands attest to the importance of agriculture to the area's economy.

Arroyo Grande

The Spanish words *arroyo grande*, meaning wide gulch, big ditch or stream bed, depending upon the translator, were first used by Spanish explorers who discovered the creek flowing west from the Santa Lucia Mountain Range to the Pacific Ocean. Arroyo Grande Valley, the wide, fertile area on either side of the creek, has been a major agricultural region in San Luis Obispo County since its first cultivation by the padres of Mission San Luis Obispo.

The town of Arroyo Grande was founded in 1862, making it the oldest town

in South County. Five years passed, however, before the first two structures—a schoolhouse and blacksmith shop—were built. Arroyo Grande continued to grow along Branch Street, parallel to the creek, which soon presented a problem for those living on the other side. A rope bridge was built to span the creek in the 1880s and later evolved into the Swinging Bridge, still used by pedestrians. Other, more permanent bridges were added as the town grew: Bridge Street Bridge (1908), Branch Street Bridge (1914) and Mason Street Bridge (1923).

Today many buildings along East Branch Street have been restored or rebuilt to reflect the 1890s, and this area is known as Arroyo Grande Village. The city has also grown to the west and features modern businesses and shopping centers to serve approximately 15,000 residents.

Two of the town's historic buildings have been turned into bed and breakfast inns. *The Guest House*—A New

Lopez Lake is a wonderful place to relax.

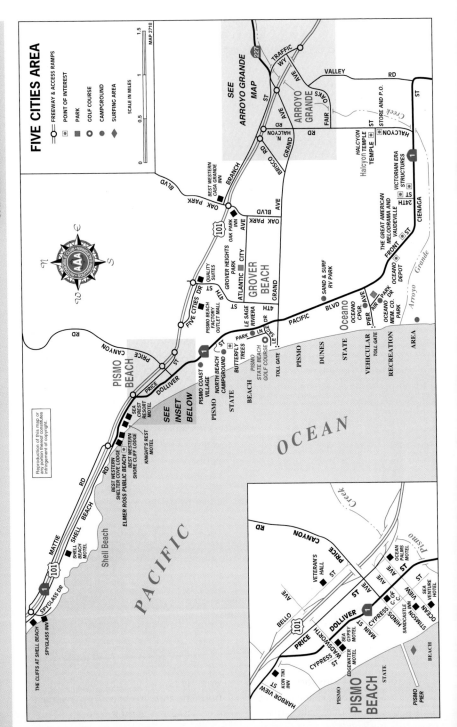

FIVE CITIES AREA

- ══ FREEWAY & ACCESS RAMPS
- ▣ POINT OF INTEREST
- ■ PARK
- ● GOLF COURSE
- ● CAMPGROUND
- ◆ SURFING AREA

SCALE IN MILES

0   0.5   1   1.5

MAP 2718

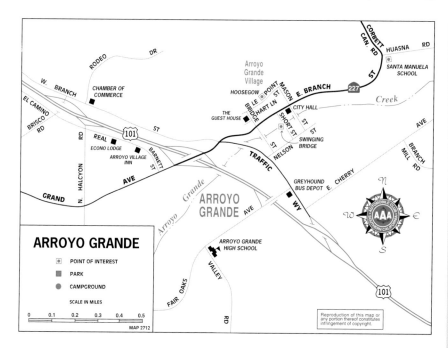

ARROYO GRANDE

- Point of Interest
- Park
- Campground

SCALE IN MILES

0   0.1   0.2   0.3   0.4   0.5

MAP 2712

Reproduction of this map or any portion thereof constitutes infringement of copyright.

England Colonial structure, built in the late 1850s by a Massachusetts sea captain, is decorated with many period pieces; located at 120 Hart Lane, (805) 481-9304. *Crystal Rose Inn*—This four-story, rose-colored mansion, originally built in 1885 on a large walnut farm, offers views of the Oceano sand dunes from the upper floors; located at 789 Valley Road, (805) 481-1854.

Agriculture is still Arroyo Grande Valley's leading business, with more than 2500 acres cultivated with two, sometimes three, crops during a single year. Commodities include flowers, bell peppers, broccoli, garbanzo beans, celery and Chinese vegetables such as snow peas and bok choy. Iceberg lettuce is a $30 million crop, and 225 acres of strawberries yield a gross revenue of close to $6 million. Visitors interested in seeing crops under cultivation will find numerous farms along Halcyon Road, Huasna Road and Lopez Lake Drive.

ARROYO GRANDE VILLAGE *Located ¼ mile east of US 101 along E. Branch St.* The village, where the town of Arroyo Grande began, harks back to the 1890s with its carefully built or restored wooden facades, boardwalk and color-ful storefronts. Housed in these build-ings is a mix of antique shops and more prosaic shops that invite investi-gation by casual strollers.

For those interested in the village's dozen or so historic structures, a brochure entitled "Historic Village Area Walking Tour" is distributed by the Arroyo Grande Chamber of Commerce, 800 West Branch Street, in the South County Regional Center; (805) 489-1488.

When entering the village from US 101, the largest and most visible of the his-toric buildings is the brightly painted former Methodist Church (1887), which currently houses an interior decorator's shop. The adjacent one-time parsonage now contains a photography shop.

Hoosegow *Le Point St. between Mason and Nevada Sts.* Built in 1906, this tiny concrete jail housed lawbreakers until the 1930s. It now stands on a hillside in a small park, one block north of Branch Street.

Swinging Bridge *At the end of Short Street, one block south of Branch Street.* Perhaps the town's best-loved reminder of its past is this suspension footbridge over Arroyo Grande Creek. In the 1800s, William Short built the first one, a rope and board bridge without handrails, to shorten the trip between his house on one side of the creek and his orchard on the other. The bridge washed out several times during floods, but was always rebuilt. Handrails were added to the bridge after 1902, and it was given to the city by the Short family in 1911. In 1969, it was completely renovated. A San Luis Obispo County Historical Landmark, the bridge is 171 feet long and is suspended about 40 feet above the creek bed. Kiwanis Park skirts the creek for one block on

either side of the bridge. It contains paths that wind down to the creek, picnic tables, and a gazebo which is used for community events. A farmer market is held weekly in the parking lot off Short Street (see Farmers Markets).

FARMERS MARKETS A wide variety of fruits, vegetables, nuts, honey, eggs, flowers, plants and herbs are sold at these farmers markets in South County.

Short Street *Parking lot behind City Hall, off E. Branch St. (near Swinging Bridge);* (805) 489-1488. *Sat noon to 3 p.m.*

Oak Park Plaza Shopping Center *1500 block of W. Branch St.; use Oak Park Blvd. exit off US 101;* (805) 489-1488. *Wed. 9 to 11:30 a.m.*

HARVEST FESTIVAL *Various locations in Arroyo Grande.* Held each year on the last weekend in September, this event celebrates the bountiful harvest of produce and flowers from the Arroyo Grande region. Area folklore claims that since the festival began, sometime

A picturesque suspension footbridge swings over scenic Arroyo Grande Creek.

in the late 1800s, contest records have been set by a 19-pound carrot and a 154-pound beet! Whether or not these claims are accurate, it is documented that the Burpee Seed Company disqualified entries from the Arroyo Grande Valley in its national produce competition because of "unfair circumstances"—namely the rich soil.

Area businesses and shopkeepers help carry out the 1890s theme of the festival with costumes and decorations. Events include a carnival with food and game booths, agricultural exhibits and a two-hour parade.

SANTA MANUELA SCHOOL *Branch St. and Huasna Rd. (805) 489-7242. Open for docent-conducted tours Sat. through Sun. 1 to 3 p.m.* Constructed in 1877, this former one-room schoolhouse was rebuilt in 1901 after a fire and continued in use until 1957. In 1968, when its location was threatened by the construction of Lopez Dam, the schoolhouse was moved to a knoll above the impending waterline. It has since been moved into Arroyo Grande. The schoolhouse retains furnishings from the early 1900s.

STRAWBERRY FESTIVAL *Branch and Bridge sts.* Thousands of pounds of strawberries take such forms as shortcake, sundaes, chocolate dipped and just plain delicious at this celebration held during Memorial Day weekend. The festival includes a large arts and crafts show, entertainment, ethnic food booths and a farmers market.

WINERIES *Hours are subject to change; please call ahead. More complete descriptions of wineries offering tours appear in the Auto Club's* California Winery Tours *book.*

Maison Deutz Winery *1 mile south of Arroyo Grande off US 101 at 453 Deutz Dr., 93420. (805) 481-1763. Open Wed. through Mon. 11 a.m. to 5 p.m., except major holidays. Fee for tasting; tours by appointment.* This winery produces only sparkling wines.

Talley Vineyards *3031 Lopez Dr., just north of Orcutt Rd., 93420. (805) 489-0446. Open 10:30 a.m. to 4:30 p.m.; daily in summer, Thur. through Sun. rest of year.* This winery's specialties are Chardonnay and Pinot Noir. Picnic area.

Avila Beach

The two-mile drive to this quiet seaside town from US 101 along Avila Beach Drive parallels Obispo Creek on its way to the ocean. As the road winds through lush vegetation, it passes two mineral hot springs spas and the San Luis Bay Golf Course (see *Recreation*).

Avila Beach, established in 1867 on San Luis Obispo Bay, retains the close interaction between land and sea that existed even before the town was founded. Nearby Cave Landing, a natural promontory, served as a fishing site for Chumash Indians and as a port during the Mission and Rancho periods.

Today, Front Street, Avila Beach's main oceanfront thoroughfare, extends five blocks. Along the mile-long beach are picnic tables, barbecues and a beach ramp for small day-use boats. On the other side of the street are businesses that offer food, souvenirs and fishing supplies. With luck and patience, you can snag red snapper, perch and halibut or rock crab off Avila Pier. (The first thing you see as you step onto the pier from the sidewalk is the tidy little San Luis Yacht Club, established in 1936.)

Just west of Avila Beach, San Luis Bay serves as a departure point for year-round sportfishing for salmon, halibut, albacore or rockcod.

AVILA STATE BEACH *Along Front St.* This level stretch of beach boasts weather that is usually mild (an annual average of 70 degrees), and gentle ocean breezes make this a popular place for swimming, surfing and sailing. Picnickers can take advantage of tables and fire rings. These activities are quite likely to be interrupted during November through April by seasonal storms, brisk winds or fog.

HOT SPRINGS Dozens of hot and cold mineral springs rise above ground throughout San Luis Obispo County. Two of the hot springs bubbling to the surface in an area paralleling San Luis Obispo Creek have drawn bathers since the Chumash. One popular spa resort was established in 1897 along the present Avila Beach Drive. Several years later, while drilling for oil nearby, workers discovered another source of the 130-degree mineral water at 900 feet, and by 1907, a bathhouse and

swimming pool were built there. During the 1920s and '30s many Hollywood stars, such as W.C. Fields, Rudolph Valentino and Charlie Chaplin, stopped to "take the waters" on their way to Hearst Castle in San Simeon.

Today these two establishments still offer hot mineral water baths. Avila Hot Springs is at 250 Avila Beach Drive, San Luis Obispo 93405; (805) 595-2359, and Sycamore Mineral Springs is at 1215 Avila Beach Drive, San Luis Obispo 93405; (805) 595-7302. (Note: Neither spa has been inspected nor recommended by the Automobile Club of Southern California; they are listed only as information.)

PORT SAN LUIS *At the end of Avila Beach Dr.* (805) 595-5400. Commercial development of the port first occurred in the late 1850s when a wharf and warehouse were built at Cave Landing. The site became known as Mallagh's Wharf when in 1864 it was purchased by Captain David Mallagh, who for the next nine years controlled all freight

A clean and sandy shoreline beckons families to Avila Beach.

and passenger traffic on San Luis Obispo Bay. In 1869 businessman John Harford and a group of local merchants erected a new 1800-foot pier called "People's Wharf" near present-day Avila Pier. Because of existing contracts, most steamships continued to call at Mallagh's Wharf, and Harford eventually asked Mallagh to manage People's Wharf. Mallagh abandoned Cave Landing, and the facilities there soon fell into disuse.

Harford, not satisfied with the vulnerable location of People's Wharf, sought a more protected site in the lee of Point San Luis at the western edge of the bay. He completed a 540-foot wharf here in 1873 and linked it to the town of Avila with a horse-drawn, narrow-gauge railroad that his workers painstakingly constructed along two miles of rocky shoreline. Harford's all-season landing quickly drew several steamship lines away from People's Wharf and soon became the port of choice on the bay. People's Wharf has since been destroyed by storms, and all that

remain are the stubs of broken pilings, visible only at extremely low tides.

Today, the Port San Luis Harbor District, established in 1954 to develop the recreational and commercial aspects of San Luis Obispo Bay, oversees two of the three piers and portions of the bay's tidelands. Tons of salmon, crab, albacore, halibut, rockcod, shark and swordfish are brought in each year by about 70 commercial boats.

Harford Pier supports on its 1460-foot length a charter boat company, Paradise Sportfishing, (see *Recreation*), fishing platforms, three fish markets, fast food service, a restaurant and saloon. Located nearby are facilities for boat launching and hoist; a marine supply store; diesel fuel; a 24-hour cafe; and a bait and tackle shop.

SAN LUIS OBISPO LIGHTHOUSE

Located on Point San Luis at the west end of San Luis Obispo Bay. This two-story Victorian lighthouse station, set on 30 acres overlooking San Luis Obispo Bay, cost $50,000 to build in 1890, when it

Between Avila Beach and Port San Luis lies a beautiful bay.

began operation. The original whale-oil lamp had nine ground lenses rotating around the wick. Once visible for 20 miles at sea, the light is now on display in the San Luis Obispo County Historical Museum. A subsequent light-house beacon was replaced by an automatic light in 1969. The structure is currently owned by the Port San Luis Harbor District. Future plans include regularly scheduled tours.

Although the interior of the lighthouse is currently closed to the public, guided coastal hikes to the lighthouse are offered two or three times each week throughout the year. These seven-mile hikes offer dramatic views of the coastal terrain, flora and fauna. For more information on hikes call (805) 541-8735.

SEE CANYON SCENIC DRIVE *See Canyon and Prefumo Canyon rds.* A popular weekend destination for local residents, See Canyon has increasingly become a favorite tourist attraction as well. The canyon lies two miles northeast of Avila Beach off San Luis Bay Drive (one mile west of US 101). See Canyon Road runs through the canyon, then on for 13 miles over the coastal hills to Los Osos Valley. The narrow road winds into the tree-shaded canyon passing a half-dozen apple orchards, small pastures and a Christmas tree farm in the first 4½ miles. During fall, visitors may purchase apples, fresh cider and other products here, and at some orchards customers can pick their own apples.

Beyond the orchards, the road climbs out of the canyon to open grasslands that stretch across the hilltops. Parts of the road in this area are unpaved, but these sections are covered with gravel and generally are good, albeit dusty. From the rounded hilltops motorists are afforded panoramic views of Morro

Bay and the curving Pacific shoreline. The horizon to the east is dominated by a chain of prominent volcanic peaks, and at several spots San Luis Obispo can be seen in the distance.

At mileage 8.5 the road drops below a canopy of oak and sycamore into Prefumo Canyon, following a small stream where deer sometimes pause to drink. The road passes several small farms and then emerges from the canyon into rapidly developing Los Osos Valley. The street, signed at this end as Prefumo Road, terminates at Los Osos Valley Road. To the left are Morro Bay and its surrounding communities; to the right is Madonna Road, 1½ miles southwest of US 101.

Grover Beach

D.W. Grover founded this coastal town in 1887. His obvious pride in that accomplishment surfaced again several years later when he declared that South County was Grover City; all other towns were merely "territories." However, the town's real growth did not begin until after incorporation in 1959, and in 1992 became Grover *Beach*.

Today the city's residents number a respectable 12,250, with a 3- to 4-percent increase each year. Originally planned as an area for retirees, Grover Beach has evolved into a bedroom community for workers at large establishments in surrounding areas, such as Vandenberg Air Force Base, California Men's Colony and Diablo Canyon Nuclear Power Plant.

The city's amenities include a nine-hole golf course (see *Recreation*), several fine community recreation parks (see *Recreation*), and a well-developed shopping district along the main street, Grand Avenue. The Chamber of

Commerce also reports 286 days of sunshine out of each 365 and an annual average temperature of 68 degrees.

Grover Beach is probably best known for the stretch of Pismo State Beach on its western boundary. An entrance ramp where Grand Avenue meets the ocean allows convenient access for passenger cars and recreational vehicles to drive along the hard beach sand. During high tide, however, it is recommended that only four-wheel-drive vehicles enter the beach. There is a $4 day-use fee (see Pismo State Beach).

Halcyon

This is a tiny town with an interesting history. The 95-acre community, just east of Oceano and north of SR 1, was founded in 1903 as the new home for a religious group, the Temple of the People. Theosophists Francia A. La Due and William H. Dower, M.D., who had formed the Temple five years earlier in Syracuse, New York, founded Halcyon

as an "intentional community" with a common philosophy, not as a utopian society. Dr. Dower began a sanatorium in a three-story Victorian mansion, the Coffee Rice Home, where he treated tuberculosis, alcoholism and drug abuse, and was one of the first doctors to use x-rays.

Today, more than half of Halcyon's population are members of the Temple, which studies a variety of eastern and western religious beliefs. The focal point of the town is the white, pillared Temple building (1922), an equilateral triangle with bowed sides, located on Halcyon Road and Temple Street. The Temple grounds include a variety of native plants. Visitors may attend a 10:30 a.m. Sunday service and a 15-minute service daily at noon.

Other points of interest near the Temple include the Halcyon Store and Post Office (established in 1907) at Halcyon Road and La Due Street. It is open Monday through Saturday 9 a.m.

This temple, with its unusual and majestic design, is a Halcyon landmark.

to 5 p.m., Sunday until 4 p.m. The William Quan Judge Library, just north of the store and post office, has about 9000 volumes on philosophy and theosophy. The library is open by appointment. The University Center, located behind the Temple, contains exhibits of local artists' works; open by appointment. For information call the Temple office at (805) 489-2822.

Lopez Lake

13 miles east of Arroy Grande via Branch St., Huasna Rd. and Lopez Dr.

Supervisor, Lopez Recreation area, *6800 Lopez Dr., Arroyo Grande 93420. (805) 489-2095. Open year round for day use from 6 a.m. to 9 p.m.; campers admitted at any time, space permitting. Day-use admission, $4 per vehicle; $4 extra per boat; camping fees vary.*

This popular recreation area lies east of Arroyo Grande in the oak-dotted, rolling foothills of the Santa Lucia Range. Formed in 1968 by the construction of Lopez Dam, the lake and adjacent recreation lands are administered by the county.

Lopez Lake Recreation Area encompasses 4276 acres, which contain the 974-acre lake (with 22 miles of shoreline), 355 campsites, a marina and boat-launching ramp, general store, bait shop, picnic and barbecue facilities and playgrounds (see *Recreation* and *Campgrounds & Trailer Parks*). There is also a privately owned water slide and hot springs area.

Every inland water sport imaginable is accommodated here. Fishermen reel in catches of bass, bluegill, catfish, crappie, rainbow trout, redear and sunfish. Relatively warm water and breezes off the Pacific Ocean provide especially

good conditions for sailing, sailboarding, swimming and water-skiing. (See *Recreation*.)

On any of the 10 trails throughout the park, hikers are likely to see some of the area's abundant wildlife. During the cool early morning hours or just before sunset, visitors may encounter deer (which are tame enough to wait while their pictures are taken), foxes, raccoons, squirrels or turkeys (see *Recreation*, Hiking).

MUSTANG WATER SLIDE & HOT SPRINGS *Near Mustang Campground in the northeastern area of the park; P.O. Box 2098, Orcutt 93457. (805) 489-8898. Open June through Aug. daily; May and Sept., Sat. and Sun.; Mon. through Fri. 10:30 a.m. to 4:30 p.m., Sat. and Sun. 9:30 a.m. to 5:15 p.m. Admission $5.75 for one hour; half-day and all-day admission offered at a reduced rate.* Four hot tubs and two 600-foot-long water slides offer a change of pace from traditional lake recreation.

Nipomo

The southernmost town in San Luis Obispo County, Nipomo was founded in 1882. Its name comes from the area's large Spanish land grant and rancho, which in turn kept a variation of the Chumash name for the area, "Nepomah," meaning "at the foot of the hills."

Rancho Nipomo, consisting of 38,000 acres, was granted in 1837 to William G. Dana, a Boston sea captain. (His cousin, Richard Henry Dana, wrote *Two Years Before the Mast*, an account of a sea voyage that called at several California ports.)

The ranch and the adobe home Dana built there served for many years as an important stop on El Camino Real, "The Royal Highway," between missions San Luis Obispo and Santa Barbara. Dana raised stock, farmed, made soap and furniture and engaged in trade. He was well known as a generous host who gave lavish fiestas—sometimes lasting a week—which included food and wine, music, dances, bullfights, cockfights and horse races.

Dana demonstrated his hospitality, up to a point, when Captain John C. Frémont and 430 soldiers stopped at the rancho on their way south to Los Angeles in 1846. Dana ordered 40 head of cattle slaughtered for a barbecue and complied with Frémont's request for 30 fresh horses. When the soldiers left, Frémont also took three of the Dana family's favorite steeds. That evening several of Dana's men visited Frémont's camp, reclaiming the three—and the 30—horses.

Today, Nipomo continues as an agricultural area with a variety of crops raised in its rich alluvial soil, washed down from the Nipomo Foothills at the eastern edge of town. Within this town of 7000, located on either side of US 101, are citrus orchards, vegetable farms and commercial nurseries. Eucalyptus trees cover the mesa area of Nipomo, where Black Lake Golf Course is located (see *Recreation*). Thousands of the blue gum eucalyptus were planted as seedlings on the mesa in 1908 by two men from Pasadena, who formed Los Berros Forest Company with the idea of selling the trees as hardwood. Fortunately for the area's scenic beauty today, the mature eucalyptus did not yield good timber.

DANA ADOBE *East of US 101 near Story St. at 671 Oakglen Rd., 93444. (805) 543-0638. Open Sun. 2 to 4 p.m.* William G. Dana initiated construction

of this adobe on Rancho Nipomo in 1839. Originally a one-story dwelling, the adobe acquired a second story and two wings as the Dana family grew. Over the years the rancho became a trading center for such items as soap, candles and furniture that were manufactured there. The land on which the adobe stands is still a working ranch, and the adobe is undergoing restoration by the San Luis Obispo County Historical Society.

FARMERS MARKET Swap Meet *263 North Frontage Rd. (805) 929-3878. Fri., Sat. and Sun. 6 a.m. to 6 p.m.* This event presents abundant and varied merchandise, including produce.

NIPOMO COUNTY REGIONAL PARK *¾ mile west of US 101 on W. Tefft St., at Pomeroy Rd.* A 144-acre park, shaded with eucalyptus, oak and pine trees, contains facilities for a number of activities: tennis, handball, basketball, softball and horseshoes. Picnic tables and barbecues are located throughout the park, and a natural area features a ring and trails for equestrians. A playground on the south side provides a good stopping place for travelers with children.

OLD ST. JOSEPH'S CHURCH *Tefft St. and Thompson Ave.* This former church, built in 1902, lost its beautiful original stained glass windows (circa 1898) and bell to the new St. Joseph's when it was built in 1970. The old building has become Victorian Bells Wedding Chapel.

WINERY *Hours are subject to change; please call ahead. More complete descriptions of wineries offering tours appear in the Auto Club's* California Winery Tours *book.*

Ross-Keller Winery *Off US 101 via Tefft St.; 985 Orchard Ave., 93444. (805) 929-*

3627. Open daily noon to 5 p.m. Grapes for red and white varietals are purchased from Central Coast vineyards and vinted in small batches, using virtually no additives nor processing. Muscat Canelli and white Zinfandel are among the offerings here. Picnic area.

Oceano

The southernmost coastal community in the county, Oceano offers such diverse activities as off-road driving in sand dunes and attending an evening performance at the melodrama. Today's town of about 6200 residents was originally laid out in 1893 by R.E. Jack and C.H. Phillips, who anticipated the Southern Pacific Railroad's arrival in the area. When the railroad steamed in three years later, Oceano was ready with a new train depot and produce to be shipped by rail. Beach resort subdivisions were laid out in 1905, but were largely unsuccessful. The real economic successes were the produce packing sheds, which flourished along the rail line from the early 1900s to the late 1950s. Then, with the advent of field packaging and truck transport, the packing sheds disappeared, railroad traffic declined, and Oceano again concentrated on the tourists attracted to its beach and sand dune recreation areas.

VICTORIAN-ERA STRUCTURES Two private homes built near the turn of the century still stand in Oceano. Neither of them is open to the public, but passersby can admire their impressive exteriors. The *Baughman House* (1894) is at the corner of 24th and Beach streets. The *Coffee Rice Home* (1885), at 25th and Cienaga (SR 1) streets, stands within a mobile home park.

THE GREAT AMERICAN MELO-DRAMA AND VAUDEVILLE *3 miles south of Pismo Beach at 1863 Front St.*

(SR 1), 93445. (805) 489-2499, Mon. through Sat. 10 a.m. to 6 p.m., Sun. 11 a.m. to 5 p.m. Performances Wed. and Thur. 7 p.m., Fri. 8 p.m., Sat. 4:30 and 8:30 p.m., Sun. 6 p.m.; theater closed major holidays. Tickets $10.50 to $13.50; seniors and under age 12, $1 off each ticket. An evening's entertainment at the Melodrama transcends the stage area—the entire theater building becomes the show. Costumed performers greet, serenade and seat playgoers, as well as serve food and drink at the bar during intermission. On stage, the performers' high level of energy continues as they dance, sing, laugh and act their way through melodramas, comedies and thrillers.

OCEANO DEPOT *1634 Front St. (SR 1), north of Paso Robles St. (805) 489-5446 Mon. through Sat. or (805) 489-5782 Sun. One room open Sun. 1:30 to 4:30 p.m. Guided tours of the building by appointment.* This two-story depot figured prominently in the growth of Oceano when the railroad brought people and commerce to the area. The original station, built in 1896, stood at the west end of Ocean Street and Highway 1, about 100 yards south of the present location.

When the original structure burned down in 1903, a similar station, probably from the San Francisco Bay area, was disassembled and sent to Oceano. Redwood, pine and fir pieces, 47 windows and 12 doors (six for people and six for freight) were reassembled, with metal smokestacks replacing the old depot's brick chimney. This type of station—the "combination 22"—was spacious enough to accommodate families of railroad employees, so the architectural plans were used repeatedly, with only minor decorative variations.

As railroad passenger travel to the area ceased, the depot became a celery-heart packing shed and finally shut down completely in 1973. After it was moved to its present location two years later, restoration began and is ongoing. When the depot is completely restored, it will serve as a community center and house a museum with railroad memorabilia and local historical exhibits.

Pismo Beach

Although the city of Pismo Beach was at one time best known for the Pismo clams that covered the area's wide sandy beaches, today other attractions and activities claim the attention of visitors. Those who want to try their hand at capturing the tasty bivalve, however, can still do so (see *Recreation*).

"Pismu" was the Chumash word meaning tar, a substance used by them to caulk their seaworthy canoes. Eventually the word became "pismo" and was assigned to the Rancho el Pismo land grant, first owned in 1849 by José Ortega. At that time, the large rancho was used primarily for raising cattle and horses. Legend says that the next owner, Isaac Sparks, won El Pismo in a card game. One of Sparks' employees, Englishman John Price, gradually acquired land and livestock until he owned about 7000 acres of the rancho stretching from present-day Pismo Beach to Oceano. Brothers D.J. and Michael Meherin are credited with constructing the first wharf in Pismo Beach, which provided a shipping port for South County agricultural products. John Price, who became Michael's father-in-law, founded the city of Pismo Beach in 1886.

The popularity of the city's clams targeted it as a tourist resort, and hundreds of visitors arrived via the new railroad. One hotel, needing more space for an overflow of tourists, erected "Tent City," a group of army tents resting on wooden planks. Rates for "Tent City," which was used until 1927, ranged from $8 to $22 per week, plus an extra 25¢ charge for the bathhouse. Clams were plentiful (you just "wiggled your feet around in the sand," according to one account).

After visitors had their fill of clamming for the day, many would wait in lines blocks long for admittance to the Pavilion, a popular dance hall that was built on pilings over the water and featured well-known orchestras. (The Pavilion burned down in 1945.) In 1946 voters agreed to permanent city incorporation, reversing a one-year trial incorporation in 1939 that had failed.

Visitors who initially came to hunt clams undoubtedly returned for other outdoor activities, which people still enjoy, including beautiful scenery, sunsets and the relaxed atmosphere. As a result of its history as a tourist town, Pismo Beach offers the largest number of accommodations and restaurants in South County.

The 1200-foot Pismo Beach Pier is a popular spot with fishermen, whose catches usually yield such bottom fish as red snapper and lingcod. Bicycles and scuba equipment can be rented near the beach, and tennis courts are located in the city (see *Recreation*). Walking, whether it be on the beach or through Pismo Beach shops, is another popular pastime.

BUTTERFLY TREES *Just south of North Beach Campground; park on dirt shoulder and enter through gate in fence.* A grove of eucalyptus and Monterey pine trees plays host to thousands of migrating monarch butterflies each year. From late November through March, the butterflies cluster together so thickly that their orange and black wings appear as yellowish leaves on the trees. On warm winter days, as the monarchs leave the clusters in search of food, the sky around the trees teems with the beautiful creatures.

Docent-led walks, lasting about 45 minutes, go through the butterfly groves November through February on Saturday and Sunday at 11 a.m. and 2 p.m. The walks last about 45 minutes. For more information, call (805) 489-1869 or 549-3312.

ELMER ROSS PUBLIC BEACH *Access via Shore Cliff Lodge parking lot at 2555 Price St.* This tiny crescent of beach is surrounded by high bluffs and can be reached only by a spiral staircase. During low tide, tide pools are revealed; however, be prepared to get wet even then. No matter what the status of the tide, the staircase affords spectacular views of the coast: high bluffs meeting the sea to the north, sandy beaches and the Pismo Beach Pier to the south. Also to the north, the lighthouse beacon at Point San Luis appears at regular intervals.

FARMERS MARKET *Dolliver St. and Main Ave. (805) 773-1661. Held May through Oct., Tue. from 4 p.m. to dusk.*

PISMO BEACH CLAM FESTIVAL The first festival was held on New Year's Day 1945 and was so popular that

▼ *The Monarch of the Coast*

Gorgeous! That's the best word to describe the annual gathering of monarch butterflies in the eucalyptus and pine groves around Pismo Beach. The orange and black pattern on the butterfly wings comes from a mosaic of scales that is layered like shingles, and from a distance the butterfly clusters resemble yellow leaves.

The butterflies appear during late October or early November and hang around, literally, through February or March. They come from as far away as Canada to escape the extreme winter cold and lack of nectar. While their initial journey south is leisurely, on the return trip they can reach speeds of 30 miles per hour.

The seemingly hearty constitution that allows the monarchs to fly long distances belies their sensitivity to cold. Each butterfly clusters on a tree with its wings covering the body of the one below to provide some warmth and shelter from rain. The weight of the cluster helps to steady it during windy periods and to keep butterflies from falling off. If a butterfly is dislodged from the group, it cannot fly when temperatures drop below 55 degrees and cannot move at less than 40 degrees.

Since monarch mating takes place before and during the migration, several generations will be born during that time. Many of the creatures who leave their northern home never return, because a monarch's lifetime is just nine short months.

it's still a big event more than a half century later; it is now held in October (specific dates vary). The numerous events associated with the annual clam festival include crowning a festival queen, complimentary clam chowder, a fishing derby, an arts and crafts show and, of course, a clam dig for prizes.

Pismo Dunes Preserve

The Pismo Dunes are considered the finest, most extensive coastal dunes in California. Because of this status, motor vehicles are prohibited from two protected areas established to preserve the ecosystem. Although no trails exist, visitors are welcome to walk through the dunes but should be careful not to damage the fragile vegetation.

Oso Flaco Lake affords access to the dunes. Take SR 166 off US 101 to SR 1 and go west on Oso Flaco Lake Road. At the end of the road is a parking lot open daily from 8 a.m. to 6 p.m. A boardwalk stroll of five or ten minutes leads past both branches of the lake and on into the dunes. There is a $4 day-use fee.

The dunes were formed between the Ice Ages when sand, brought from the mountains by rivers and creeks, accumulated offshore, was deposited back onshore by waves and then was blown inland. The Chumash used the area for food collection and preparation; accounts by early Spanish sailors report seeing natives camping there. The first Spanish land expedition to pass through the area camped at the dunes.

During the 1930s and '40s, the dunes housed the "Dunites," a group comprising mystics, nudists, artists, writers and hermits who believed the dunes were a center of creative energy. Movie makers have made such features there as "The Sheik," with Rudolph

Valentino and, several decades later, "Jonathan Livingston Seagull."

A wide variety of plant and animal life inhabits the dunes. Wildflowers, California sagebrush, sand verbena and bush lupine grow here, as does the rare giant golden coreopsis daisy. Animal tracks left in the sand include those of dune mice, coyote, fox, deer and rabbit. Shorebirds are plentiful, and other species such as hawks and peregrine falcons have been spotted from the dunes.

Pismo Dunes State Vehicular Recreation Area

The dramatic Pismo Dunes, with their gentle west-facing slopes and steep eastern "slipfaces," provide exciting off-road entertainment. Off-highway vehicle enthusiasts from all over California come to Pismo Dunes to ride dune buggies, ATVs (all-terrain vehicles) and motorcycles. All off-highway vehicles must be transported to post No. 2 before unloading, but then drivers have nearly 2000 acres to explore. Fenced and signed areas are closed to vehicles to protect dunes and private property.

Motoring around the dunes is an exciting—but sometimes dangerous—sport, as well as potentially damaging to the ecology. To minimize the danger and to protect plant and animal life in the area, please follow these rules by California's Department of Parks and Department of Motor Vehicles. For further information, call Pismo Dunes SVRA at (805) 473-7220.

1. The speed limit is 15 mph on the beach and within 50 feet of any camp or group of people. California's basic speed laws apply in the dune area.

Off the road and onto the dunes at Pismo Dunes State Vehicular Area!

2. Drinking and driving is strictly forbidden.

3. Motor vehicles must stay out of vegetated areas. Fenced and signed areas are closed to vehicular use.

4. Drivers under age 18 may only operate ATVs on public land if they have an ATV Safety Certificate of Completion. Call (800) 255-6787 for further information.

5. All vehicles operating in the dunes must be equipped with an adequate muffler and a 10-foot whip with a 6-by-12-inch orange or red flag. Except for motorcycles, all vehicles must have an adequate roll bar and a secure seat with seat belts for the driver and each passenger.

6. Drivers of ATVs and motorcycles are required by law to wear a helmet.

7. All riders are advised to wear a helmet and proper protective clothing.

BJ'S ATV RENTALS *197 Grand Ave., Grover City 93433. (805) 481-5411.* ATVs can be rented for use in Pismo Dunes SVRA. This company rents four-wheel vehicles, gives instructions and delivers vehicles to the off-highway area. A deposit is required. ATVs rent for about $25 for one hour, $40-$55 for two hours.

Pismo State Beach

Pismo State Beach extends for about eight miles along the coast of South County, running through the cities of Oceano, Grover City and Pismo Beach. Known primarily for the dune area where off-highway vehicles roam, the beach also contains a dune preserve, beach campsites and entrance ramps where passenger cars can drive onto the hard-packed beach sand. In addition to the novel recreational activities here, typical beach sports abound, such as beachcombing, surf fishing, surfing and swimming. Other activities include clam digging, hiking and horseback riding.

Information on recreational opportunities at Pismo State Beach can be found under *Recreation*; for information on campgrounds see *Campgrounds & Trailer Parks*.

Passenger vehicles may enter the beach to drive along the sand from entrance ramps at Grand Avenue in Grover Beach and Pier Avenue in Oceano. State park personnel at each entrance collect a $4-per-vehicle fee and advise of high tide or other unsafe conditions. Only street-legal vehicles are allowed between Grand Avenue and post No. 2. Vehicles are required to drive on beach sand which has varying degrees of softness.

Shell Beach

Although it retains a separate name and identity, Shell Beach lies entirely within the municipal boundaries of Pismo Beach. Unlike Pismo's typically wide, sandy shoreline, however, the coast at Shell Beach is composed of steep bluffs and small, rocky beaches. A number of small cliff-top parks have benches for leisurely enjoyment of the panorama of sea and sky, and several stairways offer beach access. Rather than shells, tide pools are the main attraction (look, but don't touch).

The main street through town, Shell Beach Road, closely parallels US 101 and is lined by a variety of businesses. The rest of Shell Beach is made up of residential streets built on the coastal bluffs.

San Luis Obispo City

The city of San Luis Obispo sits serenely in a green valley ringed by hills and volcanic peaks. In the winter and spring, oak-dotted hillsides become vivid green. In summer and fall, the colors turn tawny.

Although urban growth is pushing housing developments into the surrounding countryside, the central part of San Luis Obispo retains much of the feel and appearance it's had for many years: neighborhoods of neat, well-maintained houses face tree-lined streets, and a downtown with a friendly mix of an inviting park, historical sites and attractive shops.

San Luis Obispo was originally established in 1772 as a mission—the fifth in the chain of 21 in California; its founder was the famed Padre Junípero Serra, assisted by Padre José Cavaller. The community that developed around the mission remained tiny through the Spanish, Mexican and early American periods. Not until the coming of the Southern Pacific Railroad in 1894 did San Luis experience anything close to a boom. (By the way, it is considered acceptable to refer to the city as "San Luis" but totally incorrect, according to residents, to call the town "San Louie Obispo" or—worse—"SLO Town.")

With the founding in 1901 of a vocational school that would evolve into the renowned California Polytechnic State University, and in following years the development of a state hospital, a major prison, numerous government offices and a military base, San Luis developed an increasingly stable economic base. Nevertheless, the city has displayed no intention of relinquishing its tranquil way of life for dubious "progress." The city's 42,000 residents are highly protective of their quality of life and guard it vigorously.

They are equally rigorous in celebrating the talent and vibrancy of their community, as demonstrated by the numerous events held throughout the year. Notable are La Fiesta in May, the Central Coast Renaissance Faire in July, the Mozart Festival in August and the Christmas Plaza Festival in December.

Opportunities exist for a variety of musical and theatrical events. Cal Poly and Cuesta College (see listings) both offer seasons of performing arts. For information on San Luis Obispo County Symphony Orchestra concerts, call (805) 543-3533. Theater is represented by the San Luis Obispo Little Theatre in San Luis Obispo, (805) 543-3737.

An excellent introduction to San Luis Obispo is provided by the Chamber of Commerce Tourist Information Office at 1039 Chorro Street, downtown. The office is open Monday 9:30 a.m. to 5 p.m; Tuesday through Friday 8 a.m. to 5 p.m.; Saturday and Sunday 10 a.m. to 5 p.m. (closed some holidays). The

Young Chumash Girl with Grizzly Bear *stands near Mission San Luis Obispo de Tolosa.*

SAN LUIS OBISPO COUNTY

▼ *A Quick Guide to San Luis Obispo Information*

Population: 43,400

Elevation: 230 ft.

Telephone numbers are in the 805 area code, unless noted otherwise.

Emergency 911

Police (non-emergency) 781-7317

Emergency Road Service for AAA Members (800) 400-4222

Hospitals

Sierra Vista Regional Medical Center
1010 Murray Ave.
San Luis Obispo 93405
546-7600

French Hospital Medical Center
1911 Johnson Ave.
San Luis Obispo 93401
543-5353

Time: 767-2676

Weather: 925-0909

Highway Conditions: (800) 427-7623

Radio and TV

Radio station KVEC (920 AM) in San Luis Obispo offers news and traffic reports. KCPX (90.1 FM) is a member of National Public Radio. San Luis Obispo's Spanish and Portugese language station is KIGS (620 AM).

Network television channels are 3 (ABC), 4 or 6 (NBC), 12 (CBS). The PBS channel is 8. For a complete list of radio and television programs, consult the daily newspapers.

Automobile Club of Southern California

San Luis Obispo District Office
1445 Calle Joaquin, San Luis Obispo

Mailing address: P.O. Box 4040,
San Luis Obispo 93403-4040
Phone: 543-6454
Office hours: Mon. through Fri.
9 a.m. to 5 p.m.

Visitor Services

San Luis Obispo Chamber of
  Commerce
1039 Chorro St.
San Luis Obispo 93401
781-2777
Office hours: Mon. 9:30 a.m. to 5 p.m., Tues. through Fri. 8 a.m. to 5 p.m., Sat. and Sun. 10 a.m. to noon and 2 to 5 p.m.

San Luis Obispo County Visitors
  & Conference Bureau
1041 Chorro Street, Ste. E
San Luis Obispo 93401
(805) 541-8000 or (800) 634-1414
Office hours: Mon. through Fri.
8 a.m. to 5 p.m.

Newspapers

The major daily newspapers in the San Luis Obispo area are *The Daily News-Press* and the San Luis Obispo County edition of the *Los Angeles Times*; both contain local events and entertainment information.

Public Transportation & Taxis

San Luis Obispo Transit operates buses in San Luis Obispo. For schedule and route information call 541-2877.

Yellow Cab provides service in the San Luis Obispo area; call 543-1234. Other taxi companies are listed in the yellow pages of the local telephone directory.

friendly staff offers valuable information and distributes a variety of tourist-oriented brochures.

One item of particular interest is the informative *San Luis Obispo Chamber of Commerce Visitor Guide* ($2.95). The guide includes an outline for the "Path of History" walking tour, a two-hour self-guided stroll through central San Luis that highlights many landmarks of historic or architectural interest. Attractions along the walk range from Spanish-period adobes to a building designed by America's most famous architect, Frank Lloyd Wright. Also notable are many beautifully

restored Victorian houses and a number of architecturally distinguished churches.

Downtown San Luis Obispo contains, within a few square blocks, historic sites, inviting restaurants, interesting shops and a tree-shaded plaza. The area has parking garages and metered street parking. Once you park the car, take the Old SLO Trolley to shop or visit downtown attractions. The open-sided, old-fashioned trolley runs within a core framed by Nipomo, Marsh, Osos and Palm streets. This free service is available Monday through Wednesday and Friday from noon to 5:30 p.m.,

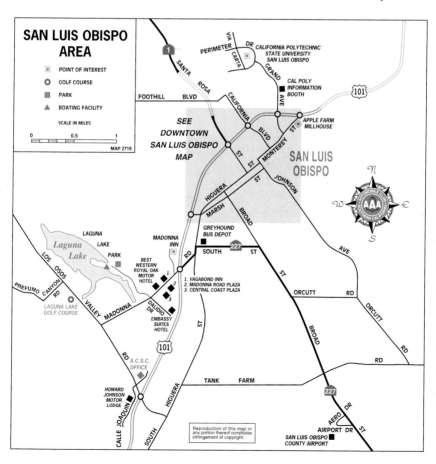

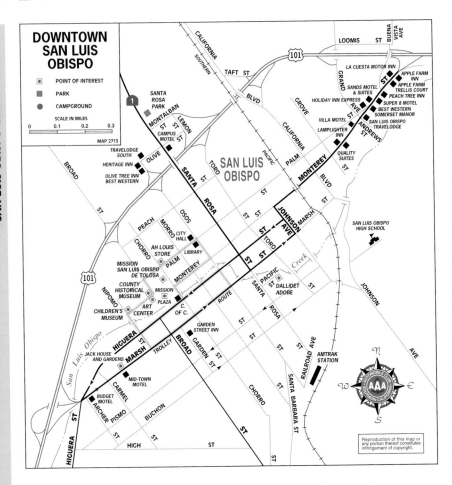

DOWNTOWN SAN LUIS OBISPO

- ◉ POINT OF INTEREST
- ■ PARK
- ● CAMPGROUND

SCALE IN MILES
0   0.1   0.2   0.3

MAP 2713

Reproduction of this map or any portion thereof constitutes infringement of copyright.

Thursday noon to 9:30 p.m., Saturday and Sunday noon to 5 p.m.

AH LOUIS STORE *800 Palm St., 93406. (805) 543-4332.* This store is about all that remains of San Luis Obispo's once-thriving Chinatown. Founded in 1874 by Ah Louis, an immigrant from China, it was originally a post office, bank and general store. The store eventually became the hub of Chinatown activities and Ah Louis an important spokesman for the Chinese—2000 of whom were railroad laborers. Designated a State Historical Landmark (No. 802), it is still owned by the Louis family and operates as a gift shop specializing in Oriental imports.

APPLE FARM MILLHOUSE *2015 Monterey St., off US 101 behind the Apple Farm restaurant (mailing address: 890 Monterey St., 93401). (805) 544-2040. Open daily 9 a.m. to 6 p.m. Free.* Modeled after the water-powered mills of the 19th century, this working replica was designed and built with painstaking attention to detail. Several of the mechanical parts were salvaged from old mills around the country, and the redwood for the flume and

Situated by the waters of San Luis Obispo Creek, this 14-foot wheel drives machinery inside the Apple Farm Millhouse.

millhouse ceiling was cut in Yosemite more than 75 years ago.

The mill's 14-foot-high water wheel drives an elaborate mechanism of gears, shafts, pulleys and belts that power a gristmill, ice cream maker and cider press. Products made at the mill are sold on the premises or in the adjacent restaurant.

CALIFORNIA POLYTECHNIC STATE UNIVERSITY (CAL POLY) *Approximately 2 miles north of downtown San Luis Obispo via Santa Rosa St. (SR 1) and Highland Dr. or, in town, north on Grand Ave. off Monterey St. (mailing address: San Luis Obispo 93407). (805) 756-1111.* Cal Poly is a key ingredient in the character of San Luis Obispo. Its student body of more than 13,000 is highly visible on the streets, and much interaction between "town and gown" is apparent at both formal and informal gatherings. The university

occupies a 6051-acre site at the base of the Santa Lucia Mountains, most of it open countryside (the developed campus area is just 374 acres). The idyllic setting no doubt contributes to the popularity of this Central Coast campus.

Also contributing to its popularity is the university's worldwide reputation for providing a practical, profession-oriented, hands-on learning experience. The fields of engineering, business, agriculture and architecture are particularly notable, with science, mathematics, education and the humanities also well represented.

Many campus activities and events are open to the public. For the latest information about the visual and performing arts, call (805) 756-1421; for all other activities, call (805) 756-2476. Student-led walking tours of the campus are available; call (805) 756-2792.

The Robert E. Kennedy Library adorns the Cal Poly campus.

Throughout the year visitors are welcome to come onto campus to purchase fruits, vegetables and dairy items produced by the students, visit the Shakespeare Press Museum, hike into Poly Canyon (an outdoor laboratory of experimental architecture and construction), attend an arts or sporting event or stroll through the Botanic Garden and ornamental horticulture greenhouses, where plants may be purchased.

Campus parking is scarce on weekdays and heavily restricted; stop at the information booth at the Grand Avenue entrance for a visitor parking permit, which costs $1.50.

CUESTA COLLEGE *6 miles northwest of downtown San Luis Obispo on SR 1 (mailing address: P.O. Box 8106, 93403-8106). (805) 546-3100.* This two-year college, located in a mountain-framed setting, has a student enrollment of over 8000. Curricula are provided in the arts and sciences in preparation for upper division courses, and technical and occupational classes prepare students for employment. The college relates closely to the community through its extensive Public Events Program, which features outstanding national and international touring productions. For information about current activities, call (805) 546-3131.

Hollister Adobe *Located on Cuesta College campus. Open Oct. through May, first and third Sun. of each month 1 to 4 p.m.; (805) 543-7831. Free.* This historic adobe dates from the early 1840s. The Hollisters were prominent settlers and citizens for over six generations in central California, where their name identifies, among other things, a town and a mountain peak. The restored Hollister residence houses a museum featuring Chumash and other American Indian artifacts, as well as more recent items.

DALLIDET ADOBE *Pacific St., between Santa Rosa and Toro sts. (mailing address: P.O. Box 1391, 93406). Open Memorial Day to Labor Day, Sun. 1 to 4 p.m. Group tours can be arranged by appointment. Open occasionally for special events and tours—contact the County Historical Museum for details, (805) 543-0638. Free.* This adobe has been proclaimed California Historical Landmark No. 720. It was built by French immigrant Pierre Hypolite Dallidet, who established one of California's earliest important wineries (he combined the mission and Italian grapes to produce a mellow wine that aged appealingly).

The Dallidet family prospered and became well established in San Luis Obispo. Paul Dallidet, Pierre's youngest son, donated the house to the Historical Society in 1953, just 100 years after Pierre arrived in San Luis Obispo. On the adobe grounds are a vintage boxcar, the first Southern Pacific Railroad depot built in San Luis Obispo, a horse-drawn street car and a Victorian garden. Many original furnishings still grace the interior of the adobe.

Heritage Day at the Dallidet is held on the first Sunday after the Fourth of July. From noon to 4 p.m. visitors can watch historic skills being put to the test as artisans form adobe bricks, a blacksmith makes the sparks fly, quilters create works of art, and other crafts are demonstrated. There is also traditional music, such as barbershop quartet singing and a town band. Admission is free.

FARMERS MARKETS A variety of fruits, vegetables, nuts, honey, eggs, flowers, herbs and plants are sold at these farmers markets in San Luis Obispo.

Gottschalk's *Central Coast Plaza parking lot off Madonna Rd. near Dalidio Dr. Sat. 8 to 11 a.m.*

Higuera Street *Between the 600 and 900 blocks. A large market and street festival Thur. evenings; see listing.*

Dallidet Adobe reflects San Luis Obispo's pioneer days.

The Market Place *#6*
Higuera St. Tues 3 to 6 p.m.

HIGUERA STREET
*between Toro and Nipomo
sts.* Downtown San Luis
Obispo's main street is
reminiscent of the
bustling main streets
that once characterized
nearly all American
cities. Shops and eating
establishments of all
sorts line both sides,
many of them occupy-
ing buildings that have
been imaginatively
restored.

**Thursday Night
Farmers Market** is a
popular weekly festival
that takes place year
round. The 600 through
900 blocks of Higuera
Street are closed to
motor traffic from 6 to
9 p.m. to make way for
stalls of fresh produce
brought in by local
growers, barbecue
stands, street dancing
and a variety of planned
and spontaneous entertainment,
including bands, puppet shows
and jugglers.

JACK HOUSE AND GARDENS *536
Marsh St., 93406. (805) 781-7299. Open
May through Oct., Wed. and Fri. 1 to 4
p.m. and Nov. through Apr., first Sun.
of each month 1 to 4 p.m. $2 donation.*
This beautifully maintained Victorian
residence was built in the early 1880s.
Its builder, Robert Jack, was an important citizen of San Luis Obispo, a man
involved in many business and government concerns. Many early-day social

Jack House and its grounds enhance downtown San Luis Obispo.

gatherings took place in the charming
Jack House gardens, which are notable
for exotic trees and plants. The interior
has been restored and the gardens
enhanced since the house was deeded
to the city in 1975.

LAGUNA LAKE PARK *Madonna Rd.,
½ mile southwest of US 101. Open daily
during daylight hours. Free.* The main
feature of this 450-acre park is Laguna
Lake, a popular spot with sailboarders
and fishermen (it's stocked with trout,
catfish, bass and crappie). Boats operated by electric motors over one horse-

power and gasoline motors are prohibited. Picnicking facilities, a playground and two fitness trails (1½ miles and 3½ miles) are located in the park, much of which is undeveloped. Volcanic peaks form the northern horizon.

MADONNA INN *Adjacent to US 101 at Madonna Rd. exit, 100 Madonna Rd., 93405. (805) 543-3000.* People from all over the world come to stay in the Madonna Inn, which includes 109 guest rooms, a restaurant and coffee shop, a bakery, gift shops and an arena for rodeos. The main attraction of this famous inn, however, is its appearance, which is best described as beyond description. The exterior is a combination of Victorian, Swiss and English Tudor elements carried out with giant boulders and pink trim. Inside, imagination has been allowed even greater latitude, with each room decorated in a different style, ranging from rock-walled cavern to Mae West boudoir. The inn is, in short, not to be missed (see *Lodging & Restaurants*).

MISSION PLAZA *Monterey and Chorro sts.* One of California's most attractive urban amenities, Mission Plaza is a lovely park tying together Mission San Luis Obispo with the downtown shopping district. Scarcely more than a back-lot dump after World War II, it was redesigned and landscaped in the mid-60s by Santa Barbara architect Richard Taylor. It has since become a major focal point for the city, attracting residents and tourists alike. Through the plaza winds picturesque San Luis Obispo Creek, a popular wading spot for the area's youngsters, as well as a major destination for brown-baggers at lunch time.

Reinforcing the plaza's importance as a town focus are the San Luis Obispo Art Center and the historic Judge Walter Murray Adobe, both of which are located within its boundaries. Just

"Colorful and exuberant" best describe the Madonna Inn.

opposite the plaza stands the San Luis Obispo County Historical Museum (see listing). Mission Plaza is the location of many community events throughout the year: major ones include La Fiesta in May and celebrations at Christmastime and the Fourth of July.

Murray Adobe *Opposite the mission.* This small restored house has a shady courtyard that is a popular public sitting area. Once a portion of the home of Judge Walter Murray—a prominent writer, editor and jurist—it is now most notable for its original adobe wall dating from the mid-1800s (don't touch, please; it's very fragile). The interior of the adobe is not open to the public.

San Luis Obispo Art Center *In Mission Plaza, 1010 Broad St., 93406. (805) 543-8562. Open Tues. through Sun. noon to 5 p.m. Free.* This visual arts facility showcases changing exhibits of paintings, prints, photographs, sculpture, ceramics and jewelry. Artists' demonstrations and special events are featured regularly.

MISSION SAN LUIS OBISPO DE TOLOSA *Chorro and Monterey sts. (mailing address: 782 Monterey St., 93401). (805) 543-6850. Open summer, daily 9 a.m. to 4:30 p.m.; rest of the year, daily 9 a.m. to 4 p.m.; closed Jan. 1, Easter, Thanksgiving and Dec. 25. Donations.* Established in 1772 by Fathers Junípero Serra and José Cavaller, the mission (and city) was named for Saint Louis, Bishop of Toulouse, France. The fifth of California's 21 missions to be built, San Luis Obispo is commonly referred to as "Prince of the Missions" and has been designated State Historical Landmark No. 325.

Like the other missions, it was established by Spain as a means, along with presidios and pueblos, to lay claim to a distant part of a far-flung

empire. With dissolution of the Spanish Empire and secularization of mission lands after Mexico came to power, the mission went into a period of decline not completely shaken until full restoration in 1930. Nevertheless, this mission functioned as a parish church through good times and bad, becoming the nucleus around which the city of San Luis Obispo would develop.

A sad chapter in the mission's history was the death of great numbers of Chumash who were drawn to the mission unaware of the dangers of European diseases to which they had developed no immunity.

The mission museum includes Chumash artifacts and relics from the mission's earliest days. Also notable are the mission gardens and the L-shape design of the main sanctuary.

SAN LUIS OBISPO CHILDREN'S MUSEUM *Nipomo and Monterey sts. (mailing address: 1010 Nipomo St., 93406). (805) 544-5437. Open July through Aug., daily 10 a.m. to 5 p.m.; Sept. through June, Thur. through Sat. 10 a.m. to 5 p.m., Sun. noon to 5 p.m. Admission $3 for ages 2 and over. Under age 16 must be accompanied by an adult.* The museum's more than 25 lively hands-on exhibits and experiences for children include "driving" a real car, performing in a mini-theater, operating a computer, "flying" a Cessna 150, exploring a reproduction of a Chumash cave, examining what goes into constructing a house and sliding down a dinosaur's tail. Special weekend events are occasionally scheduled; call for details.

SAN LUIS OBISPO COUNTY HISTORICAL MUSEUM, *696 Monterey St., opposite the mission (mailing address:*

Once a library, this imposing building now houses an important museum.

P.O. Box 1391, 93406). (805) 543-0638. *Open Wed. through Sun. 10 a.m. to 4 p.m.; closed major holidays and Dec. 24. Donations.* Housed in a Romanesque-style granite, brick and sandstone building that was once the city's Carnegie Library, this historical museum provides valuable insights into the varied past of San Luis Obispo County. Knowledgeable docents are on hand to explain the exhibits, which include a reconstructed Victorian parlor, photographs of San Luis Obispo's early days, old-time musical instruments and numerous artifacts tracing the county's history from the Chumash period to the present.

WINERIES *Hours are subject to change; please call ahead. More complete descriptions of wineries offering tours appear in* the Auto Club's *California Winery Tours* book.

Corbett Canyon Vineyards *8 miles southeast of San Luis Obispo off SR 227 at 2195 Corbett Canyon Rd., P.O. Box 3159, 93403. (805) 544-5800. Open Mon. through Fri. 10 a.m. to 4:30 p.m., Sat. and Sun. 10 a.m. to 5 p.m. Tours Sat. and Sun. by appointment.* Estate Chardonnay and Pinot Noir are among the wines produced here. The winery includes a picnic area.

Edna Valley Vineyard *5 miles southeast of San Luis Obispo off SR 227; 2585 Biddle Ranch Rd., 93401. (805) 544-9594. Open daily 10 a.m. to 4 p.m.* Among table wines at Edna Valley, the focus is on Chardonnay. Additionally, they produce sparkling wine.

North Coast

The North Coast of San Luis Obispo County, roughly extending from Point Buchon in the south to the Monterey County line, encompasses some of the most spectacular coastal scenery in North America. The Santa Lucia Mountains rise abruptly from the rugged coastline in the northern reaches and provide a dramatic backdrop to narrow coastal lowlands farther south. The upper elevations are forested, particularly in the north, while oak-studded grasslands and chaparral predominate on the coastal hills and plains.

The region's population is concentrated in the coastal lowlands along SR 1, the area's primary north/south transportation corridor. Traditionally a sparsely populated agricultural area focusing on cattle ranching and dairy farming, the North Coast has in recent years experienced a considerable influx of new residents, especially retirees. Since Hearst Castle was opened to the public in 1958, tourism has grown steadily, accounting for a major portion of the region's economy today.

Motorists and sun worshippers alike need to keep in mind that dense coastal fog occurs periodically throughout the year. It is most common during early summer mornings, but typically burns off in the afternoon, leaving the skies mostly clear and sunny.

Baywood Park/Cuesta-By-The-Sea/Los Osos (The South Bay)

Clustered at the southern edge of the Morro Bay estuary, these three compact communities began as separate developments but have since grown together. Known collectively as the South Bay, residents still consider the communities distinct from one another, but there are no official boundaries, and it is difficult to obtain a consensus on the matter from those who live here.

In 1919, Baywood Park was carved out of the rolling, wooded countryside as a residential development, followed by Cuesta-by-the-Sea in the 1920s. Los Osos, the last of the trio to develop, takes its name from Los Osos Valley, an area originally populated by Chumash and visited by Spanish explorer Gaspar de Portolá in the 1700s. Portolá's men called the valley Cañada de Los Osos, or Valley of the Bears, because of the large number of grizzly bears that inhabited the area at the time.

Today the communities remain primarily residential, with most commercial activity and public services found along a half-mile stretch of Los Osos Valley Road, west of South Bay Boulevard. The quiet, small-town character of the South Bay has traditionally

---

"La Casa Grande," the main residence at Hearst Castle, contains more than 100 rooms.

appealed to an eclectic blend of artists, retirees and families. With the influx of urban expatriots from California's metropolitan centers, however, the area has grown considerably in the last few years, and residents are trying to deal with the subsequent effects on their tranquil environment.

LOS OSOS OAKS STATE RESERVE (known locally as Pygmy Oaks)

On the south side of Los Osos Valley Rd., ½ mile east of South Bay Blvd. A ½-mile self-guided trail leads visitors into the eerie, dimly lit world beneath the low canopy of these 600- to 800-year-old coast live oaks where Chumash once lived. The leaf-covered trail winds among the trees' gnarled gray trunks and the mushrooms, wild cucumbers, hollyleaf cherry and other flora that flourish in the shaded soil. A second trail of about a mile leads into an area of native chaparral. Visitors should be wary of another less hospitable member of the reserve's plant community—poison oak, with shiny leaves lining the trail in many places.

MONTAÑA DE ORO SCENIC DRIVE

Los Osos Valley and Pecho rds. From South Bay Boulevard, the route heads west through the village of Los Osos for 1½ miles on Los Osos Valley Road. Near the edge of the community it swings southwest onto Pecho Road (Montaña de Oro Road). Approaching Montaña de Oro State Park (see listing), the winding road rises with the rolling, brush-covered foothills affording dramatic views of Morro Bay and its surroundings. From unpaved turnouts, the vista encompasses the bay and its estuary, the community of Morro Bay and the long, finger-like Morro Bay sandspit pointing northward with Morro Rock near its tip.

The road passes through dense stands of eucalyptus trees that host swarms of migrating monarch butterflies each fall. After about 3½ miles the road descends into forested Hazard Canyon, where a popular hiking trail leads a short distance to a rocky beach with tide pools. Emerging from the canyon, the road sets out across open coastal bluffs and then drops abruptly to the edge of Spooner Cove, which in years past provided smugglers with a secluded port for their clandestine trade. On a bluff overlooking the cove is the Montaña de Oro park office, housed in the former home of the Spooner family who ranched the area during the 1800s. The road continues for 1⁷⁄₁₀ miles, following the chaparral-covered coastal plain that in spring is carpeted with the golden wildflowers that inspired the park's name, Montaña de Oro or "Mountain of Gold."

PYGMY OAKS (see Los Osos Oaks State Reserve)

SOUTH BAY COMMUNITY PARK *Los Osos Valley Rd. at Palisades Ave. (west of the commercial district).* Complete with neatly manicured landscaping, tennis courts, rest rooms and a well-planned playground, this small, imaginatively designed park is a pleasant place for walking or picnicking, and it is a good spot to let auto-bound children burn off excess energy. It also is the site of the Los Osos Valley School, constructed in 1872. The one-room schoolhouse is now open occasionally for special functions. Adjacent to the park is a community center.

SWEET SPRINGS NATURE PRESERVE *North side of Ramona Ave., ⅛ mile west of 4th St.* Walking trails lead through Monterey cypress and eucalyptus trees, across two graceful wooden bridges over freshwater ponds and around a salt marsh to the bayshore. Various types of water-fowl, including white heron, are attracted to the ponds and marshes, and turtles share the sanctuary with them. Care should be taken to stay on the trail, since there are several places where poison oak grows alongside.

Cambria

The engaging community of Cambria rests among the forested slopes of the coast range, 33 miles northwest of San Luis Obispo. A convenient starting point for trips to nearby Hearst Castle and other attractions along the rugged central California coast, this quaint

village of artists and artisans has itself become a popular vacation destination. The town enjoys a mild year-round climate and offers visitors a casual, relaxed atmosphere. Shopping, dining and relaxing head a list of popular pastimes, which also includes beach-combing, hiking and photography.

Fishing, whaling, lumbering and mercury (quicksilver) mining first attracted settlers to the area during the mid-1800s, but it was not until dairymen and farmers began settling along Santa Rosa Creek about 1866 that the town actually developed. By the 1880s Cambria was an established mining and dairy center with a population of more than 7000. The town entered a

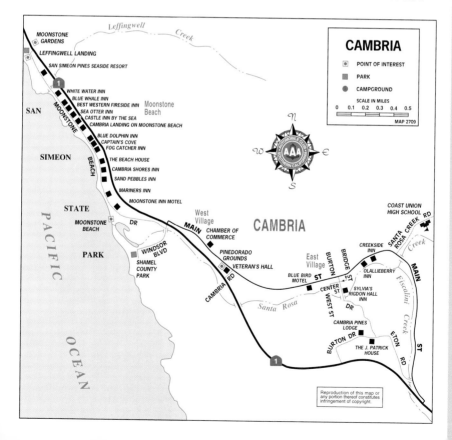

period of decline during the first part of this century, but when Hearst Castle was opened to the public in 1958, the village reemerged as a tourist town.

The town's population has since rebounded to nearly 5500, largely made up of artists, writers, craftsmen, business owners and retirees. Its original center, now called "Old Town" or "East Village," lies about one mile from SR 1 in a pine-studded cleft of the hills. A little to the north, the newer portion of Cambria, "West Village," is located adjacent to the highway. Most business activity in Cambria is found along Main Street, the link between the two parts of town.

The Pewter Plough Playhouse in Cambria offers theatrical performances; call (805) 927-3877.

East Village boasts a number of gift and specialty shops, galleries and restaurants concentrated on Burton Drive near its intersection with Main Street (location of the town's only stop sign). A two-story Victorian-style complex called the Old Village Mercantile houses art galleries and specialty shops. Across the street, a cottage-style structure built in 1874 and since enlarged, accommodates The Brambles Dinner House. East Village also has more prosaic businesses, such as a bank and the town's post office.

West Village was developed in 1927 as a subdivision called "Cambria Pines," a name that is sometimes still used. Here restaurants, art galleries and antique shops abound. Many free brochures, including a guide to the area's art galleries, are available at Cambria's Chamber of Commerce, 767 Main Street. Shops offer collectibles and gifts. One of the best-known shops, The Soldier Factory, manufactures and sells detailed miniature soldiers and a host of other figures made of pewter.

Inviting shops abound in Cambria's East Village.

Across the highway from West Village is Shamel County Park. Located on the beach, the park is equipped with a playground, a public swimming pool (open in summer), picnic tables and barbecues. To the north is Moonstone Beach.

Accommodations are plentiful in Cambria; reservations, however, are essential from May through October, and they are recommended for weekends and holidays throughout the year. Most motels and bed-and-breakfast establishments are located in East Village and parallel to SR 1 on Moonstone Drive.

FARMERS MARKET Pinedorado Grounds *Main St. and Cabria Rd., West Village. Fri. from 2:30 to 5:30 p.m.* From outdoor booths, local growers offer vegetables, fruits and flowers for sale.

LEFFINGWELL LANDING *On Moonstone Beach Dr., 1½ miles north of Cambria off SR 1. Picnic and parking area open 8 a.m. to sunset.* William Leffingwell constructed the area's first sawmill on this picturesque coastal site in the 1860s. Now a state day-use area, this bluff-top vantage point offers impressive views of the rocky shoreline and crashing surf below. Sea lions, otters and, on occasion, whales can be seen from trails that lead from the parking lot. Tide pools at the base of the cliffs can be reached during low tide. The area has picnic tables, barbecues and rest rooms.

MOONSTONE BEACH *Off Moonstone Beach Dr. (exit SR 1 at Windsor Blvd.).* Named for the smooth, milky-white moonstones that are often found here, this gently sloping, sandy beach is popular for walking, beachcombing and rock collecting (the water is too cold for swimming). In addition to moonstone, careful observers can pick

A pleasant walking path winds across the cliffs above Moonstone Beach.

up agates, bits of California "jade," quartz, driftwood and other finds. Sea otters are sometimes spotted in the surf, or sea lions may haul themselves onto rocks just off shore. In January and February migrating California gray whales commonly pass close to shore during their annual trek to the warm lagoons of Baja California. Along the street are several motels and restaurants that look out onto the ocean.

MOONSTONE GARDENS *2 miles north of Cambria on SR 1 (mailing address: Hwy. 1, 93428). (805) 927-3535. Gardens and restaurant open daily 11:30 a.m. to 9 p.m.; closed Sun. after Thanksgiving through Dec. 25. Free.* Over 400 varieties of cacti and other succulents adorn this three-acre arboretum and nursery. Paths meander through the grounds, with plants at every turn, and potted succulents may be purchased.

All manner of plants have found a home in Moonstone Gardens.

The Hamlet Restaurant at Moonstone Gardens offers outdoor and indoor dining, with a view of the sea (See *Lodging & Restaurants*).

PINEDORADO GROUNDS *Main St. and Cambria Rd., West Village*. This is a popular gathering place for the town's outdoor events. Adjacent to the grounds is the old Santa Rosa School, built in 1881; it now houses the Allied Arts Association Schoolhouse Gallery. Nearby is the Cambria "hoosegow," a small wooden one-cell jail that was constructed in 1908 after the original jail burned down. Some of the iron-work on the structure is said to have been salvaged from the original.

Pinedorado *At the Pinedorado Grounds*. This popular three-day event has been celebrated in Cambria each Labor Day weekend since 1948. The festivities include a beef and chicken barbecue, game and food booths, a melodrama, music, square dancing and a parade on Saturday featuring entries from throughout California.

SANTA ROSA CREEK SCENIC DRIVE From its junction with Main Street in Cambria's East Village, Santa Rosa Creek Road leads through the wooded valley of Santa Rosa Creek for 16 miles. The narrow road passes a number of orchards, small farms and ranches as it winds into the coastal hills. Soon after the turnoff is McCall Farm, a "U-pick" apple orchard, and ½ mile beyond is Linn's Fruit Bin, a popular stopping place where motorists can purchase fresh fruit, homemade preserves and fresh-baked fruit and berry pies. Also for sale are dried flowers and hand-made goods.

At mile 11, a hairpin turn marks the beginning of the steep switchback climb to a summit where there are good views of the ocean; the vista is particularly impressive at sunset. From here the road drops steeply, continuing to Green

▼ A What *Kind of Berry?*

In San Luis Obispo County you'll likely encounter a word on a restaurant menu, a label on a jar of preserves or a sign at a roadside stand: "olallie-berry." It looks like a blackberry, but it has a more interesting pedigree. It was developed in 1949 in Oregon, and it's two-thirds blackberry and one-third European red raspberry. It's just slightly tart, making it a natural for pies and preserves.

Don't be shy—try some olallies; they're the berries!

Valley Road (SR 46). To the right the road leads 11½ miles to SR 1, at a point about two miles south of Cambria. A left turn on SR 46 is the beginning of a 9½-mile drive past a number of vineyards and wineries to US 101.

STATEWIDE WOODCARVERS SHOW
Coast Union High School, Santa Rosa Creek Rd., approximately 1 mile from Main St. (805) 927-4718. On a weekend near the end of September, woodcarvers from throughout California come together to display their skills and imagination, taking form in all shapes and sizes. The show includes whittling contests and demonstrations of carving.

Cayucos

Originally inhabited by the Chumash, the pleasant coastal region where Cayucos stands today was included in an 18th-century Spanish land grant. The area experienced little settlement during this early period, and it was not until after the California Gold Rush that the region began to develop.

In 1867 an Englishman, "Captain" James Cass, constructed a warehouse here and began work on a deep-water wharf. With the completion of the wharf in 1875, Cayucos soon developed into an important Central Coast seaport and commercial center that, by the turn of the century, rivaled Morro Bay. Italian, Swiss and Portuguese immigrants established ranches and prosperous dairy farms in the surrounding countryside, shipping beef, cowhides, butter and cheese to markets in San Francisco and Los Angeles.

Cass's wharf has since been replaced by Cayucos Pier, and the once busy seaport is today a small, pleasant beachfront town. The community lies at the northern end of Estero Bay, sandwiched between SR 1, Cayucos County Beach and Morro Strand State Beach.

Most commercial activity and tourist services in Cayucos are found along Ocean Avenue, the town's main thoroughfare. Merchants on the street serve the needs of both residents and visitors. Among antique shops, art galleries and restaurants are nestled more mundane businesses. Several motels are clustered at the southern end of the street, while other tourist-oriented businesses are concentrated toward the north end of town near the pier.

Long sandy beaches provide opportunities for swimming, sunbathing, fishing, sailboarding and kayaking. At shops near the pier, fishing trips can be arranged.

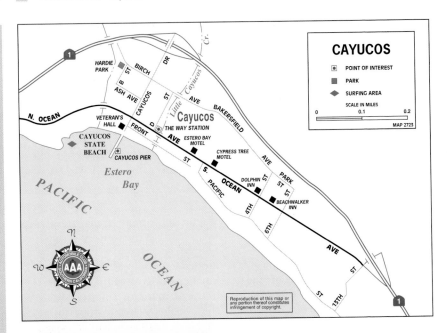

CAYUCOS

- ◉ POINT OF INTEREST
- ■ PARK
- ◆ SURFING AREA

SCALE IN MILES

0   0.1   0.2

MAP 2723

Reproduction of this map or any portion thereof constitutes infringement of copyright.

Visitors to Cayucos Pier enjoy this sculpture of graceful, leaping dolphins.

Fishing tackle and scuba gear are among the equipment for rent (see *Recreation*).

CAYUCOS PIER *At the foot of Cayucos Dr.* At this site in 1875 stood a 1360-foot deep-water wharf where cheese, butter and other products from local farms were shipped to San Francisco and Los Angeles. Construction of the wharf helped establish Cayucos as a major Central Coast port during the late 1800s.

Aging and repeatedly damaged by storms, the wharf was replaced in the 1930s by the present pier, which is 972 feet in length and is used primarily by fishermen. Night fishing is popular on the lighted pier during summer months (a fishing license is not required to fish from the pier). At the foot of the structure is a playground, rest rooms with showers and a shop where fishing tackle can be rented.

THE WAY STATION *78 Ocean Ave.* Built in the 1890s as a hotel and restaurant, this typical western-style structure, with a wooden boardwalk and false front, was a way station for stagecoach travelers. In later years the building housed a succession of businesses, including a bar, general store and bus station. It was left vacant after World War II, but in 1974 the structure was restored.

The Way Station now contains a restaurant with an outdoor garden dining area, a beauty salon and a candy shop specializing in saltwater taffy.

Harmony

This small town of about 20 residents developed around a dairy in the latter part of the 19th century. In 1907 the Harmony Valley Cooperative Dairy was established here, and the village became the center of the region's dairy industry, producing milk, cream, cheese and butter. By the late 1950s, however, events forced the dairy to

close, and except for the post office, the town was abandoned.

In 1972 new owners began the restoration of the town as an arts and crafts center. The creamery and adjacent buildings house a working pottery shop, an art gallery and shops selling handmade clothing. The village also offers wine tasting, glass blowers and sculptors. A dinner house that also features Sunday brunch and a bar are located on the premises, and for couples wishing to "tie the knot" in Harmony, a cheese storage vault has been converted into a small wedding chapel. The Harmony post office, opened in 1914, is still in operation. Shops are generally open daily from 10 a.m. to 5 p.m. For information, call (805) 927-8288.

WINERY *Hours are subject to change; please call ahead. More complete descriptions of wineries offering tours appear in the Auto Club's* California Winery Tours *book.*

These shapes and colors are definitely in Harmony.

Harmony Cellars *3255 Harmony Valley Rd. (mailing address: P.O. Box 2502, Harmony 93435). (800) 432-9239. Open daily 10 a.m. to 5 p.m.* Fee for tasting; self-guided tours. Wines available here include White Zinfandel, Johannisberg Riesling and Christmas Blush. Picnic area.

Montaña De Oro State Park

Along Pecho Valley Rd., 1 mile south of Los Osos Valley Rd.

Chief Ranger, *3220 S. Higuera St., #311, San Luis Obispo, CA 93401. (805) 528-0513. Open all year, 24 hours. Free day-use; camping fees vary.*

Located 2¼ miles south of the small community of Los Osos, this 8000-acre, mostly undeveloped park offers visitors a wealth of natural beauty and excellent opportunities for hiking, camping and horseback riding, as well as shore fishing and diving (see *Recreation* and *Campgrounds & Trailer Parks*).

Acquired by the State of California in 1965, the park was originally included in a large land grant, and in later years the property became part of the Spooner Ranch. The park office, built in 1892, was the Spooner home. The white frame structure stands in a grove of graceful cypress trees and overlooks a secluded cove bearing the ranch family's name. The calm water and isolated location of the cove proved to be an ideal port for smugglers during the Mission period and for Prohibition-era bootleggers.

Although the property has been used for cattle grazing since the late 1800s, it is virtually unspoiled, supporting lush natural vegetation and providing a primitive habitat for a variety of wildlife. The park was named Montaña de Oro, "Mountain of Gold," for the abundant fields of poppies, fiddlenecks, wild mustard and other golden

Montaña de Oro State Beach is a picture-perfect place.

wildflowers that blanket the landscape each spring. Deer, fox, weasels and a few mountain lions are among the animals that roam the grass- and chaparral-covered foothills and coastal plains that once were the dominion of the now-extinct California grizzly bear.

The park's six miles of rocky and sandy beaches and ocean waters sustain an abundance of marine life—the area is a haven for over 100 species of native and migrating birds, including the brown pelican, black oyster-catcher and the elusive pigeon guillemot, which nests in inaccessible holes along the steep sandstone coastal bluffs.

More than 50 miles of hiking and equestrian trails provide access to the park's backcountry, wooded stream canyons, tidepools and hidden coves and beaches. Bluff Trail, following the edge of the coastal cliffs, provides spectacular views of the tilted and twisted strata of the rocky shoreline and, in the distance, Morro Rock and the Morro Bay sandspit. Sea otters are often seen feeding in the surf here, and during winter months migrating California gray whales can be spotted near shore. At several points along the trail, paths lead down the bluffs to clusters of tidepools tucked away in secluded coves.

One of the most popular trails runs through Hazard Canyon. Like many of the park's trails, it begins along Pecho Valley Road, the paved road leading from Los Osos and on through the park. The ½-mile Hazard Reef trail starts in a dense stand of eucalyptus trees and meanders through the canyon next to a small, intermittently flowing stream to a rock-strewn beach. Tidepools are plentiful here, and a short distance to the north begins the long sandspit that protects Morro Bay.

Spooner Cove delights visitors to Montaña de Oro State Beach.

Each October swarms of migrating monarch butterflies, seeking the milder temperatures of the southern coastal regions, are attracted to the aromatic eucalyptus trees in the canyon. The butterflies feed during the day on nectar of the flowering trees and at night cluster on their branches for protection from the elements. In March the monarchs begin their long flight northward.

Morro Bay

While it's hard to miss towering Morro Rock as you drive past Morro Bay on SR 1, some people are unaware that Morro Bay is also the name of the bayside town which has grown up near the rock. A turn off the highway into the town reveals a pleasant seaside resort community offering visitors a wide range of sights and activities.

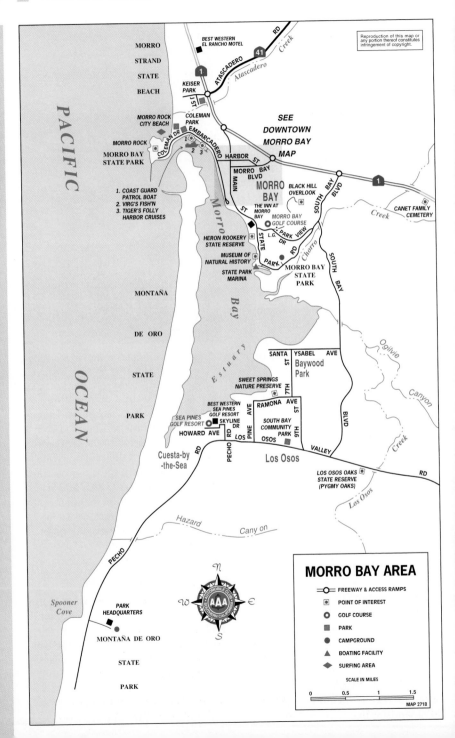

Reproduction of this map or any portion thereof constitutes infringement of copyright.

MORRO STRAND STATE BEACH

BEST WESTERN EL RANCHO MOTEL

KEISER PARK

MORRO ROCK CITY BEACH

COLEMAN PARK

MORRO ROCK

MORRO BAY STATE PARK

PACIFIC

1. COAST GUARD PATROL BOAT
2. VIRG'S FISH'N
3. TIGER'S FOLLY HARBOR CRUISES

HERON ROOKERY STATE RESERVE

MUSEUM OF NATURAL HISTORY

STATE PARK MARINA

MONTAÑA

DE ORO

STATE

OCEAN

PARK

SEA PINES GOLF RESORT

BEST WESTERN SEA PINES GOLF RESORT

SKYLINE DR

HOWARD AVE

Cuesta-by-the-Sea

SWEET SPRINGS NATURE PRESERVE

SANTA ST

YSABEL AVE

Baywood Park

RAMONA AVE

SOUTH BAY COMMUNITY PARK

LOS OSOS

Los Osos

SEE DOWNTOWN MORRO BAY MAP

MORRO BAY BLVD

MORRO BAY

BLACK HILL OVERLOOK

THE INN AT MORRO BAY

MORRO BAY GOLF COURSE

CANET FAMILY CEMETERY

MORRO BAY STATE PARK

Ogilvie

Canyon

Creek

LOS OSOS OAKS STATE RESERVE (PYGMY OAKS)

Los Osos RD

Hazard Canyon

PECHO

Spooner Cove

PARK HEADQUARTERS

MONTAÑA DE ORO

STATE

PARK

MORRO BAY AREA

- ═○═ FREEWAY & ACCESS RAMPS
- ▣ POINT OF INTEREST
- ◉ GOLF COURSE
- ■ PARK
- ▦ CAMPGROUND
- ▲ BOATING FACILITY
- ◆ SURFING AREA

SCALE IN MILES

0   0.5   1   1.5

MAP 2718

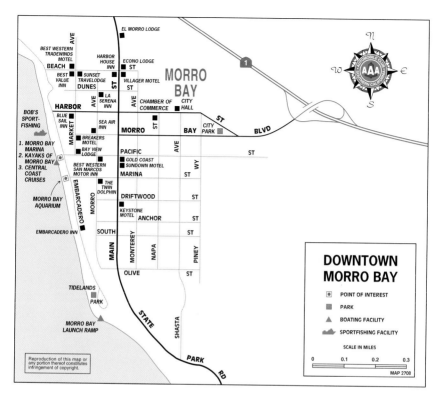

The town developed in the 1870s as a port for the region's cattle ranching and dairy industry and later emerged as an important center for commercial fishing and oyster farming. Morro Bay still maintains a large commercial fishing fleet, but increasingly the area's natural beauty, mild climate and abundant waters have attracted tourists.

Today, sportfishing, boating, golf, surfing, whalewatching, hiking and camping lure visitors to Morro Bay (see *Recreation*), as do the town's many art galleries, antique shops, boutiques and artisan shops. Bird watching also is a popular pastime for both tourists and local residents—the entire town is designated a bird sanctuary, and the area is an important West Coast stopover for hundreds of species of migrating birds.

With over 40 motels, accommodations are plentiful in Morro Bay, and numerous restaurants specializing in seafood dishes welcome visitors all year. The summer months bring the largest crowds, and during this time reservations are recommended for accommodations, dining and other activities. The town is generally not crowded most other times of the year, affording visitors a measure of tranquility.

ART IN THE PARK *Morro Bay City Park, Morro Bay Blvd. and Harbor St. (805) 772-2504.* On three separate occasions during the summer—Memorial Day, Fourth of July and Labor Day weekends—100 artists and craftspeople exhibit and sell their wares.

CANET FAMILY CEMETERY *2 miles east of Morro Bay on Canet Rd., ⁹⁄₁₀ mile* *from SR 1*. Resting on a gentle slope next to a quiet country road is the small, fenced cemetery of the Canet family. The Canets ran a cattle ranch here on a large Mexican land grant during the 1800s, and family descendants continue to raise cattle in the area.

THE EMBARCADERO *On the waterfront*. Originating in the 1800s as the center of port activity in Morro Bay, the Embarcadero has since evolved into the town's main tourist area. Fronting on the bay, this string of art galleries, specialty and souvenir shops, fish markets and seafood restaurants is a good starting point to begin exploring the community. Bay cruises leave from here, sportfishing trips can be arranged, and during winter months visitors can board special whale-watching cruises. Several small parks and observation areas along the way are good spots in which to pause and observe the small-craft harbor, the long Morro Bay sandspit across the bay and, in the distance near the harbor mouth, Morro Rock.

On the bluff overlooking the harbor, within easy walking distance of the Embarcadero, are several good motels and restaurants. Along the northern section of the Embarcadero are the commercial fishing docks. Here fishermen unload their catches or ready their crafts for the next day. Beyond the docks is an incongruous and impossible-to-miss local landmark—the Pacific Gas and Electric power plant, with its trio of smoke stacks reaching 450 feet into the sky. (The power plant is not open to the public.)

Central Coast Cruises
Embarcadero and Pacific sts. (mailing address: 1220 Beach St., San Luis Obispo 93401). (805) 541-1435. Departures once each day late June through Labor Day; call for schedule. Fare $19.95; over age 55, $17.95; ages 8-12, $15. Two-hour narrated nature cruises go several miles along the Central Coast. One-hour sunset cocktail cruises are also offered during the summer; fare $10; over age 55, $9; ages 8-12, $6. Reservations are recommended for all cruises.

Morro Rock stands watch over fishing boats in the harbor.

Morro Bay Aquarium *595 Embarcadero, 93442. (805) 772-7647. Open daily; during summer 9 a.m. to 6:30 p.m.; rest of the year 9 a.m. to 5 p.m. Admission $1; ages 5-11, 50¢.* The aquarium maintains a collection of over 300 live marine specimens. On display in 14 small tanks are eels, abalone, small sharks and other marine life. Several sea lions and harbor seals are also on exhibit in outdoor tanks, and visitors may purchase food to feed them. The aquarium also houses the Morro Bay Marine Rehabilitation Center where sick or injured animals are nursed back to health and then either returned to their natural habitat or placed in a suitable environment. **(See ad above.)**

Tiger's Folly Harbor Cruises *1205 Embarcadero (Harbor Hut Restaurant), 93442. (805) 772-2257. Fare $6; ages 5-12, $3. Call for schedule.* One-hour narrated tours of Morro Bay are offered aboard the 64-foot sternwheeler *Tiger's Folly II.* The boat makes frequent daily departures during summer months, and in winter it sails only on weekends and holidays. Brunch cruises and private charters are also available (reservations required).

U.S. Coast Guard Patrol Boat *1279 Embarcadero, 93443. (805) 772-2167, 772-1293.* Berthed at the northern end of the harbor with the commercial fishing boats is the U.S. Coast Guard patrol boat *Point Heyer.* When in port, this 82-foot vessel is often open to the public on weekends; call for specific times. (Telephone will not be answered when the ship is at sea.)

FARMERS MARKETS Friday Night Market *North end of the Embarcadero. Fri. 4 to 7 p.m.* Arts and crafts are offered, in addition to fresh produce, seafood chowder, seafood kabobs and fresh fish.

Young's Giant Food Supermarket *2650 Main St., just east of SR 1 at Atascadero Rd. (SR 41). Thur. 3 to 5 p.m.* Each week, growers from around the county gather to sell locally grown fruits, vegetables and flowers.

Morro Bay Estuary

The Morro Bay estuary is one of the largest unspoiled coastal marshes in California. Fresh water, silt and organic material flow into the estuary from two local streams and mix with ocean waters, producing a nutrient-rich environment of varying salinity. These wetlands are an essential factor in the marine food chain and are a major food source for the marine life of the Central Coast. It is estimated that as much as 80 percent of the area's sea life either originates in the estuary or spends some part of its life cycle here. The estuary's vast mud flats are home to oysters, clams, crabs, snails and other shellfish, while its shallow waters serve as a nursery to such fish as halibut, perch and smelt.

The estuary is a bird watcher's paradise, and it is an important point on the Pacific Migratory Bird Flyway. Its abundant waters, combined with a plentiful supply of seeds from the surrounding grass- and brush-covered hills, attract over 250 species of native and migrating birds. Among its native residents is the great blue heron, which nests in eucalyptus groves at the water's edge. With the aid of binoculars, marsh birds can be observed from numerous spots along the shore. For an even closer look, observers can explore the estuary in a kayak (rentals are available at Kayaks of Morro Bay, see Water Recreation, Morro Bay).

Morro Bay State Park

South end of town of Morro Bay, off State Park Rd.

State Beaches, *3220 S. Higuera St., #311, San Luis Obispo 93401. (805) 772-2560. Open daily year round. Day-use, free; camping fees vary.*

Morro Bay State Park is spread over 1965 acres of verdant rolling landscape just south of the town of Morro Bay. The forested park is laid out around a picturesque 18-hole golf course (see *Recreation*). It encompasses a primitive natural area, a portion of the prolific Morro Bay estuary and tree-shaded camping and picnic grounds. Perched on a rocky outcropping overlooking the bay is the park's natural history museum, and below at the shoreline is one of the state's foremost heron rookeries. The park's marina and small-boat harbor offer launching facilities, moorings, boat rentals and a cafe (see *Recreation*).

Black Hill Overlook *Black Hill Rd., Morro Bay State Park.* This paved observation area is located north of the park's golf course on 661-foot-high Black Hill, which, like Morro Rock, is one of seven ancient volcanic cones in San Luis Obispo County known as the "Seven Sisters." On clear days the view from the parking area stretches from Point Buchon in the south, northward along the crescent-shaped shore of Estero Bay

to Piedras Blancas Lighthouse. The panorama includes most of Morro Bay and its surrounding communities, although views of the harbor and Morro Rock are partially obstructed by treetops. For a more sweeping view, walk the well-maintained trail ¾ of a mile from the parking lot to the top of the hill.

Trails traverse the Black Hill area, and each May and June the scrub- and chaparral-covered slopes are blanketed with colorful wildflowers. One-hour guided walks through the area are also conducted by the volunteer staff of the park's Museum of Natural History. To reach the overlook, follow Black Hill Drive through Morro Bay Golf Course and drive up the hill to the end of the road. (A gate near the intersection of Black Hill and Park View drives is locked from 9 p.m. to 6 a.m.)

Heron Rookery State Reserve *State Park Rd., Morro Bay State Park.* This dense stand of tall eucalyptus trees on the shore of Morro Bay is the last remaining great blue heron rookery of its size between San Francisco and the Mexican border. Under pressure from the local Audubon Society, the 5.7-acre site on Fairbanks Point was purchased by the state in 1972 and is now part of Morro Bay State Park. Although the rookery is fenced, the birds can be observed from many points around the reserve perimeter. Parking is available along State Park Road across from the golf course. One-hour guided walks to the rookery are offered by the Museum of Natural History. A general schedule of the heron's mating and offspring-rearing activity follows:

> Pair formation - February
> Courtship - February, March
> Incubation - March, April, May
> Brooding - April, May, June
> Fledgling - June, July

Museum of Natural History *State Park Rd., Morro Bay State Park (mailing address: 3220 South Higuera St., #311, San Luis Obispo 93401) (805) 772-2694. Open daily 10 a.m. to 5 p.m.; closed Jan. 1, Thanksgiving and Dec. 25. Admission $2; ages 6-12, $1.* The museum overlooks Morro Bay from White Point, a high rocky outcropping at the edge of the bay. The museum includes interpretive displays and dioramas of the animals and marine life of the Central Coast, the area's geology and the lives of the Chumash who once made their home around the bay. Audio-visual presentations, nature walks and lectures are featured for visitors of all ages.

From the museum, visitors can look out across the bay to Morro Bay sandspit and harbor, Morro Rock and one of the largest heron rookeries on the coast. Outside the museum, trails lead to the top of White Point where even broader vistas can be enjoyed; mortar holes used by the Chumash to grind meal can be spotted in the weathered rock along the way.

MORRO ROCK An important navigational landfall for over 300 years, Morro Rock was first named in 1542 by Portuguese explorer Juan Rodríguez Cabrillo, who called it El Moro, thinking it looked like a Moor's turban. Rising 578 feet, the dome-shaped rock is of volcanic origin and is the westernmost in a chain of seven volcanic peaks reaching to the city of San Luis Obispo.

Originally standing as an island at high tide, the rock eventually was linked to the mainland by an earth and rock causeway which facilitated extensive quarrying of the monolith. Between 1880 and 1963 the shape of the rock was changed dramatically as over one million tons of rock were blasted from its base. The material was

Sunset turns the water to gold at Morro Bay.

used in the construction of breakwaters here and elsewhere along the coast, including nearby Port San Luis. In 1968, under pressure from local residents, Morro Rock was declared a State Historical Landmark (No. 821). The peak has since been designated a wildlife refuge for the endangered peregrine falcon, which nests on top of the rock. To insure the bird's safety, climbing on the rock is strictly prohibited.

Automobiles can be driven across the causeway to the rock. Ample parking is available at a broad open area on the rock's northeast side and along Coleman Drive which continues around to the breakwater on the south side. Fishing is permitted from the rocks on the edge of the parking area, and the sandy beach to the north is a popular place for walking and jogging. The harbor side of the causeway is a good vantage point from which to

Piedras Blancas Lighthouse stands guard along the Central Coast.

19th century it became apparent that a lighthouse was needed. Construction began in 1874 on one of the few parcels of land in the area not owned by Senator George Hearst (father of William Randolph Hearst).

The structure stood 110-feet high and was equipped with a French-made Fresnel lens, which produced a beam of light that was visible for 25 miles out at sea; the lens was replaced with an automated light in the 1940s. The lighthouse is under the jurisdiction of the U.S. Coast Guard; however, the facility is occupied by scientists from the U.S. Fish and Wildlife Service who are conducting sea life research. The lighthouse is not open to the public.

observe boats passing in and out of the harbor, while from the ocean side of the breakwater playful sea otters can sometimes be observed in the surf. (Because large waves often crash onto the breakwater, caution should be exercised when climbing on its rocks.)

PIEDRAS BLANCAS LIGHTHOUSE
SR 1, 5½ miles north of San Simeon. Point Piedras Blancas, named by Portuguese explorer Juan Rodríguez Cabrillo in 1542, is one of the most prominent and picturesque headlands on the California coast. ("Piedras blancas" is Spanish for white rock.) The point presented a serious navigational hazard for early seafarers, and as shipping increased from local ports in the

San Simeon

San Simeon is actually two distinct entities. The town itself is located on the shore of San Simeon Bay, across SR 1 just north of the entrance to the Hearst Castle Visitor Center. South on SR 1, about 2½ miles, is a newer, tourist-oriented community known as San Simeon Acres.

In the 1850s whalers, who hunted migrating gray whales, established a village on San Simeon Point, about one-half mile from where the town is today. When whaling declined some years later, the village was abandoned. The town was reestablished in its present location in the 1870s by Senator George Hearst, who by then had purchased most of the ranch land in the area. A general store (later to become known as Sebastian's Store) was moved from the site of the whaling village to the new town in 1878. Hearst also constructed a warehouse and a 1000-foot wharf here that same year. San Simeon subsequently became a busy port, shipping mercury and agricultural products aboard coastal steamers. But the Hearst family's near-complete ownership of the land discouraged settlement and permanently stifled the town's growth.

During construction of Hearst Castle, which began in 1919, George Hearst's son, William Randolph, built several Spanish-style houses here for his employees, and more warehouses were constructed to store building materials and treasures destined for the castle. Adjacent to the town is William Randolph Hearst Memorial State Beach, an ocean-front plot of land that was donated to the state by the Hearst Corporation in 1951, following Hearst's death.

Hearst Castle was deeded to the state and opened to the public in 1958. A State Historical Monument (No. 640), the castle has since attracted millions of visitors to the area each year. The resulting need for accommodations and other tourist services spawned the development of San Simeon Acres. Today motels and inns, restaurants and gift shops lie on either side of SR 1. Except for holiday weekends, motel reservations are usually not necessary between October and May, but from Memorial Day weekend through September reservations should be made at least 60 days in advance.

HEARST-SAN SIMEON STATE HISTORICAL MONUMENT (HEARST CASTLE) *Off SR 1 (mailing address: 750 Hearst Castle Rd., 93452-9741).*

(805) 927-2020. Open daily; closed Jan. 1, Thanksgiving and Dec. 25. Tours depart every 10 to 60 minutes, depending on the season; in summer 8 a.m. to 5 p.m.; rest of the year 8:20 a.m. to 3 p.m.; ticket office open daily, except holidays noted above, 8 a.m. to 4 p.m. Day tour $14; ages 6-12, $8. Evening tour, available during spring and fall, $25; ages 6-12, $13. Wheelchair-accessible tours are available; call (805) 927-2020 for details. Reservations are recommended and may be made up to 8 weeks in advance. To charge tickets to American Express, Discover, MasterCard or VISA by phone, call (800) 444-4445. Mail-in requests should be sent with VISA or MasterCard number, or check or money order (payable to MISTIX) to MISTIX, P.O. Box 85705, San Diego, CA 92186-5705. Ten days should be allowed for processing. For reservation forms and information, call (800) 444-4445.

Overlooking the Pacific Ocean 41 miles north of San Luis Obispo and 9 miles north of Cambria is the lavish hilltop monument to the wealth and extravagant tastes of publisher William Randolph Hearst. An insatiable collector, Hearst furnished his massive dwelling and its three separate mansion-sized guest houses with priceless works of art and antiques from around the world. Resembling a towering cathedral of Mediterranean and Gothic design, the estate's main residence, known as "La Casa Grande," has more than 100 rooms, with 41 bathrooms. The grounds and formal gardens of the 127-acre estate are ornamented with statuary, fountains and tiled pools.

Construction began in 1919 and continued for 28 years under the careful direction of publicity-shy architect Julia Morgan. Construction ended in 1947 when Hearst left the castle because of poor health. After Hearst's death in

The Neptune Pool is among the many wonders at Hearst San Simeon State Historical Monument.

1951, the castle was turned over to the state and opened to the public in 1958.

Four 1¾-hour day tours of the estate are offered:

Tour 1, suggested for the first-time visitor, includes the lower level of the main residence, the theater, one guest house, the grounds and outdoor and indoor swimming pools.

Tour 2 views the upper levels of the main residence, including Mr. Hearst's living quarters, his private Gothic suite, the main library, the kitchen and both pools.

Tour 3 visits the north wing of the main residence, a guest house, pools and gardens and includes a video presentation of the castle's construction.

Tour 4 includes gardens, a "hidden" terrace, the wine cellar, a guest house and both pools. This tour is offered only April through October.

Evening tours, available Fridays and Saturdays during spring and summer months, show highlights of the estate, including a living history program; call for schedule.

Tours depart from the 44,000-square-foot Visitor Center complex located just off SR 1. From here visitors are transported by bus five miles up the hill to the castle. The center has free parking, food service, a gift shop, ticket and information counters, lockers and rest rooms. Through viewing windows visitors can see conservators restoring the castle's many works of art. Also within the center is an exhibition of artifacts, documents, photographs and film that portray William Randolph Hearst's life and career, and the construction of the castle.

SEBASTIAN'S STORE *SLO San Simeon Rd. (mailing address: P.O. Box 133, 93452-0133). (805) 927-4217.* This store was built in 1852 on San Simeon Point, about one-half mile from where it stands today. It was constructed at the site of a whaling village and served the needs of the whalers and people who lived and worked on the surrounding ranchos. In 1878, with whaling in decline, the store was moved to its present location, on the ocean side of SR 1 just north of the entrance to the Hearst Castle Visitor Center.

The store was one of the few pieces of property in the area not owned by Senator George Hearst, who purchased over 45,000 acres here in 1865. In 1914, Portuguese immigrant Manual Sebastian bought the store, and the property, now owned by his descendants, is designated California Historical Landmark No. 726. The store includes a post office and is open daily at 8:30 a.m.

North County

North County, the northeastern two-thirds of San Luis Obispo County, is a land of rolling hills, where oak trees grow and cattle graze. Here too are the white fences and green grass of horse ranches, wineries presiding over extensive vineyards, farmlands with symmetrical rows of vegetables or grain, and orchards offering a variety of fruits and nuts.

Low-lying mountains shelter many-fingered lakes. The largest of these are Lake Nacimiento and Lake San Antonio, near the county's northern border. To the south, approximately seven miles southeast of the town of Santa Margarita, Santa Margarita Lake feeds the Salinas River.

Often little more than a narrow stream, the Salinas River flows northward, roughly paralleling US 101. Along the river and highway are towns and villages that reflect a friendly, informal way of life. An old Spanish mission and a modern military base add to the character of North County.

Atascadero

Envisioned as a model community, Atascadero Colony was founded in 1913 by publisher Edward G. Lewis. He had purchased the 23,000-acre Atascadero Rancho, and under his direction, engineers, horticulturists, planners and workmen began to build a town. Unfortunately, before it could be completed, financial problems arose: Lewis went into bankruptcy in 1924; later the Great Depression took its toll, and for many years there was little community development. In 1954, a state hospital was established near Atascadero's southern boundary; the town began a steady growth, attracting people who wanted to live in a semi-rural atmosphere, and in 1979 Atascadero achieved incorporation.

Today tree-lined streets lead past neatly landscaped residential areas. Roads originating at the center of town wind through green rolling hills to orchards, farms, horse ranches, oak groves, or to the Pacific Ocean and the county's coastal attractions. The city boasts its own fishing and boating lake, and less than an hour's drive away lie three other popular recreational lakes: Nacimiento and San Antonio to the north, and Santa Margarita to the south.

Atascadero is a Spanish word which, roughly translated, means muddy or marshy place. The town is on a firm foundation now, with attractions that include an inviting park affording access to both a lake and a zoo. In the center of town the imposing City Administration Building affirms Atascadero's earlier aspirations. For those who enjoy shopping, Atascadero offers antique shops and modern boutiques; once a week there is a farmers market.

This picturesque bell tower is part of Mission San Miguel.

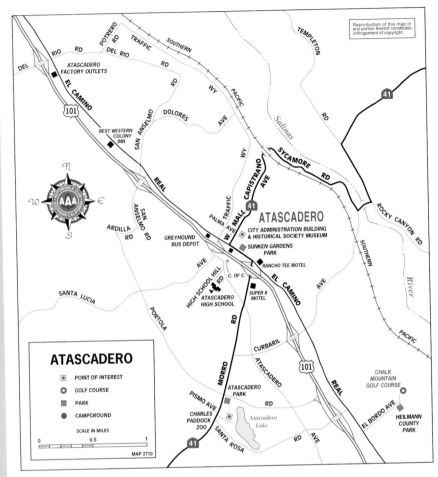

E.G. Lewis' dream of a near-perfect colony may not have materialized, but the town that developed is one that is well worth exploring.

ATASCADERO CITY ADMINISTRATION BUILDING *Palma Ave., between East and West malls.* Unquestionably the most imposing structure in Atascadero, this Italian Renaissance-style building stands in a park-like setting graced by fountains and statuary. Constructed in 1918 of reinforced concrete and locally produced brick, it was initially headquarters for E.G. Lewis and his Atascadero Colony.

Following that, the building's functions at various stages were that of bank, private boys' school and veterans' memorial. Today it is a registered California Historical Landmark (No. 958) and contains Atascadero's municipal government offices. The Atascadero Historical Society occupies the first-floor rotunda.

Atascadero Historical Society Museum *(mailing address: 6600 Lewis Ave., 93422.) Open Mon. through Sat. 1 to 4 p.m.; closed major holidays. (805) 466-8341. Donations. Under age 16 must be accompanied by an adult.*

The Atascadero City Administration Building, built in 1918, faces Sunken Gardens Park.

Atascadero Lake is a large natural reservoir fed by Atascadero Creek and other smaller streams. In 1915 it was expansively extolled as "the lake at the head of the central valley which is being preserved as a park for the enjoyment of the residents." Decades later the lake became part of the city of Atascadero, and over the years the shoreline has been enhanced by trees and picnic tables contributed by community groups.

It is possible to drive or walk around most of the lake's nearly two-mile perimeter. On foot, visitors may at some point find ducks or geese walking alongside, quacking for handouts. A variety of waterfowl inhabit the area, vying with fishermen for the lake's trout, bass and catfish (see *Recreation*).

ATASCADERO PARK *Adjacent to Atascadero Lake.* This park presents a pleasant green and tree-shaded area, complete with playground equipment, picnic tables, benches and fishing areas. The Pavilion is an attractive lakeside structure that offers meeting rooms and performance areas. The Pavilion's snack bar has an outdoor seating area overlooking the lake.

CHARLES PADDOCK ZOO *9305 Pismo St., 93422. (805) 461-5080, 461-7603. Open daily; Memorial Day through Labor Day 10 a.m. to 5 p.m.; rest of the year 10 a.m. to 4 p.m.; closed Jan. 1, Thanksgiving and Dec. 25. Admission $2; seniors, $1.25; ages 3-16, $1.* Located next to Atascadero Park, the Charles Paddock Zoo is a joint venture of the city of Atascadero and the Zoological Society of San Luis

The Administration Building's graceful first-floor rotunda, with its beautifully detailed domed ceiling, houses treasures of Atascadero history. Among the artifacts is a comprehensive pictorial history of the area. Personal possessions of early settlers include furniture, clothing and kitchenware. Representative items are displayed from two doll factories, "Dooley" and "Scarey Ann," that flourished in Paso Robles in the 1920s. Changing exhibits of locally crafted art works are also included.

ATASCADERO LAKE *Between Portola and Santa Rosa rds., east off SR 41.*

A flamingo in the Charles Paddock Zoo does a balancing act.

Obispo County. The zoo's nicely land-scaped three-acre site is home to nearly 100 animal species. Among them are bears, monkeys, meerkats, exotic birds and a pair of Bengal tigers.

COLONY DAYS CELEBRATION *Various venues in Atascadero. (805) 466-2044.* This week-long October event includes a Colony Days tea for early pioneers, bands, entertainment, a dance and a gymkhana. Festivities are capped by a two-hour parade whose entrants depict Atascadero's early days.

FARMERS MARKET Sunken Gardens *In front of City Administration Building, Palma Ave., between East and West malls. Wed. 3 to 6:30 p.m.* Produce from both the southern and northern portions of the county is offered. Among the variety of fresh seasonal fruits, nuts and vegetables are strawberries, dates, oranges, avocados and snow peas.

SPRING ART MART *Sunken Gardens Park in front of the City Administration Building. (805) 466-2044.* This two-day event is held each May on Mother's Day weekend. Artists and craftsmen display and sell their wares, such as paintings, glassware, woodcarvings, pottery and leather goods.

Camp Roberts Military Reservation

Off US 101 at Camp Roberts exit, approximately 4½ miles north of San Miguel, this area is a "closed military installation." Prior approval for entrance is required; call (805) 238-8206 for further information.

Camp Roberts was among the largest military training installations in the United States during World War II. Today this 42,500-acre base is a mobilization station and training center for active and reserve components of U.S. military services.

Carrizo Plain

Approximately 50 miles east of Santa Margarita lies the northern edge of the Carrizo Plain, a 45-mile-long expanse of deceptively calm and level land. Knowledgeable observation of the plain's creek beds and bordering hills, however, make it apparent that this is no ordinary landscape. The San Andreas Fault lies beneath the surface, and there is dramatic earthquake evidence in ancient and more recent scarps (lines of cliffs produced by faulting), sag ponds (water-filled depressions) and fault offset stream channels (formed by opposing movement of tectonic plates).

At one time the Chumash people lived here, and something of their history remains on Painted Rock. From the mid-1800s into the 1980s, cattle and sheep ranches occupied the land; a few herds still graze here. In the 1960s land speculation hit the area, but all that remains of the "boom" is the little town of California Valley, some street signs and a few houses.

CARRIZO PLAIN NATURAL AREA

Bounded roughly by 7 Mile Rd., the crest of the Temblor Range, SR 33/166 and the eastern base of the Caliente Range; about 50 miles east of Santa Margarita on SR 58, south on the road to California Valley. At the intersection of Soda Lake and 7 Mile roads is the sign proclaiming "Carrizo Plain Natural Area." The natural area was established in 1988 jointly by the U.S. Bureau of Land Management, California Department of Fish and Game and The Nature Conservancy to preserve rare and endangered wildlife and plants. Among the fauna protected here are the San Joaquin kit fox and the blunt-nosed leopard lizard. Feathered creatures include the sandhill cranes that winter at Soda Lake. March and April are usually good months to see such wildflowers as larkspur, goldfields and poppies.

Limited primitive camping is available in the Carrizo Plain; call (805) 391-6000 for information. With the exception of a portion of Soda Lake Road, all roads are unpaved and can be impassable following heavy rain. No services are available within the natural area.

Guy C. Goodwin Education Center (Visitor Center) *Off Soda Lake Rd., 6½ miles south of 7 Mile Rd. Generally open Dec. through May, Thur. through Sun. 9 a.m. to 5 p.m. (805) 475-2131.* The center houses exhibits on the area's natural and human history. Visitors can learn about current research and management programs. Information on guided tours and interpretive programs is available.

Painted Rock, significant in Chumash and Yokuts tribal culture, is a natural feature of the landscape that stands about 2½ miles south of the center.

Soda Lake *Best viewed from Soda Lake Overlook, a short walk uphill on the west side of Soda Lake Rd., 2⅒ miles south of 7 Mile Rd.* The 3000-acre lake, dry most of the year and covered with a white alkali crust, holds a variable amount of water, depending upon winter rains. Winter also brings hundreds of sandhill cranes, long-legged gray birds that measure up to four-feet high, sport long graceful tail feathers and have a trumpet-like cry that carries for miles. Among other "snow birds" of the feathered variety that winter here are plovers from Wyoming and Colorado, and hawks from Idaho, Oregon and the Arctic.

The Carrizo Plain is home to tranquil Soda Lake.

Wallace Creek *From 7 Mile Rd. south 5⁹⁄₁₀ miles on Soda Lake Rd. to Simmler Rd., 6⁸⁄₁₀ miles north to Elkhorn Rd., southeast 1⁵⁄₁₀ miles to Wallace Creek sign, continue ³⁄₁₀ miles; park just past the cattle guard.* **Do not park over tall grasses—extreme fire hazard.** *Walk ³⁄₁₀ mile north along barbed wire fence.* If you're interested in earthquakes, this is worth the trip, for now you are on the San Andreas Fault. In 1857 a quake with an estimated magnitude of 8.3 was centered near here, with the west side of the fault moving 30 feet relative to the east side. The surface of the fault ruptured for a distance of over 200 miles from near the San Luis Obispo County/Monterey County line to Cajon Pass in San Bernardino County, and shaking was felt from San Diego to Sacramento.

Wallace Creek is perhaps the best example of a fault offset, stream drainage in the world, for here you can observe a nearly 430-foot offset caused by faulting over the last 3700 years.

Cholame

Set in the midst of ranchland, Cholame is a tiny community where even a one-room post office is a thing of the past. Enlivening the landscape is a roadside restaurant and a "rebellious" film star's memorial which stands nearby.

JAMES DEAN MONUMENT *SR 46.* This simple, dignified monument is built around a small, graceful tree of heaven. Benches invite the visitor to rest or contemplate. A large metal plaque outlines the life of James Dean, a popular film actor, who in 1955 was killed in an automobile accident 900 yards from the monument. A matching plaque expresses the philosophy of Seita Ohnishi, the artist who designed the monument.

Lake Nacimiento

17 miles northwest of Paso Robles off US 101, via County Rd. G14.

Lake Nacimiento Resort, *Star Route, Box 2770, Bradley 93426. (805) 238-3256. Open year round for day use, sunrise to sunset. Day-use admission Apr. through Sept. $10 per vehicle; rest of year $7 per vehicle; camping fees vary.*

This reservoir, in a valley of oak and pine trees, was formed by a dam on the

Among San Luis Obispo County's recreational lakes is beautiful Nacimiento.

Nacimiento River. (The Spanish *nacimiento*, meaning birth or origin, was bestowed on the area by early Spanish explorers.) Numerous coves are part of the lake's 165 miles of shoreline and provide good fishing for bass, bluegill, catfish and perch. Watersports enthusiasts can enjoy boating, waterskiing and swimming, and campsites are also available (see *Recreation* and *Campgrounds & Trailer Parks*).

Lake San Antonio

31 miles northwest of Paso Robles off US 101, via County Rd. G14.

Monterey County Parks, *Star Route, Box 1610, Bradley 93426. (805) 472-2311, (800) 310-2313. Open year round for day use sunrise to sunset. Day-use admission $6 per vehicle; camping fees vary.*

The 16-mile-long reservoir has many fingers and coves that curve around rocky cliffs and reach into oak-covered hills. Although Monterey County contains all of Lake San Antonio's shoreline, San Luis Obispo County residents and visitors alike enjoy the lake's ample recreational facilities: on both the north and south sides are campgrounds, picnic areas, launch ramps and marinas. Waterskiing is a popular sport here, and fishermen can find bass, perch, striper, bluegill and catfish. Other amenities include a restaurant, general store and service station on the south shore. (See *Recreation* and *Campgrounds & Trailer Parks*).

EAGLE WATCH TOURS *Lake San Antonio, South Shore Store; Star Route 2610, Bradley, CA 93426. For reservations, call (408) 755-4899. Tours given early Dec. through mid-Mar., Fri. at 12:30 p.m.; Sat. 9:30 a.m. and 12:30 p.m.; Sun. brunch tours 8:30 a.m.; regular tours 12:30 p.m. Regular tour fare $8 per person; brunch tour $17 per person; senior citizens $6 on selected tours. Reservations are suggested, $3 reservation fee.* Each winter hundreds of bald eagles migrate southward from as far away as Alaska, staying for a few months at lakes like San Antonio. Because the lake is a good food source of fish and waterfowl and has little human development, it can support a population of from 30 to 40 bald eagles from early December through March. Standing about two-feet tall and having a six-foot wingspan, the majestic birds are easy to spot. Additionally, there are golden eagles and some ospreys.

Eagle Watch Tours takes up to 60 people aboard a pontoon boat to view the eagles from the water; binoculars are provided. The boat leaves from the South Shore Store.

Paso Robles

In 1857, Daniel and James Blackburn and Lazarus Godchaux purchased the Mexican land grant Paso Robles Rancho, an area of hot sulphur springs. As people traveled to the area for the therapeutic springs, a resort hotel and other commercial ventures sprang up. Designated "Hot Springs" in 1867, the town's name was changed within the same year to *El Paso de Robles*—Spanish for "Pass of the Oaks."

The railroad reached the area in 1886, and within the next few years the town was plotted, land was cleared and buildings were erected. The population gradually increased, and in 1889 Paso Robles was incorporated.

Now the hot springs are just a memory, and today's Paso Robles offers other attractions. The beauty of the area includes clear, clean air, graceful oaks on gently rolling hills, the green grass

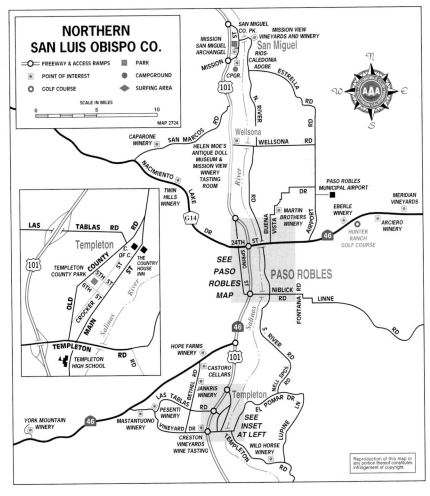

and white fences of horse ranches, and a profusion of blossoming fruit and nut trees in early spring, followed by fields of wildflowers. There are numerous motels and restaurants in town, as well as campgrounds at three lakes within easy driving distance. Wineries offer tours and tasting, and a farmers market sells county-grown produce. Museums and an art gallery provide year-round enjoyment, while annual events add their own excitement. Theatrical events are presented by the Pioneer Players; (805) 239-1638.

The most important attractions of all, however, may be the relaxed pace and friendly hospitality found in this, the North County's largest town.

AGRI-BUSINESS TOUR *First Wed. of May.* (805) 238-0506. *Tour includes lunch and steak dinner; price not available at press time. Reservations are necessary and can be made anytime after Mar. 1.* This bus tour visits agriculturally oriented businesses and may include wineries, bird farms, horse ranches, orchards and processing facilities.

CALIFORNIA MID-STATE FAIR

California Mid-State Fairgrounds, Riverside Ave. between 21st and 24th sts. (805) 238-3565, 239-0655. Annually, first part of Aug. Entrance fees vary. Each year Paso Robles hosts one of California's most popular state fairs. Numerous agricultural, livestock, domestic arts and commercial displays are located throughout the attractively landscaped fairgrounds.

Perhaps the most noteworthy aspect of the fair is its star-quality entertainment. Within recent years, performers such as Kenny Rogers, Diana Ross, Julio Iglesias, Clint Black and the Beach Boys have delighted fairgoers.

CALL-BOOTH HOUSE GALLERY

1315 Vine St., 93446. (805) 238-5473. Open Wed. through Sun. 11 a.m. to 3 p.m.,

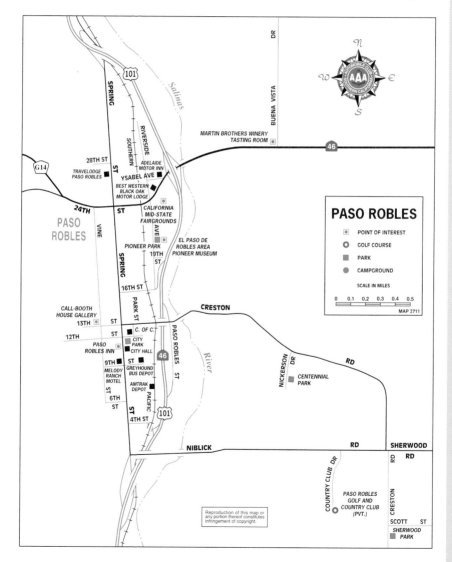

Call-Booth House Gallery is one of Paso Robles' Victorian showplaces.

closed major holidays. Free. This beautifully restored Queen Anne cottage, with its adjoining garden, was built in the 1890s by Dr. Samuel Call and later sold to his sister, Susanna Booth. Visitors can enjoy a well-blended combination of art works and Victorian ambience. Amid original fixtures and antique furnishings, the Paso Robles Art Association displays the paintings, sculpture and other works of local and guest artists; shows change every six weeks. (Display items can be purchased.)

EL PASO DE ROBLES AREA PIONEER MUSEUM *Riverside Ave., between 19th and 20th sts. (mailing address: 1225 Park St., 93446). (805) 238-0506. Open Sat. and Sun. 1 to 4 p.m.; closed major holidays and during Mid-State Fair. Free.* Farm equipment dating back more than a half century, antique wagons and buggies, and turn-of-the-century home and office furniture are among the items housed in the three large buildings on land adjacent to Pioneer Park. Larger examples of farm equipment, including a windmill, remain outside.

FARMERS MARKETS 14th Street *Just east of Spring St. (805) 238-0506. Tues. 10 a.m. to 1 p.m.* Locally grown fruits, vegetables and nuts vary according to season, and can include kiwis, avocados, pumpkins, mushrooms, apples, almonds and pistachios. Unique to this area are the dry-land almonds and watermelons.

Market on the Square *12th St. next to Paso Robles City Park. (805) 238-0506. Fri. 4 to 7 p.m.* Fresh locally-grown produce and locally-made arts and crafts are available. Barbecued meats and other prepared foods are offered, and entertainment is provided.

HELEN MOE'S ANTIQUE DOLL MUSEUM *Junction US 101 and Wellsona Rd., 4 miles north of Paso Robles (mailing address: P.O. Box 332, 93446). (805) 238-2740. Open Mon. through Sat. 9:30 a.m. to 5:30 p.m.; closed major holidays. Admission $3*

for one adult, $4 for two adults; ages 5-12,
$1. Nearly 700 dolls of varying styles,
eras and countries are displayed, often
wearing detailed, handmade costumes.
Exhibits include doll houses, antique
toys and two large mechanical dolls
that perform to music at the touch of a
button. In one large display case a doll-
sized living room recreates the clothing,
furnishings and toys from Christmas
1907. There is also a shop well stocked
with doll-related and other gift items.

PASO ROBLES INN *1103 Spring St.,
93446. (805) 238-2660.* This Paso
Robles landmark has its roots in the
19th century, the original hotel having
been built in 1891 for travelers who
had come to enjoy the medicinal
springs. That hotel was destroyed by
fire in 1940, and within a few years the
inn of today was erected on the same
site. Much of the original red pressed
brick salvaged from the fire went into
the new construction. The public is
welcome to stroll through the inn's
gardens that are landscaped with flower
beds, trees, streams and fish ponds.

**WALK WHERE PADEREWSKI
WALKED** *Various locations; brochure
available at the Chamber of Commerce,
1225 Park St., 93446. (805) 238-0506.*
Ignace Paderewski, renowned Polish
concert pianist, composer and states-
man, lived in Paso Robles during the
early 1900s. This tour retraces his walks
through the historic area of Paso Robles.
A number of Victorian-era and other historic structures can be seen on this tour.

WINE FESTIVAL *City Park, Spring St.
between 11th and 12th sts. Third Sat.
of May, noon to 5 p.m. (805) 238-0506.*
More than 20 wineries offer tasting of
a wide variety of red and white wines.
Food booths, merchandise such as wine
glasses and T-shirts, and live music are

featured. The day before and after the
festival, additional events take place at
many of the participating wineries.

WINERIES *Hours are subject to change;
please call ahead. More complete descriptions of wineries offering tours appear in
the Auto Club's* California Winery Tours
book.

Arciero Winery *6 miles east of Paso
Robles on SR 46 (mailing address: P.O. Box
1287, 93447). (805) 239-2562. Open daily
10 a.m. to 5 p.m.; during summer Sat. and
Sun. until 6 p.m.* Arciero produces 10
varietal wines. Picnic area. Five-acre
rose garden and race car exhibit.

Caparone *7½ miles northwest of Paso
Robles, off Nacimiento Lake Dr. at 2280
San Marcos Rd., 93446. (805) 467-3827.
Open daily 11 a.m. to 5 p.m.* The output
here is limited to such red wines as
Cabernet Sauvignon, Merlot and
Zinfandel.

Eberle Winery *3½ miles east of Paso
Robles on SR 46 (mailing address: P.O.
Box 2459, 93447. (805) 238-9607.
Open May through Sept. daily 10 a.m.
to 6 p.m.; until 5 p.m. rest of year.* Tours
limited to groups by appointment
only. Wines here are from Eberle's
estate-grown grapes.

Hope Farms Winery *1 mile west of US
101 on SR 46 at 2175 Arbor Rd. (mailing
address: P.O. Box 3260, 93447). (805)
238-6979. Open for tasting only, daily
11 a.m. to 5 p.m.; closed major holidays.
$2 tasting fee, includes glass.* Among the
wines produced here are Muscat Canelli,
Zinfandel and Cabernet Sauvignon.

Justin Vineyards and Winery *13½
miles west of Paso Robles off Nacimiento
Lake Dr. at 11680 Chimney Rock Rd.,
93446. (805) 238-6932. Open daily 10
am. to 6 p.m.* Among Justin wines are
Chardonnay, port and a red bordeaux-

style blend of Cabernet Sauvignon, Merlot and Cabernet Franc called Isosceles. A bed and breakfast, The Just Inn, is located here.

Laura's Vineyard *6 miles east of Paso Robles at 5620 SR 46 E., Paso Robles (mailing address: P.O. Box 304, San Miguel 93451). (805) 238-6300. Open daily 10 a.m. to 6 p.m.* Wines include Johannisberg Riesling, White Zinfandel and Syrah.

Martin Brothers Winery *1 mile east of Paso Robles off SR 46 at 2610 Buena Vista Dr. (mailing address: P.O. Box 2599, 93447). (805) 238-2520. Open daily 11 a.m. to 5 p.m.* Wines here are made from classic Italian varieties. Tours by appointment. Summer concerts.

Meridian Vineyards *7 miles east of Paso Robles at 7000 SR 46 (mailing address: P.O. Box 3289, 93447). (805) 237-6000. Open for tasting only, Wed. through Mon. 10 a.m. to 5 p.m.* A variety of award-winning wines can be sampled. Picnic area.

Norman Vineyards, Inc. *4 miles west off SR 46 at 7450 Vineyard Dr., Paso Robles 93446. (805) 237-0138. Open Sat., Sun. and holidays 11 a.m. to 5:30 p.m., or by appointment. Additional tasting Mon. through Sat. 10 a.m. to 5 p.m. at Adelaida Floral, 300 Main St., Templeton. (805) 434-2997.*

Tobin James Cellars *8 miles east of Paso Robles off SR 46 at 8950 Union Rd., Paso Robles 93446. (805) 239-2204. Open daily 10 a.m. to 6 p.m. for tasting and self-guided tours; guided tours are by appointment.* Chardonnay, Merlot, Cabernet Sauvignon, Pinot Noir, Zinfandels and Syrah are among the wines produced here. Picnic area.

Twin Hills Winery *Junction of Nacimiento Dr. and Mustard Creek Rd. at 2025 Nacimiento Lake Rd., 93446. (805)*

238-9148. Open for tasting only, summer daily 11 a.m. to 5 p.m.; winter, Mon. through Fri. noon to 4 p.m., Sat. and Sun. 11 a.m. to 5 p.m. Among the estate-bottled wines here are port and sherry. Picnic area. Art gallery and gift shop.

San Miguel

MISSION SAN MIGUEL ARCANGEL *East side of US 101 at 775 Mission St., 93451. (805) 467-3256. Self-guided tours daily 9:30 a.m. to 4:30 p.m.; closed Jan. 1, Good Friday, Easter, Thanksgiving and Dec. 25. Admission 50¢ per person, $1 per family.* Named for the archangel St. Michael, the 16th California mission was founded in 1797 by Franciscan Father Fermín de Lasuén. The present structure was completed in 1818, and the church is still administered by Franciscan fathers.

Although the white exterior of the church is almost severely plain, the

The church of the 1797 Mission San Miguel glows with its original hues.

First a home, then a stagecoach stop, the Rios-Caledonia Adobe still stands in San Miguel.

interior decorations and altar glow with warm colors that are the original hues. A self-guided tour of various rooms enables visitors to visualize the mission's activities in the days of the Spanish padres. Among the artifacts is a large, colorful, 17th-century wood carving of St. Michael the Archangel victorious over Satan. Brochures outlining the tour are available in the gift shop, which is the starting point.

RIOS-CALEDONIA ADOBE *East side of US 101, south of Mission San Miguel (mailing address: P.O. Box 326, 93451). (805) 467-3357. Open Wed. through Sun. 10 a.m. to 4 p.m; closed Jan. 1 and Dec. 25. Free.* Constructed in the 1840s as a hacienda and ranch headquarters for the Petronillo Rios family, original building material included handmade tiles and rafters made of pine poles tied with rawhide strips. By 1868 the building had been sold to George Butchart and become the Caledonia Inn, a stagecoach stop on the San Francisco to Los Angeles run. Following the coming of the railroad in 1886, the adobe housed various enterprises over the years.

In 1968 San Luis Obispo County and Friends of the Adobes banded together to restore and preserve the original appearance of this State Historical Landmark (No. 936). Picnic tables and a gift shop are located on the premises. Brochures are available for a self-guided tour of the grounds. Overnight camping is also available (see *Campgrounds & Trailer Parks*).

WINERIES *Hours are subject to change; please call ahead. More complete descriptions of wineries offering tours appear in the Auto Club's* California Winery Tours *book.*

Mission View Vineyards and Winery *1½ miles east of US 101 at 13350 N. River Rd. (P.O. Box 129, 93451). (805) 467-3104. Tasting room at junction of US 101 and Wellsona Road open daily 10 a.m. to 5 p.m.* Among the wines produced are Sauvignon Blanc and Zinfandel. Tours by appointment. Picnic area.

Silver Horse Vineyards *East off SR 46 at 2995 Pleasant Rd., San Miguel (mailing address: P.O. Box 2010, Paso Robles 93447). (805) 467-9463. Open Thur. through Mon. 11 a.m. to 5 p.m.* Tours are self guided. Cabernet Sauvignon, Zinfandel, Chardonnay, Pinot Noir and White Zinfandel are produced here.

Santa Margarita Lake

Approximately 18 miles southeast of Santa Margarita off SR 58, via Pozo Rd.

Information Officer, *Star Route Box 34-A, Santa Margarita, CA 93453. (805) 438-5485. Open year round for day use; during Pacific Daylight Time from 6 a.m. to 8 p.m.; earlier closing during standard time. Day-use admission, $4 per vehicle; $4 per extra boat; camping fees vary.*

With much of its shoreline bordered by gently rolling hills and some portions backed by high stone cliffs, this warm-water lake entices fishermen with bass, bluegill, catfish, crappie, trout and striper. Since the lake is a domestic water supply, swimming and waterskiing are prohibited. There are two paved launch ramps, several picnic areas and a group campground.

A full-service marina store provides bait, tackle, food, gasoline and boat rentals. The park also offers an extensive trails system for hikers, equestrians and bicyclists (see *Recreation* and *Campgrounds & Trailer Parks*).

Templeton

In 1886 the Southern Pacific Railroad decided to run track to this area, from which point travelers could transfer to a stagecoach bound for San Luis Obispo. As a result, C.H. Phillips of the West Coast Land Company directed that 160 acres bordering the Salinas River be laid out in business and residential lots. Within a few months, thanks to advertisements placed in newspapers nationwide, Templeton was a thriving community that counted 18 saloons among its other business establishments. A raging fire in 1897 destroyed much of the downtown area, and since the railroad roundhouse had been moved away in 1891, the town's boom days were over.

Today, a stroll down Templeton's Main Street can give a visitor the feeling of being in an honest-to-Old-West cow town. The look of the buildings harks back to the late 1800s, and there are inviting benches along the way. Near the north end of Main Street is the Templeton Livestock Market, a lively place on Tuesday nights from May through October, when teams of two or three cowboys compete in herding cattle into pens ("team penning"), and spectators can enjoy barbecue and beer.

A few antique shops are located along Main Street, and about a quarter mile off Main Street on Ramada Drive is the barn-sized Vineyard Antique Mall. Merchandise here includes furniture, toys, jewelry, Tiffany lamps, dishes, saddles and saddle blankets. Within easy driving distance of Templeton are several wineries, many of which are open for tasting and tours (see *Wineries* in this section).

Among the town's amenities is a tree-shaded park at Old County Road and 6th Street, with picnic tables, an old-fashioned bandstand and a public swimming pool that is open in summer. Attractive structures from the 19th century include the First Presbyterian Church at 6th and Crocker streets, and Bethel Lutheran Church at Third and Crocker streets, both constructed in 1887. The Country House Inn, 91 Main Street, was built in 1886 as a house for C.H. Phillips. Now a bed-and-breakfast accommodation furnished with antiques, it is set among 100-year-old trees and well-tended gardens.

FARMERS MARKET Templeton County Park *Bounded by Old County Rd., Fifth, Crocker and Sixth sts. (805) 434-4900. Sat. 9:30 a.m. to 1 p.m.* Growers display the many kinds of fruits, nuts and vegetables for which San Luis Obispo County is well known. Local arts and crafts are sometimes found among the produce.

SYCAMORE FARMS *3 miles west of Templeton on south side of SR 46 (mailing address: Route 1, Box 49A, Paso Robles 93446). (805) 238-5288. Open daily 10:30 a.m. to 5:30 p.m.; closed the first two weeks in Jan. and major holidays. Free.* Forty acres are devoted to growing colorful, fragrant, culinary and medicinal herbs and wine grapes. Potted, fresh-cut and dried herbs are for sale, and a gift shop includes food stuffs, books on herbs and cooking, as well as gardening items. Tastings for Bonny Doon Winery are also offered.

WINERIES *Hours are subject to change; please call ahead. More complete descriptions of wineries offering tours appear in the Auto Club's* California Winery Tours *book.*

Castoro Cellars *1¼ miles west of US 101 at 1315 N. Bethel Rd., Templeton 93465. (805) 238-2602. Open daily 11 a.m. to 5:30 p.m.* Among the wines here are Merlot, Chardonnay and Cabernet.

Creston Vineyards *14 miles east of Santa Margarita on SR 58 at 679 Calf Canyon Hwy., Creston 93432. (805) 238-7398. Tasting room in Templeton at US 101 and Vineyard Dr. Open daily 10 a.m. to 5 p.m.* Tours of vineyard by appointment only. The winery produces a large number of varietal wines each year.

Jankris Winery *Off US 101, west on SR 46 to Bethel Rd. (mailing address: Route 2,*

Box 40, Bethel Rd., Templeton 93465). (805) 434-0319. Open daily 11 a.m. to 5:30 p.m. Among the wines offered for tasting are Pinot Blanc, Syrah, Gamay and White Zinfandel.

Live Oak Vineyards *1 mile west of US 101 on SR 46 at 1480 N. Bethel Rd., Templeton 93446. (805) 227-4766. Open 10 a.m. to 6 p.m.* Originally a one-room schoolhouse, the tasting area offers Chardonnay, Sauvignon Blanc, White Zinfandel and Zinfandel, Merlot, and Cabernet Sauvignon.

Mastantuono Winery *4 miles west of Templeton at Vineyard Dr. and SR 46 (mailing address: 100 Oak View Rd., 93465). (805) 238-0676. Open daily for tasting only; May to Oct. 10 a.m. to 6 p.m.; rest of year 10 a.m. to 5 p.m.* Zinfandel and Muscat are the notable wines here. Picnic area.

Pesenti Winery *3 miles west of Templeton at 2900 Vineyard Dr., 93465. (805) 434-1030. Open for tasting only, Mon. through Sat. 8 a.m. to 6 p.m., Sun. from 9 a.m.* Premium varieties of red and white wines are available.

Wild Horse Winery *2½ miles south of Vineyard Dr. off Templeton Rd. at Wild Horse Court (mailing address: P.O. Box 910, 93465). (805) 434-2541. Open for tasting only, daily 11 a.m. to 5 p.m.* Wines are produced from both estate-grown grapes and those purchased from other Central Coast vineyards.

York Mountain Winery *10 miles west of Templeton via SR 46 on York Mountain Rd. (mailing address: Route 2, Box 191, 93465). (805) 238-3925. Open daily 10 a.m. to 5 p.m.; closed major holidays.* Pinot Noir, sherry, port and sparkling wine are among the wines available here. Tours by appointment.

Los Padres National Forest

A major portion of the Central Coast's backcountry lies within Los Padres National Forest, the third largest national forest in California. Rugged mountains and deep, remote valleys comprise most of its two million acres that sprawl through five counties: Ventura, Kern, Santa Barbara, San Luis Obispo and Monterey. Sightseeing is a popular pastime in accessible portions of Los Padres, and recreational opportunities include hiking and camping (see Recreation *and* Campgrounds & Trailer Parks*).*

Los Padres National Forest Headquarters *6144 Calle Real, Goleta 93117; (805) 683-6711. Open Mon. through Fri. 8 a.m. to 4:30 p.m.*

Mt. Pinos Ranger District *34580 Lockwood Valley Rd. (mailing address: HC-1, Box 400, Frazier Park 93225). (805) 245-3731. Open Mon. through Fri. 8 a.m. to 4:30 p.m.*

Ojai Ranger District *1190 E. Ojai Ave., Ojai 93023. (805) 646-4348. Open Mon. through Fri. 8 a.m. to 4:30 p.m.*

Santa Barbara Ranger District *Star Route, Santa Barbara 93105; (805) 967-3481. Open Mon. through Sat. 8 a.m. to 5 p.m.*

Santa Lucia Ranger District *1616 N. Carlotti Dr., Santa Maria 93454-1599. Open Mon. through Fri. 8 a.m. to 4:30 p.m.*

The lower slopes of Los Padres alternate between grassland and oak forest. Middle elevations are chaparral covered, and higher altitudes are forested with pines and firs. These varied environments provide habitats for nearly 500 species of animals and birds, including black bear, fox, deer, golden eagle and peregrine falcon. The endangered California condor, North America's largest bird, has recently been reintroduced to its natural habitat, deep in the wilderness area of the forest in Ventura County. Although it is very difficult to view the condors, their survival is being monitored by wildlife biologists.

Summers are usually warm and dry in Los Padres, with little rain falling from May to October except for an occasional afternoon thundershower near the higher peaks. Winter is generally cool and wet, although some winter days are sunny and mild. Wildflowers help make the forest most appealing in the spring, and bright colors at higher elevations add beauty to fall.

Ventura County offers two well-maintained, paved roads that venture through a sizable portion of Los Padres: SR 33 heads north into the Forest from Ojai and intersects with Lockwood Valley Road going northeast. Cuddy

In Los Padres National Forest a waterfall feeds a branch of Matilija Creek.

Valley and Frazier Mountain roads, just over the boundary with Kern County, go west and east respectively off Lockwood Valley Road. Secondary paved and unpaved roads lead off these main routes to scenic areas, trail heads, picnicking spots and campgrounds. A word of warning: Following a season of heavy rain, creek beds which cross highways may contain deep water, making crossing difficult. Signs along Lockwood Valley Road warn, "Next 17 miles, road may be impassable due to rain or snow."

In case you thought that it never snows in Southern California, be aware that where Ventura and Kern counties meet in Los Padres, there may often be two to three feet of the white stuff in winter. That's when the hiking trails around Mount Pinos become cross-country skiing trails. Obviously, it's best to bring tire chains when visiting that area in winter.

In Santa Barbara County, a major portion of the forest comprises the roadless San Rafael and Dick Smith wilderness areas, largely untouched except for dauntless backpackers with wilderness permits. Several paved and dirt roads provide access to picnic areas and campgrounds at the edge of the forest. Notable are Gibraltar Road and Camino Cielo near Santa Barbara, Figueroa Mountain and Happy Canyon roads above the Santa Ynez Valley, and Tepusquet Road east of Santa Maria. All of these require slow, careful driving. Pavements are narrow and, in places, rough; curves are frequent and sharp. In wet weather these roads may be closed to motor vehicles.

State Routes 166 and 154 are the only major, frequently traveled roads in Santa Barbara County going into Los Padres, and together they total less than 20 miles within forest boundaries. SR 166 goes east off US 101 north of Santa Maria and about 10 miles into the forest gives access to Sierra Madre Road. This unpaved, dusty, frequently rough road ventures approximately 30 miles into Los Padres backcountry and borders the San Rafael Wilderness. Needless to say, this road should not be attempted in inclement weather.

SR 154 leaves US 101 northwest of Santa Barbara, and as it cuts through Los Padres, becomes San Marcos Pass, a road that gives access to an ancient cave, a graceful bridge and a historic tavern, as described below.

While San Luis Obispo County claims comparatively little of Los Padres National Forest, most of the county's mountainous regions lie within Los Padres' boundaries. A sizable part of the forest is designated the Santa Lucia Wilderness. This scenic region includes a 3000-foot-high mountain ridge that separates the valleys containing Lopez and Santa Margarita lakes. Access to the wilderness is by foot or horseback only.

The most accessible areas of Los Padres in San Luis Obispo County lie northeast of Santa Margarita Lake. On the east side of the town of Santa Margarita, Pozo Road leads south off SR 58, passes the lake, then goes east to Park Hill Road. After about 2½ miles, Park Hill becomes Black Mountain Road. Just over 1½ miles east of Park Hill Road off Pozo Road, a rugged dirt road (Pozo Grade) heads north to Pozo Summit. Both Black Mountain and Pozo Grade roads lead to scenic vistas and campsites. Except for Pozo Grade, these roads are paved. They are all narrow and winding, though, and as always in the backcountry, bad weather is a time to exercise particular caution.

Popular Lake Piru lies near Ventura County's eastern border.

Lake Piru Recreation Area

LAKE PIRU *Approximately 7½ miles east of Fillmore off SR 126, north on Piru Canyon Rd., through the town of Piru (mailing address: Lake Piru Recreation Manager, P.O. Box 202, Piru 93040). (805) 521-1645. Fees for day use and camping.* This four-mile-long lake, formed by the Santa Felicia Dam, takes its name from the Chumash word for the reeds that once grew on the site. In addition to its recreational uses, Lake Piru provides water for homes and industries in Ventura County.

Although the northern portion of Lake Piru lies within Los Padres National Forest, the lake is administered by the United Water Conservation District in Santa Paula. Regardless of who's in charge, there's plenty to do: boating, camping, fishing, swimming and water-skiing (see *Recreation* and *Campgrounds & Trailer Parks*).

San Marcos Pass Area

CHUMASH PAINTED CAVE STATE HISTORIC PARK *2 miles northwest of Santa Barbara via SR 154 and Painted Cave Rd.* This park consists of a shallow cave and surrounding terrain. On the cave walls the Chumash long ago left their mark in brightly colored designs. These pictographs are a fine example of American Indian art and are thought to have played a part in Chumash religion. A locked, metal screen protects the designs but allows a view of the interior. The road leading to the cave is narrow and winding; parking near the cave consists of pulling off onto a narrow shoulder.

COLD SPRING ARCH BRIDGE *Best seen ¼ mile below Cold Spring Tavern on Stagecoach Rd.* This graceful steel structure leaps Cold Spring Canyon in one 700-foot span, providing a spectacular sight for travelers on Stagecoach Road 400 feet below. Completed in 1963, the

Cold Spring Arch Bridge, a 700-foot single span, crosses Cold Spring Canyon along SR 154.

bridge was constructed so that motorists on SR 154 might avoid the twisting route through Cold Spring Canyon.

COLD SPRING TAVERN *½ mile southwest of SR 154 on Stagecoach Road, 14 miles northwest of Santa Barbara (mailing address: 5995 Stagecoach Rd., Santa Barbara 93105). (805) 967-0066.* After completion of the San Marcos Pass toll road in the 1880s, a small restaurant was opened here to accommodate stagecoach passengers. Travelers today also can enjoy food and drink in the

Cold Spring Tavern, a stagecoach stop in the 1880s, is still open to travelers.

▼ *The Past of the Pass*

San Marcos Pass, SR 154, runs from Santa Barbara through Los Padres National Forest, passes Lake Cachuma, crosses the road to Santa Ynez and Solvang, goes through Los Olivos and ends at US 101. This 32-mile-long road has been deservedly designated a scenic highway, with mountains, valleys, the lake, vineyards, ranches and, on a clear day from near the summit, a view of the channel islands.

SR 154 is a well-paved, thoughtfully engineered highway traversed daily by hundreds of motorists without a second thought. It was not always so. In 1901 the first car over San Marcos Pass was a De Dion-Bouton Motorette, owned by L.L. Whitman of Pasadena. Mr. Whitman had to ford the Santa Ynez River by constructing a stone roadway down the bank, across the river, and up the other side. Mr. Whitman had thoughtfully carried a canvas to cover the Dion—he didn't want horses spooked at the sight of this strange machine.

During the next few years while the roads remained narrow and winding, they were difficult to navigate, and too often a motorist found himself walking into Santa Ynez to place a telephone call or send a wire for help. For a night or two a local hotel welcomed him while he waited for the requisite auto parts to arrive from Los Angeles.

tavern, which still occupies the original structure. Another building set in this tree-shaded spot formerly served as a bottling plant for the spring water and now houses the Wagon Wheel Back Bar.

Zaca Lake Area

ZACA LAKE *Off Zaca Station Rd., 12 miles northeast of US 101 and Zaca Station Rd. junction (mailing address: Zaca Lake Lodge, P.O. Box 187, Los Olivos 93441). (805) 688-4891. Fees for day use, accommodations and camping.* This small, privately owned lake is virtually hidden away amidst tree-covered hills in Los Padres National Forest. Public access is along nearly a mile of paved road followed by about 3½ miles of a rough dirt and gravel road that fords five streams and can be hazardous after winter rainstorms. The road ends with another mile of paved road.

Zaca Lake offers primitive camping, picnicking facilities, swimming and rental boats (see Water Recreation in *Recreation* chapter); fishing and motorized craft are prohibited. Overnight accommodations are available, and meals are served in the lodge dining room (reservations required).

Annual Events

In addition to things to see and do all through the year, the Central Coast hosts a variety of once-a-year events. Special-interest displays, holiday celebrations, parades, music, athletics—you name it, you can probably find it here. While most events are free, a few do charge admission. For more detailed information, call the telephone numbers shown.

February

FHP HEALTH CARE CLASSIC (SENIOR PGA TOUR) *Ojai Valley Inn, Ojai. (805) 640-2800.* In the course of one week, well-seasoned professional golfers compete in this event.

MARDI GRAS JAZZ FESTIVAL *Various locations, Pismo Beach. (805) 773-4382; (800) 443-7778.* For three days, noteworthy Dixieland bands perform at local establishments. (Advance-purchase badges are available.)

MARDI GRAS PARADE *San Luis Obispo. (805) 541-2183 (information recording available in Jan.).* A parade celebrating the pre-Lenten season features floats, balloons and masked figures; an evening ball is also scheduled.

STORYTELLING FESTIVAL *Various locations, Solvang. (805) 688-8000.* Professional and amateur storytellers share their tales during this 12-hour event.

March

BEANS & JEANS JAMBOREE *Veteran's Hall, Cambria. (805) 927-3624.* Participants enjoy a day of western dance workshops and a chili cook-off.

CAMBRIA WELSH FESTIVAL *Various locations, Cambria. (805) 927-3624.* Participants enjoy a four-day celebration of Welsh music, story-telling and dancing.

INTERNATIONAL FILM FESTIVAL *Various locations, Santa Barbara. (805) 963-0023.* This 10-day festival premieres U.S. and international films and includes workshops, seminars and evenings with selected actors.

INTERNATIONAL ORCHID SHOW *Earl Warren Showgrounds, Santa Barbara. (805) 967-6331.* For a three-day period, spectacular displays compete for awards. A commercial sales area is included.

PADEREWSKI FESTIVAL *Various locations, Paso Robles. (805) 238-0506.* This three-day event features music and Zinfandel wine to celebrate the life of Ignace Paderewski, renowned Polish concert pianist of the early 1900s, who is credited with introducing the Zinfandel grape to the Paso Robles area.

ST. PATRICK'S DAY PARADE AND FESTIVAL *Mission Park, Ventura. (805) 648-2075.* The weekend before St. Patrick's Day is marked with a hometown-style parade, followed by Irish dancing, arts and crafts, and entertainment.

Costumes and dances are part of Old Spanish Days, held during August in Santa Barbara.

SOLVANG CENTURY BIKE RIDE
Begins and ends in Solvang. (805) 943-9440. Participants compete in a one-day, 100-mile bicycling course through the Santa Ynez Valley.

TASTE OF SOLVANG *Various locations, Solvang. (800) 468-6765.* A three-day food festival includes live entertainment, a dessert showcase, walking smorgasbord and the "World's Largest Danish."

April

CALIFORNIA BEACH PARTY *Harbor Blvd. and California St., Ventura. (805) 654-7830.* Live music, wind-surfing, 5K and 10K runs and walks, food, and arts and crafts highlight this spring weekend event.

CAMARILLO COMMUNITY EXPOSITION *Camarillo Community Center, Camarillo. (805) 484-4383.* Local businesses, including restaurants, showcase their products and services for two days.

CHANNEL ISLANDS HARBOR FOOD & WINE FESTIVAL *Harbor and Channel Islands blvds., Oxnard. (800) 994-4852.* Local musicians provide a background for food, beverages and children's activities during this three-day event.

CONEJO VALLEY DAYS *Various locations, Thousand Oaks. (805) 373-6000.* A celebration of the community features parades, art contests, Miss Conejo Pageant and a five-day carnival.

I MADONNARI ITALIAN STREET PAINTING FESTIVAL *Mission San Luis Obispo courtyard, San Luis Obispo. (805) 528-6492.* For two days, amateur and professional artists and children create sidewalk drawings with vivid pastels.

LA FIESTA *Mission Plaza, San Luis Obispo. (805) 543-1710.* Festivities for one week include music, costumes, ethnic food, dancing, arts and crafts booths, a carnival and parade.

OJAI TENNIS TOURNAMENT *Libbey Park and other tennis courts, Ojai. (805) 646-2494.* In this four-day event, more than 1500 amateur tennis players compete in 34 divisions, which include the Big West Championships and the PAC 10 Championships.

PAINT-O-RAMA *California Mid-State Fairgrounds, Paso Robles. (805) 238-0506.* This four-day equestrian event is a gathering of paint horses that compete in English and Western classes; a gymkhana is included.

SANTA BARBARA COUNTY VINTNER'S FESTIVAL *Santa Ynez. (805) 688-0881.* Wine, food and entertainment highlight this two-day festival.

SANTA BARBARA FAIR & EXPO *Earl Warren Showgrounds, Santa Barbara. (805) 687-0766.* For five days, a carnival, livestock exhibits, commercial and competitive displays, food booths and entertainment make up a down-sized country fair.

SANTA YNEZ VALLEY CARRIAGE CLASSIC *Various locations, Santa Ynez. (805) 688-4454.* For three days, carriages, coaches and wagons compete for honors and share the spotlight with beautifully groomed horses.

SPRING ARTS FESTIVAL *Ryon Park, Lompoc. (805) 735-8511.* This three-day festival features arts, crafts, entertainment, a chili cook-off, food booths and antique cars.

May

ANTIQUE SHOW *Coast Union High School, Cambria. (805) 927-3624.* During Memorial Day weekend scores of dealers display their antiques and collectibles for browsers and buyers. There is a nominal admission fee.

ARABIAN HORSE SHOW *Earl Warren Showgrounds, Santa Barbara. (805) 967-6331.* This three-day event puts beautiful animals through their paces.

BEACHFEST *Various locations, Pismo Beach. (805) 773-4382.* For two days there are such activities and competitions as volleyball tournaments, surfing contests, jet ski races and a swimsuit fashion show.

CAJUN/CREOLE MUSIC FESTIVAL *Los Angeles Ave. near Tapo Canyon Rd., Simi Valley. (805) 526-3900.* Simi Sunrise Rotary Club sponsors Cajun and Creole flavored food, music, arts and crafts, and dancing during Memorial Day weekend.

CALIFORNIA STRAWBERRY FESTI-VAL *College Park, Oxnard. (805) 385-7578.* This weekend celebration of the delicious berry includes arts, crafts and food booths, entertainment and children's activities. Admission fee.

CAMBRIA VILLAGE STORYTELLING FEST *Various locations, Cambria. (805) 927-3624.* For three days, professional storytellers celebrate the art of telling tales.

CELEBRATE NIPOMO *Dana Adobe, Nipomo. (805) 929-1583.* Local artisans and crafts people demonstrate art and techniques of the past; food and music are included in this one-day event.

CINCO DE MAYO CELEBRATION *City Park, Paso Robles. (805) 238-0506.* Paso Robles' Hispanic heritage is the theme of this one-day celebration which includes food, music and dancing.

EAGLE POINT POW-WOW *Lake Casitas. (805) 640-0400.* A two-day cel-ebration of American Indian music and dance presents an opportunity to enjoy Indian culture, foods, arts and crafts.

EARLY CALIFORNIA DAYS FESTIVAL *Various locations, Fillmore. (805) 524-0351.* A four-day celebration of Fillmore's heritage includes parades, a carnival, barbecues, hot air balloon rides, food and game booths.

GOURMET CENTURY BIKE RIDE *Santa Ynez Valley. (805) 688-6385.* Participants bicycle a one-day, 100-mile course through the Santa Ynez Valley and enjoy gourmet offerings at several stations along the way.

GREAT WESTERN BICYCLE AND WEST KOAST KUSTOMS CUSTOM CAR RALLY *Various locations, Paso Robles. (805) 238-0506.* Over 400 custom cars and over 2000 bicyclists participate in three days of shows and races.

HUCK FINN FISHING DERBY *Rancho Simi Community Park, Simi Valley. (805) 584-4400.* For one day, children under age 15 compete for prizes in catching fish from the park's freshly stocked lagoon.

MOTHER'S DAY MINI-CIRCUIT *California Mid-State Fairgrounds, Paso Robles. (805) 238-0506.* For three days, quarter horses compete in English and Western classes, and there are team-penning events.

OJAI GARDEN TOUR *Various locations, Ojai and vicinity. (805) 646-8126.* Perennials, roses and home orchards are among the flowering sights to see on this one-day self-guided tour of private gardens in the Ojai Valley.

STRAWBERRY FESTIVAL *Arroyo Grande Village. (805) 489-1488.* In addition to traditional and imaginative new strawberry creations, this two-day event includes arts and crafts displays, food booths, pancake breakfast and a 10K run.

WILDFLOWER FESTIVAL *Lake San Antonio. (805) 472-2311.* Nature activities are featured for two days, along with a mountain bike race; arts and crafts; wildflower displays; entertainment and refreshments.

WINE FESTIVAL *City Park, Paso Robles. (805) 238-0506.* During this three-day event, more than 20 wineries offer samples for tasting, with entertainment and food booths. (See listing under Paso Robles, *San Luis Obispo County.*)

June

ART WALK *Exxon Company USA Building, Thousand Oaks. (805) 373-0054.* A two-day art exhibit showcases the work of California artists.

CONFEDERATE AIR FORCE AIR SHOW *Paso Robles Municipal Airport. (805) 238-4858.* One-day static and flying displays of historic and contemporary "war birds" are sponsored by a local Confederate Air Force squadron.

CUSTOM CAR SHOW *Various locations, Pismo Beach. (805) 773-4382; (800) 443-7778.* Classic cars and street rods are displayed for two days on the Pismo Beach pier and on downtown streets.

ELKS RODEO AND PARADE *Various locations, Santa Maria. (805) 922-6006.* A parade, contests, a rodeo, dances and barbecues are featured in this four-day event.

FLOWER FESTIVAL *Various locations, Lompoc. (805) 735-8511.* Tours of the flower fields, a parade, carnival, arts and crafts booths, a flower show and special entertainment highlight this five-day event.

OJAI FESTIVAL *Libbey Park, Ojai. (805) 646-2094.* This three-day event features classical music presented by professional music groups under the baton of renowned conductors.

OJAI WINE FESTIVAL *Lake Casitas. (800) 648-4881.* This is an afternoon of wine tasting, sampling the cuisine of Ojai Valley restaurants and browsing through arts and crafts displays.

OLD SANTA YNEZ DAYS *Various locations, Santa Ynez. (805) 688-5318.* For one day out of the year the town celebrates its birthday with cowboys, food, a parade and entertainment.

SUMMER SOLSTICE CELEBRATION *Various locations, Santa Barbara. (805) 965-3396.* In celebration of the coming of summer, performers and artisans display their talents for one day, and a lively parade winds through the city streets, followed by a festival featuring music, dance, food and an evening performance event.

June-August

MUSIC ACADEMY OF THE WEST SUMMER CONCERT SERIES *Various locations, Santa Barbara. (805) 969-4726.* Student and professional performances are set in gardens and theaters during an eight-week period.

June-September

THEATERFEST *Solvang Festival Theater, Solvang. (805) 922-8313.* For 18 weeks a variety of music and drama is presented in an outdoor setting.

July

CENTRAL COAST RENAISSANCE FAIRE *El Chorro Regional County Park, 5 miles north of San Luis Obispo. (805) 528-4427.* On two consecutive weekends, this re-creation of a 16th-century English fair features period foods and crafts, music, dancing, games and a reenactment of Queen Elizabeth I's resplendent court.

FOURTH OF JULY *Cambria, Cayucos, Fillmore, Morro Bay, Pismo Beach, Templeton, Thousand Oaks.* Daytime activities and/or nighttime fireworks displays are featured in these communities. For further information check with local chambers of commerce (see listings under *Tourist Information Sources*).

4TH OF JULY CELEBRATION *Downtown Ventura. (805) 654-7830.* The day begins at the Ventura Pier with a 5 a.m. fireworks display. Later in the day along Main Street, food booths, bands, games, a children's parade, and an arts and crafts show light up the city.

HERITAGE DAY AT THE DALLIDET *Dallidet Adobe, San Luis Obispo. (805) 543-0638.* Arts, crafts and entertainment of the 1800s are featured in this one-day event (see listing under *San Luis Obispo County*, San Luis Obispo City).

OBON FESTIVAL *SLO Veteran's Hall, San Luis Obispo. (805) 929-4461 or 595-2625.* Japanese exhibits include sushi, martial arts, bonsai and crafts during this one-day event.

OLD-FASHIONED FOURTH OF JULY *Mission Plaza, San Luis Obispo. (805) 781-7300.* Live entertainment, food, games and activities for all ages are featured.

PORTUGUESE CELEBRATION *Veterans Hall, Cayucos. (805) 995-1200.* This three-day event honors those whose Portuguese ancestors helped settle Cayucos and is highlighted by a parade and barbecue.

SANTA BARBARA COUNTY FAIR *Santa Barbara County Fairgrounds, Santa Maria. (805) 925-8824.* Billed as a real country fair, this one-week event includes 4-H exhibits, horse shows, animal judging, homemade food, a carnival, music and entertainment.

SANTA BARBARA KENNEL CLUB SHOW *Stevenson Field, Buellton. (818) 796-3869.* As one of the largest one-day dog shows in the nation, this event is a real treat for canine fanciers.

July-August

OJAI SHAKESPEARE FESTIVAL *Libbey Bowl, Ojai. (805) 646-9455.* For two weeks, Saturday and Sunday matinee and evening performances of at least two of the bard's plays take place in an outdoor setting.

August

CALIFORNIA MID-STATE FAIR *California Mid-State Fairgrounds, Paso Robles. (805) 239-0655, 238-3565.* The two-week-long fair features livestock exhibitions, food booths and entertainment (see listing under *San Luis Obispo County*, Paso Robles).

CLASSIC CAR SHOW *Various locations, Atascadero. (805) 466-2044.* An evening of cruising up and down El Camino Real is followed by a dance, and next day, cars from the '30s through the '50s are displayed in Atascadero Park.

DUNE RUN-RUN *Grover Beach. (805) 489-9091.* A 5K walk, 10K run, Tour de Nipomo (a bicycle poker run), food booths and entertainment are featured in this one-day event.

MISSION SANTA INES FIESTA *Mission Santa Inés, Solvang. (805) 688-4815.* Food and game booths, a barbecue and folk dancing highlight this weekend event that raises money for mission restoration.

ANNUAL EVENTS

MOZART FESTIVAL *Most events in San Luis Obispo, with selected single concerts in Los Osos, Arroyo Grande, Paso Robles, Pismo Beach, Atascadero, Morro Bay and Cambria. (805) 781-3008.* This 10-day classical music event encompasses recitals, concerts and lectures.

OLD SPANISH DAYS FIESTA *Various locations, Santa Barbara. (805) 962-8101.* Arts and crafts displays, two parades, two marketplaces, a rodeo and free variety shows are a few of the fiesta's exciting, colorful activities. This 10-day extravaganza, enjoyed every year for over half a century, celebrates the city's Spanish and Mexican heritage.

ST. ANTHONY CELEBRATION *Portuguese Grounds in Pismo Beach. (805) 773-4382, (800) 443-7778 (in California).* Three days of festivities include dances, a parade and a sopas feast.

VENTURA COUNTY FAIR *Fairgrounds and Seaside Park, Ventura. (805) 648-3376.* Included in this 12-day seaside fair are livestock auctions, a chili cookoff, free entertainment, a carnival, rodeo and fireworks over the ocean every night.

September

BOWLFUL OF BLUES *Libbey Park, Ojai. (805) 646-7230.* In the course of one day, top-flight musicians celebrate American music in blues, zydeco and gospel.

CENTRAL COAST WINE FESTIVAL *Mission San Luis Obispo, San Luis Obispo. (805) 546-4231.* For one day, wines from over 30 Central Coast wineries are offered for tasting, accompanied by food and entertainment.

CONCOURS D'ELEGANCE *Santa Barbara City College, Santa Barbara. (805) 965-7212.* This one-day event features a winner's parade follows the exhibiting and judging of classic and vintage cars.

DANISH DAYS *Various locations, Solvang. (805) 688-3317, 688-6144.* For three dyas, parades, entertainment, dancing and special foods reflect Solvang's pride in its Danish heritage.

FALL OJAI RENAISSANCE FESTIVAL *Lake Casitas. (805) 649-2233.* For one weekend, music and plays, jousting and archery, food and crafts are set in a recreation of a Renaissance village.

GROVER BEACH ETHNIC STREET FAIR *Ramona Garden Park and other sites, Grover Beach. (805) 489-9091.* For two days, food and craft booths and performances represent the diverse ethnic make-up of the Grover Beach area.

HARVEST FESTIVAL *Various locations, Arroyo Grande. (805) 489-1488.* A two-hour parade highlights this festival, which over two days also includes giant vegetable contests, a quilt show, an agricultural tour and a carnival (see listing under *San Luis Obispo County*, Arroyo Grande).

MEXICAN FIESTA *Libbey Park, Ojai. (805) 646-5997.* Mariachi, ballet folklorico and authentic Mexican food are all part of a weekend fiesta to benefit Mexican-American scholarships.

MISSION SAN MIGUEL FIESTA AND BARBECUE *Mission San Miguel, San Miguel. (805) 467-3256.* For one day, a barbecue, games and entertainment are held on the mission grounds.

PINEDORADO *Pinedorado Grounds, Cambria. (805) 927-3624.* Labor Day weekend festivities include a barbecue and melodrama, games, booths and a parade (see listing under *San Luis Obispo County*, Cambria).

SIMI VALLEY DAYS *Southeast corner of Los Angeles Ave. and Madera Rd., Simi Valley. (805) 526-3900.* There's something for everyone during the three consecutive weekends of this Rotary Club event: barn dance, chili cook-off, horse show, parade, carnival, 5K and 10K runs and a golf tournament.

STATEWIDE WOODCARVERS SHOW *Coast Union High School, Cambria. (805) 927-4718.* For one weekend, art works in wood are featured, along with whittling contests and demonstrations of carving.

WESTERN DAYS *Various locations, Pismo Beach. (805) 773-4382; (800) 443-7778 (in California).* Western-style dancing takes place at five venues. There are also dance clinics and exhibitions, country food and a Western art exhibition during this three-day event. (Advance-purchase badges are available.)

ZOO-B-QUE *Santa Barbara Zoological Gardens, Santa Barbara. (805) 962-5339.*

This one-day event features a family barbecue and entertainment help support the zoo.

October

APPLE FESTIVAL *County Park, Templeton. (805) 434-4900.* For one day, food booths, apple tasting and live music welcome the apple-harvest season.

ARTISTS' STUDIOS TOUR *Various locations, Ojai. (805) 646-8126.* For one weekend, many of Ojai's finest painters, sculptors, print makers and potters open their private studios to visitors.

CALIFORNIA AVOCADO FESTIVAL *Along Linden Ave., Carpinteria. (805) 684-0038.* A two-day food fair honoring the avocado joins live entertainment, an art fair, athletic events and exhibits.

COLONY DAYS *Various locations, Atascadero. (805) 466-2044.* A pancake

"Ojai Mountains" are interpreted by Ojai artist Gayel Childress.

ANNUAL EVENTS

breakfast, street dancing, barbecue, parade and gymkhana are all part of this weekend celebration (see listing under *San Luis Obispo County*, Atascadero).

DAY IN THE COUNTRY *Los Olivos. (805) 688-5083.* This one-day event includes crafts, music, food and buggy rides in the country.

DIXIELAND JUBILEE BY THE SEA *Various locations, Pismo Beach. (805) 773-4382; (800) 443-7778 (in California).* Top Dixieland bands perform over three days in various Pismo Beach locations. (Advance-purchase badges are available.)

GOLETA LEMON FESTIVAL *Stow House, Goleta. (805) 967-4618.* Lemonade, pies and everything else that's lemony has a part in this one-day event that also includes arts and crafts, children's activities and entertainment.

HARBOR FESTIVAL *North end of Embarcadero, Morro Bay. (805) 772-1155.* Seafood Faire and wine tasting, harbor activities, marine-related events and exhibits, arts and crafts and live entertainment highlight the two-day festivities.

HARVEST ARTS FESTIVAL *Ryon Park, Lompoc. (805) 736-4567.* A 12x48-foot mural is painted in one day by 15 professional artists. The weekend event also features hands-on art activities, entertainment and food booths.

OCTOBER FESTIVAL *Nipomo Regional County Park, Nipomo. (805) 929-1583.* One-day festivities include live entertainment, arts and crafts, food booths and a 5K run.

PIONEER DAY *Various locations, Paso Robles. (805) 238-0506.* One-day festivities include an antique car show, roping and gymkhana exhibitions, contests, a parade and a free bean feed.

PISMO BEACH CLAM FESTIVAL *Various locations, Pismo Beach. (805) 773-4382; (800) 443-7778.* This two-day festival includes a parade, clam chowder cookoff, sand sculpture contest, food, arts and crafts (see listing under *San Luis Obispo County*, Pismo Beach).

PT. MUGU AIR SHOW *Naval Air Weapons Station, 4 miles south of Port Hueneme via Las Posas Rd. off SR 1. (805) 989-8786.* For one weekend, military and civilian pilots perform air maneuvers in a variety of aircraft—from vintage to current experimental. The Blue Angels team performs every other year. Free admission; fee for grandstand seats.

November

DIXIELAND JAZZ FESTIVAL *Various locations, Solvang. (805) 688-8000.* Top Dixieland jazz bands from around the country provide crowd-pleasing music over three days.

EAGLE CRUISES *Lake Cachuma. (805) 568-2460.* Cruises to observe the American bald eagle in its winter habitat take place on weekends during November through March (see listing under *Santa Barbara County*, Lake Cachuma).

INTERNATIONAL FILM FESTIVAL *Various locations, San Luis Obispo. (805) 543-0855.* On view are films from independent film makers, documentary and short film series, and seminars on film-making and appreciation are enjoyed over four days.

MARCHING BAND REVIEW *Judkins Junior High School, Pismo Beach. (805) 773-4382; (800) 443-7778 (in California).* For one day, more than 30 competing high school marching bands participate in a downtown parade and field exercises.

PRO-AM GOLF TOURNAMENT *Santa Barbara area golf course; not designated by press time. (805) 568-5828.* Professionals and celebrities join amateurs in this one-day event; spectators are welcome. Proceeds benefit Saint Francis Medical Center of Santa Barbara.

December

CHRISTMAS IN THE VILLAGE *Arroyo Grande Village, Arroyo Grande. (805) 489-1488.* Activities during a three-week period include street caroling, breakfast with Santa, a Christmas tree-decorating contest and concerts.

CHRISTMAS PARADES *Fillmore, Grover Beach, Paso Robles, San Luis Obispo and Santa Maria.* Parades that feature jolly ol' Santa himself swing down a main thoroughfare one day during the holiday season. Arts and crafts fairs and other delights are also offered in some communities. Lighted holiday boat parades are held in Morro Bay and Ventura. For further information check with local chambers of commerce (see listings under *Tourist Information Sources*).

HOLIDAY GAZEBO LIGHTING *County Park, Templeton. (805) 434-4909.* On an evening in early December, lights are festooned on a small town focal point to shine during the holidays.

HOLIDAY STREET FESTIVAL *Main St., downtown Ventura. (805) 654-7830.* A one-day celebration with food booths, bands, choirs and plenty of arts and crafts start off the holiday season.

OLDE FASHIONED CHRISTMAS *Los Olivos. (805) 688-5083.* For one day, entertainment, food booths and buggy rides are featured, while shops hold open house.

PARADE OF LIGHTS *Channel Islands Harbor, Oxnard. (800) 994-4852.* For one evening, illuminated, animated and decorated boats circle the harbor.

PARADE OF LIGHTS *Ventura Harbor, off Spinnaker Dr., Ventura. (805) 644-0169.* During the annual boat parade, millions of colored lights sparkle over the water for one night.

VINE STREET SHOWCASE *Various locations, Paso Robles. (805) 238-0506.* An evening walking tour of historic Victorian houses, with Christmas lights, displays and caroling. Trolley rides, hayrides and refreshments are also offered.

WILD WINTER WONDERLAND *Santa Barbara Zoological Gardens, Santa Barbara. (805) 962-5339.* For two days, children can play in machine-made snow and enjoy other wintery activities, while zoo animals frolic in the sun.

WINTERFEST *Various locations, Solvang. (805) 688-6144.* During all of December, parades, evening carriage rides, caroling, tree-lighting ceremonies and special store window displays celebrate the Christmas season.

Recreation

Thanks to the weather and terrain in the Central Coast, there is something for everyone in the way of outdoor recreation. Among the possibilities are hiking on paths that lead through city parks or up mountain trails; fishing from ocean-going vessels or from boats on lakes; golfing on relaxing, lakeside links or challenging, tree-dotted courses. Then there's bicycling, horseback riding, swimming or tennis. They're all here, and they're all available almost any time of year.

If your idea of outdoor recreation is to just relax and enjoy the view from a bench in a park or at the beach, you'll find that's also possible.

BICYCLING

The Central Coast's generally mild climate and its wide valleys and gently rolling hills make for enjoyable bicycling, whether the routes are relaxing or challenging. Many communities have marked routes, and most state highways are wide enough to accommodate cyclists, along with motor vehicles.

Following is a sampling of bike paths throughout the three counties, listed alphabetically by city; in most cases, lengths, classifications and difficulty ratings are given. Class I paths have been constructed exclusively for use by cyclists and offer the most pleasant recreational riding. Class II bikeways share an existing right-of-way with automobiles. A lane of the roadway is marked for bicycle use by a painted stripe, offering limited protection from automobile traffic. A difficulty rating

of "A" indicates that the ride is level throughout. "B" denotes a partially or moderately hilly route, not too strenuous for the average cyclist.

For bike paths within Ventura County marked with a (V), a comprehensive map of designated bike paths, with a list of local bicycle clubs, is available. Contact Ventura County Transportation Commission, 950 County Square Drive, Suite 207, Ventura, CA 93003; phone (800) 438-1112.

Goleta

ATASCADERO RECREATIONAL TRAIL *7⁷⁄₁₀ miles; Class I and II; Difficulty Rating A.* This point-to-point route offers a leisurely trip along Atascadero Creek in Goleta. The trail begins at the corner of Encore Drive and Modoc Road and follows residential streets for about ½ mile before entering the Atascadero Creek levee. It then travels southwest past stables and rural acreage, with wooden bridges crossing the creek at several points. The route officially terminates at Goleta Beach County Park, but cyclists can continue on a Class I spur

*Strolling or pedaling—Santa Barbara's Cabrillo Bikeway is **the** place.*

to the University of California at Santa Barbara campus.

GOLETA VALLEY BIKEWAY *9‰ miles; Class I; Difficulty Rating B.* This route follows Cathedral Oaks Road between San Marcos Pass Road and Alameda Avenue. The bikeway passes through both suburban and semi-rural areas, making the ride alternately lively and tranquil. A spur heading south along Turnpike Road connects the Goleta Valley Trail with the Atascadero Recreational Trail, a Class I bikeway paralleling Atascadero Creek. Additional east-west branches run along Calle Real and Hollister Avenue, and a spur runs to Goleta Beach County Park near the University of California at Santa Barbara.

Lompoc

LOMPOC VALLEY *36-mile loop; not classified; not rated.* The 36-mile loop trip between Lompoc and Buellton takes riders through scenic terrain and offers pleasant places to stop for sightseeing and recreational activities. The route begins in Lompoc at Ocean Avenue (SR 1) and H Street, goes east on Ocean to the junction with SR 1/SR 246 and then proceeds south on SR 1 for about 1½ miles to Santa Rosa Road. Cyclists then turn left on Santa Rosa and travel about 16½ miles to Buellton in the Santa Ynez Valley. The road passes over gently rolling hills, skirting a few vineyards and paralleling the Santa Ynez River much of the way. At the halfway point, Santa Rosa County Park offers picnic sites, barbecue pits, a volleyball court, horseshoe pits and a small playground for children. To return from Buellton, ride west on the wide shoulder of SR 246 through the rolling Santa Rita Valley and back into Lompoc where the highway becomes

Ocean Avenue (SR 1). SR 246 passes within a mile of La Purísima Mission State Historic Park just northeast of Lompoc.

Los Padres National Forest

While biking trails within Los Padres have not been officially rated, there are many mountain biking trails which are usually shared with hikers and equestrians. (Bicycling is not allowed in designated wilderness lands.) For information contact Los Padres National Forest, 6144 Calle Real, Goleta 93117; (805) 683-6711. A book entitled *Mountain Biking the Coast Range* is available at the national forest's Ojai District Office, 1190 East Ojai Avenue, Ojai 93023; (805) 646-4348.

Ojai

(V) **OJAI VALLEY TRAIL** *9 miles; Class I; Difficulty Rating B.* This trail, shared by hikers and equestrians, begins at Soule Park, just east of downtown Ojai on Ojai Avenue, and ends nine miles south at Foster Park, just off SR 33; there are a number of places along the trail where one can enter or exit. The trail is a wide, fenced path that offers pleasant vistas of mountains, oak groves, orchards, fields and a golf course. Trail maps are available at the Ojai Chamber of Commerce, 338 East Ojai Avenue, Ojai 92023; (805) 646-8126.

San Luis Obispo

SAN LUIS OBISPO BIKEWAY *19‰-miles; not classified; Difficulty Rating B.* This bikeway shares an existing automobile right-of-way; some of the well-marked route is striped for bicycle use only. The bikeway runs from the western city limit along Foothill Boulevard to Cal Poly, then from the campus toward the downtown area on Grand

Avenue and on to California Boulevard. The route connects with Johnson Avenue, then to Laurel Lane, Orcutt Road and Oso Street. After that it joins Johnson Avenue via Marsh Street. There are several spurs, including one along Madonna Road to Laguna Lake. Another extends south along Broad Street, west on Tank Farm Road and back to town north on Higuera Street.

Santa Barbara

CABRILLO BEACHWAY *3‰ miles; Class I; Difficulty Rating A.* This point-to-point trail runs along the north side of Cabrillo Boulevard from the Andree Clark Bird Refuge to Milpas Street. Then it follows the shoreline of the Santa Barbara Channel to a small-craft harbor just east of Leadbetter Beach. Signs are placed every quarter mile, and route maps are posted at three locations.

Santa Maria

SANTA MARIA VALLEY *13 miles; not classified; not rated.* This level valley invites cyclists of all abilities to explore the region. A flat 13-mile ride goes from the junction of SR 135 (Broadway) and SR 166 (Main Street) in Santa Maria, west on SR 166 through the town of Guadalupe to Rancho Guadalupe Dunes County Park on the Pacific Ocean. Riders can stop and surf fish or explore the sand dunes at the county park. The road from Guadalupe to the park is rough and potholed, but it carries very little traffic. More experienced cyclists might like to pedal over the Casmalia Hills on SR 1 from the Santa Maria gate at Vandenberg Air Force Base to the SR 1/SR 135 junction. This 6‰-mile ride along SR 1, a two-lane, divided highway, is very steep, but it provides some spec-tacular views of the Santa Maria Valley, and the highway is wide enough to ac-commodate both cyclists and motorists.

Santa Paula

(V) SANTA PAULA *2 miles; Class II; Difficulty Rating A.* This ride offers a good look at Santa Paula and some of its Victorian houses. Beginning at the intersection of SR 150 and Santa Paula Street, bicyclists can continue west to Peck Road, south to Telegraph Road, then turn west through the countryside. Another pleasant ride is Santa Paula Street west to Palm Avenue, then south to Santa Maria Street and east to the airport.

Simi Valley

(V) SIMI VALLEY *3½ miles; Class I; Difficulty Rating A.* A good introduction to Simi Valley is afforded by this ride through the city. Beginning at Madera Road near Easy Street, the route follows the Arroyo Simi waterway, skirts Rancho-Simi Community Park, and just east of Sycamore Drive goes north to Los Angeles Avenue or south to Hollister Street.

Thousand Oaks

(V) THOUSAND OAKS *Approximately 7 miles; Class II; Difficulty Rating B.* This ride begins at the intersection of Potrero Road and Westlake Boulevard. Westlake Boulevard leads to Kanan Road, through foothills and valleys that shelter upscale homes and country clubs. (This journey can be combined with a challenging, uphill bike ride from the coast on SR 23 that ends at the intersection of Potrero Road and Westlake Boulevard.)

Ventura Coast

(V) Ventura Harbor Area *3 miles; Class I; Difficulty Rating B.* The north-west end of this bikeway starts at the Ventura River Group Camp near the intersection of US 101 and SR 33. It continues to the Ventura County Fairgrounds and winds along the beach, past the Ventura Pier to San Buenaventura State Beach.

(V) **Ventura to Port Hueneme** *5 miles; Class II; Difficulty Rating A.* This bikeway runs from Harbor Boulevard and Olivas Park Drive, passes McGrath State Beach and Mandalay State Beach before entering seaside residential areas and ending at Channel Islands Harbor.

BICYCLE RENTALS

Lake Casitas

CYCLES 4 RENT, INC. *1131 Santa Ana Rd.,Ventura 93001. (805) 652-0462.* Rentals include bicycles, mountain bikes, three-wheelers, four-wheel surreys, bike trailers and car-carry racks. (Locks and helmets provided.) With minimum order, free delivery in Ventura and Santa Barbara.

Ojai

BICYCLES AND COLLECTABLES *108 Canada St. (805) 646-7736.* This shop rents only mountain bicycles.

BICYCLE DOCTOR AND RENTALS *212 Fox St. (805) 646-7554.* Beach cruisers only.

Pismo Beach

PISMO BIKE RENTALS *519 Cypress St. (805) 773-0355.* In addition to various kinds of bicycles, including surreys, this establishments also rents a variety of beach paraphernalia, including wet suits, and surf and boogie boards.

San Simeon

CENTRAL COAST ADVENTURES *Plaza de Cavalier (mailing address: P.O. Box 160, San Simeon 93452).* Bicycles

for rent, as well as kayaks. Guided hiking tours are also offered.

San Luis Obispo

ALAMO BICYCLE TOURING COMPANY *Mailing address: 1108 Vista del Lago, San Luis Obispo 93405. (805) 781-3830.* Bicycles for rent are delivered to various locations throughout San Luis Obispo County. This company also offers guided bike tours.

Santa Barbara

CYCLES 4 RENT, INC. *Three locations: 101 State St., (805) 966-3804; 633 E. Cabrillo Blvd in Fess Parker's Red Lion Resort, (805) 564-4333, extension 444; and 1111 E. Cabrillo Blvd. in the Radisson Hotel Santa Barbara, (805) 963-0744 (mailing address: 3875 Telegraph Rd., Ste. A-242; Ventura 93003).* Rentals include bicycles, mountain bikes, three-wheelers, rollerblades, four-wheel surreys, bike trailers and car-carry racks. (Locks and helmets provided.) With minimum order, free delivery in Ventura and Santa Barbara.

Solvang

SURREY CYCLE & BICYCLE RENTALS *475 First St. (805) 688-0091.* This establishment rents mountain bikes, beach cruisers, surrey cycles (quad bikes) and roller skates.

Thousand Oaks

MICHAEL'S BICYCLES *2253 Michael Dr. (805) 498-6633.* From Memorial Day through Labor Day Michael's rents mountain bikes, tandems, racing and BMX bikes and trailers.

NEWBURY PARK BICYCLE SHOP *1536-A Newbury Rd. (805) 498-7714.* This shop rents mountain bikes and tandems.

GOLFING

The temperate climate of the Central Coast helps to make golfing a year-round pleasure. Following is information on public, semi-private and private courses, listed by community. Each golf course listing includes name, location, mailing address, phone number and facilities, plus yardage, par and slope and USGA ratings (all from men's white tees). Unless otherwise stated, each course is open daily all year. The abbreviation N/A means the information was not available. Greens fees are given for weekday and weekend play during peak season. Many courses have senior citizen rates. Military golf courses show greens fees that apply to civilian guests of military personnel.

The listings have been made as complete as possible; a few courses, however, have been intentionally omitted at the request of the operators. All semi-private and private courses have restrictions on public play ranging from members and guests only to liberal reciprocal agreements with members of other courses. It is impossible to list all of the restrictions for each course, so please telephone the course directly if in doubt. Reservations are advised at most courses; some country clubs require reservations months in advance.

Each golf course listing gives general street directions from the nearest freeway.

Atascadero

CHALK MOUNTAIN GOLF COURSE (Public)
½ mile east of US 101 off El Camino Real, in Heilman County Park at 10000 El Bordo Ave., 93422.
(805) 466-8848.

The course is 18 holes; 5926 yards; par 72; 116 slope; 68.6 rating. Rates: $20 weekdays, $26 weekends. Golf shop, professional, power carts, rental clubs, driving range; coffee shop.

Avila Beach

AVILA BEACH GOLF RESORT (Public)
2 miles west of US 101 at Avila Beach Dr., 93444.
(805) 595-2307. Closed Dec 25.

The course is 18 holes; 6443 yards; par 71; 122 slope; 70.9 rating. Rates: $23 weekdays, $30 weekends. Clubhouse, golf shop, professional, power carts, rental clubs, driving range; restaurant, snack bar.

Buellton

ZACA CREEK GOLF COURSE (Public)
¼ mile west of US 101 via Avenue of the Flags at 223 Shadow Mountain Dr., 93427.
(805) 688-2575.

The course is 9 holes; 1544 yards; par 29; N/A slope; N/A rating. Rates: $6 weekdays, $7 weekends. Clubhouse, golf shop, professional, hand carts, rental clubs, driving range; tennis; coffee shop, snack bar.

Camarillo

CAMARILLO SPRINGS GOLF COURSE (Public)
South of US 101 at 791 Camarillo Springs Rd., 93012.
(805) 484-1075.

The course is 18 holes; 6375 yards; par 72; 115 slope; 70.2 rating. Rates (mandatory golf cart included): $22 weekdays, $50 weekends. Clubhouse, golf shop, professional, power carts, rental clubs, driving range (night lighting); restaurant, coffee shop, snack bar.

You may be way over par, but so is the scenery at Elkins Ranch Golf Course.

LAS POSAS COUNTRY CLUB (Private)
3 miles north of US 101 via Las Posas Rd., Crestview Ave. and Valley Vista Dr. at 955 Fairway Dr., 93010.
(805) 482-4518. Closed Jan. 1 and Dec. 25.

The course is 18 holes; 6211 yards; par 71; 124 slope; 70.1 rating. Rate N/A. Clubhouse, locker room, golf shop, professional, power carts, driving range; tennis, swimming; restaurant, coffee shop, snack bar.

SPANISH HILLS GOLF AND COUN-TRY CLUB (Private)
North of US 101 off Las Posas Rd. at 999 Crestview Ave., 93010.
(805) 388-5000. Closed Mon. and Dec. 25.

The course is 18 holes; 6749 yards; par 71; 140 slope; 73.4 rating. Rate: $75 daily. Clubhouse, locker room, golf shop, professional, power carts, rental clubs, driving range; tennis, swimming; restaurant, coffee shop.

Fillmore

ELKINS RANCH GOLF COURSE (Public)
East of SR 23, ½ mile south of Guiberson Rd. at 1386 Chambersburg Rd., 93016.
(805) 524-1121, (805) 524-1440. Closed Dec. 25.

The course is 18 holes; 6304 yards; par 71; 117 slope; 69.9 rating. Rates: $22 weekdays, $27 weekends. Golf shop, professional, power carts, rental clubs, driving range; snack bar.

Frazier Park

PINE MOUNTAIN CLUB GOLF COURSE (Private)
18 miles west of I-5 via Frazier Mountain and Cuddy Valley rds. at 2524 Beechwood Wy., 93222.
(805) 242-3788.

The course is 9 holes; 1791 yards; par 30; N/A slope; N/A rating. Clubhouse, golf shop, professional, power carts, rental clubs, driving range; tennis, swimming; restaurant.

Goleta

OCEAN MEADOWS GOLF CLUB
(Public)
*½ mile south of US 101 off Storke Rd. at
6925 Whittier Dr., 93117.*
(805) 968-6814.

The course is 9 holes; 3514 yards; par
36; 108 slope (two tees); 68.4 rating
(two tees). Rates: $12 weekdays, $14
weekends. Clubhouse, golf shop, professional, power carts, rental clubs, driving
range; restaurant, coffee shop, snack bar.

SANDPIPER GOLF COURSE (Public)
*South of US 101 off Winchester Canyon
Rd. at 7925 Hollister Ave., 93117.*
(805) 968-1541.

The course is 18 holes; 7068 yards; par
72; 134 slope; 74.5 rating. Rates: $55
weekdays, $75 weekends. Clubhouse,
golf shop, professional, power carts,
rental clubs, driving range; restaurant,
coffee shop, snack bar.

TWIN LAKES GOLF COURSE (Public)
*¼ mile south of US 101 off Fairview Ave.
at 6034 Hollister Ave., 93117.*
(805) 964-1414.

The course is 9 holes; 1504 yards; par
29; 73 slope (two tees); 53.6 rating
(two sets tees). Rates: $7 weekdays,
$8 weekends. Golf shop, professional,
hand carts, rental clubs, driving range
(night lighting).

Grover Beach

PISMO STATE BEACH GOLF COURSE
(Public)
*West of SR 1 off Le Sage Dr. at 25 Grand
Ave., 93433.*
(805) 481-5215.

The course is 18 holes; 1465 yards; par
27; N/A slope; N/A rating. Rates: $6.50
weekdays, $7.25 weekends. Clubhouse,
locker room, golf shop, professional,
rental clubs; restaurant.

Lompoc

LA PURISIMA GOLF COURSE (Public)
*12 miles west of US 101 at 3455 E. Hwy.
246, 93436.*
(805) 735-8395.

The course is 18 holes; 6657 yards; par
72; 133 slope; 72.5 rating. Rates: $25
weekdays, $35 weekends. Golf shop,
professional, power carts, rental clubs,
driving range; restaurant, coffee shop,
snack bar.

VILLAGE COUNTRY CLUB (Private)
*2 miles northwest of SR 1 via
Constellation Rd. and Burton Mesa Blvd.
at 4300 Clubhouse Rd., 93436.*
*(805) 933-3535. Closed Jan. 1 and
Dec. 25.*

The course is 18 holes; 6564 yards; par
72; 126 slope; 71.5 rating. Rates: $40
weekdays, $50 weekends and holidays.
Clubhouse, locker room, golf shop,
professional, power carts, rental clubs,
driving range; tennis, swimming;
restaurant, snack bar.

Los Osos

SEA PINES GOLF RESORT (Public)
*12 miles west of US 101 via Los Osos
Valley Rd. and Pecho Rd. at 250 Howard
Ave., 93402.*
(805) 528-1788.

The course is 9 holes; 1475 yards;
par 28; N/A slope; N/A rating. Rates:
$7.50 weekdays, $8.50 weekends.
Clubhouse, locker room, golf shop,
professional, power carts, rental clubs,
driving range, night lighting for
course and driving range; restaurant,
coffee shop, snack bar.

Morro Bay

MORRO BAY GOLF COURSE (Public)
*2 miles south of SR 1 in Morro Bay State
Park at 101 State Park Rd., 93442.*
(805) 772-4560.

The course is 18 holes; 6100 yards; par 71; 118 slope; 69.3 rating. Rates: $20 weekdays, $25 weekends. Clubhouse, locker room, golf shop, professional, power carts, rental clubs, driving range, night lighting for course and driving range; snack bar.

Nipomo

BLACK LAKE GOLF RESORT (Public)
3½ miles west of US 101 off Teft St. at 1490 Golf Course Ln., 93444.
(805) 343-1214.

The course is 18 holes; 6412 yards; par 72; 120 slope; 70.3 rating. Rates: $28 weekdays, $43 weekends; mandatory golf cart $18 for one person, $24 for two or more persons. Clubhouse, golf shop, professional, power carts, rental clubs, driving range; swimming; restaurant, coffee shop, snack bar.

Ojai

OJAI VALLEY INN & COUNTRY CLUB (Semi-Private)
1 mile west of SR 33 at 905 Country Club Dr., 93023.
(805) 646-2420.

The course is 18 holes; 6252 yards; par 70; 123 slope; 70.6 rating. Rate: $86 daily. Clubhouse, locker room, golf shop, professional, power carts, rental clubs, driving range; tennis, swimming; restaurant, coffee shop, snack bar.

SOULE PARK GOLF COURSE (Public)
6 miles east of SR 33 off SR 150 at 1033 East Ojai Ave., 93024.
(805) 646-5633. Closed Dec. 25.

The course is 18 holes; 6390 yards; par 72; 107 slope; 69.1 rating. Rates: $18 weekdays, $23 weekends. Clubhouse, locker room, golf shop, professional, power carts, rental clubs, driving range; restaurant, snack bar.

Oxnard

RIVER RIDGE GOLF CLUB (Public)
2 miles west of US 101 Vineyard Ave., Gonzales and Ventura rds. at 2401 W. Vineyard Ave., 93030.
(805) 983-4653. Closed Dec. 25.

The course is 18 holes; 6543 yards; par 72; 118 slope; 70.7 rating. Rates: $18 weekdays, $23 weekends. Clubhouse, golf shop, professional, power carts, rental clubs, driving range (night lighting); snack bar.

Paso Robles

HUNTER RANCH GOLF COURSE (Public)
2½ miles east of US 101 4041 Hwy 46 East, 93446.
(805) 237-7444.

The course is 18 holes; 6741 yards; par 72; 128 slope; 72.2 rating. Rates: $25 weekdays, $35 weekends. Clubhouse, golf shop, professional, power carts, rental clubs, driving range; restaurant, snack bar.

PASO ROBLES GOLF AND COUNTRY CLUB (Semi-Private)
2 miles west of US 101 off Niblick Rd. at 1600 Country Club Dr., 93446. (805) 238-4710. Closed Dec. 25.

The course is 18 holes; 6015 yards; par 71; 119 slope; 69.3 rating. Rate: $20 daily for public play after 11 am. Clubhouse, golf shop, power carts, rental clubs, driving range; tennis, swimming; restaurant, coffee shop.

Point Mugu

POINT MUGU GOLF COURSE (Semi-Private)
West of SR 1 off Wood Rd. at Naval Air Weapons Station Bldg. 153.
(805) 989-7109. Closed Dec. 25.

The course is 9 holes; 3000 yards; par 35; 100 slope (two tees); 66.8 rating (two tees). Rates: $9 weekdays, $12 weekends. Locker room, golf shop, professional, power carts, rental clubs, driving range (night lighting); snack bar.

Port Hueneme

SEABEE GOLF CLUB OF PORT HUENEME (Semi-Private)
5 miles south of US 101 off Ventura Rd. at Special Services, Code 19, NCBC, 93043.
(805) 982-2620. Closed Dec. 25.

The course is 18 holes; 5945 yards; par 71; 107 slope; 67.4 rating. Rates (mandatory golf cart included): $28 weekdays, $31 weekends. Clubhouse, golf shop, professional, power carts, rental clubs, driving range; snack bar.

San Luis Obispo

LAGUNA LAKE GOLF COURSE (Public)
2 miles northwest of US 101 at 11175 Los Osos Valley Rd., 93405.
(805) 781-7309. Closed Dec. 25.

The course is 9 holes; 1306 yards; par 31; N/A slope; N/A rating. Rates: $6 weekdays, $6.75 weekends. Clubhouse, golf shop, professional, hand carts, rental clubs, driving range; coffee shop.

SAN LUIS OBISPO GOLF AND COUNTRY CLUB (Private)
7 miles north of US 101 off SR 227 at 255 Country Club Dr., 93401.
(805) 543-4035. Closed Mon. and Dec. 25.

The course is 18 holes; 6390 yards; par 72; 124 slope; 70.8 rating. Guest rate: $35 daily. Clubhouse, locker room, golf shop, professional, power carts, rental clubs, driving range; tennis, swimming; restaurant, coffee shop, snack bar.

Santa Barbara

BIRNAM WOOD GOLF CLUB (Private)
½ mile north of US 101 off Sheffield Dr. at 2031 Packing House Rd., 93108.
(805) 969-0919. Closed Dec. 25.

The course is 18 holes; 5990 yards; par 70; 121 slope; 68.7 rating. Rate (mandatory golf cart included): $95 daily. Clubhouse, locker room, golf shop, professional, power carts, rental clubs, driving range; tennis.

HIDDEN OAKS COUNTRY CLUB (Public)
1½ miles south of US 101 off Turnpike Rd., Hollister Ave. and Puente Dr. at 4760-G Calle Camarada, 93110.
(805) 967-3493.

The course is 9 holes; 1118 yards; par 27; N/A slope; N/A rating. 18-hole rates: $12 weekdays, $14 weekends. Clubhouse, golf shop, professional, hand carts, rental clubs; tennis, swimming; coffee shop, snack bar.

LA CUMBRE GOLF AND COUNTRY CLUB (Private)
¼ mile south of US 101 off Las Palmas Dr. at 4015 Via Laguna, 93110.
(805) 682-3131. Closed Dec. 25.

The course is 18 holes; 6352 yards; par 71; 128 slope; 70.8 rating. Guest rate (mandatory golf cart included): $128 daily. Clubhouse, locker room, golf shop, professional, power carts, rental clubs, driving range; tennis, swimming; restaurant, snack bar.

MONTECITO COUNTRY CLUB (Private)
Declined to be listed.

SANTA BARBARA GOLF CLUB (Public)
1 mile north of US 101 off Las Positas Rd. at 3500 McCaw Ave., 93105.
(805) 687-7087. Closed Dec. 25.

The course is 18 holes; 6014 yards; par 70; 103 slope; 67.2 rating. Rates: $18 weekdays, $20 weekends. Clubhouse, golf shop, professional, power carts, rental clubs, driving range; restaurant, snack bar.

VALLEY CLUB OF MONTECITO
(Private)
1 mile north of US 101 off Sheffield Dr. at 1901 E. Valley Club Rd., 93150.
(805) 969-2215.

The course is 18 holes; 6603 yards; par 72; 133 slope; 72.1 rating. Rate (mandatory golf cart included): $100 daily. Clubhouse, locker room, golf shop, professional, power carts, driving range; tennis.

Santa Maria

RANCHO MARIA GOLF CLUB (Public)
5 miles west of US 101 off Clark Rd. at 1950 Casmalia Rd., 93455.
(805) 937-2019. Closed Dec. 25.

The course is 18 holes; 6390 yards; par 72; 119 slope; 70.2 rating. Rates: $20 weekdays, $25. Clubhouse, golf shop, professional, power carts, rental clubs, driving range; coffee shop.

SANTA MARIA COUNTRY CLUB
(Private)
1½ miles west of US 101 off Santa Maria Way at 505 W. Waller Ln., 93455.
(805) 937-2027. Closed Mon., Jan. 1, Thanksgiving and Dec. 25.

The course is 18 holes; 6495 yards; par 72; 129 slope; 71.8 rating. Rate: $75 daily. Clubhouse, locker room, golf shop, professional, power carts, driving range; tennis, swimming; restaurant, snack bar.

SUNSET RIDGE GOLF COURSE
(Public)
1½ miles southwest of US 101 via Betteravia Rd. and Skyway Dr. at 1425 Fairway Ave., 93455.
(805) 347-1070.

The course is 9 holes; 1500 yards (executive golf course); par 29; N/A slope; N/A rating. Rates: $8 weekdays; $10 weekends. Golf shop, professional, power carts, driving range (night lighting); restaurant, coffee shop, snack bar, bar.

Santa Paula

MOUNTAIN VIEW GOLF COURSE
(Semi-private)
½ mile south of SR 126 at 16799 S. Mountain Rd., 93060.
(805) 525-1571.

The course is 18 holes; 260 yards; par 69; 112 slope; 65.0 rating. Rates: $12 weekdays, $18 weekends. Clubhouse, golf shop, professional, power carts, rental clubs; snack bar.

Saticoy

SATICOY COUNTRY CLUB (Private)
3 miles north of US 101 via Santa Clara Ave. and Los Angeles Ave. at 4540 N. Clubhouse Dr., 93066.
(805) 485-5216.

The course is 18 holes; 6407 yards; par 72; 128 slope; 71.0 rating. Rate: $80 daily. Clubhouse, locker room, golf shop, professional, power carts, driving range; swimming; restaurant, snack bar.

SATICOY REGIONAL GOLF COURSE
(Public)
South of SR 126 at 1025 S. Wells Rd., 93004.
(805) 647-6678.

The course is 9 holes; 2781 yards; par 34; 116 slope (two tees); 69.1 rating (two tees). Rates: $9-14.50 weekdays, $11-16.50 weekends. Golf shop, professional, power carts, rental clubs, driving range (night lighting); snack bar.

Simi Valley

SIMI HILLS GOLF COURSE (Public)
¼ mile north of SR 118 off Stearns St. at 5031 Alamo St., 93063.
(805) 522-0803.

The course is 18 holes; 6509 yards; par 71; 115 slope; 70.2 rating. Rates: $18 weekdays, $25 weekends. Clubhouse, golf shop, professional, power carts, rental clubs, driving range (night lighting); restaurant, coffee shop, snack bar.

SINALOA GOLF COURSE (Public)
2 miles south of SR 118 at 980 Madera Rd., 93065.
(805) 581-2662.

The course is 9 holes; 903 yards; par 27; N/A slope; N/A rating. Rates: $5 weekdays, $6 weekends. Clubhouse, golf shop, hand carts, rental clubs, driving range; snack bar.

WOOD RANCH GOLF CLUB (Private)
2½ miles east of SR 23 off Olsen Rd. at 301 Wood Ranch Pkwy., 93065.
(805) 527-9663. Closed Mon.

The course is 18 holes; 6972 yards; par 72; 151 slope; 75.8 rating. Rates: $50 weekdays, $75 weekends. Clubhouse, locker room, golf shop, professional, power carts, driving range, night lighting for course and driving range; restaurant, snack bar.

Solvang

THE ALISAL RANCH COURSE (Private)
1 mile south of SR 246 at 1054 Alisal Rd., 93463. (805) 688-4215.

The course is 18 holes; 6396 yards; par 72; 121 slope; 70.7 rating. Rates: $70 daily. Clubhouse, locker room, golf shop, professional, power carts ($24), rental clubs, driving range; coffee shop.

THE ALISAL RIVER COURSE (Public)
½ mile south of SR 246 at 150 Alisal Rd., 93463.
(805) 688-6042. Closed Dec. 25.

The course is 18 holes; 6830 yards; par 72; 126 slope; 73.1 rating. Rates: $35 weekdays, $45 weekends. Clubhouse, golf shop, professional, power carts, rental clubs, driving range; restaurant, coffee shop, snack bar.

Thousand Oaks

LOS ROBLES GOLF COURSE (Public)
South of US 101 at 299 S Moorpark Rd., 91361.
(805) 495-6421.

The course is 18 holes; 6274 yards; par 70; 118 slope; 69.4 rating. Rates: $15 weekdays, $20 weekends. Golf shop, professional, power carts, rental clubs, driving range; snack bar.

SUNSET HILLS COUNTRY CLUB (Private)
4 miles north of US 101 via SR 23 and Olsen Rd. at 4155 Erbes Rd. North, 91360.
(805) 495-5407. Closed Jan. 1 and Dec. 25.

The course is 18 holes; 6066 yards; par 71; 110 slope; 68.6 rating. Rates (mandatory golf cart included): $45 weekdays, $60 weekends. Clubhouse, locker room, golf shop, professional, power carts, rental clubs, driving range; tennis, swimming; restaurant, coffee shop, snack bar.

Vandenberg Air Force Base

MARSHALLIA RANCH GOLF COURSE (Semi-Private)
4 miles north of main gate off Lompoc Casmalia Rd.,Vandenberg AFB, 93437.
(805) 734-4764. Closed Mon., Jan. 1 and Dec. 25.

The course is 18 holes; 6845 yards; par 72; 130 slope; 74.1 rating. Rates: $40 weekdays, $50 weekends. Clubhouse, locker room, golf shop, professional, power carts, rental clubs, driving range; snack bar.

Ventura

BUENAVENTURA GOLF COURSE (Public)
1 mile south of US 101 off Victoria Ave. at 5882 Olivas Park Dr., 93002.
(805) 642-2231. Closed Dec. 25.

The course is 18 holes; 6146 yards; par 72; 126 slope; 69.7 rating. Rates: $16 weekdays, $20 weekends. Clubhouse, locker room, golf shop, professional, power carts, rental clubs; restaurant, coffee shop, snack bar.

OLIVAS PARK GOLF COURSE (Public) *1½ miles west of US 101 off Victoria Ave. at 3750 Olivas Park Dr., 93003. (805) 642-4303, (805) 485-5712.*

The course is 18 holes; 6353 yards; par 72; 115 slope; 69.5 rating. Rates: $17 weekdays, $22 weekends. Golf shop, professional, power carts, rental clubs, driving range (night lighting); restaurant, snack bar.

HIKING

Central Coast foothills, beaches, canyons and park trails are inviting areas for hikers, and the trails listed here are among those that afford moderate to challenging hikes.

For those interested in more extensive hiking and backpacking, contact Los Padres National Forest headquarters at 6144 Calle Real, Goleta 93117, (805) 683-6711; Santa Barbara Ranger District, Star Route, Santa Barbara 93105, (805) 967-3481; or Santa Maria Ranger District, 1616 North Carlotti Drive, Santa Maria 93454, (805) 925-9538. Fire permits are issued on an annual basis and are required for backcountry camping during fire season.

Lopez Lake

Trails in the Lopez Lake area are generally short and fairly easy, offering picturesque views of the lake and surrounding countryside. For additional information and a trail map contact the ranger office at (805) 489-1122.

BLACKBERRY SPRING TRAIL features plants used by the Chumash (pick up a self-guiding brochure at upper Squirrel Campground). This $9/10$-mile trail involves a moderate walk and a 260-foot climb and lasts about an hour.

DUNA VISTA TRAIL is reached via Two Waters Trail (see listing). A 200-foot climb leads to a high point on the peninsula, which affords good views of Pismo Dunes, the Santa Lucia Wilderness and three arms of Lopez Lake. The ½-mile trail and boat trip to the trailhead take about three hours.

HIGH RIDGE TRAIL, a 1½-mile hike from the end of Blackberry Spring Trail (see listing) to a firebreak on the park's east ridge, offers impressive views. During hot weather, the steep trail should be traveled early or late in the day. The round-trip hike lasts two to three hours.

MARINA TRAIL climbs over the 160-foot divide separating the park gate and the marina. The $9/10$-mile, easy hike features benches to enjoy views of the lake and hills. It takes only 10 to 15 minutes to traverse.

QUAIL TRAIL is ideal for winter hikes. This easy, 30- to 40-minute, $9/10$-mile walk starts at the covered bridge in Quail Campground and leads to a quiet rest area. During or just after heavy winter rains, small waterfalls spill onto the trail.

ROCKY POINT TRAIL provides access to a scenic peninsula and a popular fishing hole. The $9/10$-mile trail originates from the park road between the gate and marina.

TUOUSKI TRAIL follows lakeside bluffs on the north shore of the Wittenberg Arm of the lake. It's especially inviting in spring, when colorful wildflowers are usually profuse.

Hiking trails around Lake Lopez include scenes like this.

TURKEY RIDGE TRAIL connects with Blackberry Springs Trail (see listing) to form a loop trail. This strenuous trail, where encounters with wild turkeys are likely, leads to good views of the lake and Santa Lucia Mountains. The trailhead is located at the registration parking area, making it the most accessible of the park trails.

TWO WATERS TRAIL connects the Wittenberg and Lopez arms of Lopez Lake via a saddle 400 feet above the lake. The 1³⁄₁₀-mile, well-graded pathway, partly in oak forest, provides many scenic overviews. The trail head can be reached by way of the Tuouski Trail (see listing) or by boat at Millers Cove; total hike is about two hours.

WITTENBERG TRAIL offers a pleasant, level one-mile walk along the shore of upper Wittenberg Arm. The walk, appropriate for children and elderly persons, features good views of the lake and early-morning bird watching. This

trail offers access to the High Ridge Trail or the Tuouski Trail (see listings).

Los Padres National Forest

Following is a sampling of moderate to challenging hikes within the national forest. For a free brochure describing these and other trail lengths and difficulties, as well as backpacking opportunities, contact Los Padres National Forest, 6144 Calle Real, Goleta 93117, (805) 683-6711; or the national forest's Ojai District Office,1190 East Ojai Avenue, Ojai 93023, (805) 646-4348.

ALISO CANYON SELF-GUIDED NATURE TRAIL begins about five miles east of Paradise Road and SR 154 junction behind Sage Hill Group Camp. The trail is a three-mile, self-guided loop, with a moderately steep grade. Developed by 11- to 14-year-old students, the trail offers beautiful views and is a good introduction to local natural history.

COLD SPRINGS TRAIL begins about ½ mile east of Cold Springs Road and Mountain Drive junction. The trail runs 4½ miles to East Camino Cielo. The grade is moderate to steep, with a starting elevation of 750 feet and an elevation gain of 2650 feet. At the lower level the trail borders a creek that is filled most of the year and has lovely pools.

COZY DELL TRAIL begins about 4 miles north of Ojai east off SR 33 behind Friends Ranch Packing House. This is an easy to moderate 1⁹⁄₁₀-mile hike that ties into Foothill Trail and Cozy Dell Road. From this junction, a loop follows the Foothill Trail and continues along the road from Stewart Canyon. This is a scenic hike that includes large, shady oak trees.

DAVY BROWN TRAIL begins off Figueroa Mountain Road near the Figueroa Campground. The steep trail follows a creek the length of Fir Canyon, passing an old mine shaft and remnants of a miner's cabin. Hikers are advised to start at Figueroa Mountain Road and walk downhill to Davy Brown Campground. The trail winds through large stands of big-cone fir, pine and sycamore, so it is well shaded even in summer. Davy Brown Trail connects with Munch Canyon Trail (see listing).

GENE MARSHALL-PIEDRA BLANCA NATIONAL RECREATION TRAIL begins on the left-hand trail across the stream bed at Lion Campground (see *Campgrounds & Trailer Parks*). Turn right at the junction after ½ mile. Hiking another 2⁷⁄₁₀ miles brings you through the impressive white rocks and to Piedra Blanca Campground. Twin Fork Campground is ½ mile farther, with water most of the year. At the end of a steep, additional three-mile climb is Pine Mountain Lodge Campground, nestled in conifers. From here the Piedra Blanca Trail continues northwest to Haddock and Reyes Creek campgrounds. An eastbound trail from Pine Mountain Lodge leads to Fishbowls or Cedar Creek campgrounds in the Mt. Pinos Ranger District.

HOWARD CREEK TRAIL begins off Rose Valley Road, about ½ mile east of SR 33; the trail is on the right, going south. This is a moderately difficult three-mile hike to Nordhoff Ridge where, on a clear day, there are good views of the coastline and the Ojai Valley.

JESUSITA TRAIL begins just north of Cater Water Filtration Plant on San Roque Road, north of Foothill Road. The trail runs three miles to Inspiration Point and another mile to intersect with Tunnel Trail. The grade is moderate, with a starting elevation of 400 feet and an elevation gain of 642 feet. At lower levels are large, old trees; upper levels present views of the city and Channel Islands.

LITTLE PINE MOUNTAIN TRAIL begins at Upper Oso Campground, 22 miles northwest of Santa Barbara off SR 154 (see *Campgrounds & Trailer Parks*). The five-mile trail gains 3260 feet of elevation from its start on a dirt road at the northeast end of Upper Oso Campground to its summit next to an unusually large pine tree. Follow the dirt road for ⁷⁄₁₀ mile until it turns right. At the turn, continue straight to a sign reading "Santa Cruz Trail." From the sign, parallel Oso Creek for one mile through a canyon to the junction with a side trail to Nineteen Oaks Camp. Keep to the left, cross the stream and take switchbacks up a brush-covered slope. At ⁹⁄₁₀ mile farther, the trail comes to a grassy meadow and follows a rocky overhanging wall. After curving into a side canyon, the trail switchbacks up to another section of the brush-covered slope. At 3⁷⁄₁₀ miles, the route intersects a path leading up to a spring. Continuing past the spring, the trail climbs through a large grassy area, then levels off to reach a junction and several trail signs. Turn right at the signs. Several hundred yards farther, the trail joins an old roadbed. Turn right upon reaching a wire fence, follow a small path to a meadow of deep grass and head straight across the area to the large pine tree.

MCKINLEY TRAIL begins at Cachuma Saddle, junction of Figueroa Mountain Road and Happy Canyon Road. This trail follows an administrative road 10 miles past Cachuma Peak to a saddle west of McKinley Mountain, tracing the southern edge of the San Rafael Wilderness. The route offers good views of the Manzana drainage and Hurricane Deck to the north, and the Santa Ynez drainage to the south. Hikers should carry water because the only reliable source is at McKinley Spring trail camp, nine miles from Cachuma Saddle.

MCPHERSON PEAK TRAIL begins at Aliso campground, eight miles southwest of New Cuyama off SR 166 via Aliso Canyon Road. The six-mile trail goes to the summit of McPherson Peak and involves an elevation gain of 3000 feet. Hikers should carry their own water because the only source, at Hog Pen Spring Campground, is undependable and sometimes impure. The route begins at the southwest edge of Aliso Campground and follows an old jeep road up a canyon for 2⁷⁄₁₀ miles to Hog Pen Spring. Here a small tank may contain the only water on the mountain. Just beyond a boundary fence, a trail leads left (south) and begins climbing chaparral-covered slopes. After the second switchback, the trail forks; the left branch is the best route up the mountain. At 4⁷⁄₁₀ miles, the trail meets a fire road. Turn right and continue past a locked metal gate and some corrals. From this point, there are two options: continue northwest on the fire road for 1½ miles to a junction with a spur road, which leads to the right for ⁹⁄₁₀ mile to the summit; or, climb directly up the ridge line from the corrals on a rutted old road past an abandoned campground for 1⁷⁄₁₀ miles to the top.

MUNCH CANYON TRAIL begins off Sunset Valley Road just east of Davy Brown Campground. Evidence of old mine excavations can be seen along this four-mile trail that was constructed as a mining access road. The trail connects with the Sunset Valley and Davy Brown trails.

PIÑO ALTO SELF-GUIDED NATURE TRAIL begins two miles off Figueroa Mountain Road at the Piño Alto picnic area. This easy, ½-mile trail forms a loop requiring 30 to 45 minutes to walk. A trail guide providing information about observation points along the way is available at the picnic area. The trail and picnic area are accessible for handicapped people.

POTRERO JOHN TRAIL begins about 7½ miles north of Wheeler Springs, east off SR 33. This easy 1⁹⁄₁₀-mile hike follows a canyon bottom and has running water most of the year. It ends at Potrero John Campground, but can be explored beyond that.

RATTLESNAKE TRAIL begins at the bridge on Las Canoas Road, just north of Skofield Park. The trail runs two miles to Tin Can Junction, then branches west to meet Tunnel Trail and east to Gibraltar Road; either fork is approximately ¾ mile long. The grade is moderate, with a starting elevation of 900 feet and an elevation gain of 1550 feet. During the spring a variety of wildflowers bloom along this trail. Note: It is advisable to carry drinking water.

SULPHUR SPRINGS TRAIL begins at Cedros Saddle about 5½ miles north of Figueroa Mountain Road near Sulphur Spring. The two-mile trail to the south goes to Zaca Lake. The steep four-mile trail to the north travels from Cedros Saddle to Manzana Creek in the San Rafael Wilderness. The route drops 2100 feet as it passes through oak woodlands and areas of pine. A spring is located halfway between Cedros Saddle and Manzana Creek.

SUNSET VALLEY TRAIL parallels Sunset Valley Road from Sunset Valley southeast to Fish Creek Divide. The short, two-mile trail meanders through oak and pine trees and chaparral. The trail begins off the Munch Canyon Trail just south of Sunset Valley Road.

TUNNEL TRAIL begins at the locked gate at the north end of Tunnel Road. The trail runs five miles to East Camino Cielo; 1¹⁄₁₀ miles west on Camino Cielo is La Cumbre Peak Lookout. The grade is moderate to steep with a starting elevation of 900 feet and an elevation gain of 3000 feet. La Cumbre Peak, at an elevation of 3981 feet, is the highest point in the area immediately behind Santa Barbara. Note: Hikers should carry water and prepare for full sun since there is almost no shade along the trail.

ZACA PEAK TRAIL begins off Zaca Ridge Road about 4½ miles north of Figueroa Mountain Road. The trail follows a ridge west for two miles

from Zaca Ridge Road, with the west end of the trail dropping down to Zaca Lake. Good views of the Santa Ynez Valley and Zaca Lake basin are found along this route.

Ojai

Ojai Valley Trail begins at Soule Park in Ojai. The nine-mile trail stretches south from Soule Park to Foster Park, with pathways for walkers, bicyclists and horseback riders. The trail is open from dawn to dusk.

Pismo Dunes Preserve

This preserve, accessible from the west end of either SR 166 or Oso Flaco Lake Road, is off-limits to vehicular traffic. A hike among the sand dunes offers views of wildflowers, unusual plant life and wild animals. Early-morning hikers can occasionally spot coyote, fox and deer. Birds of all kinds abound. The dunes display coreopsis, sand verbena, mock heather and white-fringed asters at different seasons. There are no paths in the dunes, and hikers must be careful not to damage the fragile vegetation.

Thousand Oaks

Los Robles Trail System begins at 482 Greenmeadow Drive near the Oak Creek Canyon Whole Access Interpretive Trail (see listing). Five trails that vary in difficulty from easy to moderate to strenuous have their trailhead here. Distances covered range from ⅓ mile to 4½ miles.

WILDWOOD REGIONAL PARK Parking area at Avenida Los Arboles and Big Sky Drive (see Thousand Oaks listing under Simi and Conejo Valleys, *Ventura County*). An extensive trail system runs through the park, with varying distances and degrees of difficulty.

A hike through the Pismo Dunes Preserve leads past Oso Flaco Lake.

HORSEBACK RIDING

There are good trails for horseback riding in various parts of the Central Coast, but a relatively small number of stables that rent horses. Many of the hiking trails in Los Padres National Forest, particularly in the Mt. Pinos Ranger District, are also suitable for horses; contact Los Padres National Forest, 6144 Calle Real, Goleta 93117; (805) 683-6711 for information.

Avila Beach

ROCKING D RIDING STABLES *555 Avila Beach Dr., 93424. (805) 595-7407.* Horses can be rented to ride in the Avila Beach and nearby areas.

Goleta

CIRCLE BAR B RANCH STABLES *3½ miles north of US 101 at 1800 Refugio Rd., 93117. (805) 968-3901.* Guides lead riders along mountain and canyon trails.

Montecito

SAN YSIDRO STABLES *900 San Ysidro Ln., 93108. (805) 969-5046.* Escorts take riders on trails through the mountains.

Oceano

THE LIVERY STABLE *1207 Silver Spur Pl., 93445. (805) 489-8100.* Horses can be rented for riding on Pismo State Beach.

Ojai

In the Ojai Valley, equestrians are welcome on the Ojai Valley Trail. (See Hiking, this chapter.)

OJAI VALLEY INN & COUNTRY CLUB *Country Club Rd., 93023. (805) 646-5511, ext. 456.* Trail rides are offered from a nearby working ranch. Reservations are required within at least 48 hours of the day you wish to ride; call number shown above.

Paso Robles

FULL SAIL FARM *6 miles east of Paso Robles at 5715 Linne Rd. (805) 238-2802.* Full Sail Farm **does not rent horses**, rather it has overnight stabling facilities for people traveling with their horses. Owners can provide their own feed or buy it at the farm. Blanketing and feed are provided; exercise facilities may be reserved. The nightly fee is $10, plus a $5 cleaning deposit. Self-contained motorhomes or campers can stay overnight at the farm at no additional charge.

HIGHCOUNTRY HORSEBACK ADVENTURES *2 miles east of Paso Robles at 7055 Adelaida Rd, 93446. (805) 238-5483.* Reservations at least 24 hours in advance are required for rental horses and trail rides over scenic terrain, ranging from two hours to overnight trips.

San Miguel

CHOLAME CREEK RANCH *18 miles east of San Miguel off SR 46 (mailing address: RFD Box 3653, San Miguel 93451). (805) 463-2320.* This working ranch has experienced wranglers to escort trail rides, moonlight rides and cattle round-ups; there are gentle horses for beginners. Call for reservations. Bed and breakfast accommodations are available.

HUNTING

Within Los Padres National Forest and certain other areas of the Central Coast, a variety of game can be hunted **in season**. A hunting license is required for anyone age 16 and over. For specific information regarding seasons, regulations, limits and fees contact the California Department of Fish and Game at (310) 590-5126.

Among the animals which can be legally hunted are bear, bobcat, deer, fox, wild pig and quail.

PICNICKING

The parks listed are usually within ½ mile of a highway or major city street or are picnic areas within a designated county or state recreation area. Each of these parks offers picnic tables, drinking fountains and public rest rooms. Other amenities are noted. No fees are charged.

Arroyo Grande

BIDDLE COUNTY PARK *6 miles northeast of Arroyo Grande on Lopez Dr.* Barbecues.

STROTHER PARK *Huasna Rd. and Bearwood Ave.* Barbecues

Atascadero

ATASCADERO PARK *SR 41 and Portola Rd.* Barbecues, boat rentals, fishing, zoo, playgrounds.

HEILMANN COUNTY PARK *Off El Camino Real on El Bordo Ave.* Barbecues, tennis courts.

Camarillo

CAMARILLO GROVE COUNTY PARK *2 miles east of Camarillo, off US 101.* Barbecues, playground, equestrian trails, horseshoe pits, softball field.

COMMUNITY CENTER PARK *Carmen Dr. and Burnley St.* Barbecues, horseshoe pits, playground, bocci ball lane, volleyball court.

CRESTVIEW PARK *Earl Joseph Dr. and Bradford Ave.* Barbecues, playground, volleyball area.

DOS CAMINOS PARK *Belota Rd. and Ponderosa Dr.* Barbecues, playground.

FOOTHILL PARK *Cranbrook St. and Lathan Ave.* Barbecues, playground, volleyball court.

FREEDOM PARK *Pleasant Valley Rd. and Freedom Park Dr.* Barbecues, playground, horseshoe pits, softball field, volleyball court, soccer fields.

MISSION OAKS PARK *Mission Oaks Blvd. between Oak Canyon Rd. and Butterfield St.* Barbecues, playground, softball field, tennis courts, volleyball court.

PLEASANT VALLEY PARK *Ponderosa Dr. and Brookhaven Ave.* Barbecues, playground, horseshoe pits, softball field, swimming pool open in summer, tennis courts, volleyball court.

Cambria

LEFFINGWELL LANDING *1½ miles north of Cambria off Moonstone Beach Dr.* Barbecues, view sites (see listing).

SHAMEL COUNTY PARK *Windsor Blvd. off SR 1.* Barbecues, fire rings; swimming pool open in summer.

Carpinteria

RINCON BEACH COUNTY PARK *2 miles south of Carpinteria, off US 101 at the Santa Barbara/Ventura county line.* Barbecues.

Fillmore

KENNEY GROVE PARK *2 miles northwest of Fillmore at 823 N. Oak Ave.* Barbecues, horseshoe pits, playground, softball field.

Goleta

GOLETA BEACH COUNTY PARK *3 miles south of US 101, off SR 217.* Playground, fishing pier.

LAKE LOS CARNEROS COUNTY PARK *Off Los Carneros Rd., just north of*

US 101. Includes South Coast Railroad Museum and Stow House (see listings).

STOW GROVE COUNTY PARK *Borders La Patera Ln. south of Cathedral Oaks Rd.* Barbecues, playground.

Grover Beach

GROVER HEIGHTS PARK *8th St. and Atlantic City Ave.* Barbecues, tennis courts.

Lake Casitas

LAKE CASITAS RECREATION AREA *5 miles southwest of Ojai, off SR 150.* Barbecues, boating, fishing, playgrounds. Day-use fee. (See Lake Casitas listing under *Ventura County,* Ojai and Santa Paula Areas; also, Water Recreation, this chapter.)

FOSTER COUNTY PARK *1 mile south of Casitas Springs, off SR 33.* Barbecues, equestrian path, horseshoe pits, playground, softball field, volleyball area.

Lompoc

RIVER PARK *SR 246 and River Park Rd.* Barbecues, children's fishing pond.

RYON PARK *Ocean Ave. and O St.* Barbecues, playground.

Los Alamos

LOS ALAMOS COUNTY PARK *Centennial St., ½ mile south of SR 166.* Barbecues, playground.

Los Olivos

LOS OLIVOS PARK *Grand Ave, 2 blocks south of SR 154.*

Montecito

MANNING COUNTY PARK *1 mile north of US 101 off San Ysidro Rd.* Barbecues, playground.

Los Alamos County Park: a serene setting off the beaten path.

Morro Bay

COLEMAN PARK *At the Embarcadero and Coleman Dr.* Barbecues; fishing and swimming in the bay.

KEISER PARK *At Atascadero Rd. and SR 1.* Barbecues.

MORRO ROCK CITY BEACH *Foot of Coleman Dr.* Barbecues, fishing, swimming and surfing in the bay.

TIDELANDS PARK *Embarcadero between Olive and Fig sts.* Fishing and swimming in the bay.

Ojai

CAMP COMFORT COUNTY PARK *Creek Rd, 2 miles south of Ojai.* Barbecues, playground, horseshoe pits, softball field.

LIBBEY PARK *Downtown Ojai on Ojai Ave.* Tennis courts.

SARZOTTI PARK *East of downtown Ojai on Park Rd.* Ball field, barbecues, playground.

SOULE COUNTY PARK *Off Ojai Ave. on Boardman Rd.* Baseball field, tennis courts, volleyball area.

Oxnard

COMMUNITY CENTER PARK *2 blocks east of Ventura Rd. on 7th St.* Playground, basketball court, tennis courts, volleyball area, wading pool.

DEL SOL PARK *Camino de la Raza and Rose Ave.* Playground, basketball court, soccer field, volleyball area.

LATHROP MEMORIAL PARK *2 blocks east of Saviers Rd. on Gisler Ave. at E. Hemlock St.* Playground, basketball court, wading pool, volleyball area.

PENINSULA PARK *South end of Peninsula Rd. off Channel Islands Blvd.* Playground, tennis courts.

RUDOLPH BECK PARK *1 block west of Saviers Rd. at Laurel and C sts.* Playground, basketball court, tennis courts.

SIERRA LINDA PARK *3 blocks east of Ventura Rd. on Holly Ave. at Lantana St.* Playground, tennis courts, jogging path, volleyball court.

SOUTHWINDS PARK *2 blocks west of Saviers Rd. on Clara St.* Playground, basketball court, tennis courts, shuffleboard, volleyball court.

WILSON PARK *2 blocks west of Oxnard Ave. on Palm Dr. at C St.* Playground, tennis courts, jogging path, shuffleboard.

Paso Robles

CENTENNIAL PARK *Nickerson Dr. just south of Creston Rd.* Barbecues, swimming pool open in summer, tennis courts.

PASO ROBLES CITY PARK *12th and Spring sts.* Barbecues.

PIONEER PARK *Riverside Ave. and 21st St.* Barbecues.

Port Hueneme

BUBBLING SPRINGS PARK *4 blocks east of Ventura Rd. on Bard Rd. at Park Ave.* Playground.

PORT HUENEME BEACH PARK *South end of Ventura Rd. at Surfside Dr.* Playground, fire rings, fishing pier, ocean swimming.

San Luis Obispo

LAGUNA LAKE PARK *Off Madonna Rd., west of US 101.* Barbecues, fishing, playground. (See listing under Water Recreation, this chapter.)

SANTA ROSA PARK *Santa Rosa and Oak sts.* Barbecues.

San Miguel

SAN MIGUEL COUNTY PARK *2 blocks west of Mission St. between 12th and 13th sts.* Barbecues, swimming pool open in summer.

Santa Barbara

CHASE PALM PARK *Cabrillo Blvd., foot of Santa Barbara St.*

EAST BEACH *Cabrillo Blvd., foot of Por la Mar Dr.* Volleyball courts, barbecues and snack bar. Fitness Center provides showers, dressing rooms, weight-lifting room, lockers and beach equipment rentals; center open daily except Jan. 1,

The essence of Southern California: beach volleyball in Santa Barbara.

Thanksgiving and Dec. 25. Call (805) 965-0509 for further information.

LEADBETTER BEACH *Shoreline and Loma Alta drs.* Barbecues.

MACKENZIE PARK *State St. and Las Positas Rd.* Barbecues.

OAK PARK *300 W. Alamar Ave.* Barbecues; children's wading pool open in summer.

ROCKY NOOK COUNTY PARK *Mission Canyon Rd. just north of Mountain Dr. near Santa Barbara Museum of Natural History.* Barbecues, playground.

SAN ANTONIO CANYON COUNTY PARK *San Antonio Creek Rd. just north of Cathedral Oaks Rd.* Playground.

SHORELINE PARK *La Marina and Shoreline drs.* Barbecues.

STEVENS PARK *258 Canon Dr.* Barbecues.

WEST BEACH *Cabrillo Blvd., foot of Chapala St.* Children's wading pool open in summer.

Santa Maria

MEMORIAL PARK *Pine and Tunnell sts.* Barbecues, playground.

PREISKER PARK *¼ mile north of SR 135 off Preisker Ln.* Barbecues, playground.

RUSSELL PARK *1 block south of SR 166 at 200 S. Russell Ave.* Playground.

SIMAS PARK *500 S. McClelland St.* Playground.

WALLER COUNTY PARK *Orcutt Expy. (SR 135) and Waller Ln.* Barbecues, playground, fishing pond, pony rides.

Santa Paula

CHARLES M. TEAGUE PARK *Harvard Blvd. and Steckel Dr.* Barbecues, basketball court, playground, soccer field, softball field.

EBELL PARK *Main and 7th sts.*

GEORGE HARDING PARK *1330 E. Harvard Blvd.* Barbecues, playground, soccer field, softball field.

MILL PARK *Ojai Rd. and Bedford St.* Barbecues, basketball court, horseshoe pits, playground.

STECKEL COUNTY PARK *4 miles north of Santa Paula off SR 150.* Barbecues, horseshoe pits, playground, softball field, volleyball area.

Santa Ynez

SANTA YNEZ PARK *Just north of SR 246 on Cuesta St.* Barbecues, playground.

Shandon

CRAWFORD W. CLARK MEMORIAL PARK *SR 41 and First St.* Barbecues, tennis courts; swimming pool open in summer.

Simi Valley

RANCHO SIMI COMMUNITY PARK *Royal Ave. and Erringer Rd.* Basketball courts, horseshoe pits, lagoon, playgrounds, shuffleboard courts, softball diamonds, tennis courts, swimming pool open in summer. (See Fishing, this chapter.)

SANTA SUSANA PARK *6503 Katherine Rd.* Baseball diamond, basketball court, rock-climbing area, train depot, volleyball area.

RANCHO SANTA SUSANA COMMUNITY PARK *5005 Los Angeles Ave.* Basketball and volleyball courts, softball diamonds, soccer fields, playgrounds.

Go fly a kite—in Conejo Creek Park, Thousand Oaks.

RANCHO TAPO COMMUNITY PARK
3700 Avenida Simi. Barbecues, basketball courts, horseshoe pits, jogging course, playgrounds, softball diamond.

Solvang

HANS CHRISTIAN ANDERSEN PARK
Off Atterdag Rd., 3 blocks north of Mission Dr. Barbecues, playground, tennis courts.

NOJOQUI FALLS COUNTY PARK *7 miles southwest on Alisal Rd.* Barbeques, playgrounds, softball diamonds, volleyball courts, horseshoe pits.

Summerland

LOOKOUT BEACH COUNTY PARK
Foot of Evans St., south of US 101. Barbecues, playground.

Templeton

TEMPLETON COUNTY PARK *Old County Rd. between 5th and 6th sts.*

Barbecues; swimming pool open in summer.

Thousand Oaks

CONEJO CREEK NORTH PARK
¼ mile east of SR 23; 1370 E. Janss Rd. Barbecues, fitness/jogging trail, playgrounds, volleyball courts.

FORT WILDWOOD PARK *6850 Avenida de los Arboles.* Barbecues, playground, trailhead to Wildwood Regional Park.

STAGECOACH INN PARK *51 S. Ventu Park Rd. in Newbury Park.* Barbecues, basketball court, playground, access to Stagecoach Inn Museum (see separate listing for Stagecoach Inn Museum, *Ventura County*).

THOUSAND OAKS COMMUNITY PARK *2625 N. Moorpark Rd.* Basketball court, fitness trail, playground, softball fields, tennis courts, volleyball court.

WILDWOOD REGIONAL PARK *550 W. Avenida de los Arboles.* Barbecues, hiking and nature trails, nature center (see separate listing for Wildwood Regional Park, *Ventura County*).

Ventura

ARROYO VERDE PARK *Day and Foothill rds.* Barbecues, playground, basketball court, horseshoe pits.

CAMINO REAL PARK *Dean Dr. and Varsity St.* Barbecues, playgrounds, baseball fields, basketball courts, soccer space, softball fields, tennis courts, volleyball court.

CHUMASH PARK *Petit Ave. at Waco St.* Barbecues, playground, basketball court.

HOBERT PARK *Telegraph Rd. at Petit and Cambria aves.* Barbecues, playground.

MARINA PARK *South end of Pierpont Blvd.* Barbecues, boat dock, fishing, volleyball court.

PLAZA PARK *Santa Clara and Chestnut sts.* Playground.

SURFERS' POINT *Seaside Park, Figueroa St. at the Promenade.*

TENNIS

All public tennis courts listed here are outdoors; the courts with lights are noted. With few exceptions, no fees are charged for use of the courts; occasionally there is a nominal fee for lights. No reservations are taken; play is on a first-come, first-play basis. As a courtesy, players should limit themselves to one set or one hour if others are waiting.

Atascadero

HEILMANN COUNTY PARK *Off El Camino Real on El Bordo Ave.* 2 courts.

Camarillo

MISSION OAKS PARK *Mission Oaks Blvd. between Oak Canyon Rd. and Butterfield St.* 5 lighted courts.

PLEASANT VALLEY PARK *Ponderosa Dr. and Brookhaven Ave.* 6 lighted courts.

VALLE LINDO PARK *Coe St. and Harris Ave.* 5 lighted courts.

Cayucos

HARDIE COUNTY PARK *Birch Ave. and B St.* 2 lighted courts.

Grover Beach

GROVER HEIGHTS PARK *8th St. and Atlantic City Ave.* 2 lighted courts.

MENTONE TENNIS COURTS *Trouville Ave. between 14th and 16th sts.* 1 lighted court.

Lompoc

RYON PARK *Ocean Ave. and O St.* 2 lighted courts.

Los Osos

SOUTH BAY COMMUNITY PARK *Los Osos Valley Rd. and Palisades Ave.* 2 courts.

Montecito

MANNING COUNTY PARK *1 mile north of US 101 off San Ysidro Rd.* 1 court.

Morro Bay

MONTE YOUNG PARK *South St. and Napa Ave.* 2 courts.

Nipomo

NIPOMO REGIONAL COUNTY PARK *Pomeroy Rd and Tefft St.* 2 lighted courts.

Ojai

LIBBEY PARK *Downtown Ojai on Ojai Ave.* 8 courts.

SOULE COUNTY PARK *Off Ojai Ave. on Boardman Rd.* 4 lighted courts.

Oxnard

COMMUNITY CENTER PARK *2 blocks east of Ventura Rd. on 7th St.* 8 lighted courts; fee.

PENINSULA PARK *South end of Peninsula Rd. off Channel Islands Blvd.* 2 courts.

RUDOLPH BECK PARK *1 block west of Saviers Rd. on Laurel St. at C St.* 2 lighted courts; fee.

SIERRA LINDA PARK *3 blocks east of Ventura Rd. on Holly Ave. at Lantana St.* 2 courts.

SOUTHWINDS PARK *2 blocks west of Saviers Rd. on Clara St.* 2 courts.

WILSON PARK *2 blocks off Oxnard Ave. on Palm Dr. at C St.* 2 courts.

Paso Robles

CENTENNIAL PARK *Nickerson Dr., just south of Creston Rd.* 4 lighted courts.

SHERWOOD PARK *Scott St. and Creston Rd.* 4 lighted courts.

Pismo Beach

PALISADES TENNIS COURTS *Shell Beach Rd. near Hermosa Dr.* 2 lighted courts.

PISMO BEACH CITY HALL COURTS *Wadsworth Ave. and Bello St.* 2 lighted courts.

Port Hueneme

MORANDA PARK *1 block off Port Hueneme Rd. at south end of Moranda Pkwy.* 8 courts; fee.

San Luis Obispo

SINSHEIMER PARK *900 Southwood Dr.* 6 courts.

Santa Barbara

OAK PARK *300 W. Alamar Ave. at Quinto St.* 2 courts.

Note: A $2 daily permit is required for each player 18 years of age and over to use the following public tennis facilities. Permits can be purchased at the courts.

If tennis is your racket, try Santa Barbara.

LAS POSITAS COURTS *1002 Las Positas Rd.* 6 lighted courts.

MUNICIPAL TENNIS CENTER *1414 Park Pl.* 12 courts.

PERSHING PARK *100 E. Castillo St. at Cabrillo Blvd. junction.* 8 courts.

Santa Maria

ATKINSON PARK *1000 N. Railroad Ave.* 4 lighted courts.

MINAMI COMMUNITY CENTER *600 W. Enos Dr.* 6 lighted courts.

Shandon

CLIFFORD W. CLARK MEMORIAL PARK *Old Hwy. 41 and First St.* 1 lighted court.

Simi Valley

RANCHO SIMI COMMUNITY PARK *1765 Royal Ave.* 8 lighted courts.

Solvang

HANS CHRISTIAN ANDERSEN PARK *Off Atterdag Rd., 3 blocks north of Mission Dr.* 4 courts.

Thousand Oaks

BORCHARD PARK *190 Reino Rd., Newbury Park.* 4 lighted courts.

THOUSAND OAKS COMMUNITY PARK *2625 N. Moorpark Rd.* 4 lighted courts.

WILDFLOWER PLAYFIELD *635 Avenida de los Arboles.* 4 lighted courts.

Ventura

CAMINO REAL PARK *Dean Dr. and Varsity St.* Information not available at press time; call (805) 658-8175.

WATER RECREATION

Whether it's water-skiing, deep-sea fishing, strolling on a pier or hanging ten, California's Central Coast abounds with salty or fresh water recreational opportunities. Following are the names of communities, lakes, beaches, bays, harbors and parks where it is possible to engage in water-related recreation.

Boating listings indicate where boats can be launched or moored. Entries include each establishment's location and phone number and give additional information on rental equipment, fuel, boat repairs and other facilities and services available nearby.

A California State Fishing License is required for anyone over age 16 fishing in either freshwater lakes or the ocean; a license is not required, however, for fishing from a public saltwater pier. Fishing listings often indicate the type of fish which may be caught, and in the case of pier fishing, whether lights are available for night fishing.

Sportfishing establishments offer half-day, three-quarter-day and all-day open-party or charter trips. Reservations are advisable year round and essential on summer weekends. Most boats provide bait, and often tackle can be rented. Whale-watching trips are sometimes offered by these companies during the winter; call for availability, prices and schedules.

Swimming listings indicate ocean areas safe for swimming and inland water recreation areas that include public pools.

Water-skiing listings simply mean that water-skiing is allowed in that particular area.

CLAMMING

Pismo clams are not as abundant as they once were (too many people like their taste), but it is still possible to bag a limit of 10 clams at Pismo Beach. All clammers need is a clamming fork, a California State Fishing License and some patience. Clams are buried four to six inches under the sand and up to several hundred feet offshore. The best time to dig is at minus low tide. Clammers that dig in deeper water will have more success but should remember that the ocean is warm only in mid-summer. Clams measuring less than 4½ inches in diameter must be reburied.

FISHING

Depending upon where you are (and how lucky you are), fishing in ocean waters along the Central Coast provides varied bounty for fishermen. Pier fishermen can catch halibut, bonito, mackerel, barracuda, calico bass and white sea bass.

Surf fishermen can probably snag four species of surf perch, cabezon, kelp bass and halibut. Arroyo Burro Beach, Goleta Beach, Isla Vista Beach, Jalama Beach, Lookout Park, Ocean Beach, Rancho Guadalupe Dunes and Rincon Beach are all considered good spots for surf fishing.

Go deep-sea fishing and you're likely to find albacore, barracuda, white sea bass, bonito, halibut, calico bass, lingcod, mackerel, rockfish, sculpin, sheephead and silver salmon.

SAILBOARDING

Sailboarding has become a popular water sport along the Central Coast. Morro Bay and San Luis Obispo Bay, especially, offer good ocean sailboarding spots. Calmer and usually warmer waters can be found at Laguna Lake, Lake Nacimiento, Lake San Antonio and Lopez Lake. People who want to engage in this sport should have their own equipment; shops that rent sailboards are few and far between.

SKIN AND SCUBA DIVING

If you want to get up close and personal with the fish and underwater plants, there are several areas along the Central Coast that afford good skin and scuba diving. The best diving areas off Ventura County's coastline are the reefs and kelp beds that enrich the waters of the channel islands.

The most popular skin and scuba diving areas along Santa Barbara County's coastline are off Arroyo Burro County Beach and Shoreline Park in Santa Barbara and at the foot of Butterfly Lane in Montecito. Carpinteria beaches and Refugio State Beach are good, and Channel Islands National Park also offers excellent skin and scuba diving.

In San Luis Obispo County, skin and scuba diving are best in the waters off Shell Beach and Avila Beach, in San Simeon Bay, off Montaña de Oro State Park, at Morro Rock and in the vicinity of Cayucos Point.

The variety of fish and shellfish in Central Coast waters includes red abalone, lingcod, rockfish, surf fish and game fish. A valid California sportfishing license is required to spearfish in the waters off the mainland and the islands.

Following are establishments where rental equipment, air refills and information on water conditions and charter dive boats are available:

Arroyo Grande

SCUBA ADVENTURES *1039 Grand Ave. (805) 473-1111.* Rental equipment, air refills and information on water conditions and charter dive boats are available.

Camarillo

AQUA VENTURES *2172 Pickwick Dr. (805) 484-1594.* Rental equipment, air refills and information on water conditions and charter dive boats are available.

Cayucos

BILL'S SPORTING GOODS *At the pier. (805) 995-1703.* Rental equipment, air refills and information on water conditions and charter dive boats are available.

Goleta

THE DIVE LOCKER *5708 Hollister Ave. (805) 967-4456.* Rental equipment, air refills and information on water conditions and charter dive boats are available.

Waiting for the perfect wave near Cayucos Pier.

SANTA BARBARA AQUATICS *5370 Hollister Ave. (805) 964-8680.* Rental equipment, air refills and information on water conditions and charter dive boats are available.

Pismo Beach

SEA WINK *750 Price St. (805) 773-4794.* Rental equipment, air refills and information on water conditions and charter dive boats are available.

Santa Barbara

ANACAPA DIVE CENTER *22 Anacapa St. (805) 963-8917.* Rental equipment, air refills and information on water conditions and charter dive boats are available.

UNDERWATER SPORTS *Breakwater. (805) 962-5400.* Rental equipment, air refills and information on water conditions and charter dive boats are available.

Ventura

CHANNEL ISLANDS SCUBA *4255-4 E. Main St. (805) 644-3483.* Rental equipment, air refills and information on water conditions and charter dive boats are available.

SURFING

Surfing in the Ventura County coastal area is possible off a number of beaches. At Rincon Point the surfing is poor in summer, but excellent in winter, with surf at four to ten feet. At Solimar Beach, there is a fair winter surf, three to five feet. San Buenaventura State Beach offers surfing for novice and intermediate, with a good winter surf at four to eight feet. A three-to-eight-foot winter surf can be experienced at Hollywood and Silver Strand County beaches in Ventura County. At the Los Angeles/Ventura county line off SR 1, one mile west of Leo Carrillo State Beach, there is good year-round surf at two to three feet.

It's a good day for an outing at Carpinteria State Beach.

Surfing along Santa Barbara County's coast is best at Rincon Point, three miles south of Carpinteria. This spot is particularly good during the winter, when surf averages from two to four feet with swells to 12 feet during storms. A designated surfing zone at Refugio State Beach usually has winter surf from three to six feet. Surfing is also possible at El Capitan State Beach and Arroyo Burro Beach. Farther north, surfing is good at Tarantula Point, ½ mile south of Jalama Beach County Park near Lompoc and at Rancho Guadalupe Dunes County Park, west of Santa Maria.

Along San Luis Obispo County's coastline, surfing is best in Estero Bay near Atascadero, Cayucos and Morro Strand state beaches. Pismo State Beach and Pismo City Beach near the pier also offer good year-round surf. Surfers occasionally use Avila State Beach also, but this area is generally better for swimming.

SWIMMING

Ocean swimming in Ventura County is good at San Buenaventura State Beach, with lifeguards on duty in summer. At Channel Islands Beach Park, near Victoria Avenue and Pelican Way, there is good swimming in small, lifeguarded areas. Port Hueneme Beach Park offers swimming; lifeguards are there during the summer.

Calm waters off Santa Barbara County's south-facing beaches provide good ocean swimming, but west-facing shores north of Point Conception receive high winds and severe riptides that make swimming dangerous. During the summer months, lifeguards are on duty at state park beaches along the coast; at Arroyo Burro, Goleta and Lookout Park county beaches; and at Carpinteria City Beach (no lifeguard at Isla Vista and Rincon Beach county parks).

San Luis Obispo County's beaches and lakes provide numerous opportunities for swimming. Atascadero and Morro Strand state beaches and Cayucos County Beach are good swimming beaches, as is Estero Bay. At the beaches north of Cayucos, water is considered too cold and rough for swimming; however, boardsurfing with wetsuits is popular in San Simeon Cove at William Randolph Hearst Memorial State Beach. In the southern portion of the county, Avila and Pismo state beaches have cool, calm ocean waters.

Cove and beach areas for swimming in warmer, calmer waters are designated at lakes Lopez, Nacimiento and San Antonio.

WATER-SKIING

Water-skiing is good off East Beach in Santa Barbara and in Ventura County's Lake Piru. It is possible to water-ski in the ocean at San Luis Obispo and Estero bays; the water, however, is cold and often rough. Inland, lakes Lopez, Nacimiento and San Antonio provide good water-skiing.

LAKES

Atascadero Lake

Between Portola and Santa Rosa rds., east off SR 41 (mailing address: Supervisor, Dept. of Parks & Recreation, City of Atascadero, 6500 Palma Ave., Atascadero 93422). (805) 461-5000. Free.

BOATING

Atascadero Lake *9100 Morro Rd., Atascadero 93422. (805) 461-5000. Open daily in summer.* Rentals: pedal boats in summer. Miscellaneous: food concession, picnic area, horseshoe pits and volleyball.

FISHING

Bass, catfish, crappie and trout.

Laguna Lake (San Luis Obispo)

Madonna Rd. near Dalidio Dr., ½ mile southwest of US 101 (mailing address: San Luis Obispo Parks and Recreation Dept., 860 Pacific St., San Luis Obispo 93401). (805) 781-7300. Free.

BOATING

Near park entrance. Open daily all year. Hand-launching ramp. Only boats with electric motors under 1 horsepower are permitted; gasoline motors are prohibited. Rentals: none. Miscellaneous: jogging trail, picnic area, playground.

FISHING

Bass, catfish, crappie and trout.

Lake Cachuma

Approximately 18 miles northwest of Santa Barbara off SR 154 (mailing address: Star Rte., Santa Barbara 93105). (805) 688-4658. Day-use fee, $5 per vehicle.

BOATING

Cachuma Lake Boat Rentals, Inc. *On south shore, 1 mile north of SR 154. (805) 688-4040. Open daily.* Paved ramp, temporary mooring, slips, dry storage, boat fuel. Rentals: rowboats, motorboats (4½ to 9 hp), pedal boats, pontoon boats, fishing tackle. Miscellaneous: marine hardware, bait, groceries, ice, snack bar, picnic area, lake tours.

FISHING

Good fishing year round for bass, crappie, catfish, bluegill and trout.

SWIMMING

Although swimming in the lake is prohibited, two pools within the recreational area are open during the summer (fee).

Lake Casitas

Approximately 3 miles west of junction SR 150 and SR 33 off Santa Ana Rd. (mailing address: 1131 Santa Ana Rd., Ventura 93001). (805) 649-2233. Day-use fee, $5 per vehicle; $4 per boat.

BOATING

Casitas Boat Rentals *Santa Ana Rd. (805) 649-2043. Open daily.* Slips, dry

All systems are go for a launch at Lake Casitas.

storage, boat fuel, engine repairs. Rentals: rowboats, motorboats (4 to 10 hp), pedal boats, fishing tackle. Miscellaneous: bait, ice, snack bar, picnic area.

Lake Casitas Recreation Area *Santa Ana Rd. (805) 649-2233. Open daily.* Facilities: paved ramp (fee). Rentals: none. Miscellaneous: groceries, ice, tent and RV sites.

FISHING

Trout, bass, crappie, channel catfish and redear sunfish.

Lake Nacimiento

Approximately 17 miles northwest of Paso Robles off US 101, via County Rd G14 (mailing address: Star Rte, Box 2770, Bradley 93426). (805) 238-3256. Day-use fee, $10 per vehicle Apr. through Sept.; $7 per vehicle Oct. through Mar.

BOATING

Lake Nacimiento Resort *On east shore 1½ miles southwest of Nacimiento Dam.*

(800) 323-3839. Open daily. Paved ramp (fee), temporary mooring, slips, dry storage, boat fuel. Rentals: ski boats, rowboats, motorboats (10 to 225 hp), canoes, fishing tackle, pedal boats, water-skis. Miscellaneous: bait, groceries, ice, restaurant, lodging, tent and RV sites, picnic area.

FISHING

Bass, bluegill, catfish and crappie.

SWIMMING

An unheated pool is available at Lake Nacimiento Resort. The day-use fee includes use of pool. Call for hours.

WATER-SKIING

The water is warm in summer and usually calm. Equipment can be rented at Lake Nacimiento Resort.

Lake Piru

Approximately 7½ miles east of Fillmore off SR 126, north on Piru Canyon Rd., through the town of Piru (mailing address: P.O. Box

If you don't catch any fish at Lake Piru, you can just enjoy the scenery.

202, Piru 93040). (805) 521-1645. Day-use fee, $6 per vehicle; $6 per boat.

BOATING

Lake Piru Marina *On west shore on Piru Canyon Rd. (805) 521-1231. Open daily.* Temporary mooring, slips, dry storage, boat fuel. Rentals: motorboats (6 hp), pontoon boats, fishing tackle, water-skis. Miscellaneous: bait, groceries, ice, snack bar, picnic area.

Lake Piru Recreation Area *On west shore on Piru Canyon Rd. (805) 521-1500. Open daily.* Paved ramp (free), temporary mooring, slips, dry storage, boat fuel. Rentals: motorboats (6 hp), fishing tackle, water-skis. Miscellaneous: bait, groceries, ice, restaurant, tent and RV sites, picnic area.

FISHING

Rainbow and brown trout, black bass, catfish, bluegill, sunfish and crappie.

WATER-SKIING

Water-skiing is permitted in the area just off Piru Canyon Road, between sun-up and sunset.

Lake San Antonio

Approximately 31 miles northwest of Paso Robles off US 101, via County Rd. G14 (mailing address: Star Rte., Box 2610, Bradley 93426). (805) 472-2311, (800) 310-2313. Day-use fee, $6 per vehicle.

BOATING

Harris Creek and Lynch Launching Ramps *On south shore northeast of Interlake Rd. (805) 472-2311. Open daily.* Paved ramp (fee). Rentals: fishing boats, pontoon boats. Miscellaneous: rest rooms, tent and RV sites, picnic area, fish-cleaning station.

Lake San Antonio Resort *On north shore at Pleyto Campground (see* Campgrounds & Trailer Parks). (800) 310-2313. *Open daily.* Slips, dry storage, boat fuel, marine waste station. Rentals: fishing boats, pontoon boats. Miscellaneous: bait, groceries, ice, snack bar, tent and RV sites, picnic area.

Lake San Antonio Resort *On south shore at Lynch Campground (see* Campgrounds & Trailer Parks). (800)

310-2313. Open daily. Slips, dry storage, boat fuel, marine waste station. Rentals: fishing boats, pontoon boats, water-skis. Miscellaneous: bait, groceries, ice, snack bar (summer only), tent and RV sites, picnic area.

Lynch Launching Ramp *On south shore 3½ miles north of Interlake Rd. (805) 472-2311. Open daily.* Paved ramp (fee). Rentals: fishing boats, pontoon boats.

Pleyto Launching Ramp *On north shore 4½ miles south of Co. Rd. G18. (805) 472-2311. Open daily.* Paved ramp (fee). Rentals: fishing boats, pontoon boats. Miscellaneous: rest rooms, tent and RV sites, picnic area, fish-cleaning station.

FISHING

Bass, bluegill, catfish, crappie, redear and striper.

WATER-SKIING

The water is warm in summer and usually calm. Equipment can be rented at Lake San Antonio Resort.

Lopez Lake

13 miles east of Arroyo Grande along Branch St., Huasna Rd. and Lopez Dr. (mailing address: 6800 Lopez Dr., Arroyo Grande 93420). (805) 489-1122. Day-use fee, $4 per vehicle; $4 per boat.

BOATING

Lopez Lake Marina, Inc. *1 mile from entrance on north shore. (805) 489-1006. Open daily.* Paved ramp, slips, boat fuel. Rentals: motorboats (7½ hp), pedal boats, pontoon boats, fishing tackle, water-skis. Miscellaneous: bait, groceries, ice, snack bar in summer.

FISHING

Bass, bluegill, catfish, crappie, redear and trout.

WATER-SKIING

Skis, vests and ropes may be rented at Lopez Lake Marina.

Los Padres National Forest

LOS PADRES NATIONAL FOREST HEADQUARTERS *6144 Calle Real, Goleta 93117; (805) 683-6711. Open Mon. through Fri. 8 a.m. to 4:30 p.m.*

FISHING

Davy Brown and Manzana creeks *Off Sunset Valley Rd near Davy Brown Campground (see* Campgrounds and Trailer Parks*).* Catchable-size trout; best during spring months following stocking.

Santa Ynez River *Off SR 154 near Paradise Campground (see* Campgrounds and Trailer Parks*).* Trout and bluegill; best during late winter and early spring, following stocking.

Sespe Creek *Lion Canyon Campground to Cherry Canyon (see* Campgrounds and Trailer Parks*).* Rainbow trout; best February through May, following stocking.

Rancho Simi Community Park, Simi Valley

Royal Ave. and Erringer Rd. (mailing address: 1692 Sycamore Dr., Simi Valley 93065). 805-584-4400. Free.

FISHING

Children under age 15 and seniors over 55 can fish in the park's lagoon during the summer, when it is stocked with channel catfish, bluegill, large-mouth bass and crappie. (A fishing license is not required.)

Santa Margarita Lake

Approximately 18 miles southeast of Santa Margarita off SR 58, via Pozo Rd. (mailing address: Star Rte., Box 34-A,

Santa Margarita 93453). (805) 438-5485. Day-use fee, $4 per vehicle; $4 per boat.

BOATING
½ mile off Pozo Rd. Open daily. Paved ramps. Rentals: fishing boats. Miscellaneous: picnic areas.

FISHING
Bass, bluegill, catfish, crappie, trout and striper.

SWIMMING
Unheated pool. Fee for use of pool, in addition to day-use fee.

Zaca Lake

Off Zaca Station Rd., 12 miles northeast of US 101 and Zaca Station Rd. junction (mailing address: Zaca Lake Lodge, P.O. Box 187, Los Olivos 93441). (805) 688-4891.

BOATING
On east shore. (805) 688-4891. Open daily. Graded ramp (free). Rentals: rowboats, pedal boats, canoes. Miscellaneous: ice, restaurant, rustic lodging, picnic area.

OCEAN

Cayucos

(See city listing.)

PIER FISHING
Cayucos Pier *Foot of Cayucos Rd.* Lit for night fishing.

Gaviota State Park

32 miles west of Goleta off US 101 (mailing address: #10 Refugio Beach Rd., Goleta 93117). (805) 968-3294. Day-use fee, $5 per vehicle.

BOATING
In the park, ½ mile south of US 101. Open daily all year. Boat hoist (fee), slings not provided. No rentals. Miscellaneous: bait, groceries, ice (available daily during summer months; weekends rest of year), picnic area.

Goleta Beach County Park

2 miles south of Goleta off US 101 and SR 217 (mailing address: 5905 Sandspit Rd., Goleta 93117). (805) 967-1300. Free.

BOATING
Goleta Pier *East of Sandspit Rd. Open daily.* Sling hoist and launch ramp (open Sat., Sun. and holidays only). No rentals. Miscellaneous: bait, snack bar, restaurant, picnic area.

PIER FISHING
Goleta Pier Lit for night fishing.

SWIMMING
Daily lifeguard service in summer is provided.

Morro Bay

(See city listing.)

BOATING
Kayaks of Morro Bay *699 Embarcadero, #9 (805) 772-9463. Open daily all year.* Kayaks can be rented here for exploring the bay. Single kayaks, $3 for ½ hour; double kayaks, $5 for ½ hour; singles and doubles, $20 for ½ day. Guided kayak tours offered.

Morro Bay Fuel Dock, Inc. *201 S. Main St., Morro Bay 93442. (805) 772-8617.* Open daily all year. Slips and boat fuel. Rentals: none. Miscellaneous: limited marine hardware and snack bar.

Morro Bay Launch Ramp *100 Embarcadero; c/o Harbor Master, 1275 Embarcadero, Morro Bay 93442. (805) 772-6254. Open daily.* Paved ramp (free). Rentals: none.

Headline: "Bakersfield Man Catches Morro Bay Fish."

State Park Marina *Opposite Morro Bay State Park; c/o #10 State Park Rd., Morro Bay 93442. (805) 772-8796. Open daily.* Slips. Rentals: canoes, kayaks, rowboats. Miscellaneous: restaurant, tent and RV sites.

SPORTFISHING

Bob's Sportfishing *845 Embarcadero, Morro Bay. (805) 772-3340.*

Virg's Fish'n *1215 Embarcadero, Morro Bay. (805) 772-1222.*

Oceano Memorial County Park *In Oceano, west of SR 1, off Air Park Dr. (805) 781-5219.*

FISHING

Ocean fishing is possible just a short distance from the park.

SWIMMING

Ocean waters near the park are suitable for swimming.

Oxnard, Channel Islands Harbor

Between west end of Channel Islands Blvd. and south end of Victoria Ave. (mailing address: Harbor Dept., 3900 Pelican Way, Oxnard 93035). (805) 385-8697.

BOATING

Channel Islands Harbor Public Launch Ramp *¼ mile south of Channel Islands Blvd. on Victoria Ave, Oxnard. (805) 385-8693. Open daily.* Paved ramp (free); parking fee. Rentals: none. Miscellaneous: bait, groceries, restaurant, picnic area.

Channel Islands Landing *3821 S. Victoria Ave., Oxnard. (805) 985-6059. Open daily.* Eyebolt and sling hoist, temporary mooring, slips, dry storage. Rentals: sailboats. Miscellaneous: bay cruises.

SPORT FISHING

Cisco Sportfishing *4151 S. Victoria Ave., Oxnard. (805) 985-8511.*

Port Hueneme

(See city listing.)

PIER FISHING

Port Hueneme Pier *South end of Ventura Rd. at Surfside Dr.*

Take two kayaks, add ocean waves, mix well; makes hours of fun.

SPORTFISHING

Port Hueneme Sportfishing *301 W. Hueneme Rd. (805) 488-1000.*

SWIMMING

The ocean is safe for swimming here; lifeguards on duty in summer.

San Luis Obispo Bay

(See Avila Beach city listing.)

BOATING

Port San Luis Harbor District *Pier 3 (mailing address: P.O. Box 249, Avila Beach 93424). (805) 595-5400. Open daily.* Hand-launching beach ramp (free).

Port Side Marine *Pier 3 (mailing address: P.O. Box 456, Avila Beach 93424). (805) 595-7214. Open daily.* Sling hoist, temporary mooring, dry storage, boat fuel. Miscellaneous: marine hardware, bait, groceries, ice, snack bar, restaurants, picnic area.

SPORTFISHING

Paradise Sportfishing *Harford Pier, Avila Beach. (805) 595-7200.*

Gold Coast Charter Fishing *Avila Beach. (805) 773-5612.*

Santa Barbara Harbor

Between foot of State St. and Breakwater, Santa Barbara (mailing address: 132-A Harbor Way, Santa Barbara 93109). (805) 564-5520.

BOATING

Sailing Center of Santa Barbara *At the public launch ramp (mailing address: Breakwater, Santa Barbara 93109). (805) 962-2826. Open daily; closed Jan. 1, Thanksgiving and Dec. 25.* Rentals: motorboats (13 ft.), sailboats (21 to 51 ft.), from May to October, wave runners and jet boats can be rented. Miscellaneous: sailing school, boat charters, whale-watch trips, dinner cruises and sailing excursions aboard a 50-ft. catamaran.

Santa Barbara Municipal Harbor *On the breakwater (mailing address: 132-A Harbor Way, Santa Barbara 93109). (805) 564-5520. Open daily 24 hours.* Paved launching ramp (fee), slips. Hull repairs, hoist launching, marine fuel. Rentals: see Sailing Center of Santa Barbara. Miscellaneous: bait, ice, snack bars, restaurants, groceries, harbor cruise.

Union Marine Station *On the break-water (mailing address: Breakwater, Santa Barbara 93109). (805) 962-7186. Open daily; closed Jan. 1, Thanksgiving and Dec. 25.* Marine fuel, marine waste station. Miscellaneous: oil, batteries, filters. No rentals.

PIER FISHING
Stearns Wharf *Foot of State St.* Lit for night fishing.

SPORTFISHING
Captain Don's Deep-Sea Fishing *219 Stearns Wharf, foot of State St., opposite Moby Dick's. (805) 969-5217.*

Sea Landing Sport Fishing *Cabrillo Blvd at Bath St.; 301 W. Cabrillo Blvd. (805) 963-3564.*

SWIMMING
Daily lifeguard service in summer is provided at East, West and Leadbetter beaches. Los Baños del Mar Pool at 401 Shoreline Drive is open for recreational swimming during summer months. Call (805) 564-5418 for further information.

WATER-SKIING
There is a good area for water-skiing off East Beach, away from harbor traffic.

Ventura Harbor
Spinnaker Dr., west off Harbor Blvd. (mailing address: P.O. Box 99, Ventura 93002-0099). (805) 654-3951.

BOATING
Ventura Port District *1603 Anchors Way Dr., off Harbor Blvd., Ventura. (805) 642-8538. Open daily.* Paved ramp (free), slips, dry storage, boat fuel, engine and hull repairs, marine waste station. Rentals: pedal boats, fishing tackle. Miscellaneous: marine hardware, bait, groceries, ice, snack bar, restaurant, picnic area.

PIER FISHING
Ventura Pier *Just east of south end of California St.* Lit for night fishing.

SPORTFISHING
Ventura Sportfishing Landing *1516 Anchors Way. (805) 650-1255, 644-7363.*

Transportation

Take a plane, drive your car, hop aboard a bus or train. By whatever means you get to the Central Coast, it's more than worth the trip.

Air

Oxnard Airport is located on West Fifth Street, between Ventura Road and Victoria Avenue; (805) 385-8685. This airport services commuter flights to Ventura County.

Santa Barbara Municipal Airport is located in Goleta, about ½ mile south of US 101, off Fairview Avenue; (805) 683-4011. Limited long-distance jet service and commuter flights go to and from Northern and Southern California cities, as well as Denver.

Santa Maria Public Airport is on Skyway Drive off SR 135; (805) 928-9100. This airport services three commuter airlines. Nonstop flights to Santa Maria originate in Los Angeles. The airport is about 30 minutes from Lompoc.

San Luis Obispo County Airport is located just south of the city of San Luis Obispo off SR 227 (Broad Street); (805) 781-5205. Three airlines offer direct passenger service between a number of California communities and this airport.

Comprehensive information regarding travel to these and other airports can be obtained by contacting any Automobile Club Travel Agency office.

General aviation airports for private and charter planes are located in Camarillo off Pleasant Valley Road at Freedom Park Drive, phone (805) 388-4274; and in Santa Paula, off Santa Maria Street, just east of Eighth Street,

phone (805) 933-1155. The airports at Oxnard, Santa Barbara, Santa Maria and San Luis Obispo also serve private and charter planes.

Automobile

The majority of travelers who choose the Central Coast as their destination arrive by automobile. US 101 is usually the route of choice since it is a multi-lane, divided highway with limited access. The city of Ventura is situated on US 101, 65 miles northwest of Los Angeles and 369 miles southeast of San Francisco. Santa Barbara lies about 30 miles northwest of Ventura on 101, and San Luis Obispo is approximately 100 miles northwest of Santa Barbara.

From Santa Barbara, US 101 runs west along the coast, makes a turn north through Gaviota Pass, and a few miles farther on meets State Route 1. Scenic SR 1 runs through Lompoc and tiny Guadalupe, rejoins 101 at Pismo Beach and stays with it until San Luis Obispo. At this point the motorist can choose to follow SR 1 up the coast through Cambria and San Simeon or head northeast on 101 through the interior of San Luis Obispo County to Paso Robles, visiting Atascadero and Templeton along the way.

Taking either SR 1 or US 101 is not an irrevocable decision. At Atascadero, SR 41 leads from 101 to 1, as does SR 46 just north of Templeton; 46 is a particularly scenic drive to the coast between Harmony and Cambria.

Should you need to connect with the Central Coast from Interstate 5 in Los Angeles County, take SR 126 from Valencia west through Fillmore and Santa Paula to Ventura. Out of Kern County north of the junction with SR 99, SR 166 goes west to just north of Santa Maria, passing through a portion of Los Padres National Forest on the way. SR 46 at the Lost Hills turnoff leads from I-5 to Paso Robles, while SR 41 at the Kettleman City turnoff heads southwest to Atascadero. Both 46 and 41 pass through Cholame and Shandon.

Bus

Greyhound Bus Lines offers service to many Central Coast communities from almost every town in California. One-way tickets can be purchased up to two months prior to departure and up to 12 months in advance for round-trip tickets.

For information, contact Greyhound at (800) 231-2222 or one of the following bus terminals.

Arroyo Grande
400 Traffic Way   (805) 489-5922

Atascadero
5945 Entrada Ave.   (805) 466-3431

Oxnard
201 E. 4th St.   (805) 487-2706

Paso Robles
845 9th St.   (805) 238-1242

San Luis Obispo
150 South St.   (805) 543-2121

Santa Barbara
34 W. Carrillo St.   (805) 965-3971

Santa Maria
313-A N. Broadway   (805) 925-8841

Ventura
291 E. Thompson Blvd. (805) 653-0164

Train

Amtrak's *San Diegan*, a daily passenger train, starts at the Santa Fe (Amtrak) Depot in San Diego, making stops in San Diego and Orange counties before reaching Los Angeles (Union Station). From there the train makes stops at Glendale, Burbank Airport, Van Nuys, Chatsworth, Simi Valley, Moorpark, Camarillo, Oxnard, Ventura and Santa Barbara.

Amtrak's *Coast Starlight* provides daily service to San Luis Obispo from Union Station in Los Angeles. The train stops to take on and discharge passengers in Glendale, Simi Valley, Oxnard and Santa Barbara before arriving in San Luis Obispo.

For information contact Amtrak at (800) 872-7245 or one of the following stations.

Camarillo
30 Lewis Rd.   No telephone*

Oxnard
201 E. 4th St.   (805) 487-8787

San Luis Obispo
1011 Railroad Ave.   (805) 541-0505

Santa Barbara
209 State St.   (805) 963-1015

Ventura
Harbor Blvd. &
Figueroa St.   No telephone*

*Camarillo and Ventura stations are pick-up/drop-off points only; there are no ticket sales available.

For reservations and help in arranging connecting trains from cities without direct service, contact any Travel Agency office of the Automobile Club of Southern California.

Lodging & Restaurants

The lodging and restaurant properties listed in these pages have been inspected at least once in the past year by a trained representative of the Automobile Club of Southern California. In surprise inspections, each property was found to meet AAA's extensive and detailed requirements for approval. These requirements are reflective of current industry standards and the expectations of the traveling public. Less than two-thirds of the lodgings establishments open for business are listed in AAA publications.

Virtually all listings include AAA's esteemed "diamond" rating, reflecting the overall quality of the establishment. Many factors are considered in the process of determining the diamond rating. In lodging properties, the facility is first "classified" according to its physical design—is it a motel, a hotel, a resort, an apartment, etc. Since the various types of lodging establishments offer differing amenities and facilities, rating criteria are specific for each classification. For example, a motel, which typically offers a room with convenient parking and little if any recreational or public facilities, is rated using criteria designed only for motel-type establishments—it is not compared to a hotel with its extensive public and meeting areas, or to a resort with its wide range of recreational facilities and programs. The diamonds do, however, represent standard levels of quality in all types of establishments.

There is no charge for a property to be listed in AAA publications. Many lodgings and restaurants, however, choose to advertise their AAA approval by displaying the AAA 🅰🅰🅰 emblem on the premises and using it in their adver-

tising. These properties are especially interested in serving AAA members.

Properties are listed alphabetically under the nearest town, with lodging facilities first and restaurants second. The location is given from the center of town or from the nearest major highway.

Nearly all lodging and restaurant facilities accept credit cards as forms of payment for services rendered. The following symbols are used to identify the specific cards accepted by each property.

AE	American Express
CB	Carte Blanche
DI	Diner's Club International
DS	Discover
ER	En Route (European)
JCB	Japanese credit card
MC	MasterCard
VI	VISA

Some lodgings and restaurants listed in Auto Club publications have symbols indicating that they are accessible to individuals with disabilities. The criteria used in qualifying these listings are consistent with, but do not represent the full scope of, the Americans with

Disabilities Act of 1990. AAA does not evaluate recreational facilities, banquet rooms or convention and meeting facilities for accessibility. Individuals with disabilities are urged to phone ahead to fully understand an establishment's facilities and accessibility.

In accommodations, a 🚹 indicates that at least one fully accessible guest room exists and that an individual with mobility impairments will be able to park and enter the building, register, and use at least one food and beverage outlet. For restaurants, the symbol indicates that parking, dining rooms and rest rooms are accessible.

The ⊡ at the end of a lodging listing means that the following elements are provided: closed captioned decoders; text telephones; visual notification for fire alarms, incoming phone calls and door knocks; and, phone amplification devices.

Lodging

The following accommodations classifications appear in this book.

Bed & Breakfast—Usually a small establishment emphasizing personal attention. Individually decorated guest rooms provide an at-home feeling but may lack some amenities such as TVs, phones, etc. Usually owner-operated with a common room or parlor where guests and owners can interact during evening and breakfast hours. May have shared bathrooms. A continental or full hot breakfast is included in the room rate.

Complex—A combination of two or more kinds of lodgings.

Cottage—Individual bungalow, cabin or villa, usually containing one rental unit equipped for housekeeping. May

have a separate living room and bedroom(s). Parking is usually at each unit.

Country Inn—Similar in definition to a bed and breakfast. Offers a dining room reflecting the ambience of the inn. At a minimum, breakfast and dinner are served.

Hotel—A multi-story building usually including a coffee shop, dining room, lounge, room service, convenience shops, valet, laundry and full banquet/meeting facilities. Parking may be limited.

Lodge—Typically two or more stories with all facilities in one building. Located in vacation, ski, fishing areas, etc. Usually has food and beverage service. Adequate on-premises parking.

Motel—Usually one or two stories; food service, if any, consists of a limited facility or snack bar. Often has a pool or playground. Ample parking, usually adjacent to guest rooms.

Motor Inn—Usually two or three stories, but may be a high-rise. Generally has recreation facilities, food service and ample parking. May have limited banquet/meeting facilities.

Apartment—Usually four or more stories with at least half the units equipped for housekeeping. Often in a vacation destination area. Units typically provide a full kitchen, living room and one or more bedrooms, but may be studio-type rooms with kitchen equipment in an alcove. May require minimum stay and/or offer discounts for longer stays. This classification may also modify any of the other lodging types.

Condominium—A destination property located in a resort area. Guest units consist of a bedroom, living room and kitchen. Kitchens are separate from bedrooms and are equipped with a stove, oven or microwave, refrigerator, cooking utensils and table settings for the maximum number of people occupying the unit. Linens and maid service are provided at least twice weekly. This classification may also modify any of the other lodging types.

Historic—Accommodations in restored, pre-1930 structures, reflecting the ambience of yesteryear and the surrounding region. Rooms may lack some modern amenities and have shared baths. Usually owner-operated and provides food service. Parking is usually available. This classification may also modify any of the other lodging types.

Resort—May be a destination in itself. Has a vacation atmosphere offering extensive recreational facilities for such specific interests as golf, tennis, fishing, etc. Rates may include meals under American or Modified American plans. This classification may also modify any of the other lodging types.

Suite—Units have one or more bedrooms and a living room, which may or may not be closed off from the bedrooms. This classification may also modify any of the other lodging types.

A property's **diamond rating** is not based on the room rate or any one specific aspect of its facilities or operations. Many factors are considered in calculating the rating, and certain minimum standards must be met in all inspection categories. If a property fails approval in just one category, it is not listed in Club publications. The inspection categories include housekeeping, maintenance, service, furnishings and decor. Guest comments received by AAA may also be reviewed in a property's approval/rating process.

These criteria apply to all properties listed in this publication:

- Clean and well-maintained facilities
- Hospitable staff
- Adequate parking
- A well-kept appearance
- Good quality bedding and comfortable beds with adequate illumination
- Comfortable furnishings and decor
- Smoke detectors
- Adequate towels and supplies
- At least one comfortable easy chair with adequate illumination
- A desk or other writing surface with adequate illumination

Lodging ratings range from one to five diamonds and are defined below:

♦ —Good but unpretentious. Establishments are functional. Clean and comfortable rooms must meet the basic needs of privacy and cleanliness.

♦ ♦—Shows noticeable enhancements in decor and/or quality of furnishings over those at the one-diamond level. May be recently constructed or an older property. Targets the needs of a budget-oriented traveler.

♦ ♦ ♦ —Offers a degree of sophistication with additional amenities, services and facilities. There is a marked upgrade in services and comfort.

♦ ♦ ♦ ♦ —Excellent properties displaying high levels of service and hospitality and offering a wide variety of amenities and upscale facilities, inside the room, on the grounds and in the common areas.

♦ ♦ ♦ ♦ ♦—Renowned for an exceptionally high degree of service, attractive and luxurious facilities and many extra amenities. Guest services are executed and presented in a flawless manner. Guests are pampered by a very professional, attentive staff. The property's facilities and operations set standards in hospitality and service.

Occasionally a property is listed without a rating, as when an establishment was under construction or undergoing renovations at press time, and a rating could not be determined. A few non-rated bed & breakfast facilities are included as a courtesy to our readers.

Room rates shown in the listings are provided by each establishment's management for publication by the Auto Club. **All rates are subject to change.** During special events or holiday periods rates may exceed those published and special discounts or savings programs may not be honored. High-season rates are always shown; off-season rates are listed if they are substantially lower than the rest of the year. Rates are for typical rooms, not special units, and do not include taxes.

Many properties make special and discounted rates available exclusively to AAA members; two publications list these rates: The AAA *TourBook*, published annually, offers two additional rate options: *Guaranteed Rates*, meaning the management has agreed to honor the published rates for AAA members; *AAA Special Value Rates*, which gives AAA members at least 10 percent off the published rates. The monthly *Member $aver*, published by the Automobile Club of Southern California, lists many short-term rates and packages offering a minimum of 20 percent off published rates for reservations made through the Auto Club. Both publications are available to Auto Club members at no charge through Auto Club offices.

Some properties offer discounts to senior citizens, or special rate periods such as weekly or monthly rentals. Inquiries as to the availability of any special discounts should be made at the time of registration. Typically, a property will allow a guest to take advantage of only one discount during their stay (i.e., a guest staying at a property offering both the *AAA Special Value Rates* and senior discount may choose only one of the two savings plans).

Each rate line gives the dates for which the rates are valid, and the rates for one person (abbreviated 1P), two persons with one bed (2P/1B), two persons with two beds (2P/2B), and the rate for each extra person (XP) not included in the family rate. Figures following these abbreviations are the price(s) for the specified room and occupants. Most rates listed are European plan, which means that no meals are included in the rate. Some lodgings' rates include breakfast [BP] or continental breakfast [CP]. At a few properties you will find the American Plan [AP] which includes three meals, or a Modified American Plan [MAP] which offers two meals, usually breakfast and dinner.

All baths have a combination tub and shower bath unless noted otherwise. Since nearly all establishments have air conditioning, telephones and color TV, only the absence of any of these items is noted in the listing. Check-in time is shown only if it is after 3 p.m.; check-out time is shown only if it is before 10 a.m. Service charges are not shown unless they are $1 or more, or at least five percent of the room rate. If the pet acceptance policy varies within the establishment, no mention of pets is made; it is best to call ahead to verify policy. By U.S. and Canada laws, pet restrictions do not apply to guide dogs. A heated pool is heated when it is reasonable to expect use of a pool. Outdoor pools may not open in winter.

Reservations are always advisable in resort areas and may be the only way to assure obtaining the type of accommodations you want. Deposits are almost always required. Should your plans change and you need to cancel your reservation, be aware of the amount of notice required to receive a refund of your deposit. AAA members may make reservations through any AAA office.

Many properties welcome children in the same room with their parents at no additional charge; individual listings indicate if there is an age limit. There may be charges for additional equipment, such as roll-aways or cribs. Some properties offer a discount for guests age 60 and older—be aware that the Senior Discount cannot usually be taken in conjunction with or in addition to other discounts.

Fire warning and protection equipment are indicated by the symbols Ⓓ (all guest rooms have smoke detectors) and Ⓢ (all guest rooms have sprinklers). Many properties have reserved rooms for non-smokers; look for the ⊘ symbol in the listing and if you desire a non-smoker room, be sure to make that request both when you make a reservation and upon registration.

Restaurants

Restaurants listed in this publication have been found to be consistently good dining establishments. In metropolitan areas, where many restaurants are above average, we select some of those known for the superiority of their food, service and atmosphere and also those offering a selection of quality food at moderate prices (including some cafeterias and family restaurants). In smaller communities the restaurants considered to be the best in the area may be listed.

The type of cuisine featured at a restaurant is used as a means of classification for restaurants. You will find listings for Steakhouses and Continental cuisine as well as a range of ethnic foods, such as Chinese, Japanese, Italian and yes, American. Special menu types, such as early bird, a la carte, children's or Sunday brunch, are also listed. We have tried to indicate something about each restaurant's atmosphere and appropriate attire. The availability of alcoholic beverages is shown, as well as entertainment and dancing.

Prices are given in ranges of $10-dollar increments. Taxes and tips are not included.

Restaurant ratings are applied to two categories of operational style—full-service eating establishments, and self-service, family-dining operations such as cafeterias or buffets.

♦ —Good but unpretentious dishes. Table settings are usually simple and may include paper placemats and napkins. Alcoholic beverage service, if any, may be limited to beer and wine. Usually informal with an atmosphere conducive to family dining.

♦ ♦ —More extensive menus representing more complex food preparation and, usually, a wider variety of alcoholic beverages. The atmosphere is appealing and suitable for either family or adult dining. Service may be casual, but host or hostess seating can be expected. Table settings may include tablecloths and cloth napkins.

♦ ♦ ♦ —Extensive or specialized menus and more complex cuisine preparation requiring a professional chef contribute to either a formal dining experience or a special family meal. Cloth table linens, above-average quality table settings, a skilled service staff and an inviting decor should all be provided. Generally, the wine list includes representatives of the best domestic and foreign wine-producing regions.

♦ ♦ ♦ ♦ —An appealing ambience is often enhanced by fresh flowers and fine furnishings. The overall sophistication and formal atmosphere visually create a dining experience more for adults than for families. A wine steward presents an extensive list of the best wines. A smartly attired, highly skilled staff is capable of describing how any dish is prepared. Elegant silverware, china and correct glassware are typical. The menu includes creative dishes prepared from fresh ingredients by a chef who frequently has international training. Eye-appealing desserts are offered at tableside.

♦ ♦ ♦ ♦ ♦ —A world-class operation with even more luxury and sophistication than four-diamond restaurants. A proportionally large staff, expert in preparing tableside delicacies, provides flawless service. Tables are set with impeccable linens, silver and crystal glassware.

Arroyo Grande

ARROYO VILLAGE INN   ♦♦♦ Bed & Breakfast
Adjacent to US 101; exit Grand Ave, west side via Barnett St to 407 El Camino Real (93420).
(805) 489-5926.

All year [BP]	1P $ 75-105	2P/1B $ 95-195	2P/2B $ 95-165

XP $25. Senior discount; mid-week discount. Reservation deposit required; 14-day refund notice. Weekly rates. 3 stories; interior corridors. 7 rooms. Victorian style inn, beautifully decorated in antiques and Laura Ashley prints. TV and phone by request. No pets. AE, DI, DS, MC, VI. Ⓓ ⊘ Outside smoking area.

BEST WESTERN CASA GRANDE INN ⒶⒶⒶ   ♦♦♦ Motor Inn
1 block east of US 101 at 850 Oak Park Rd (93420).
(805) 481-7398; FAX (805) 481-4859.

All year [CP]	1P $ 55- 90	2P/1B $ 55- 95	2P/2B $ 55- 95

XP $10; children age 18 and under free. Reservation deposit required; 30-day cancellation notice. 2 stories; exterior corridors. 103 rooms; 2 2-bedroom units; 7 efficiency suites. Movies; some refrigerators. Heated pool, saunas, whirlpools, exercise room. Coin laundry. Meeting rooms. AE, CB, DI, DS, MC, VI. Restaurant, 7 am-10 pm, Sun 9 am-9 pm; $10-19; cocktails. Ⓓ ⊘

ECONO LODGE ⒶⒶⒶ   ♦♦♦ Motel
Adjacent to US 101, northbound exit Brisco, southbound exit Halcyon Rd to 611 El Camino Real (93420).
(805) 489-9300; FAX (805) 473-8318.

All year	1P $ 40-110	2P/1B $ 40-110	2P/2B $ 45-125

XP $10. Senior discount. Reservation deposit required; 3-day cancellation notice. 2 stories; exterior corridors. 40 rooms. Cable TV; some microwaves and refrigerators; no air conditioning. Pool. Pets, $10 (designated rooms). AE, CB, DI, DS, MC, VI. Restaurant nearby. D ⊘

THE GUEST HOUSE			Bed & Breakfast

120 Hart Ln (93420).
(805) 481-9304.

All year [BP]	1P $ 45	2P/1B $ 60	2P/2B ...

XP $10. No specified check-in or check-out times. Reservation deposit required; 36-hr cancellation notice. 2 guest rooms with 1 shared bath. New England Colonial-style house with antique furnishings is set among old-fashioned gardens; located in Arroyo Grande Village. No pets; two resident cats. Full breakfast served in the parlor or on the terrace. Beverages served in the afternoon. Smoking permitted in the public rooms only

Atascadero

BEST WESTERN COLONY INN ⓐⓐⓐ			♦♦♦ Motor Inn

East side of US 101; exit San Anselmo Rd, ½ mile north to 3600 El Camino Real (93422).
(805) 466-4449; FAX (805) 466-2119.

5/12-9/11	1P $ 49- 69	2P/1B $ 49- 75	2P/2B $ 58- 83
9/12-5/11	1P $ 46- 59	2P/1B $ 50- 65	2P/2B $ 56- 72

XP $8; children age 11 and under stay free. Credit card guarantee. Senior discount. 2-3 stories; interior corridors. 75 units. Cable TV, movies, refrigerators; some whirlpools. Heated pool, saunas; whirlpool. Pets, $100 deposit. Meeting rooms. AE, CB, DI, DS, MC, VI. Restaurant, 6 am-11 pm; $9-16; cocktails. D ⊘

RANCHO TEE MOTEL ⓐⓐ			♦♦ Motel

On SR 41, 1 block north of Jct US 101 at 6895 El Camino Real (93422).
(805) 466-2231; FAX (805) 466-0214.

Fri-Sat	1P $ 75	2P/1B $ 85	2P/2B $ 95
Sun-Thu	1P $ 46	2P/1B $ 50	2P/2B $ 50

XP $5; children age 12 and under stay free. Reservation deposit required; 7-day cancellation notice. Weekly rates. Senior discount. 2 stories; exterior corridors. 27 rooms; 2 kitchens. Cable TV, movies; some refrigerators. Pool. Pets, $5; $30 deposit. AE, DS, MC, VI. Coffee shop nearby. D ⊘

SUPER 8 MOTEL			♦ Motel

On SR 41, ½ block west of jct US 101 at 6505 Morro Rd (93422).
(805) 466-0794.

5/16-8/31	1P $ 49- 59	2P/1B $ 53- 64	2P/2B $ 64- 95
9/1-5/15	1P $ 39- 49	2P/1B $ 48- 59	2P/2B $ 49- 64

XP $8; children age 12 and under stay free. Reservation deposit required; 10-day cancellation notice. Senior discount. 2 stories; exterior corridors. 30 rooms. Cable TV, movies, coffee makers. Small pets only, $5; $100 deposit. AE, CB, DS, MC, VI. D ⊘

Ballard

LODGING

THE BALLARD INN   ◆◆◆◆ Bed & Breakfast
3½ miles northeast of Solvang via Alamo Pintado Rd; 2436 Baseline Ave (93463).
(805) 688-7770; FAX (805) 688-9560.

All year [BP]   1P $160-195   2P/1B $160-195   2P/2B …

10% service charge. Credit card guarantee; 7-day cancellation notice. 2 stories;
interior/exterior corridor. 15 rooms. A charming inn with individually decorated
rooms, 7 with fireplace. Telephone jacks, cable TV hookups; some shower baths.
Rental bicycles. No pets. AE, MC, VI. Afternoon tea & beverages. Ⓓ Smoke-free
premises

RESTAURANT

THE BALLARD STORE RESTAURANT   ◆◆◆ Continental
3½ miles northeast of Solvang via Alamo Pintado Rd; 2436 Baseline Ave (93463).
(805) 688-5319.

$11-20; prixe fixe menu, $17.95. Open 5:30-9:30 pm; Sat 6-9:30 pm; Sun 10:30 am-
2 & 5-8:30 pm; closed Mon, Tue, 12/24 and 12/25. Reservations suggested. Fine
dining in a French country atmosphere. International cuisine. Extensive selection
of California wines. Casual attire. Children's menu, early bird specials, gourmet picnic boxes available with advance arrangements. Cocktails. AE, MC, VI. ⊘

Buellton

LODGING

BEST WESTERN PEA SOUP ANDERSEN'S INN 🅰🅰   ◆◆◆ Motel
1 block west of jct US 101 at 51 E Hwy 246 (Box 197, 93427).
(805) 688-3216; FAX (805) 688-9767.

5/1-9/30 [CP]   1P $ 55- 70   2P/1B $ 55- 80   2P/2B $ 55- 70
10/1-4/30 [CP]   1P $ 45- 60   2P/1B $ 45- 60   2P/2B $ 45- 60

XP $10; children age 12 and under stay free. Monthly rates. Reservation deposit
required. 2 stories; exterior corridors. 97 rooms. Cable TV; some microwaves, refrigerators. Putting green; heated pool, whirlpool; playground. No pets. Meeting
rooms. AE, CB, DI, DS, MC, VI. Restaurant nearby. Ⓓ ⊘

ECONO LODGE 🅰🅰   ◆◆ Motel
*Adjacent to US 101; southbound first Buellton exit; northbound Frontage Rd exit, then 1
block west over the frwy; 630 Ave of Flags (93427).*
(805) 688-0022; FAX (805) 688-7448.

All year   1P $ 30- 60   1P/1B $ 40- 70   2P/2B $ 40- 70

XP $10; children age 18 and under stay free. Reservation deposit required in sum-
mer. Weekly & monthly rates. Senior discount. 2-3 stories; interior/exterior corridors. 60 rooms; 16 efficiencies, $59.95-68.95 for 2 persons. Cable TV, movies.
Coin laundry. Small pets only. AE, DS, MC, VI. Ⓓ Ⓢ ⊘

RAMADA INN AT THE WINDMILL ⦿

♦♦♦ Motel

Adjacent to US 101 at 114 E SR 246 (93427).
(805) 688-8448; FAX (805) 686-1338.

Fri-Sat 5/24-9/21	1P	$ 88	2P/1B	$ 94	2P/2B	$ 94	
Sun-Thu 5/24-9/21	1P	$ 56- 62	2P/1B	$ 66- 72	2P/2B	$ 66- 72	
Fri-Sat 9/22-5/23	1P	$ 86	2P/1B	$ 92	2P/2B	$ 92	
Sun-Thu 9/22-5/23	1P	$ 44- 54	2P/1B	$ 50- 60	2P/2B	$ 50- 60	

XP $6; children age 18 and under stay free. Senior discount. Monthly rates. 2 stories; exterior corridors. 110 rooms. Cable TV, movies; some refrigerators, microwaves. Heated pool, whirlpool. Coin laundry. No pets. Meeting rooms. AE, CB, DI, DS, JCB, MC, VI. Cocktail lounge. Ⓓ ⊘

SANTA YNEZ VALLEY INN CROWN PLAZA RESORT ⦿

♦♦♦ Motor Inn

Formerly Holiday Inn-Solvang Buellton. Adjacent to US 101, exit SR 246, ¼ mile north to 555 McMurray Rd (93427).
(805) 688-1000; FAX (805) 688-0380.

All year	1P	$ 69-105	2P/1B	$ 69-105	2P/2B	$ 69-105

XP $10; children age 18 and under stay free. Senior discount. 4 stories; interior corridors. 149 rooms; 7 suites with heart-shaped whirlpool tub. Located in center of town. Cable TV, free and pay movies, bars, coffee makers; rental refrigerators. Heated pool, steam room, 2 indoor whirlpools, racquetball court, 1 tennis court; fee for massage, tanning bed, video game room. Coin laundry. Local transportation. No pets. Meeting rooms, data ports. AE, CB, DI, DS, JCB, MC, VI. Coffee shop, 7 am-10 pm; see separate listing for Federico's. Ⓓ Ⓢ ⊘

RESTAURANTS

A J SPURS ⦿

♦♦ American

On SR 246, ¼ mile east of US 101 at 350 E SR 246 (93427).
(805) 686-1655.

$11-20; extra plate fee $6.95. Open 4-9:30 pm; closed 1/1, Thanksgiving, 12/24 & 12/25. Reservations suggested. Casual, western-style family dining featuring steaks, ribs, barbecue chicken & seafood. Large portions. Children's menu, early-bird specials. Cocktails & lounge. AE, MC, VI. X

FEDERICO'S

♦♦ Mexican

At Santa Ynez Valley Inn Crown Plaza Resort, 585 McMurray Rd (93427).
(805) 688-0606.

$11-20. Open 11:30 am-10 pm; Sun 10:30 am-9 pm. Large dining area, attractively decorated. Small gift shop. Casual attire. Children's menu, senior menu. Cocktails & lounge. AE, CB, DI, DS, JCB, MC, VI. Smoke-free premises

THE HITCHING POST II

♦♦ Steakhouse

On SR 246, ½ mile east from jct US 101 at 406 E SR 246 (93427).
(805) 688-0676.

$11-20. Open 5-10 pm; Sun 4-9 pm; closed major holidays. Reservations suggested. Well-known for steak & barbecue specialties. Children's menu, early-bird specials. Cocktails & lounge. AE, MC, VI. Smoke-free premises

Camarillo

LODGING

BEST WESTERN CAMARILLO INN ⬛　　　　◆◆◆ Motel
Adjacent to US 101; ¼ mile northeast, exit Los Posas Rd to 295 E Daily Dr (93010).
(805) 987-4991; FAX (805) 388-3679.

| All year [CP] | 1P $ 52 | 2P/1B $ 57 | 2P/2B $ 60 |

XP $5; children age 12 and under stay free. Reservation deposit required; 3-day cancellation notice. 2 stories; exterior corridors. 58 rooms. Movies; some refrigerators, whirlpools. Small heated pool, whirlpool. No pets. Conference facilities, meeting rooms. AE, CB, DI, DS, JCB, MC, VI. Restaurant nearby. Ⓓ ⊗

COMFORT INN ⬛　　　　◆◆ Motel
Adjacent to US 101, ½ mile southeast; exit Central Ave to 984 Ventura Bl (93010).
(805) 987-4188; FAX (805) 987-3450.

| 5/1-9/15 | 1P $ 47 | 2P/1B $ 53 | 2P/2B $ 59 |
| 9/16-4/30 | 1P $ 45 | 2P/1B $ 49 | 2P/2B $ 53 |

XP $6; children age 17 and under stay free. Reservation deposit required; 3-day cancellation notice. Weekly & monthly rates. 3 stories; exterior corridors. 70 rooms; 11 suites, $65-69. Cable TV, movies; some refrigerators. Small heated pool, whirlpool. Pets, $5. Meeting rooms. AE, CB, DI, DS, JCB, MC, VI. Ⓓ Ⓢ ⊗

COUNTRY INN AT CAMARILLO ⬛　　　　◆◆◆ Motel
Adjacent to US 101, north side, ½ mile west; exit Central Ave to 1405 Del Norte Rd (93010).
(805) 983-7171; FAX (805) 983-1838.

| All year [BP] | 1P $ 66 | 2P/1B $ 66 | 2P/2B $ 66 |

XP $10; children age 12 and under stay free. 3 stories; interior corridors. 100 rooms. Refrigerators; some VCPs. Heated pool, whirlpool. Coin laundry. No pets. AE, CB, DI, DS, JCB, MC, VI. Complimentary evening beverages. Ⓓ Ⓢ ⊗

COURTYARD BY MARRIOTT　　　　◆◆◆ Motor Inn
Adjacent north side of US 101, exit Pleasant Valley Rd/Santa Rosa Rd to 4994 Verdugo Wy (93012).
(805) 388-1020; FAX (805) 987-6274.

| Sun-Thu | 1P $ 66 | 2P/1B $ 66 | 2P/2B $ 66 |
| Fri-Sat | 1P $ 64 | 2P/1B $ 64 | 2P/2B $ 64 |

Credit card guarantee. Weekly rates. Senior discount. 2 stories; interior corridors. 130 rooms. Many patios or balconies. Cable TV, free and pay movies; some microwaves, refrigerators. Heated pool, whirlpool. Coin laundry. No pets. Conference facilities, meeting rooms, data ports. AE, CB, DI, DS, MC, VI. Restaurant; 6:30-10:30 am, Sat & Sun 7-11 am; cocktails. Ⓓ Ⓢ ⊗

DAYS INN ⬛　　　　◆◆ Motel
Adjacent to US 101; exit Los Posas Rd to 165 Daily Dr (93010).
(805) 482-0761.

| All year [CP] | 1P $ 48 | 2P/1B $ 53 | 2P/2B $ 58 |

XP $5; children age 12 and under stay free. Reservation deposit required; 3-day cancellation notice. 2 stories; exterior corridors. 82 rooms. Adjacent to shopping plaza. Movies; some shower baths, whirlpools; rental refrigerators, VCPs. Heated pool. No pets. AE, CB, DI, DS, JCB, MC, VI. Restaurant nearby. D ⊘

DEL NORTE INN ▦   ◆◆◆ Motel
Adjacent to US 101, north side; exit Central Ave; 4444 E Central Ave (93010).
(805) 485-3999; FAX (805) 485-1820.

All year [CP]	1P $ 49	2P/1B $ 49	2P/2B $ 49

XP $10; children age 12 and under stay free. Reservation deposit required. Senior discount. 3 stories; interior corridors. 110 rooms, 24 efficiencies. Patio or balcony. Cable TV; refrigerators; some microwaves, VCPs. Small heated pool, whirlpool. Coin laundry. No pets. Data ports. AE, CB, DI, DS, JCB, MC, VI. Restaurant nearby. D S ⊘

RESTAURANTS

GIOVANNI'S   ◆◆ Northern Italian
2½ miles northeast of US 101, exit Dawson Rd (Mission Oaks Plaza) to 5227 Mission Oaks Bl (93012).
(805) 484-4376.

$11-20. Open 11 am-2:30 & 5-10 pm; Sat & Sun from 5 pm; closed Mon. Reservations suggested. Homemade pasta, fresh fish & eastern veal. Semi-formal atmosphere. Carryout, a la carte. Cocktails & lounge. AE, MC, VI. ⊘

OTTAVIO'S   ◆◆ Italian
½ block southeast of US 101; exit Carmen Dr to 1620 Ventura Bl (93010).
(805) 482-3810.

$11-20; minimum charge $5.50 weekends. Open 11 am-10 pm; Sun to 9 pm; closed 12/25. Reservations suggested weekends. Selection of seafood, steaks & pasta. Informal atmosphere. Children's menu, carryout, a la carte. Buffet lunch Mon-Fri 11:30 am-1:30 pm. Cocktails & lounge. AE, CB, DI, DS, MC, VI. ⊘

Cambria

LODGING

THE BEACH HOUSE BED & BREAKFAST ▦   ◆◆ Bed & Breakfast
2 miles north, adjacent to SR 1 at 6360 Moonstone Beach Dr (93428).
(805) 927-3136.

All year [BP]	1P $120-150	2P/1B $125-155	2P/2B …

Closed 12/24-25. Reservation deposit required; 7-day cancellation notice. 3 stories; interior/exterior corridors. 7 rooms. Across from beach. Attractive rooms with full or partial ocean view, some with fireplace. Cable TV, movies; some shower baths; no air conditioning, phones. No pets. MC, VI. D Designated smoking area

BEST WESTERN FIRESIDE INN ▦   ◆◆◆ Motel
2¼ miles north adjacent to SR 1 at 6700 Moonstone Beach Dr (93428).
(805) 927-8661; FAX (805) 927-8584.

6/30-9/5 [CP]	1P	$ 95-135	2P/1B	$ 95-135	2P/2B	$ 95-105
Fri-Sun 9/6-6/29 [CP]	1P	$ 85-120	2P/1B	$ 85-120	2P/2B	$ 85-120
Mon-Thu 9/6-6/29 [CP]	1P	$ 75-115	2P/1B	$ 75-115	2P/2B	$ 75- 85

XP $10; children age 17 and under stay free. Reservation deposit required. Monthly rates. Interior/exterior corridors. 46 rooms. Across from beach. Spacious rooms; many with gas fireplace. Cable TV, movies, refrigerators, coffee makers; some rooms with whirlpool; no air conditioning. Heated pool; whirlpool. No pets. AE, CB, DI, DS, JCB, MC, VI. Ⓓ ⊘

BLUE BIRD MOTEL ◍   ♦♦ Motel
In East Village area, 2 blocks west of Burton Dr at 1880 Main St (93428).
(805) 927-4634.

All year	1P	$ 38- 78	2P/1B	$ 42- 78	2P/2B	$ 44- 78

XP $6; children age 12 and under stay free. Reservation deposit required. 2 stories; exterior corridors. 37 rooms; 1 2-bedroom unit; some new creekside rooms and suites with refrigerator and fireplace. Cable TV; some shower baths, coffee makers, refrigerators, phones, VCPs; no air conditioning. No pets. AE, CB, DI, DS, JCB, MC, VI. Restaurant nearby. Ⓓ ⊘

BLUE DOLPHIN INN ◍   ♦♦♦♦ Motel
2½ miles north; adjacent to SR 1 at 6470 Moonstone Beach Dr (93428).
(805) 927-3300.

4/1-10/31 &						
Fri-Sat 11/1-3/31 [CP]	1P	...	2P/1B	$ 85-165	2P/2B	$ 85-165
Sun-Thu 11/1-3/31 [CP]	1P	...	2P/1B	$ 75-145	2P/2B	$ 75-145

XP $5. Credit card guarantee; 3-day cancellation notice. 2 stories; interior corridors. 18 rooms. Across from beach. French country decor, rooms with gas fireplace, some with ocean view. Cable TV, free and pay movies, VCPs, refrigerators; some rooms with whirlpool, extra charge; no air conditioning. No pets. AE, DI, MC, VI. Ⓓ Ⓢ ⊘

BLUE WHALE INN BED & BREAKFAST ◍   ♦♦♦♦ Bed & Breakfast
2¼ miles north, adjacent to SR 1 at 6736 Moonstone Beach Dr (93428).
(805) 927-4647.

All year [BP]	1P	$135-170	2P/1B	$135-180	2P/2B	...

Reservation deposit required; 10-day cancellation notice. 2-night minimum stay on weekends. Exterior corridors. 6 rooms. Overlooking the ocean. Beautifully decorated rooms in European country decor with canopy beds and gas fireplaces. Cable TV, refrigerators; no air conditioning. No pets. MC, VI. Complimentary afternoon refreshments. Ⓓ Smoke-free premises

CAMBRIA LANDING ON MOONSTONE BEACH ◍   ♦♦♦ Motel
2¼ miles north, adjacent to SR 1 at 6530 Moonstone Beach Dr (93428).
(805) 927-1619.

Fri-Sat [CP]	1P	$ 75-200	2P/1B	$ 75-200	2P/2B	$ 85-120
Sun-Thu [CP]	1P	$ 75-150	2P/1B	$ 75-150	2P/2B	$ 75-120

XP $5. Credit card guarantee; 7-day cancellation notice. 2 stories; interior corridors. 26 rooms; 6 cottages with whirlpool tub. Across from beach. All rooms with gas fireplace, some with balcony and ocean view. Cable TV, VCPs, refrigerators; no air conditioning. 2 indoor whirlpools. No pets. DS, MC, VI. Restaurant nearby. Ⓓ Ⓢ

CAMBRIA PINES LODGE ⊕ ♦♦ Motor Inn
From SR 1, take Burton Dr ½ mile north; 2905 Burton Dr (93428).
(805) 927-4200. FAX (805) 927-4016.

2/1-5/25 & 9/4-12/23	1P $ 60-110	2P/1B $ 60-110	2P/2B $ 60-110
5/26-9/3 & 12/24-1/31	1P $ 65-115	2P/1B $ 65-115	2P/2B $ 65-115

XP $5. Reservation deposit required. On several acres of open and pine-shaded grounds. Accommodations vary from rustic cabins and motel rooms to large, nicely furnished 1-bedroom suites with microwave and refrigerator. 2 stories; interior/exterior corridors. 125 rooms. Cable TV, coffee makers, rental VCPs; some shower baths; no air conditioning. Heated indoor pool, whirlpool. No pets. Meeting rooms, data ports. AE, DI, DS, MC, VI. Restaurant; 7 am-2 & 5-9 pm, Fri & Sat -10 pm; $13-$18; cocktails. Ⓓ ⊘

CAMBRIA SHORES INN ⊕ ♦♦ Motel
2 miles north; adjacent to SR 1 at 6276 Moonstone Beach Dr (93428).
(805) 927-8644.

All year [CP]	1P $ 45- 95	2P/1B $ 45- 95	2P/2B $ 55-110

XP $5. Reservation deposit required; 3-day cancellation notice. Exterior corridors. 24 rooms. Across from beach. Nice lawn area overlooking ocean. Cable TV, refrigerators, coffee makers; some shower baths; no air conditioning. Pets. AE, DS, MC, VI. Ⓓ ⊘

CAPTAIN'S COVE ⊕ ♦♦♦ Motel
2½ miles north; adjacent to SR 1 at 6454 Moonstone Beach Dr (93428).
(805) 927-8581.

Sun-Thu 10/1-4/30 [CP]	1P $ 75	2P/1B $ 75	2P/2B $ 75
5/1-9/30 & Fri-Sat 10/1-4/30 [CP]	1P $ 95	2P/1B $ 95	2P/2B $ 95

XP $10; children age 17 and under stay free. Credit card guarantee. 1 story; exterior corridors. 4 rooms. Across from beach. Charming cottage-type units nicely decorated in early American motif. Microwaves, refrigerators, cable TV, VCPs. No pets. JCB, MC, VI. Ⓓ Smoke-free premises

CASTLE INN BY THE SEA ⊕ ♦♦ Motel
2¼ miles north; adjacent to SR 1 at 6620 Moonstone Beach Dr (93428).
(805) 927-8605; FAX (805) 927-3179.

5/15-10/15	1P $ 55-100	2P/1B $ 55-100	2P/2B $ 65-100
10/16-5/14	1P $ 45-100	2P/1B $ 45-100	2P/2B $ 55-100

XP $5. Reservation deposit required. 2 stories; exterior corridors. 31 rooms. Across from beach. Many ocean-view rooms. Cable TV; some shower baths, refrigerators; no air conditioning. Heated pool; whirlpool. No pets. AE, DS, MC, VI. Restaurant nearby. Ⓓ

CREEKSIDE INN ⊕ ♦♦ Motel
¼ mile east of the East Village business area at 2618 Main St (93428).
(805) 927-4021.

| 4/2-11/30 | 1P | $ 35- 85 | 2P/1B | $ 45- 85 | 2P/2B | $ 45- 85 |
| 12/1-4/1 | 1P | $ 35- 70 | 2P/1B | $ 35- 70 | 2P/2B | $ 35- 70 |

XP 5; children age 12 and under stay free. Reservation deposit required; 3-day cancellation notice. 2 stories; exterior corridors. 21 rooms. 13 creekside rooms with balcony. Cable TV, VCPs, coffee makers; some shower baths; no air conditioning; pay movies. No pets. DS, MC, VI. ▣ ⊘

FOG CATCHER INN 🆎 ◆◆◆ Motel

2½ miles north; adjacent to SR 1 at 6400 Moonstone Beach Dr (93428).
(805) 927-1400.

| 5/26-9/5 [BP] | 1P | $ 90-145 | 2P/1B | $ 95-145 | 2P/2B | $ 90-145 |
| 9/6-5/25 [BP] | 1P | $ 70-135 | 2P/1B | $ 70-135 | 2P/2B | $ 70-135 |

XP $5. Credit card guarantee. 1-2 stories; exterior corridors. 60 rooms; 1 large unit with private balcony and ocean view, $160. Across from beach. Charming English village motif. Attractively landscaped grounds. Country decor with gas fireplace. Cable TV, coffee makers, microwaves, honor bars; no air conditioning. Heated pool; whirlpool. No pets. AE, DS, MC, VI. ▣ ⊘

THE J PATRICK HOUSE BED AND BREAKFAST INN ◆◆◆ Bed & Breakfast

½ mile north at 2990 Burton Dr (93428).
(805) 927-3812.

| All year [CP] | 1P | $105-145 | 2P/1B | $105-145 | 2P/2B | ... |

XP $30. Reservation deposit required; 5-day cancellation notice. 2 stories; interior corridors. 8 rooms. Rustic log home and guest house on nicely landscaped, tree-shaded grounds. Country decor. 6 rooms with fireplace, 1 with wood-burning stove; some shower baths; no air conditioning, phones or TVs. No pets. MC, VI. ▣ Smoke-free premises

MARINERS INN 🆎 ◆◆ Motel

1¾ miles north; adjacent to SR 1 at 6180 Moonstone Beach Dr (93428).
(805) 927-4624; FAX (805) 927-3425.

1/1-1/31 [CP]	1P	$ 32- 89	2P/1B	$ 36-115	2P/2B	$ 45-125
2/1-5/14 &						
10/1-12/31 [CP]	1P	$ 36-105	2P/1B	$ 38-105	2P/2B	$ 48-125
5/15-6/30, 9/1-9/30 &						
Sun-Thu 7/1-8/31 [CP]	1P	$ 45-135	2P/1B	$ 55-135	2P/2B	$ 58-135
Fri-Sat 7/1-8/31 [CP]	1P	$ 65-135	2P/1B	$ 65-135	2P/2B	$ 70-135

XP $10. Credit card guarantee. Senior discount. 1 story; exterior corridors. 26 rooms. Across from beach. Sun deck overlooking ocean. Many rooms with gas fireplace. Cable TV, movies; some refrigerators; no air conditioning. Whirlpool. Small pets. AE, DS, MC, VI. ▣ ⊘

MOONSTONE INN MOTEL 🆎 ◆◆◆ Motel

1¾ miles north; adjacent to SR 1 at 5860 Moonstone Beach Dr (93428).
(805) 927-4815.

| All year [CP] | 1P | $ 91-131 | 2P/1B | $ 91-135 | 2P/2B | ... |

XP $10. Reservation deposit required; 7-day cancellation notice. 2 stories; exterior corridors. 7 rooms; 6 units with gas fireplace and refrigerator. A small, charming motel with the friendly atmosphere of a country inn. Across from beach. Ocean view. English Tudor decor. Cable TV, movies, VCPs, shower baths; some whirlpools; no air conditioning. Whirlpool. No pets. AE, CB, DI, DS, MC, VI. Complimentary afternoon refreshments. Designated smoking area

OLALLIEBERRY INN 🅐🅐🅐   ♦♦♦ Historic Bed & Breakfast
2 blocks east of Burton Dr in East Village area at 2476 Main St (93428).
(805) 927-3222.

All year [BP]	1P $ 85-120	2P/1B $ 85-120	2P/2B ...

Reservation deposit required; 5-day cancellation notice. Senior discount. 2 stories; interior corridors. 6 rooms. Restored 1873 wooden house furnished with turn-of-the-century antiques. Some shower and tub baths; 3 gas fireplaces; no air conditioning, phones, TV. No pets. MC, VI. Ⓓ Smoke-free premises

SAND PEBBLES INN 🅐🅐🅐   ♦♦♦♦ Motel
2 miles north, adjacent to SR 1 at 6252 Moonstone Beach Dr (93428).
(805) 927-5600.

4/1-10/31 &			
Fri-Sat 11/1-3/31 [CP]	1P ...	2P/1B $ 85-165	2P/2B $ 85-165
Sun-Thu 11/1-3/31 [CP]	1P ...	2P/1B $ 75-145	2P/2B $ 75-145

XP $5. Credit card guarantee; 3-day cancellation notice. 2 stories; interior corridors. 23 rooms. Across from beach. French country decor. Many rooms with ocean view, all with gas fireplace. Cable TV, free and pay movies, VCPs, refrigerators; some rooms with whirlpool, extra charge; no air conditioning. No pets. AE, CB, DI, MC, VI. Ⓓ Ⓢ ⊘

SAN SIMEON PINES SEASIDE RESORT 🅐🅐🅐   ♦♦♦ Motel
3 miles north; adjacent to SR 1 on Moonstone Beach Dr (Box 117, San Simeon, 93452).
(805) 927-4648.

All year	1P ...	2P/1B $ 70- 98	2P/2B $ 70- 84

Reservation deposit required. 1-2 stories; exterior corridors. 60 rooms; 22 rooms with fireplace. Spacious, tree-shaded and nicely landscaped grounds. Private access to beach. Cable TV, coffee makers, safes; some shower baths; no air conditioning. Heated pool, playground. No pets. AE, MC, VI. Ⓓ ⊘ **(See ad below.)**

SEA OTTER INN 🆎 ♦♦♦ Motel
2¼ miles north; adjacent to SR 1 at 6656 Moonstone Beach Dr (93428).
(805) 927-5888.

5/25-10/31 &					
Fri-Sat 11/1-5/24	1P	$ 65- 90	2P/1B	$ 70-100	2P/2B $ 70-110
Sun-Thu 11/1-5/24	1P	$ 55- 75	2P/1B	$ 60- 80	2P/2B $ 60- 80

XP $5. Reservation deposit required. Exterior corridors. 25 rooms. Across from beach. Attractive grounds. Gas fireplace, cable TV, VCPs, refrigerators, coffee makers; some whirlpools; no air conditioning. Heated pool, whirlpool. No pets. CB, DI, DS, MC, VI. Ⓓ

SYLVIA'S RIGDON HALL INN 🆎 ♦♦♦ Suite Motel
In East Village, 2 blocks south of Main St at 4036 Burton Dr (93428).
(805) 927-5125.

All year [CP]	1P ...	2P/1B	$ 79-120	2P/2B ...

Reservation deposit required; 3-day cancellation notice. 2 stories; interior corridors. 8 rooms. A charming inn in the East Village shopping area. Very spacious, beautifully furnished 1-bedroom suites. Cable TV, coffee maker, refrigerator, microwave; no air conditioning. No pets. AE, MC, VI. Complimentary evening refreshments. Ⓓ ⊘

WHITE WATER INN 🆎 ♦♦♦ Motel
2½ miles north; adjacent to SR 1 at 6790 Moonstone Beach Dr (93428).
(805) 927-1066; FAX (805) 927-5902.

All year [CP]	1P ...	2P/1B	$120	2P/2B	$100

XP $10. Reservation deposit required; 3-day cancellation notice. Exterior corridors. 17 rooms; 2 rooms with private patio and whirlpool, $160. Across from beach. Many ocean-view rooms. Cable TV, movies, VCPs, refrigerators, gas fireplaces; some whirlpools; no air conditioning. No pets. AE, CB, DI, DS, MC, VI. Ⓓ Smoke-free premises

RESTAURANTS

THE BRAMBLES DINNER HOUSE 🆎 ♦♦ American
In East Village area, 2 blocks south of Main St at 4005 Burton Dr.
(805) 927-4716.

$11-20. Open 4-9:30 pm, Sat to 10 pm, Sun 9:30 am-2 and 4-9:30 pm. Reservations suggested. Selection of steaks, prime rib, chicken and seafood. Several dining areas in a charming English cottage. No air conditioning. Casual attire. Children's menu, early bird specials, Sun brunch. Cocktails & lounge. AE, CB, DI, DS, MC, VI. ⊘

THE HAMLET RESTAURANT AT MOONSTONE GARDENS ♦♦ American
3 miles north on SR 1, across from jct Moonstone Beach Dr; SR 1, (93428).
(805) 927-3535.

$11-20. Open 11:30 am-9 pm; closed 11/29-12/25. Reservations suggested. Ocean-view dining. Luncheon served in the outdoor patio garden area. Dinner served in downstairs dining room, light suppers served in upstairs lounge. No air conditioning. Casual attire. Cocktails and lounge. MC, VI.

IAN'S
♦♦♦ American

In East Village area, ½ block west of Burton Dr at 2150 Center St (93428).
(805) 927-8649.

$11-20. Open 5-9 pm, Fri to 10 pm, Sat 11 am-2 & 5-10 pm; closed 12/25. Reservations suggested. Four individually decorated dining rooms. Nice selection of beef, lamb and seafood. Casual dress. Cocktails & lounge. AE, MC, VI. ⊘

LINN'S
♦ American

In East Village, 1 block east of Burton at 2277 Main St (93428).
(805) 927-0371.

Up to $10. Open 8 am-10 pm; to 9 pm in winter; closed 12/25. Nice selection of soups, salads, sandwiches and entrees. Chicken and beef pot pies a specialty. Home-baked pies and pastries. No air conditioning. Casual dress. Children's menu, carryout, Sun brunch. Beer and wine. Gift shop. DS, MC, VI. ⊘

MOONSTONE BEACH BAR AND GRILL
♦♦ American

2¼ miles north; adjacent to SR 1 at 6550 Moonstone Beach Dr (93428).
(805) 927-3859.

$11-20. Open 11 am-9 pm, Sun from 10 am. Reservations suggested. Attractive setting with ocean view. Indoor and outdoor patio dining. No air conditioning. Casual attire. Sun brunch. Cocktails. MC, VI. ⊘

MUSTACHE PETE'S ITALIAN EATERY ⏺
♦♦ Italian

In East Village area, 1 block south of Main St at 4090 Burton Dr (93428).
(805) 927-8589.

$11-20. Open 11 am-10 pm, Sun 10 am-9 pm; closed 12/25. Casual family dining. Selection of seafood, chicken, beef, pizza and pasta entrees. No air conditioning. Early bird specials, children's menu, carryout, Sun brunch. Cocktails. AE, CB, DI, DS, MC, VI. ⊘ **(See ad below.)**

THE OLD HARMONY PASTA FACTORY
♦♦ Italian

5 miles south on SR 1.
(805) 927-5882.

$11-20. Open 5 pm-8:30, Fri & Sat to 9 pm, Sun 9:30 am-2 & 5-8:30 pm; closed Thanksgiving. Reservations suggested. Quaint, rustic atmosphere in a former creamery building. Large selection of homemade pasta entrees. Also seafood and gourmet pizza. No air conditioning. Casual attire. Sun brunch. Beer & wine. AE, MC, VI. Smoke-free premises

ROBIN'S Ⓐ   ◆◆ Ethnic
In East Village, 1 block south of Main St at 4095 Burton Dr (93428).
(805) 927-5007.

$11-20. Open 11 am-9 pm, Sun 5-9 pm; closed 11/24, 12/25. Reservations suggested on weekends. A variety of ethnic cuisines, including Indian, Mexican, Italian, Thai and Chinese. No air conditioning. Casual attire. Beer & wine. AE, MC, VI. Smoke-free premises

SEA CHEST RESTAURANT & OYSTER BAR   ◆◆ Seafood
6216 Moonstone Beach Dr (93428).
(805) 927-4514.

$11-20. Open 6-9:30 pm; closed Tue and 11/24-12/26. Reservations not accepted. Cozy, quaint California coast atmosphere. Features a nice selection of fresh seafood. No air conditioning. Casual attire. Beer and wine. Smoke-free premises

THE SOW'S EAR CAFE   ◆◆ American
In East Village area, ½ block east of Burton Dr at 2248 Main St (93428).
(805) 927-4865.

$11-20. Open 5:30-9 pm, Sat to 10 pm; closed Thanksgiving, 12/24-12/25. Reservations suggested. A cozy, comfortable restaurant with nice selection of fresh seafood, baby back ribs and chicken. Breads and dessert made on premises. No air conditioning. Street parking. Casual attire. Children's menu. Beer & wine. MC, VI. Smoke-free premises

Carpinteria

BEST WESTERN CARPINTERIA INN Ⓐ   ◆◆ Motor Inn
Adjacent to US 101; northbound exit Santa Monica Rd, southbound exit Reynolds Ave;
4558 Carpinteria Ave (93013).
(805) 684-0473; FAX (805) 684-4015.

| 5/1-10/1 | 1P $105-125 | 2P/1B $125-135 | 2P/2B $115-125 |
| 10/2-4/30 | 1P $ 91-111 | 2P/1B $105-115 | 2P/2B $ 95-105 |

XP $10; children age 11 and under stay free. Reservation deposit required; 3-day cancellation notice. 3 stories; interior corridors. 146 rooms. Many rooms with patio or balcony surrounding landscaped garden area. Some smaller rooms. Cable TV; some coffee makers, radios; rental VCPs. Small heated pool, whirlpool. Pets, $25 deposit. Meeting rooms. AE, CB, DI, DS, MC, VI. Dining room, 7-10 am & 5-9:30 pm; $9-18; cocktails. Ⓓ Ⓢ ⊘

Cayucos

BEACHWALKER INN Ⓐ   ◆◆ Motel
501 S Ocean Ave (93430).
(805) 995-2133.

Sun-Thu 6/15-9/15	1P $ 55-110	2P/1B $ 55-110	2P/2B $ 60- 65
Fri-Sat 6/15-9/15	1P $ 65-110	2P/1B $ 65-110	2P/2B $ 70- 75
Sun-Thu 9/16-6/14	1P $ 45- 80	2P/1B $ 45- 80	2P/2B $ 50- 55
Fri-Sat 9/16-6/14	1P $ 55- 95	2P/1B $ 55- 95	2P/2B $ 60- 65

XP $10; children age 12 and under stay free. Reservation deposit required. Weekly rates. 2 stories; exterior corridors. 24 rooms; rooms and 1-bedroom suites with efficiency, can be combined into 2-bedroom suites. 1 block to beach. Gas fireplace, cable TV, VCPs, coffee makers; no air conditioning. No pets. AE, CB, DI, DS, MC, VI. Ⓓ ⊘

CYPRESS TREE MOTEL ♦♦ Motel
125 S Ocean Ave (93430).
(805) 995-3917.

5/22-9/15	1P ...	2P/1B	$ 50- 60	2P/2B	$ 60- 75
9/16-5/21	1P ...	2P/1B	$ 31- 56	2P/2B	$ 35- 59

XP $5. Credit card guarantee. Senior discount. 1-2 stories; exterior corridors. 11 rooms. 3 kitchens, $10 extra. 1 block to beach. Cable TV, VCPs; some shower baths; no air conditioning. No pets. AE, DS, MC, VI. Restaurant nearby. Ⓓ

DOLPHIN INN 🆔 ♦ Motel
On SR 1 business route at 399 S Ocean Ave (93430).
(805) 995-3810.

Fri-Sat 6/30-9/30 [CP]	1P	$ 55- 95	2P/1B	$ 65-105	2P/2B	$ 75- 85
Sun-Thu 6/30-9/30 [CP]	1P	$ 45- 85	2P/1B	$ 45- 85	2P/2B	$ 55- 75
Fri-Sat 10/1-6/29 [CP]	1P	$ 45- 75	2P/1B	$ 45- 85	2P/2B	$ 45- 65
Sun-Thu 10/1-6/29 [CP]	1P	$ 35- 45	2P/1B	$ 35- 65	2P/2B	$ 45- 55

XP $10; children age 10 and under stay free. Reservation deposit required. Weekly rates. 1 story; exterior corridors. 18 rooms; 5 rooms with kitchen and whirlpool. Cozy motel units and cottages. Limited rooms. Cable TV, movies, coffee makers; some shower baths; no air conditioning. Pets. AE, DS, MC, VI. Ⓓ

ESTERO BAY MOTEL 🆔 ♦♦ Motel
On SR 1 business route at 25 S Ocean Ave (93430).
(805) 995-3614.

5/1-10/15	1P	$ 50- 82	2P/1B	$ 50- 82	2P/2B	$ 55- 85
10/16-4/30	1P	$ 30- 72	2P/1B	$ 30- 75	2P/2B	$ 45- 85

XP $8. Reservation deposit required; 5-day cancellation notice. Weekly rates. Senior discount. 1 story; exterior corridors. 12 rooms; 4 kitchens & 1 efficiency, $10 extra. ½ block to beach. Cable TV, movies, VCPs, coffee makers; some shower baths; no air conditioning. Pets, $10. AE, MC, VI. Ⓓ

Fillmore

BEST WESTERN LA POSADA MOTEL 🆔 ♦♦ Motel
½ mile west on SR 126 at 827 Ventura St (93015).
(805) 524-0440; FAX (805) 524-1463.

All year	1P	$ 45- 55	2P/1B	$ 50- 60	2P/2P	$ 50- 70

XP $6. Reservation deposit required. Senior discount. 2 stories; exterior corridors. 49 rooms. Orange trees in planting areas. Cable TV, movies; some shower baths, radios, VCPs. Pool, sauna, whirlpool. No pets. AE, CB, DI, DS, MC, VI. Restaurant nearby. Ⓓ ⊘

Grover Beach

OAK PARK INN Ⓐ ♦♦♦ Motel
1 block west of US 101, exit Oak Park Blvd; 775 Oak Park Blvd (93433).
(805) 481-4448; FAX (805) 473-3609.

5/15-10/1 [CP]	1P	$ 49- 79	2P/1B $ 59- 89	2P/2B $ 59- 95
10/2-5/14 [CP]	1P	$ 49- 65	2P/1B $ 55- 75	2P/2B $ 55- 79

XP $5; children age 15 and under stay free. Reservation deposit required. Senior discount. 3 stories; interior corridors. 35 rooms; 4 rooms with whirlpool tub and gas fireplace, $95-120. Attractive hillside location. Cable TV, movies. Heated pool, whirlpool, exercise room. No pets. Data ports. AE, CB, DI, DS, MC, VI. Restaurant nearby. Ⓓ Ⓢ ⊘

Lompoc

LODGING

BEST WESTERN PORTO FINALE INN Ⓐ ♦♦♦ Motel
1 mile east on SR 1 & 246 at 940 E Ocean Ave (93436).
(805) 735-7731; FAX (805) 736-8925.

3/1-9/30 [BP]	1P	$ 38- 45	2P/1B $ 45- 49	2P/2B $ 55- 60
10/1-2/28 [BP]	1P	$ 38- 42	2P/1B $ 38- 42	2P/2B $ 45- 52

Reservation deposit required; 3-day cancellation notice. Weekly & monthly rates. 2 stories; exterior corridors. 82 rooms. Well appointed rooms; nicely landscaped grounds. Cable TV, refrigerator; rental microwaves. Heated pool, whirlpool. Coin laundry. Pets, $10. Meeting rooms. AE, DI, DS, MC, VI. Ⓓ ⊘

EMBASSY SUITES HOTEL ♦♦♦ Suite Motor Inn
1¼ miles north on SR 1 at 1117 N H St (93436).
(805) 735-8311; FAX (805) 735-8459.

All year [BP]	1P	$ 75	2P/1B $ 85	2P/2B …

XP $10; children age 12 and under stay free. Reservation deposit required. Senior discount. 3 stories; exterior corridors. 156 2-room suites surrounding outdoor pool and garden area; 1 2-bedroom apartment, $175. Cable TV, free and pay movies, refrigerators, microwaves; some shower baths. Heated pool, whirlpool, exercise room. Coin laundry. No pets. Meeting rooms. AE, CB, DI, DS, JCB, MC, VI. Complimentary evening beverages. Restaurant nearby. Ⓓ Ⓢ ⊘

INN OF LOMPOC Ⓐ ♦♦♦ Motel
1¼ miles north on SR 1 at 1122 N H St (93436).
(805) 735-7744; FAX (805) 736-0421.

All year [CP]	1P	$ 51	2P/1B $ 57	2P/2B $ 57

XP $6; children age 12 and under stay free. Weekly & monthly rates. Senior discount. 2 stories; interior/exterior corridors. 90 rooms. Downtown location. Cable TV, movies, coffee makers, refrigerators; some shower baths; rental microwaves. Heated indoor pool, whirlpool, exercise room. Coin laundry. Pets, $25. Meeting rooms. AE, CB, DI, DS, JCB, MC, VI. Restaurant nearby. Complimentary evening beverages. Ⓓ ⊘

LODGING & RESTAURANTS

QUALITY INN & EXECUTIVE SUITES 🆎   ♦♦♦ Motel
1¾ miles north on SR 1 at 1621 N H St (93436).
(805) 735-8555; FAX (805) 735-8566.

All year [CP]   1P $ 54- 75   2P/1B $ 59- 80   2P/2B $ 59- 80

XP $5; children age 18 and under stay free. Reservation deposit required. Breakfast and package plans. 3 stories; interior corridors. 218 rooms; 91 executive suites with efficiency, $75-80. Downtown area. Cable TV, free and pay movies, coffee makers; some microwaves, refrigerators. Heated pool, whirlpool; fee for massage. Coin laundry. Pets, $15. Meeting rooms. AE, CB, DI, DS, JCB, MC, VI. Restaurant nearby. Complimentary evening beverages. Ⓓ Ⓢ ⊘

REDWOOD INN 🆎   ♦ Motel
1¼ miles north on SR 1 at 1200 N H St (93436).
(805) 735-3737; FAX (805) 735-3510.

All year   1P $ 40- 45   2P/1B $ 40- 45   2P/2B $ 40- 45

XP $2. Reservation deposit required; 4-day cancellation notice. Weekly & monthly rates. Senior discount. 2 stories; interior/exterior corridors. 60 rooms. Downtown location. Cable TV, movies, refrigerators; some shower baths; no air conditioning; rental microwaves, VCPs. Sauna. Coin laundry. Pets, $10. AE, CB, DI, DS, MC, VI. Restaurant nearby. Ⓓ ⊘

TALLY HO MOTOR INN 🆎   ♦♦ Motel
1 mile east on SR 1 & 246 at 1020 E Ocean Ave (93436).
(805) 735-6444; FAX (805) 735-5558.

All year   1P $ 29- 55   2P/1B $ 29- 55   2P/2B $ 45

Reservation deposit required. Weekly & monthly rates. 2 stories; exterior corridors. 53 rooms; few smaller economy rooms; 4 2-room units with efficiency, $55. Cable TV; some refrigerators, microwaves, coffee makers; rental VCPs. Sauna, indoor whirlpool. Coin laundry. Pets, $10. AE, CB, DI, DS, JCB, MC, VI. Ⓓ ⊘ **(See ad below.)**

RESTAURANT

THE OUTPOST   ♦ American
Corner of 7th St at 1501 E Ocean Ave (93436).
(805) 735-1130.

$11-20. Open 11 am-10 pm. Country western decor. Beef, chicken and fish entrees. Hamburgers and sandwiches served all day. Casual attire. Children's menu, early bird specials, senior's menu. Cocktails & lounge; entertainment. AE, DS, MC, VI. ⊘

Los Olivos

LODGING

LOS OLIVOS GRAND HOTEL ⊛   ♦♦♦♦ Country Inn
½ mile south of SR 154 at 2860 Grand Ave (PO Box 526, 93441).
(805) 688-7788; FAX (805) 688-1942.

Fri-Sat	1P	$210-325	2P/1B	$210-325	2P/2B $230
Sun-Thu	1P	$160-300	2P/1B	$160-300	2P/2B $180

Credit card guarantee; 3-day cancellation notice. 2-night minimum stay on weekends. 2 stories; interior/exterior corridors. 21 rooms. Charming country inn atmosphere in the center of town. Spacious, beautifully decorated rooms with gas fireplaces. Walking distance to shops and art galleries. Cable TV, refrigerators; some VCPs, whirlpools. Heated pool, whirlpool; rental bicycles. Valet laundry. No pets. Meeting rooms. AE, DI, DS, MC, VI. Restaurant, see Remington's Restaurant. Ⓓ Ⓢ ⊘

RESTAURANTS

MATTEI'S TAVERN   ♦ American
On SR 154 (93441).
(805) 688-4820.

$11-20. Open 5:30-9 pm, Fri noon-3 pm & 5:30-9, Sat & Sun noon-3 pm & 4:30-9 pm; closed 12/25. Reservations suggested. Dining in a historic stagecoach stop. Nice selection of steaks, prime rib, seafood & other entrees. Casual dress. Cocktails & lounge. MC, VI. ⊘

REMINGTON'S RESTAURANT   ♦♦♦ Continental
In Los Olivos Grand Hotel at 2860 Grand Ave (93441).
(805) 688-7788.

$11-20. Open 7 am-3 & 5:30-9 pm, Sat & Sun 8 am-3 & 5:30-10 pm. Casual dress. Children's menu, health-conscious menu. Cocktails. AE, CB, DI, DS, MC, VI. ⊘

Los Osos

LODGING

BEST WESTERN SEA PINES GOLF RESORT   ♦♦♦ Motor Inn
1 mile west of 9th St via Los Osos Valley Rd, ¼ mile north on Pecho Rd, 1 block west on Skyline Dr to 1945 S Solano St (93402).
(805) 528-5252; FAX (805) 528-8231.

Fri-Sat 5/1-9/30	1P	$ 89-119	2P/1B	$ 89-119	2P/2B	$ 89-119
Sun-Thu 5/1-9/30	1P	$ 69- 99	2P/1B	$ 69- 99	2P/2B	$ 69- 99
Fri & Sat 10/1-4/30	1P	$ 75- 99	2P/1B	$ 75- 99	2P/2B	$ 75- 99
Sun-Thu 10/1-4/30	1P	$ 66- 89	2P/1B	$ 66- 89	2P/2B	$ 66- 89

Credit card guarantee. 2 stories; exterior corridors. 20 rooms; 3 1-bedroom suites with fireplace, $139-149. Rooms with golf course or bay view. Cable TV, coffee makers. Putting green; fee for 9-hole executive golf course. No pets. AE, DI, DS, MC, VI. Restaurant, 9 am-8 pm; $8-15; beer & wine. Ⓓ ⊘

RESTAURANT

RODNEY'S   ♦♦ American
In Baywood Park, ¼ mile south of Santa Ysabel St at 1315 2nd St (93402).
(805) 528-0459.
$11-20. Reservations suggested. Open 4:30-9 pm, Fri & Sat to 10 pm; closed Tues.
Small charming restaurant. Interesting selection of seafood, pasta, venison,
pheasant and other entrees. No air conditioning. Casual attire. Early-bird specials,
children's menu. Beer & wine. MC, VI. ⊘

Morro Bay

LODGING

BAY VIEW LODGE 🆔   ♦♦♦ Motel
1 block north of Morro Bay Bl at Market Ave and 225 Harbor St (93442).
(805) 772-2771.

6/1-10/1 &					
Fri & Sat 10/2-5/31	1P ...	2P/1B	$ 60- 74	2P/2B	$ 72- 76
Sun-Thu 10/2-5/31	1P ...	2P/1B	$ 48- 60	2P/2B	$ 60- 70

XP $8. Credit card guarantee. 2 stories; exterior corridors. 22 rooms. Some ocean-
view rooms, 16 with gas fireplace. Cable TV, movies, VCPs, coffee makers, refrigerators; some shower baths; no air conditioning. Whirlpool. Coin laundry. No
pets. AE, MC, VI. Ⓓ ⊘

BEST VALUE INN 🆔   ♦ Motel
220 Beach St at Market Ave (93442).
(805) 772-3333.

Sun-Thu	1P	$ 28- 45	2P/1B	$ 32- 50	2P/2B	$ 40- 65
Fri-Sat 5/1-9/15	1P	$ 72- 89	2P/1B	$ 72- 89	2P/2B	$ 78- 98
Fri-Sat 9/16-4/30	1P	$ 42- 62	2P/1B	$ 45- 64	2P/2B	$ 48- 72

XP $5; children age 12 and under stay free. Credit card guarantee. Weekly rates.
Senior discount. 1 story; exterior corridors. 32 rooms. 1 block from the
Embarcadero. Cable TV, movies; some shower baths, refrigerators; no air condi-
tioning. Small pets only, $6. AE, DI, DS, MC, VI. Ⓓ ⊘

BEST WESTERN EL RANCHO MOTEL 🆔   ♦♦ Motor Inn
On east side of SR 1, northbound exit SR 41, southbound exit San Jacinto St; at 2460
Main St (93442).
(805) 772-2212; FAX (805) 544-3529.

6/9-9/4	1P ...	2P/1B	$ 69- 89	2P/2B	$ 79- 99
4/7-6/8 & 9/5-10/9	1P ...	2P/1B	$ 54- 74	2P/2B	$ 59- 79
2/1-4/6	1P $ 44- 54	2P/1B	$ 49- 59	2P/2B	$ 54- 69
10/10-1/31	1P $ 39- 49	2P/1B	$ 44- 54	2P/2B	$ 49- 59

XP $5; children age 12 and under stay free. Credit card guarantee; 3-day cancella-
tion notice. Senior discount. 1 story; interior corridors. 27 rooms. Ocean views.
Cable TV, movies, VCPs, refrigerators, some shower baths, microwaves; no air
conditioning. Heated pool. Pets, $4. Coin laundry. AE, CB, DI, DS, MC, VI. Ⓓ ⊘

BEST WESTERN SAN MARCOS MOTOR INN ⊛

♦♦♦ Motel

250 Pacific St at Morro Ave (93442).
(805) 772-2248; FAX (805) 772-6844.

3/31-5/25 [CP]	1P $ 54- 94	2P/1B $ 54- 94	2P/2B $ 59- 99
5/26-9/14 [CP]	1P $ 62- 94	2P/1B $ 62- 94	2P/2B $ 67- 99
9/15-3/30 [CP]	1P $ 39- 94	2P/1B $ 46- 94	2P/2B $ 49- 99

XP $5-10. Credit card guarantee; 3-day cancellation notice. Weekly rates. 3 stories; interior corridors. 32 rooms. Many rooms with ocean view. Cable TV, movies, refrigerators, coffee makers, shower baths; no air conditioning. Whirlpool. No pets. Data ports. AE, CB, DI, DS, MC, VI. Complimentary evening beverages. Ⓓ ⊘

BEST WESTERN TRADEWINDS MOTEL ⊛

♦♦ Motel

225 Beach St at Market Ave (93442).
(805) 772-7376.

6/16-9/15	1P $ 50- 70	2P/1B $ 60- 80	2P/2B $ 65- 85
9/16-6/15	1P $ 38- 58	2P/1B $ 42- 62	2P/2B $ 44- 64

XP $5. Reservation deposit required. Senior discount. 2 stories; exterior corridors. 24 rooms. Cable TV, movies, refrigerators, coffee makers. Whirlpool. Small pets with manager's approval. AE, CB, DI, DS, JCB, MC, VI. Coffee shop nearby. Ⓓ ⊘

BLUE SAIL INN ⊛

♦♦♦ Motel

½ block north of Morro Bay Bl at 851 Market Ave (93442).
(805) 772-7132.

All year	1P ...	2P/1B $ 65- 95	2P/2B $ 65- 95

Reservation deposit required. 3 stories; interior/exterior corridors. 48 rooms. Most rooms with balcony and harbor view; 7 with gas fireplace. Cable TV, movies, refrigerators, coffee makers; no air conditioning. Whirlpool. No pets. AE, DI, DS, MC, VI. Ⓓ Ⓢ ⊘

BREAKERS MOTEL ⊛

♦♦♦ Motel

Morro Bay Bl at Market Ave (Box 1447, 93442).
(805) 772-7317.

5/1-10/15	1P ...	2P/1B $ 70- 96	2P/2B $ 70- 86
10/16-4/30	1P ...	2P/1B $ 60- 88	2P/2B $ 60- 78

XP $10. Reservation deposit required. 3 stories; exterior corridors. 25 rooms. 1 block to the Embarcadero. Nicely decorated rooms, most with ocean view. Cable TV, movies, refrigerators, coffee makers; some shower baths, wood-burning fireplaces, air conditioning. Heated pool, whirlpool. No pets. AE, CB, DI, DS, MC, VI. Restaurant nearby. Ⓓ ⊘

ECONO LODGE ⊛

♦♦ Motel

3 blocks north of Morro Bay Bl at 1100 Main St (93442).
(805) 772-5609.

Fri-Sat 5/26-9/30	1P $ 65- 85	2P/1B $ 70- 90	2P/2B $ 75-105
Sun-Thu 6/11-9/30	1P $ 40- 55	2P/1B $ 45- 60	2P/2B $ 50- 65
Fri-Sat 10/1-5/25	1P $ 44- 65	2P/1B $ 48- 70	2P/2B $ 60- 85
Sun-Thu 10/1-6/10	1P $ 38- 50	2P/1B $ 40- 55	2P/2B $ 45- 60

XP $5. Reservation deposit required. Weekly rates. Senior discount. 2 stories; exterior corridors. 18 rooms; 1 2-bedroom unit; 4 efficiencies, no utensils. Cable TV, movies. Small pets, $20 deposit plus $8 daily. AE, CB, DI, DS, MC, VI. Coffee shop nearby. Ⓓ ⊘

EL MORRO LODGE ⊕   ♦♦♦ Motel
2 blocks southwest of SR 1; exit Main St; 1206 Main St (93442).
(805) 772-5633; FAX (805) 772-1404.

All year [CP]	1P	$ 50	2P/1B	$ 55- 90	2P/2B $ 60- 90

XP $8; children age 16 and under stay free. Reservation deposit required. 2 stories; interior corridors. 27 rooms; penthouse suite with whirlpool, fireplace and private sundeck, $160-175. Spacious, nicely furnished rooms in an attractive Spanish-style building. Cable TV, movies, refrigerators, coffee makers; most rooms with balcony; 12 with gas fireplace; no air conditioning. Whirlpool. Coin laundry. No pets. AE, CB, DI, DS, MC, VI. Ⓓ

EMBARCADERO INN ⊕   ♦♦♦ Motel
South of Marina St on the Embarcadero; 456 Embarcadero (93442).
(805) 772-2700.

4/1-10/15 [CP]	1P	...	2P/1B	$ 70-120	2P/2B $100-125
10/16-3/31 [CP]	1P	...	2P/1B	$ 60- 95	2P/2B $ 85- 95

XP $10; children age 11 and under stay free. Reservation deposit required; 3-day cancellation notice. Senior discount. 3 stories; exterior corridors. 32 rooms; 3 1-bedroom suites. Spacious rooms with harbor views. Cable TV, VCPs, refrigerators, coffee makers; most units with balcony; some microwaves; 19 gas fireplaces; no air conditioning. 2 indoor whirlpools. No pets. AE, CB, DI, DS, MC, VI. Ⓓ Ⓢ ⊘

GOLD COAST ⊕   ♦♦ Motel
1 block south of Morro Bay Bl at 670 Main St (93442).
(805) 772-7740.

Fri-Sat	1P	$ 45- 85	2P/1B	$ 50- 85	2P/2B $ 55- 95
Sun-Thu	1P	$ 30- 50	2P/1B	$ 35- 55	2P/2B $ 45- 65

XP $5; discounts for children. Reservation deposit required. Senior discount. 2 stories; exterior corridors. 17 rooms. Cable TV, movies, coffee makers; no air conditioning. Small pets, $5. AE, DS, MC, VI. Ⓓ

HARBOR HOUSE INN ⊕   ♦♦♦ Motel
2 blocks north of Morro Bay Bl at 1095 Main St (93442).
(805) 772-2711.

6/1-9/30	1P	$ 60	2P/1B	$ 60- 70	2P/2B $ 65- 75
Sun-Thu 10/1-5/31	1P	$ 45	2P/1B	$ 45- 60	2P/2B $ 55- 65
Fri-Sat 10/1-5/31	1P	$ 55	2P/1B	$ 55- 65	2P/2B $ 65- 70

Reservation deposit required. 2 stories; exterior corridors. 46 rooms. Cable TV, free and pay movies, coffee makers; some shower baths, VCPs; rental refrigerators; no air conditioning. Whirlpool. No pets. AE, DI, DS, MC, VI. Restaurant nearby. Ⓓ Ⓢ ⊘

THE INN AT MORRO BAY ⓐⓐⓐ   ♦♦♦ Motor Inn
*1 mile south on Main St, at entrance to Morro Bay State Park & golf course; 60 State
Park Rd (93442).*
(805) 772-5651; FAX (805) 772-4779.

Fri-Sat 4/1-10/31	1P ...	2P/1B	$115-215	2P/2B	$115-215
Sun-Thu 4/1-10/31 &					
Fri-Sat 11/1-3/31	1P ...	2P/1B	$ 95-195	2P/2P	$ 95-195
Sun-Thu 11/1-3/31	1P ...	2P/1B	$ 70-170	2P/2B	$ 70-170

XP $15; children age 17 and under stay free. Reservation deposit required. 2 stories; exterior corridors. 96 rooms. Some small rooms. Bayfront. On nicely landscaped tree-shaded grounds. Spacious, nicely decorated rooms, many with patio or balcony. Cable TV, movies; some shower baths, refrigerators, gas fireplaces; no air conditioning. Heated pool, bicycles. No pets. Meeting rooms. AE, CB, DI, DS, MC, VI. Blue Heron Restaurant, see separate listing. Ⓓ ⊘

KEYSTONE MOTEL ⓐⓐⓐ   ♦♦ Motel
3 blocks south of Morro Bay Bl at 540 Main St (93442).
(805) 772-7503.

5/15-9/30	1P ...	2P/1B	$ 52- 75	2P/2B	$ 60- 85
10/1-5/14	1P ...	2P/1B	$ 40- 56	2P/2B	$ 56- 70

XP $5. Reservation deposit required. 2 stories; exterior corridors. 21 rooms. Some ocean-view rooms. Cable TV, movies, coffee makers; some refrigerators; no air conditioning. No pets. AE, CB, DI, DS, MC, VI. Ⓓ ⊘

LA SERENA INN ⓐⓐⓐ   ♦♦♦ Motel
2 blocks north of Morro Bay Bl at 990 Morro Ave (PO Box 1711, 93443).
Phone & FAX (805) 772-5665.

4/1-10/15 [CP]	1P ...	2P/1B	$ 69-145	2P/2B	$ 74- 94
10/16-3/31 [CP]	1P ...	2P/1B	$ 59-135	2P/2B	$ 64- 84

XP $5. Reservation deposit required; 7-day cancellation notice. 3 stories; interior corridors. 37 rooms; 4 king mini-suites with gas fireplace, $110-115; 1 2-bedroom unit. Spacious rooms. Cable TV, movies; rental refrigerators, microwaves; some ocean views. Sauna. No pets. AE, CB, DI, DS, MC, VI. Ⓓ Ⓢ ⊘

SEA AIR INN ⓐⓐⓐ   ♦♦ Motel
845 Morro Ave at Morro Bay Bl (93442).
(805) 772-4437.

5/1-9/30 &						
Fri-Sat 10/1-4/30	1P	$ 40- 60	2P/1B	$ 40- 70	2P/2B	$ 50- 80
Sun-Thu 10/1-4/30	1P	$ 30- 50	2P/1B	$ 35- 55	2P/2B	$ 40- 65

XP $5; children age 12 and under stay free. Reservation deposit required. Senior discount. 2 stories; exterior corridors. 25 rooms; 1 2-bedroom unit. Cable TV, movies, coffee makers; some refrigerators, ocean-view rooms, shower baths; no air conditioning. No pets. AE, DS, MC, VI. Restaurant nearby. Ⓓ

Room rates are subject to change.

SUNDOWN MOTEL ⊛   ◆◆ Motel
2 blocks south of Morro Bay Bl at 640 Main St (93442).
(805) 772-7381.

Fri-Sat 6/1-9/30	1P	$ 45- 65	2P/1B $ 50- 70	2P/2B	$ 55- 75
Sun-Thu 6/1-9/30 &					
Sat 10/1-5/31	1P	$ 38- 50	2P/1B $ 38- 55	2P/2B	$ 42- 60
Sun-Fri 10/1-5/31	1P	$ 30- 42	2P/1B $ 32- 48	2P/2B	$ 38- 50

XP $4; children age 8 and under stay free. Reservation deposit required. Weekly rates. Exterior corridors. 17 rooms. Cable TV, movies, shower baths; no air conditioning. Small pets 10/1-5/31 only, $5. AE, DS, MC, VI. Ⓓ ⊘

SUNSET TRAVELODGE ⊛   ◆◆ Motel
1080 Market Ave at Beach St (93442).
(805) 772-1259; FAX (805) 772-8967.

6/1-9/30	1P	$ 55- 98	2P/1B $ 65- 98	2P/2B	$ 69-125
10/1-5/31	1P	$ 39- 69	2P/1B $ 45- 69	2P/2B	$ 49- 89

XP $5-8; children age 17 and under stay free. Reservation deposit required; 7-day cancellation notice. Senior discount. 2 stories; exterior corridors. 31 rooms; 6 2-bedroom units. Cable TV, movies, coffee makers; some shower baths, microwaves, refrigerators, ocean views; no air conditioning. Heated pool. Small pets $5, $25 deposit. AE, CB, DI, DS, JCB, MC, VI. Ⓓ ⊘

THE TWIN DOLPHIN ⊛   ◆◆◆ Motel
2 blocks south of Morro Bay Bl at 590 Morro Ave (93442).
(805) 772-4483.

5/1-10/31 [CP]	1P	$ 55- 80	2P/1B $ 55- 80	2P/2B	$ 55- 80
11/1-4/30 [CP]	1P	$ 45- 65	2P/1B $ 45- 65	2P/2B	$ 55- 65

XP $10; discount for children age 10 and under. Reservation deposit required; 15-day cancellation notice. 3 stories; interior corridors. 31 rooms. Cable TV, movies, shower baths; rental refrigerators; some ocean views. Whirlpool. No pets. DS, MC, VI. Roll-in showers. Ⓓ Ⓢ ⊘

VILLAGER MOTEL ⊛   ◆◆ Motel
3 blocks north of Morro Bay Bl at 1098 Main St (93442).
(805) 772-1235.

Sun-Thu	1P	$ 35- 50	2P/1B $ 40- 55	2P/2B	$ 45- 60
Fri-Sat 6/11-9/10	1P	$ 60- 85	2P/1B $ 65- 90	2P/2B	$ 70- 95
Fri-Sat 9/11-6/10	1P	$ 45- 60	2P/1B $ 50- 65	2P/2B	$ 55- 75

XP $8. Reservation deposit required; 3-day cancellation notice. 2 stories; exterior corridors. 22 rooms. Cable TV, movies, shower baths, coffee makers; some refrigerators; no air conditioning. Indoor whirlpool. No pets. AE, CB, DI, DS, MC, VI. Coffee shop nearby. Ⓓ ⊘

AAA members can make reservations
through any office of the Automobile Club of Southern California.

RESTAURANTS

THE BLUE HERON RESTAURANT   ♦♦♦ American
At The Inn at Morro Bay, 60 State Park Rd (93442).
(805) 772-5651.

$21-30. Open 7-11 am, 11:30-2 & 5-9 pm; Sun 7 am-2 & 5:30-9 pm. Reservation suggested on weekends. Attractive dining room overlooking the bay; California/French cuisine. No air conditioning. Casual attire. Children's menu, Sun brunch, a la carte. Cocktails and lounge. AE, DI, DS, MC, VI. ⊘

BRANNIGAN'S REEF   ♦♦ American
781 Market Ave at Morro Bay Bl (93442).
(805) 772-7321.

$11-20. Open 4-9 pm, Fri to 10 pm, Sat 11:30 am-3 & 4-10 pm, Sun 10 am-2 & 4-9 pm. View of bay. Menu features a selection of seafood, steaks, prime rib, chicken and pasta. No air conditioning. Casual attire. Children's menu. Sun brunch. Cocktails & lounge. AE, MC, VI. ⊘

GALLEY RESTAURANT ⦿   ♦♦ Seafood
899 Embarcadero (93442).
(805) 772-2806.

$21-30. Open 11 am-9 pm; Sat, Sun & 6/1-9/15 to 9:30 pm; closed 12/1-12/25. Reservations suggested. Long-established family operated restaurant on waterfront overlooking bay. Seafood, beef & chicken. Casual atmosphere. No air conditioning. Children's menu. Beer & wine. MC, VI. Smoke-free premises

GREAT AMERICAN FISH COMPANY ⦿   ♦♦ Seafood
1185 Embarcadero (93442).
(805) 772-4407.

$11-20. Open 11 am-10 pm; 11/1-4/1 to 9 pm. On waterfront, overlooking bay. Nice selection of mesquite-broiled seafood and steaks. No air conditioning. Casual attire. Children's menu. Cocktails & lounge. DS, MC, VI. ⊘

HARADA JAPANESE RESTAURANT & SUSHI BAR   ♦♦ Japanese
630 Embarcadero (93442).
(805) 772-1410.

$11-20. Open 11:30 am-2 & 5-10 pm. Reservations suggested. Attractive oriental decor, overlooks the bay. No air conditioning. Casual attire. Beer & wine. MC, VI. ⊘

HARBOR HUT RESTAURANT ⦿   ♦♦ Seafood
1205 Embarcadero (93442).
(805) 772-2255.

$11-20. Open 11 am-10 pm; 11/1-4/1 to 9 pm. Reservations suggested. On waterfront overlooking bay. Casual, informal atmosphere. Nice selection of pasta, mesquite-broiled steaks & seafood. No air conditioning. Cocktails & lounge. AE, DS, MC, VI.

HOPPE'S AT 901 🎖   ♦♦♦ Continental
901 Embarcadero (93442).
(805) 772-9012.

$11-20. Open 5-9 pm; Fri 11 am-2 & 5-9 pm; Sat & Sun to 10 pm; closed Tue & 12/25. Reservations suggested. On the Embarcadero. Bay-view dining. Specializing in fresh seafood, steaks, venison, chicken & vegetarian selections. No air conditioning. Casual attire. Children's menu, a la carte, Sun brunch. Beer & wine. AE, DS, MC, VI. Smoke-free premises

ROSE'S LANDING RESTAURANT 🎖   ♦ Seafood
725 Embarcadero (93442).
(805) 772-4441.

$11-20. Open 11:30 am-3 & 5-10 pm; Sat & Sun 11:30 am-3 & 4-10 pm. Reservations suggested. On 2nd floor, overlooking bay. Nice selection of seafood. Also some chicken & steak entrees. Casual atmosphere. Children's menu, early bird specials, senior's menu. Cocktails & lounge; entertainment. AE, MC, VI. ⊘

Nipomo

THE KALEIDOSCOPE INN BED & BREAKFAST   ♦♦ Historic Bed & Breakfast
From US 101, exit Tefft/Nipomo, ½ mile east to Thompson Rd, then 1 block south to 130 E Dana St (93444).
(805) 929-5444.

All year [BP]	1P $ 75	2P/1B $ 80	2P/2B ...

XP $10. Credit card guarantee. 2 stories; interior corridors. 3 rooms. Attractive lawn and garden area. Historical Victorian house built in 1887. Some shower baths, whirlpools; no air conditioning, phones, TVs. No pets. AE, MC, VI. Ⓓ Smoke-free premises

Ojai

LODGING

BEST WESTERN CASA OJAI 🎖   ♦♦ Motel
¾ mile east on SR 150 at 1302 E Ojai Ave (93023).
(805) 646-8175; FAX (805) 640-8247.

Sun-Thu [BP]	1P $ 56- 71	2P/1B $ 66- 81	2P/2B $ 71- 86
Fri-Sat 3/11-5/26 [BP]	1P $ 85-100	2P/1B $ 95-110	2P/2B $100-115
Fri-Sat 5/27-9/29 [BP]	1P $ 90-105	2P/1B $100-115	2P/2B $100-120
Fri-Sat 9/30-3/10 [BP]	1P $ 81- 96	2P/1B $ 91-106	2P/2B $ 96-111

XP $10; children age 12 and under stay free. Reservation deposit required weekends. CP available. 2 stories; exterior corridors. 45 rooms. Cable TV, coffee makers; some refrigerators; VCPs. Heated pool, whirlpool. No pets. AE, CB, DI, DS, JCB, MC, VI. Ⓓ ⊘

LOS PADRES INN 🎖   ♦♦ Motel
¾ mile east on SR 150 at 1208 E Ojai Ave (93023).
(805) 646-4365; FAX (805) 646-0625.

Fri-Sat 5/26-10/31 [CP]	1P	$ 70- 80	2P/1B	$ 85- 95	2P/2B	$ 85- 95
Sun-Thu 5/26-10/31 &						
Fri-Sat 11/1-5/25 [CP]	1P	$ 60- 70	2P/1B	$ 75- 85	2P/2B	$ 75- 85
Sun-Thu 11/1-5/25 [CP]	1P	$ 50- 70	2P/1B	$ 65- 75	2P/2B	$ 65- 75

XP $10; children age 12 and under stay free. Reservation deposit required. 2 stories; exterior corridors. 31 rooms; 1 kitchen & 1 efficiency, $10-20 extra. Cable TV; some coffee makers, microwaves, refrigerators. Heated pool, whirlpool. Pets $10, $100 deposit. AE, CB, DI, DS, MC, VI. Restaurant nearby. Ⓓ ⊘

OJAI VALLEY INN ⓐⓐ   ◆◆◆ Resort Complex
1 mile west on SR 150, ¼ mile south; Country Club Rd (PO Box 1866, 93024-1866).
(805) 646-5511; FAX (805) 646-7969.

| All year [BP] | 1P | $195-260 | 2P/1B | $195-260 | 2P/2B | $195-260 |

XP $25; children age 18 and under stay free. Check in 4 pm. Credit card guarantee; 3-day cancellation notice. Senior discount. 2 stories; interior/exterior corridors. 212 rooms; 16 suites with fireplace. Charming resort on 200 acres of beautifully landscaped grounds. Cable TV, coffee makers; some VCPs; pay movies. 2 heated pools, saunas, whirlpool, playground, putting green, children's program, recreation program; bicycles, hiking and jogging trails; fee for massage, golf (18 holes), 8 tennis courts (4 lighted). No pets. Conference facilities, PC, secretarial services. AE, CB, DI, DS, JCB, MC, VI. Dining room, restaurant; 6:30 am-11 pm; $18-35; cocktails. 24-hour room service. Ⓓ Ⓢ ⊘

THEODORE WOOLSEY HOUSE   Bed & Breakfast
1484 E Ojai Ave (93023).
(805) 646-9779

| All year [CP] | 1P … | 2P/1B | $ 50- 95 | 2P/2B … |

XP $15. Check in 1 pm; check out noon. 2-night minimum stay on weekends. Reservation deposit required; 5-day cancellation notice. 6 guest rooms, 3 with private bath, 2 with water closet. An 1887, two-story, stone and clapboard Connecticut country farmhouse lies on seven acres 1 mile east of town. The house has two fireplaces, a screened-in patio and a garden room. Expanded continental breakfast served buffet-style in the dining room. Television in three guest rooms; two rooms with fireplace. Pool. No pets. Refreshments served in the afternoon. Smoking permitted on the outside balconies and porches

RESTAURANTS

RANCH HOUSE RESTAURANT   ◆◆◆ Continental
From jct SR 150 & 33, ¾ miles northwest on Maricopa Rd, ⅛ mile west on El Roblar,
then ½ mile south; corner of S Lomita Ave and Besa Rd (93023).
(805) 646-2360.

$21-30. Open 11:30 am-1:30 pm, seatings for dinner at 6 & 8:30 pm; Sun 1-3:30 pm, seatings for dinner at 7:30 pm; closed Mon, Tue & for lunch 10/2-4/14. Reservations required for dinner. Colorful lush garden foliage, patio dining. Homemade breads & desserts. Beef, lamb, chicken & fresh seafood. Menu changes weekly. Informal atmosphere. No air conditioning. Casual attire. A la carte. Beer & wine only. AE, DS, MC, VI. ⊘

SUZANNE'S CUISINE ♦♦ French
¾ mile west on SR 150 at 502 W Ojai Ave (93023).
(805) 640-1961.

$21-30. Open 11:30 am-8:30 pm; closed Tue. Reservations suggested Fri & Sat. Sandwiches, salads, pastas, chicken, beef, lamb chops, pork and fresh seafood prepared with an Italian flair. Patio dining. Daily selections of homemade desserts. Casual attire. A la carte, Sun brunch. Cocktails. MC, VI. ⊘

Oxnard

LODGING

CASA SIRENA MARINA RESORT ⒶⒶ ♦♦ Motor Inn
½ mile west of Victoria Bl via Channel Islands Bl at Channel Islands Harbor; 3605 Peninsula Rd (93035).
(805) 985-6311; FAX (805) 985-4329.

6/1-9/30	1P $ 89	2P/1B $ 89	2P/2B $ 89
10/1-5/31	1P $ 69	2P/1B $ 69	2P/2B $ 69

XP $10; children age 12 and under stay free. Credit card guarantee. 3 stories; interior/exterior corridors. 273 rooms; 24 2-bedroom units; 24 efficiencies. Many rooms overlooking marina. Patio or balcony. Spacious, nicely landscaped grounds. Cable TV, coffee makers, refrigerators; 24 microwaves; pay movies; no air conditioning. Heated pool, saunas, whirlpools, putting green, 1 lighted tennis court, exercise room; rental bicycles; fee for massage; hair & tanning salon. Valet laundry. No pets. Meeting rooms. AE, CB, DI, DS, JCB, MC, VI. Coffee shop; 6:30 am-2 pm; Lobster Trap Restaurant, see separate listing. Ⓓ ⊘ **(See ad below.)**

OXNARD HILTON INN ⒶⒶ ♦♦♦ Hotel
2 blocks south of US 101, exit Vineyard Ave to 600 Esplanade Dr (93030).
(805) 485-9666; FAX (805) 485-2061.

All year	1P $ 65	2P/1B $ 65	2P/2B $ 65

XP $10; family plan. Credit card guarantee. 6 stories; interior corridors. 160 rooms. Nicely landscaped patio area. Many rooms with balcony. Cable TV, free and pay movies, refrigerators. Heated pool, whirlpool, 1 lighted tennis court. Valet laundry. Fee for child care. Small pets. Conference facilities, data ports. AE, CB, DI, DS, JCB, MC, VI. Restaurant, 6:30 am-10 pm; $9-18; cocktails; entertainment. Ⓓ Ⓢ ⊘

RADISSON SUITE HOTEL AT RIVER RIDGE ⒶⒶ ◆◆◆ Apartment Motor Inn
1¾ miles southwest of US 101, exit Vineyard Ave; 2101 Vineyard Ave (93030).
(805) 988-0130; FAX (805) 983-4470.

Fri-Sat 5/15-9/30 [BP]	1P	$115-135	2P/1B	$115-135	2P/2B	$135
Sun-Thu 5/15-9/30 &						
Fri-Sat 10/1-5/14 [BP]	1P	$105-125	2P/1B	$105-125	2P/2B	$125
Sun-Thu 10/1-5/14 [BP]	1P	$ 95-115	2P/1B	$ 95-115	2P/2B	$115

XP $10; children age 17 and under stay free. Weekly & monthly rates. 2 stories; exterior corridors. 250 rooms; 60 2-bedroom units; 60 loft suites with fireplace & kitchen; 120 fireplace units. Nicely landscaped grounds. Cable TV, free and pay movies; kitchens, coffee makers, microwaves, refrigerators. 2 heated pools, whirlpools, 5 lighted tennis courts; fee for golf (18 holes). Coin laundry. Airport transportation. No pets. Conference facilities. AE, CB, DI, DS, JCB, MC, VI. Restaurant; 6:30 am-10 pm; $9-17; cocktails. Ⓓ ⊗ **(See ad below.)**

The Diamond ratings shown in this book were based on inspections done in 1994-95. Some establishments do not meet all AAA standards but are described here as a service to our readers. These property listings lack a Diamond rating.

RESTAURANTS

FURR'S CAFETERIA   ◆◆ American
1 block east of Ventura Rd at 1301 W Channel Islands Bl (93033).
(805) 483-0187.

Up to $10. Open 11 am-9 pm; closed 12/25. Casual attire. A la carte. AE, MC, VI. ⊘

GREEK AT THE HARBOR   ◆◆ Greek
From US 101, exit Seaward Ave, 1¾ mile southwest on Harbor Bl, ¾ mile west on Spinnaker Dr; in Ventura Harbor Village at 1583 Spinnaker Dr (93001).
(805) 650-5350.

$11-20. Open 11 am-10 pm; Fri & Sat to 11 pm. Reservations suggested Fri & Sat. Steaks, seafood, lamb, chicken, vegetarian plate, pasta & casseroles. Patio dining, dancing and harbor views. Casual attire. Children's menu, early bird specials, a la carte, carryout. Cocktails. MC, VI. ⊘

LOBSTER TRAP RESTAURANT   ◆◆ Steak & Seafood
In Casa Sirena Marina Resort, 3605 Peninsula Rd (93035).
(805) 985-6361.

$11-20. Open 11:30 am-10 pm; Sun brunch 10 am-2 pm. Overlooking marina. Salads, seafood, chicken, steak & prime rib. Casual attire. Cocktails & lounge; entertainment. AE, CB, DI, DS, MC, VI. ⊘

TUGS RESTAURANT   ◆ Steak & Seafood
½ mile southeast of Channel Islands Bl, via Harbor Bl at Channel Islands Harbor; 3600 S Harbor Bl (93035).
(805) 985-8847.

$11-20. Open 8 am-9 pm; closed Thanksgiving & 12/25. Located on the 2nd floor of Marine Emporium Bldg. Patio dining, weather permitting. Steaks, fresh seafood, chicken & pasta. View of harbor. No air conditioning. Casual atmosphere. Cocktails. AE, MC, VI. ⊘

Paso Robles

LODGING

ADELAIDE MOTOR INN ⊕   ◆◆◆ Motel
1 block west of US 101, exit SR 46, Fresno; 1215 Ysabel Ave (93446).
(805) 238-2770; FAX (805) 238-3497.

4/28-10/15	1P	$ 40- 48	2P/1B	$ 40- 48	2P/2B	$ 52
10/14-4/27	1P	$ 38- 45	2P/1B	$ 38- 45	2P/2B	$ 48

XP $5. Reservation deposit required. Senior discount. 1-2 stories; exterior corridors. 67 rooms; 1 2-bedroom unit with microwave, $75-84. Attractively landscaped. Cable TV, movies, refrigerators, coffee makers; some shower baths, whirlpools; rental VCPs. Heated pool. Coin laundry. No pets. Data ports. AE, CB, DI, DS, MC, VI. Restaurant nearby. Ⓓ ⊘ **(See ad opposite.)**

RELAX IN THE SUNSHINE. 🜲 ♦♦♦ (805) 238-2770
ENJOY NEARBY WINERIES, HEARST CASTLE TOURS & LAKES.
Heated Pool ■ Refrigerators ■ HBO ■ In-Room Coffee
Adjacent to Black Oak Restaurant
1215 YSABEL AVE., PASO ROBLES, CALIFORNIA 93446

BEST WESTERN BLACK OAK MOTOR LODGE 🜲 ♦♦♦ Motor Inn
Adjacent to US 101, exit SR 46 Fresno, 1 block west to 1135 24th St (93446).
(805) 238-4740; FAX (805) 238-0726.

4/30-10/12	1P $ 54- 70	2P/1B $ 54- 70	2P/2B $ 59- 68
10/13-4/29	1P $ 50- 66	2P/1B $ 48- 66	2P/2B $ 55- 64

XP $6; children age 5 and under stay free. Senior discount. 2 stories; exterior corridors. 110 rooms; 2 2-bedroom units. Cable TV, refrigerators, coffee makers; some microwaves, shower baths, whirlpools. Heated pool, wading pool, sauna, whirlpool, playground. Coin laundry. No pets. Data ports. AE, CB, DI, DS, MC, VI. Coffee shop, 6 am-8:30 pm; $6-11; beer & wine. Ⓓ ⊘

MELODY RANCH MOTEL 🜲 ♦ Motel
On US 101 business route, 2 blocks south of downtown at 939 Spring St (93446).
(805) 238-3911.

5/20-9/16	1P $ 36- 42	2P/1B $ 42- 46	2P/2B $ 44- 48
9/17-5/19	1P $ 30- 36	2P/1B $ 36- 42	2P/2B $ 38- 44

XP $3. Credit card guarantee; 3-day cancellation notice. 1 story; exterior corridors. 19 rooms. Cable TV, shower baths. Heated pool. No pets. AE, CB, DI, DS, MC, VI. Ⓓ

TRAVELODGE PASO ROBLES 🜲 ♦♦ Motel
1 mile north on US 101 business route at 2701 Spring St (93446).
(805) 238-0078; FAX (805) 238-0822.

5/1-10/1	1P $ 38- 48	2P/1B $ 42- 58	2P/2B $ 48- 75
10/2-4/30	1P $ 34- 45	2P/1B $ 38- 48	2P/2B $ 45- 65

XP $ 5; children age 17 and under stay free. Credit card guarantee; 3-day cancellation notice. Weekly & monthly rates. Senior discount. 1-2 stories; exterior corridors. 31 units. Tree-shaded lawn area. Cable TV, movies, refrigerators, coffee makers; some microwaves, shower baths. Heated pool. Pets, $4. AE, CB, DI, DS, JCB, MC, VI. Ⓓ ⊘

RESTAURANTS

BLACK OAK RESTAURANT 🜲 ♦ American
Adjacent to US 101, exit SR 46, Fresno, 1 block west to 1535 24th St (93446).
(805) 238-6330.

$11-20. Open 7 am-10:30 pm. Popular coffee shop featuring salads, sandwiches & entrees. Casual attire. Children's menu, early bird specials. Cocktails & lounge. Also, Annie's Dinnerhouse, featuring steaks, seafood, ribs and chicken. Open 4:30-10:30 pm. AE, DS, MC, VI. ⊘

VINE STREET GRILL   ◆◆ American

Formerly Joshua's. 2 blocks west of Spring St at 13th St and Vine (93446).
(805) 238-7515.

$11-25. Open 11 am-2:30 & 4:30-9 pm, Fri & Sat to 10; Sun 10 am-2 & 4-9 pm. Sun brunch 10 am-2 pm. Reservations suggested. Charming restaurant located in a converted church building. Features steaks, ribs, seafood, pasta, rack of lamb; prime rib served Fri & Sat. Large selection of local wines. Casual attire. Children's menu, early-bird specials, senior discount, a la carte. Cocktails & lounge. AE, MC, VI. ⊘

LOLO'S MEXICAN 🆔   ◆ Mexican

½ mile south on US 101 business route at 305 Spring St (93446).
(805) 239-5777.

Up to $10. Open 11 am-9 pm, Fri & Sat to 10 pm; closed Thanksgiving & 12/25. Casual atmosphere in a restored house. Outdoor patio dining available. Children's menu, carryout, a la carte. Beer & wine. MC, VI. Smoke-free premises

Pismo Beach

LODGING

BEST WESTERN SHELTER COVE LODGE 🆔   ◆◆◆ Motel

From US 101 & SR 1, northbound exit Mattie Rd, southbound exit Price St; 2651 Price St (93449).
(805) 773-3511.

	1P	2P/1B	2P/2B
6/1-10/5 [CP]	$108-118	$108-118	$108-118
10/6-5/31 [CP]	$ 88- 98	$ 88- 98	$ 88- 98

XP $ 10. 2 stories; exterior corridors. 52 rooms; 4 with fireplace. On a high bluff overlooking the ocean. Spacious rooms with balcony and ocean view. Cable TV, refrigerators, coffee makers. Heated pool, whirlpool. No pets. AE, DI, DS, MC, VI. Ⓓ Ⓢ ⊘

BEST WESTERN SHORE CLIFF LODGE   ◆◆◆ Motor Inn

From US 101 & SR 1, northbound exit Mattie Rd, southbound exit Price St; 2555 Price St (93449).
(805) 773-4671; FAX (805) 773-2341.

	1P	2P/1B	2P/2B
4/1-6/30 & 9/1-10/31	$105-120	$105-120	$105-120
7/1-8/31	$115-130	$115-130	$115-130
11/1-3/31	$ 95-110	$ 95-110	$ 95-110

XP $ 10; children age 17 and under stay free. Credit card guarantee; 3-day cancellation notice. Senior discount. 2-3 stories; interior/exterior corridors. 99 rooms; 9 efficiencies, $10 extra; 6 2-bedroom suites with kitchen, $185-210 for up to 4 persons. Located on a high bluff with a stairway down to the ocean. Spacious ocean-view rooms with balcony or patio. Cable TV, pay movies, coffee makers. Heated pool, sauna, whirlpool, 2 lighted tennis courts. No pets. Meeting rooms. AE, CB, DI, DS, JCB, MC, VI. Cocktail lounge; also, Shore Cliff Restaurant, see separate listing. Ⓓ Ⓢ ⊘

THE CLIFFS AT SHELL BEACH 🅐🅐🅐 ◆◆◆ Motor Inn
Adjacent to US 101 & SR 1, northbound exit Spyglass Dr; southbound, Shell Beach Rd.
2757 Shell Beach Rd (93449).
(805) 773-5000; FAX (805) 773-0764.

| All year | 1P $120-180 | 2P/1B $120-180 | 2P/2B $120-180 |

XP $10; children age 16 and under stay free. Reservation deposit required. 5 stories; interior corridors. 165 rooms; 27 suites with whirlpool tub, $210-300. Attractive oceanfront location. Spacious, nicely furnished rooms, many with ocean view. Cable TV, pay movies, coffee makers; some refrigerators. Heated pool, sauna, indoor whirlpool. Coin laundry. No pets. Conference facilities. AE, CB, DI, DS, MC, VI. Sea Cliffs Restaurant, see separate listing. Ⓓ Ⓢ ⊘

EDGEWATER MOTEL 🅐🅐 ◆◆ Motel
On SR 1; 2 blocks w of US 101 at 280 Wadsworth Ave (93449).
(805) 773-4811; FAX (805) 773-5121.

| All year [CP] | 1P ... | 2P/1B $ 60- 90 | 2P/2B $ 65- 90 |

Credit card guarantee. Weekly & monthly rates. 2-3 stories; exterior corridors. 93 rooms; 1 2-bedroom unit; 20 1-bedroom apartments, $85-135 for up to 4 persons. At the beach, 3 blocks north of pier. Some ocean-view rooms. Cable TV, refrigerators; some whirlpools; no air conditioning. Heated pool; whirlpool. Coin laundry. No pets. Meeting rooms. Data ports. AE, CB, DI, DS, MC, VI. Ⓓ **(See ad below.)**

KNIGHT'S REST MOTEL ◆◆ Motel
1 mile north, adjacent to US 101 & SR 1 at 2351 Price St (93449).
(805) 773-4617.

| All year | 1P $ 75 | 2P/1B $ 75 | 2P/2B $ 85 |

1 story; exterior corridors. 35 rooms. Cable TV, shower baths, coffee makers, refrigerators; 2 kitchens; no air conditioning, phones. Heated pool, wading pool. No pets. AE, DS, MC, VI. Ⓓ

Room rates may increase during special events.

KON TIKI INN ⊕   ◆◆◆ Motor Inn

From US 101, southbound exit SR 1; northbound exit Price St, then ¾ mile north; 1621
Price St (93449).
(805) 773-4833; FAX (805) 773-6541.

3/17-9/30	1P	$ 76- 90	2P/1B	$ 76- 90	2P/2B	$ 76- 90
10/1-3/16	1P	$ 70- 80	2P/1B	$ 70- 80	2P/2B	$ 70- 80

XP $14. Reservation deposit required. 3-4 stories; exterior corridors. 86 rooms;
4 rooms with gas fireplace. Nicely landscaped grounds with a private stairway to
beach. Ocean-view rooms. Cable TV, movies, refrigerators. Heated pool,
whirlpools, 2 lighted tennis courts, racquetball courts. Coin laundry. No pets. AE,
MC, VI. Restaurant, 7 am-9 pm; $14-25; cocktails; entertainment. Ⓓ ⊘

OCEAN PALMS MOTEL ⊕   ◆◆ Motel

From US 101 northbound exit Price St; southbound exit Hinds St, 2 blocks south to 390
Ocean View Ave (93449).
(805) 773-4669.

Fri- Sat	1P	$ 45- 85	2P/1B	$ 55- 95	2P/2B	$ 55-105
Sun-Thu	1P	$ 28- 38	2P/1B	$ 38- 48	2P/2B	$ 42- 52

XP $5; children age 10 and under stay free. Credit card guarantee; 3-day cancella-
tion notice. Weekly rates. Senior discount. 22 rooms. 3 blocks to beach. Cable
TV, movies; some shower baths, refrigerators; no air conditioning. Heated pool.
No pets. AE, DS, MC, VI. Restaurant nearby. Ⓓ ⊘

QUALITY SUITES ⊕   ◆◆◆ Suite Motel

2 miles south, adjacent to US 101, exit 4th St to 651 Five Cities Dr (93449).
(805) 773-3773; FAX (805) 773-5177.

All year [BP]	1P	$ 69	2P/1B	$ 69	2P/2B	$ 69

XP $6; children age 18 and under stay free. Reservation deposit required. 2 sto-
ries; exterior corridors. 133 rooms. Nicely landscaped, tree-shaded courtyard
areas. Attractively decorated 1-bedroom suites. Cable TV, refrigerators, microwaves; some VCPs. Heated pool, wading pool, whirlpool, putting green. Coin
laundry. Pets, $6. AE, CB, DI, DS, JCB, MC, VI. Complimentary beverages each
evening. Ⓓ Ⓢ ⊘

SANDCASTLE INN ⊕   ◆◆◆ Motel

3 blocks west of SR 1 at 100 Stimson Ave (93449).
(805) 773-2422; FAX (805) 773-0771.

Fri-Sat 3/3-10/14 [CP]	1P	$ 99-149	2P/1B	$ 99-149	2P/2B	$ 99-149
Sun-Thu 6/9-9/9 &						
Fri-Sat 10/15-3/2 [CP]	1P	$ 79-129	2P/1B	$ 79-129	2P/2B	$ 79-129
Sun-Thu 9/10-6/8	1P	$ 69- 99	2P/1B	$ 69- 99	2P/2B	$ 69- 99

XP $10; children age 12 and under stay free. Reservation deposit required.
Weekly rates. Senior discount. 3 stories; interior corridors. 60 rooms; suites $155-
255. On beach, ½ block south of pier. Many rooms with ocean view, patio or balcony. Cable TV, VCPs, refrigerators, coffee makers; no air conditioning.
Whirlpool. No pets. AE, CB, DI, DS, JCB, MC, VI. Ⓓ Ⓢ ⊘

SEA CREST RESORT MOTEL ◉ ♦♦♦ Motel
From US 101 & SR 1, southbound exit SR 1, northbound exit Price St, then 1 mile north;
2241 Price St (93449).
(805) 773-4608.

4/1-10/31	1P ...	2P/1B	$ 65-135	2P/2B	$ 65-135
11/1-3/31	1P ...	2P/1B	$ 55-135	2P/2B	$ 55-135

XP $10; children age 12 and under stay free. Reservation deposit required; 3-day cancellation notice. Weekly rates. Senior discount. 2-4 stories; interior/exterior corridors. 160 rooms; 5 2-bedroom units. Many ocean-view rooms. Private stairway to beach. Movies, refrigerators, coffee makers; some shower baths, whirlpool; no air conditioning. Heated pool, whirlpools. No pets. AE, CB, DI, DS, JCB, MC, VI. Restaurant nearby. Ⓓ **(See ad below.)**

SEA GYPSY MOTEL ◉ ♦♦ Condo Motel
3 blocks west of US 101 at 1020 Cypress St (93449).
(805) 773-1801; FAX (805) 773-9286.

3/25-6/30 & 9/5-10/31	1P	$ 35- 50	2P/1B	$ 40- 55	2P/2B	$ 55- 75
7/1-9/4	1P	$ 50	2P/1B	$ 60	2P/2B	$ 75-105
11/1-3/24	1P	$ 30- 45	2P/1B	$ 35- 50	2P/2B	$ 45- 70

XP $10. Check in 3:30 pm. Reservation deposit required; 4-day cancellation notice. Weekly & monthly rates. 3 stories; interior/exterior corridors. 77 rooms; 47 studio units with kitchen, queen-size murphy bed and sofa bed; 30 smaller rooms connect to studio unit to make a 1-bedroom suite. At beach, 3 blocks north of pier. Cable TV, refrigerators; some shower baths; no air conditioning. Small heated pool, whirlpool. Coin laundry. Small pets. AE, DS, MC, VI. Ⓓ

SEA VENTURE HOTEL Motor Inn
3 blocks west of US 101, northbound exit Price St, southbound exit Hinds St; 100
Oceanview Ave (93449).
(805) 773-4994; FAX (805) 773-4693.

All Year [CP]	1P	$ 89-159	2P/1B	$ 89-159	2P/2B	$ 89-159

XP $12; children age 18 and under stay free. Under major renovation. Credit card guarantee. Senior discount. 2-3 stories; interior/exterior corridors. 72 rooms; 20

1-bedroom suites with kitchen, gas fireplace, VCP, $175-225. 2 blocks south of pier. Many ocean-view rooms. Cable TV, movies; some shower baths, refrigerators, coffee makers; 20 kitchens; no air conditioning. No pets. AE, DI, DS, MC, VI. Restaurant 5-10 pm; $14-24; cocktails. D ⊘

SHELL BEACH MOTEL ⊛   ♦♦ Motel

2 miles north in Shell Beach; adjacent to US 101 & SR 1; 653 Shell Beach Rd (93449).
(805) 773-4373.

6/1-9/15	1P ...		2P/1B $ 68-110	2P/2B $ 70-120
9/16-5/31	1P ...		2P/1B $ 55- 90	2P/2B $ 59- 96

XP $5; children age 12 and under stay free. Reservation deposit required; 5-day cancellation notice. Senior discount. 1 story; exterior corridors. 10 rooms. 2 blocks from beach. Attractively decorated and furnished in charming country English decor. Cable TV, movies, coffee makers; some refrigerators, shower baths; no air conditioning. Small heated pool. No pets. AE, DS, MC, VI. D ⊘

SPYGLASS INN ⊛   ♦♦♦ Motor Inn

Adjacent to US 101 & SR 1, Spyglass Dr exit; 2705 Spyglass Dr (93449).
(805) 773-4855; FAX (805) 773-5298.

Fri-Sat 3/3-10/14	1P $ 89-130	2P/1B $ 89-130	2P/2B $ 89-130
Sun-Thu 9/10-6/10	1P $ 65-105	2P/1B $ 65-105	2P/2B $ 65-105
Sun-Thu 6/11-9/9 & Fri-Sat 10/15-3/2	1P $ 79-106	2P/1B $ 79-106	2P/2B $ 79-106

XP $6; discount for children age 12 and under. Reservation deposit required. Weekly rates. Senior discount. 2-3 stories; exterior corridors. 82 rooms; 2 1-bedroom suites with efficiency. Many ocean-view rooms. Cable TV, VCPs, coffee makers; some shower baths; no air conditioning. Heated pool, whirlpool, miniature golf. No pets. AE, CB, DI, DS, JCB, MC, VI. Restaurant 7 am-2 & 4:30-9 pm, Fri & Sat to 10 pm; $14-20; cocktails. D ⊘

RESTAURANTS

F MCLINTOCK'S SALOON & DINING HOUSE ⊛   ♦♦ Steakhouse

Adjacent to US 101 & SR 1 between Spyglass Dr and Price St exits at 750 Mattie Rd (93449).
(805) 773-1892.

$11-20. Open 4-10 pm, Sat 3-10:30 pm, Sun 9 am-9:30 pm; closed 1/1, Thanksgiving, 12/24 & 12/25. Sun ranch breakfast 9 am-1:30 pm. Very popular restaurant with ocean view. Informal western atmosphere. Nice selection of steaks, ribs, prime rib and seafood. Early-bird specials, children's menu. Cocktails & lounge; entertainment. DS, MC, VI. ⊘

MARIE CALLENDER'S   ♦ American

¾ mile north; adjacent to US 101 & SR 1; 2131 Price St (93449).
(805) 773-0606.

Up to $10. Open 7 am-10 pm, Fri & Sat to 11 pm, Sun 8 am-10 pm; closed 12/25. Nice selection of salads, sandwiches, pasta and entrees. No air conditioning. Children's menu, salad bar, Sun brunch. Beer & wine. AE, DS, MC, VI. ⊘

ROSA'S RESTORANTE ITALIANO 🆎 ♦♦ Italian
From US 101, northbound exit Price St, southbound exit Hinds St; 491 Price St (93449).
(805) 773-0551.

$11-20. Open 11:30 am-2 & 4-9:30 pm, Fri to 10 pm, Sat 4-10 pm, Sun 4-9:30 pm; closed Thanksgiving & 12/25. A charming restaurant featuring a nice selection of pasta, pizza, seafood, chicken and veal. No air conditioning. Casual attire. Children's menu, a la carte, carryout. Cocktails. AE, DS, MC, VI. ⊘

SEA CLIFFS RESTAURANT ♦♦♦ Seafood
At The Cliffs at Shell Beach, 2757 Shell Beach Rd (93449).
(805) 773-3555.

$11-20. Open 7 am-9:30 pm, Fri & Sat to 11 pm. Reservations suggested. Attractive, colorfully decorated dining room. Selection of seafood, steaks, pasta & prime rib. Valet parking. Casual attire. Early-bird specials. Cocktails & lounge. AE, DI, DS, MC, VI. ⊘

SHORE CLIFF RESTAURANT ♦♦ American
At Best Western Shore Cliff Lodge, 2555 Price St (93449).
(805) 773-4671.

$11-20. Open 7 am-9 pm, Fri & Sat to 10 pm. Reservations suggested. Located on edge of cliff overlooking the ocean. Children's menu, early-bird specials, Sun brunch. Cocktails & lounge; entertainment. AE, DI, DS, MC, VI. ⊘

SINFULLY DELICIOUS ♦♦♦ Continental
Adjacent to US 101, ¾ mile south of Spyglass Dr at 1739 Shell Beach Rd (93449).
(805) 773-1210.

$11-20. Open 5-10 pm, in summer noon-10 pm; closed 12/25. Reservations suggested. Victorian decor. Interesting menu selection, including lamb, pheasant, steaks, pasta and local seafood. Casual attire. Beer & wine. AE, MC, VI. Smoke-free premises

Port Hueneme

CASA VIA MAR INN & TENNIS CLUB 🆎 ♦♦♦ Motel
5 blocks west of Ventura Rd at 377 W Channel Islands Bl (93041).
(805) 984-6222; FAX (805) 984-9490.

Fri-Sat [BP]	1P	$ 59	2P/1B	$ 59	2P/2B	$ 59
Sun-Thu [BP]	1P	$ 55	2P/1B	$ 59	2P/2B	$ 59

XP $10; children age 5 and under stay free. Reservation deposit required. Senior discount. 2 stories; exterior corridors. 74 rooms. Some rooms with patio or balcony. Attractive Spanish exterior. Cable TV, movies, VCPs, refrigerators, coffee makers; some shower baths; 31 kitchens; no air conditioning. Heated pool, whirlpool, 6 tennis courts. Valet laundry. No pets. Meeting rooms. AE, CB, DI, DS, MC, VI. ⒟

If your plans change, don't forget to cancel your reservations.

COUNTRY INN AT PORT HUENEME ⊕   ♦♦♦ Motel
At Ventura Rd & 350 E Hueneme Rd (93041).
(805) 986-5353; FAX (805) 986-4399.

Sun-Thu [BP]	1P $ 76	2P/1B $ 76	2P/2B $ 76
Fri-Sat [BP]	1P $ 69	2P/1B $ 69	2P/2B $ 69

XP $10; children age 12 and under stay free. Credit card guarantee. 3 stories; interior corridors. 135 rooms. Attractive exterior. Nicely furnished rooms. Cable TV, honor bars, microwaves, refrigerators; 8 kitchens, whirlpools. Small heated pool, whirlpool. Coin laundry. No pets. Meeting rooms. AE, CB, DI, DS, JCB, MC, VI. Complimentary beverages each evening. ⒹⓈ ⊘

San Luis Obispo

LODGING

APPLE FARM INN ⊕   ♦♦♦♦ Motor Inn
2 blocks south of jct US 101, Monterey St exit, behind Apple Farm restaurant; 2015 Monterey St (93401).
(805) 544-2040; FAX (805) 541-5497.

Fri	1P $135-195	2P/1B $135-195	2P/2B $145-180
Sat	1P $160-195	2P/1B $160-195	2P/2B $170-180
Sun	1P $135-195	2P/1B $135-195	2P/2B $145-180
Sun-Thu 7/1-8/31	1P $135-175	2P/1B $135-195	2P/2B $145-180
Sun-Thu 9/1-6/30	1P $125-160	2P/1B $125-160	2P/2B $145-155

XP $15; children age 18 and under stay free. Check in 4 pm. Reservation deposit required. 69 units. 3 stories; interior corridors. Country decor and atmosphere. Early American period furnishings. Gas fireplaces. Heated pool, whirlpool. Airport transportation. No pets. Data ports. AE, DS, MC, VI. ⒹⓈ ⊘ **(See ad below.)**

APPLE FARM TRELLIS COURT ⊕   ♦♦♦ Motel
Adjacent to US 101, Monterey St exit; 2121 Monterey St (93401).
(805) 544-2040; FAX (805) 543-3064.

Sat [CP]	1P $ 90-110	2P/1B $100-110	2P/2B $100
Fri [CP]	1P $ 85-110	2P/1B $ 85-110	2P/2B $ 95-100
Sun-Thu 7/1-8/31 [CP]	1P $ 85-100	2P/1B $ 85-100	2P/2B $ 95
Sun-Thu 9/1-6/30 [CP]	1P $ 75- 90	2P/1B $ 75- 90	2P/2B $ 85

XP $15; children age 18 and under stay free. Check in 4 pm. Reservation deposit required. 2 stories, exterior corridors. 34 units; 2 2-bedroom units. Country decor. Cable TV, gas fireplaces. Heated pool; whirlpool. No pets. AE, DS, MC, VI. Restaurant nearby. Ⓓ ⊘

BEST WESTERN ROYAL OAK MOTOR HOTEL ⊛ ♦♦♦ Motor Inn
1 block south of jct US 101, Madonna Rd exit; 214 Madonna Rd (93405).
(805) 544-4410; FAX (805) 544-3026.

4/29-6/30 &					
9/5-11/13 [CP]	1P $ 63- 80	2P/1B $ 69- 89	2P/2B $ 69- 89
7/1-9/4 [CP]	1P $ 63- 89	2P/1B $ 69- 89	2P/2B $ 74- 89
11/14-4/28 [CP]	1P $ 61- 79	2P/1B $ 68- 79	2P/2B $ 68- 79

XP $7; children age 11 and under stay free. Credit card guarantee. Weekly & monthly rates. Senior discount. 2 stories; interior corridors. 99 rooms. Cable TV; some refrigerators; rental VCPs; no air conditioning. Heated pool, indoor whirlpool. Coin laundry. Small pets. Data ports. AE, CB, DI, DS, JCB, MC, VI. Restaurant, 6:30 am-9:30 pm, Fri & Sat to 10 pm, Sun 7 am-4 pm; $6-9; cocktails. Ⓓ ⊘

BEST WESTERN SOMERSET MANOR ⊛ ♦♦♦ Motor Inn
2 blocks south of jct US 101, Monterey St exit; 1895 Monterey St (93401).
(805) 544-0973; FAX (805) 541-2805.

5/18-7/31 & 9/1-10/13	1P $ 52	2P/1B $ 55	2P/2B $ 58
8/1-8/31	1P $ 64	2P/1B $ 67	2P/2B $ 70
10/14-5/17	1P $ 40	2P/1B $ 43	2P/2B $ 46

XP $3. Credit card guarantee. 2 stories; exterior corridors. 40 rooms. Cable TV; some shower baths, microwaves, refrigerators. Heated pool, whirlpool. Small pets, $10; $10 deposit. AE, CB, DI, DS, JCB, MC, VI. Coffee shop; 6 am-2 pm; 7/1-10/15 6 am-10 pm; $6-16; beer & wine. Ⓓ

BUDGET MOTEL ⊛ ♦ Motel
1 block east of US 101, Marsh St exit; 345 Marsh St (93401).
(805) 543-6443; FAX (805) 545-0951.

All year [CP]	1P $ 34- 50	2P/1B $ 38- 68	2P/2B $ 48- 68

XP $2-6; children age 5 and under stay free. Credit card guarantee; 3-day cancellation notice. Senior discount. 2 stories; exterior corridors. 51 rooms; 2 2-bedroom units. 2 blocks south of downtown area. Cable TV, movies; some shower baths, air conditioning. No pets. AE, CB, DI, DS, MC, VI. Ⓓ ⊘

CAMPUS MOTEL ⊛ ♦ Motel
On SR 1 at jct US 101; 404 Santa Rosa St (93405).
(805) 544-0881.

3/25-6/9	1P ...	2P/1B $ 50- 89	2P/2B $ 60- 99
6/10-10/7	1P ...	2P/1B $ 56-110	2P/2B $ 66-120
10/8-3/24	1P ...	2P/1B $ 45- 75	2P/2B $ 55- 85

XP $5; children age 16 and under stay free. Reservation deposit required; 5-day cancellation notice. 2 stories; exterior corridors. 35 rooms. Cable TV, coffee makers, refrigerators; rental VCPs; some whirlpools, air conditioning. Heated pool. Coin laundry. Pets. Meeting rooms. AE, DS, MC, VI. Ⓓ ⊘

---

*AAA members must identify themselves upon making reservations
and at registration to receive special and discounted rates.*

EMBASSY SUITES HOTEL (AAA)   ♦♦♦ Suite Motor Inn
Formerly Pacific Suites Hotel. From US 101, exit Madonna Rd, ½ mile south, then east
on Dalidio Dr; 333 Madonna Rd (93405).
(805) 549-0800; FAX (805) 543-5273.

3/1-5/14 & 9/16-10/31 [BP]	1P	$ 89-145	2P/1B	$ 89-145	2P/2B	$ 89-145
5/15-9/15 [BP]	1P	$ 99-159	2P/1B	$ 99-159	2P/2B	$ 99-159
11/1-2/28 [BP]	1P	$ 79-129	2P/1B	$ 79-129	2P/2B	$ 79-129

XP $10; children age 12 and under stay free. Credit card guarantee. Senior discount. 4 stories; interior corridors. 195 1-bedroom suites. At Central Coast Plaza Mall. Cable TV, free and pay movies, coffee makers, honor bars. Heated indoor pool, whirlpools. Coin laundry. Airport transportation. No pets. Conference facilities; meeting rooms. AE, CB, DI, DS, MC, VI. Complimentary evening beverages. Restaurant 11:30 am-2:30 & 5-10 pm; $9-$16; cocktail lounge. Ⓓ Ⓢ ⊘

GARDEN STREET INN BED & BREAKFAST   ♦♦♦ Historic Bed & Breakfast
½ mile east of US 101, Marsh St exit; 1212 Garden St (93401).
(805) 545-9802.

All year [BP]	1P	...	2P/1B	$ 90-120	2P/2B	...

Reservation deposit required; 7-day cancellation notice. Senior discount. 2 stories; interior corridors. 13 rooms; 4 suites, $140-160. In downtown area, 1887 restored Italianate/Queen Anne-style house. Charming Victorian decor. No TVs, phones. Some gas fireplaces, whirlpools. No pets. AE, MC, VI. Ⓓ Ⓢ Designated smoking area

HERITAGE INN BED & BREAKFAST   ♦♦ Historic Bed & Breakfast
1 block west of US 101 at junction SR 1; southbound Santa Rosa exit, northbound
Morro Bay exit; l block south on Olive St; 978 Olive St (93405).
(805) 544-7440.

All year [BP]	1P	...	2P/1B	$ 85- 95	2P/2B	...

XP $10. Reservation deposit required; 7-day cancellation notice. 2 stories; interior corridors. 7 rooms. Charming rooms in a turn-of-the-century home. No air conditioning, phones, TVs. Pets. AE, MC, VI. Ⓓ Designated smoking area

HOLIDAY INN EXPRESS (AAA)   ♦♦♦ Motor Inn
2 blocks south of jct US 101; northbound Grand Ave exit, southbound Monterey St exit;
1800 Monterey St (93401).
(805) 544-8600, FAX (805) 541-4698.

Fri-Sat [CP] 5/26-9/10	1P	$ 90-100	2P/1B	$100-120	2P/2B	$100-120
Fri-Sat [CP] 9/11-5/25 & Sun-Thu [CP] 5/26-9/10	1P	$ 80- 90	2P/1B	$ 90-100	2P/2B	$ 90-100
Sun-Thu [CP] 9/11-5/25	1P	$ 70- 80	2P/1B	$ 80- 90	2P/2B	$ 80- 90

XP $10; children age 12 and under stay free. Credit card guarantee; 3-day cancellation notice. 3 stories; interior corridors. 100 rooms. Cable TV, movies, coffee makers; rental VCPs. Heated pool, whirlpool. No pets. AE, CB, DI, DS, JCB, MC, VI. Restaurant, 11:30 am-midnight; $8-12; cocktails. Ⓓ Ⓢ ⊘ **(See ad opposite.)**

HOWARD JOHNSON MOTOR LODGE   ◆◆ Motel
Adjacent to US 101, Los Osos Rd exit; 1585 Calle Joaquin (93405).
(805) 544-5300; FAX (805) 541-2823.

All year   1P $ 49- 69   2P/1B $ 59- 79   2P/2B $ 59- 79

XP $10; children age 16 and under stay free. Reservation deposit required; 3-day cancellation notice. Weekly & monthly rates. Senior discount. 2 stories; interior corridors. 64 rooms. Cable TV, movies; some refrigerators. Heated pool, wading pool. Coin laundry. Pets, $10 deposit. AE, DI, DS, MC, VI. Restaurant nearby.
Ⓓ ⊘

LA CUESTA MOTOR INN ⒶⒶⒶ   ◆◆◆ Motel
2 blocks south of jct US 101, Monterey St exit; 2074 Monterey St (93401).
(805) 543-2777; FAX (805) 544-0696.

3/1-10/31 [CP]   1P $ 75- 95   2P/1B $ 75- 95   2P/2B $ 75- 95
11/1-2/28 [CP]   1P $ 68- 85   2P/1B $ 68- 85   2P/2B $ 68- 85

XP $10; children age 12 and under stay free. 4 stories; interior corridors. 72 rooms. Cable TV, movies; some refrigerators, balconies. Pool, whirlpool. No pets. Meeting rooms. AE, CB, DI, DS, MC, VI. Afternoon tea. Restaurant nearby. Ⓓ Ⓢ
⊘ **(See ad below.)**

MADONNA INN
SAN LUIS OBISPO, CALIFORNIA
Each Room Unique

EXPERIENCE THE MAGIC at the world famous Madonna Inn. You'll marvel at the imaginative expression of fantasy in our interior design and architecture. No two rooms are alike. Each is designed with its own distinct fantasy theme.

Dine nightly in our Gold Rush Dining Room. Select from choice steaks, fresh seafood, lamb or chicken cooked over our oak pit BBQ; or enjoy the casual atmosphere of our coffee shop.

Our Bakery offers a wide array of French pastries, fruit and cream pies, assorted cookies and of course our famous "Black Forest" cakes.

Enjoy browsing through our Ladies Boutique, Men's Clothing Store and Gourmet Gift Shop. You'll find an extensive selection of unique gifts and the finest apparel selected from around the world.

Situated amidst 2200 acres of pastoral beauty in the heart of the Central Coast wine growing region, we're only minutes away from the airport, Cal Poly State Universtiy, shopping and miles of sandy beaches. Visit the historic mission San Luis Obispo de Tolosa or have our staff assist you in arranging a Hearst Castle tour. Secluded ranch rooms and rural jogging and fitness trails are also available.

805/543-3000 or toll free: 800/543-9666

LAMPLIGHTER INN ◉ ♦♦ Motel
5 blocks south of jct US 101, Monterey St exit; 1604 Monterey St (93401).
(805) 547-7777; FAX (805) 547-7787.

4/1-6/9 & 9/7-10/15 [CP]	1P	$ 39- 59	2P/1B	$ 45- 74	2P/2B	$ 54- 74
6/10-7/19 [CP]	1P	$ 45- 69	2P/1B	$ 49- 84	2P/2B	$ 64- 89
7/20-9/6 [CP]	1P	$ 54- 79	2P/1B	$ 54- 89	2P/2B	$ 69- 94
10/16-3/31 [CP]	1P	$ 37- 59	2P/1B	$ 42- 69	2P/2B	$ 49- 69

XP $5-6; discount for children age 8 and under. Credit card guarantee. Weekly rates. Senior discount. 2-3 stories; exterior corridors. 45 rooms. A variety of rooms from compact to nicely decorated suites. 6 2-bedroom units. Cable TV, movies, coffee makers; some shower baths, microwaves, refrigerators, phones. Heated pool, whirlpool. Coin laundry. No pets. AE, DS, MC, VI. ⓓ ⊘

MADONNA INN ♦♦♦ Motor Inn
Adjacent to US 101, Madonna Rd exit; 100 Madonna Rd (93405).
(805) 543-3000; FAX (805) 543-1800.

All year [CP]	1P	$ 77	2P/1B	$ 87-180	2P/2 B	$ 87-180

XP $13; children age 16 and under stay free. Reservation deposit required. Check in 4 pm. Senior discount. 3 stories, exterior corridors. 109 rooms; 2 2-bedroom units, 2 3-bedroom units; suites, some with fireplace, $130-180. On spacious grounds. Large, uniquely designed theme rooms. Some rock rooms with waterfall shower. Cable TV; some shower baths, air conditioning. No pets. CB, JCB, MC, VI. Coffee shop 7 am-10 pm; in summer to 11 pm; $7-$13; cocktails. Dining room (see separate listing). ⓓ **(See ad opposite.)**

MID-TOWN MOTEL ◉ ♦ Motel
¼ mile east of US 101, Marsh St exit; 475 Marsh St (93401).
(805) 543-4533.

Fri 5/1-9/30	1P	$ 40	2P/1B	$ 40- 45	2P/2B	$ 50- 60
Sat 5/1-9/30	1P	$ 60	2P/1B	$ 65	2P/2B	$ 70- 80
Sun-Thu 5/1-9/30	1P	$ 34- 40	2P/1B	$ 38- 42	2P/2B	$ 46- 50
10/1-4/30	1P	$ 32- 36	2P/1B	$ 34 - 38	2P/2B	$ 38- 42

XP $4-5; children age 10 and under stay free. Credit card guarantee. Weekly rates. 2 stories; exterior corridors. 32 rooms; 3 2-bedroom units. 3 blocks south of downtown area. Cable TV, movies; some radios, microwaves, refrigerators; no air conditioning. Pool. No pets. AE, CB, DI, MC, VI. ⓓ ⊘

OLIVE TREE INN BEST WESTERN ◉ ♦♦ Motor Inn
¾ block west of US 101 at jct SR 1; US 101 northbound Morro Bay exit, southbound Santa Rosa exit; 1000 Olive St (93405).
(805) 544-2800.

6/1-9/30	1P	$ 55- 58	2P/1B	$ 70- 85	2P/2B	$ 80- 83
10/1-5/31	1P	$ 48- 53	2P/1B	$ 55- 62	2P/2B	$ 58- 63

XP $4. Reservation deposit required; 3-day cancellation notice. Senior discount. 2 stories; exterior corridors. 38 rooms. 6 efficiencies, $6 extra. Cable TV; no air conditioning. Heated pool; sauna. Coin laundry. Small pets. AE, CB, DI, DS, MC, VI. Coffee shop 6:30 am-2 pm. ⓓ ⊘

PEACH TREE INN ◆◆ Motel
1 block south of jct US 101, Monterey St exit; 2001 Monterey St (93401).
(805) 543-3170; FAX (805) 543-7673.

All year [CP]	1P	$ 49- 69	2P/1B	$ 54- 75	2P/2B	$ 59- 89

XP $3-5; children age 16 and under stay free. Reservation deposit required; 3-day cancellation notice. Senior discount. Exterior corridors. 39 rooms. Cable TV, movies, coffee makers; some shower baths. No pets. AE, DI, DS, MC, VI. Restaurant nearby. Ⓓ ⊘

QUALITY SUITES Ⓐ ◆◆◆ Suite Motel
5 blocks south of jct US 101, Monterey St exit; 1631 Monterey St (93401).
(805) 541-5001; FAX (805) 546-9475.

5/22-9/7 [BP]	1P	$ 99-129	2P/1B	$109-139	2P/2B	$109-139
9/8-5/21 [BP]	1P	$ 89-119	2P/1B	$ 99-129	2P/2B	$ 99-129

XP $10; children age 18 and under stay free. 2-3 stories; exterior corridors. 138 rooms. 1-bedroom suites. Nicely landscaped, tree-shaded pool & courtyard area. Cable TV, movies, VCPs, refrigerators, microwaves. Heated pool, whirlpool. Coin laundry. No pets. Meeting rooms. AE, DI, DS, MC, VI. Complimentary evening beverages. Ⓓ Ⓢ ⊘

SANDS MOTEL & SUITES Ⓐ ◆◆ Motel
2 blocks south of jct US 101, Monterey St exit; 1930 Monterey St (93401).
(805) 544-0500; FAX (805) 544-3529.

3/24-6/8 & 9/4-10/8 [CP]	1P ...		2P/1B	$ 59- 79	2P/2B	$ 64- 84
6/9-9/3 [CP]	1P ...		2P/1B	$ 69- 99	2P/2B	$ 74-109
10/9-3/23 [CP]	1P ...		2P/1B	$ 54- 69	2P/2B	$ 59- 79

XP $7; children 12 and under stay free. Senior discount. 2 stories; exterior corridors. 70 rooms; 14 1-bedroom suites with microwave, refrigerator & wet bar. Cable TV; some VCPs, shower baths. Heated pool, whirlpool. Coin laundry. No pets. Meeting rooms. AE, CB, DI, DS, MC, VI. Restaurants nearby. Ⓓ Ⓢ ⊘ **(See ad below.)**

Be sure to read the introduction to Lodging & Restaurants.

SAN LUIS OBISPO TRAVELODGE ⓐⓐⓐ ♦♦ Motel

2 blocks south of jct US 101; northbound exit Grand Ave, southbound exit Monterey St; 1825 Monterey St (93401).
(805) 543-5110; FAX (805) 543-3406.

5/1-6/30 & 9/12-10/31	1P	$ 42- 49	2P/1B	$ 47- 52	2P/2B	$ 49- 54
7/1-9/11	1P	$ 58- 79	2P/1B	$ 78- 92	2P/2B	$ 89- 99
11/1-4/30	1P	$ 39- 48	2P/1B	$ 45- 50	2P/2B	$ 48- 52

XP $5; children age 9 and under stay free. Reservation deposit required; 7-day cancellation notice. Weekly & monthly rates. Senior discount. 2 stories; exterior corridors. 38 rooms. Cable TV, movies; some shower baths, coffee makers. Heated pool. Small pets. AE, CB, DI, DS, MC, VI. Coffee shop nearby. Ⓓ ⊘

SUPER 8 MOTEL ⓐⓐ ♦♦ Motel

2 blocks south of jct US 101, Monterey St exit; 1951 Monterey St (93401).
(805) 544-7895.

5/15-7/31 & 8/16-11/15 [CP]	1P	$ 42- 59	2P/1B	$ 42- 59	2P/2B	$ 45- 69
8/1-8/15 [CP]	1P	$ 49- 69	2P/1B	$ 54- 69	2P/2B	$ 54- 79
11/16-5/14 [CP]	1P	$ 37- 49	2P/1B	$ 39- 49	2P/2B	$ 44- 59

XP $5. Credit card guarantee. Senior discount. 2 stories; exterior corridors. 49 rooms. Cable TV, movies; some microwaves, refrigerators. Heated pool. No pets. AE, CB, DI, DS, JCB, MC, VI. Coffee shop nearby. Ⓓ Ⓢ ⊘

TRAVELODGE SOUTH ⓐⓐⓐ ♦ Motel

1 block west of US 101 at jct SR 1; US 101 northbound Morro Bay exit; southbound Santa Rosa exit; 950 Olive St (93405).
(805) 544-8886.

Fri-Sat 5/25-9/9	1P	...	2P/1B	$ 70- 90	2P/2B	$ 95-115
Sun-Thu 5/25-9/9	1P	...	2P/1B	$ 46- 60	2P/2B	$ 50- 75
Fri-Sat 9/10-5/24	1P	...	2P/1B	$ 44- 75	2P/2B	$ 60- 95
Sun-Thu 9/10-5/24	1P	...	2P/1B	$ 40- 60	2P/2B	$ 50- 70

XP $8; children age 16 and under stay free. Reservation deposit required. Weekly rates. Senior discount. 2 stories; exterior corridors. 32 rooms. 2 efficiencies, no utensils. Cable TV, movies. Whirlpool. Small pets, $8, $20 deposit. AE, CB, DI, DS, JCB, MC, VI. Ⓓ Ⓢ ⊘

VAGABOND INN ⓐⓐⓐ ♦ Motel

½ block south of jct US 101, Madonna Rd exit; 210 Madonna Rd (93401).
(805) 544-4710; FAX (805) 541-1949.

5/16-10/15 [CP]	1P	$ 55- 59	2P/1B	$ 59- 64	2P/2B	$ 65- 69
10/16-5/15 [CP]	1P	$ 44- 48	2P/1B	$ 49- 53	2P/2B	$ 53- 58

XP $5; children 18 and under stay free. Credit card guarantee. 2 stories; exterior corridors. 60 rooms; 1 2-bedroom unit. Cable TV, movies. Heated pool. Small pets, $5. AE, CB, DI, DS, MC, VI. Restaurant nearby. Ⓓ ⊘

VILLA MOTEL ⓐⓐⓐ ♦♦ Motel

4 blocks south of jct US 101, Monterey St exit; 1670 Monterey St (93401).
(805) 543-8071.

	1P ...	2P/1B	$ 37- 49	2P/2B	$ 42- 59
4/1-5/31	1P ...	2P/1B	$ 37- 49	2P/2B	$ 42- 59
6/1-9/30	1P ...	2P/1B	$ 43- 79	2P/2B	$ 53- 85
10/1-3/31	1P ...	2P/1B	$ 33- 39	2P/2B	$ 39- 49

XP $4; children age 12 and under stay free. Credit card guarantee. Weekly rates. 1-2 stories; exterior corridors. 14 units. Cable TV, movies; some shower baths, microwaves, refrigerators. Heated pool open 4/1-10/31. No pets. AE, CB, DI, DS, JCB, MC, VI. Ⓓ ⊘

RESTAURANTS

APPLE FARM RESTAURANT 🌑🌑   ♦♦ American
At Apple Farm Inn, 2015 Monterey St (93401).
(805) 544-6100.

$11-20. Open 7 am-9:30 pm; to 10 pm Fri-Sat and summer. Reservations suggested. Country charm. Serving homemade soups, desserts & varied entrees. Casual attire. Children's menu. Beer & wine. AE, DS, MC, VI. Smoke-free premises

BENVENUTI RISTORANTE   ♦♦♦ Italian
½ mile south, ¼ mile east of US 101, Marsh St exit, then ¼ mile north at 450 Marsh St (93401).
(805) 541-5393.

$11-20. Open 11:30 am-2 & 5:30-10 pm; Sat & Sun from 5:30 pm; closed 1/1, Thanksgiving & 12/25. Reservations suggested. Charming restaurant in a restored house. Nice selection of Italian cuisine. Casual attire. A la carte. Cocktails. AE, DI, MC, VI. Smoke-free premises

CAFE ROMA 🌑🌑   ♦♦ Italian
½ mile east of downtown, adjacent to train station at 1819 Osos St (93401).
(805) 541-6800.

$11-20. Open 11:30 am-2:30 & 5:30-9:30 pm, Sat 5:30-9:30 pm; closed Sun, 7/4, Thanksgiving & 12/25. Reservations suggested. Charming restaurant with nice selection of pasta, veal, chicken, scampi and pizza. Outdoor patio dining available. Casual attire. A la carte. Cocktails. AE, CB, DI, DS, MC, VI. Smoke-free premises

MADONNA INN DINING ROOM   ♦♦♦ American
In Madonna Inn at 100 Madonna Rd (93405).
(805) 543-3000.

$21-30. Open 5:30-10 pm; to 11 pm in summer. Reservations suggested. Ornate, uniquely decorated dining room. Nice selection of entrees. Casual attire. Children's menu. Cocktails & lounge; entertainment. MC, VI. Smoke-free premises

THIS OLD HOUSE 🌑🌑   ♦ American
2½ miles southwest of SR 1 (Santa Rosa St) at 740 W Foothill Blvd (93405).
(805) 543-2690.

$11-20. Open 5-9:30 pm; Fri to 10 pm; Sat 4-10 pm; Sun 4-9:30 pm; closed Thanksgiving & 12/25. Reservations suggested. Informal, Old West atmosphere. Features oak-pit barbecued steaks, chicken, ribs & seafood. No air conditioning. Casual attire. Children's menu. Cocktails & lounge. AE, DI, MC, VI. ⊘

San Simeon

LODGING

BEST WESTERN GREEN TREE INN ⓐⓐ   ♦♦♦ Motel
On SR 1 at 9450 Castillo Dr (PO Box 100, 93452).
(805) 927-4691; FAX (805) 927-1473.

6/1-9/30 [CP]	1P ...	2P/1B	$ 55- 90	2P/2B	$ 60- 95
10/1-5/31 [CP]	1P ...	2P/1B	$ 50- 80	2P/2B	$ 55- 85

XP $10; children age 17 and under stay free. Reservation deposit required; 10-day cancellation notice. 2 stories; interior/exterior corridors. 117 rooms; 25 efficiencies, no utensils. Cable TV, movies. Heated indoor pool, whirlpool, 2 lighted tennis courts. Coin laundry. No pets. AE, CB, DI, DS, MC, VI. Restaurant nearby. Ⓓ ⊘

CALIFORNIA SEACOAST LODGE ⓐⓐ   ♦♦♦ Motel
On SR 1 at 9215 Hearst Dr (93452).
(805) 927-3878.

6/1-9/30 [CP]	1P ...	2P/1B	$ 65 -100	2P/2B	$ 65- 100
10/1-5/31 [CP]	1P ...	2P/1B	$ 55- 95	2P/2B	$ 55- 95

XP $5; children age 12 and under stay free. Credit card guarantee; 3-day cancellation notice. 2 stories; interior corridors. 57 rooms. Decorated in country motif. Cable TV, movies, refrigerators; many gas fireplaces; fee for whirlpool tubs; some VCPs, ocean view; no air conditioning. Small heated pool. No pets. AE, DI, MC, VI. Ⓓ ⊘

EL REY INN ⓐⓐ   ♦♦♦ Motor Inn
3½ miles south on SR 1 at 9260 Castillo Dr (PO Box 200, 93452).
(805) 927-3998; FAX (805) 927-8268.

6/5-9/3, Fri-Sat 3/31-6/4 & Fri-Sat 9/4-10/29 [CP]	1P ...	2P/1B	$ 79- 99	2P/2B	$ 79- 99
10/30-3/30, Sun-Thu 3/31-6/4 & Sun-Thu 9/4-10/29 [CP]	1P ...	2P/1B	$ 69- 89	2P/2B	$ 69- 89

XP $5. Reservation deposit required. Senior discount. 2 stories; interior/exterior corridors. 56 rooms; 2 2-bedroom units; 2 2-room suites with whirlpool, $99-$159. Spacious rooms with patio or balcony, many with ocean or garden view. Cable TV, movies, coffee makers; some gas fireplaces, refrigerators; no air conditioning. Small heated pool; whirlpools. Coin laundry. No pets. AE, DS, MC, VI. Europa Restaurant; see separate listing. Ⓓ

QUALITY INN ⓐⓐ   ♦♦♦ Motor Inn
3½ miles south on SR 1, at 9280 Castillo Dr (93452).
(805) 927-8659; FAX (805) 927-4800.

6/1-7/31 & 9/1-9/30	1P ...	2P/1B	$ 75 -125	2P/2B	$ 83- 93
8/1-8/31	1P ...	2P/1B	$ 85 -135	2P/2B	$ 93-103
10/1-5/31	1P ...	2P/1B	$ 60 -115	2P/2B	$ 65- 75

XP $5; children age 18 and under stay free. Reservation deposit required. Senior discount. 2 stories; interior corridors. 48 rooms; 4 large rooms with refrigerator, microwave & gas fireplace. Spacious rooms with patio or balcony. Cable TV, movies; no air conditioning. Indoor whirlpool. No pets. AE, CB, DI, DS, JCB, MC, VI. Restaurant, 6:30 am-8 pm; $8-$12; beer & wine. Ⓓ ⊘

SAN SIMEON LODGE ⒶⒶ   ♦ Motor Inn
3½ miles south on SR 1 at 9520 Castillo Dr (93452).
(805) 927-4601.

6/1-9/1	1P	...	2P/1B	$ 50- 70	2P/2B	$ 50- 75
9/2-5/31	1P	...	2P/1B	$ 35- 50	2P/2B	$ 40- 50

XP $5. Credit card guarantee. 2 stories; exterior corridors. 63 rooms; 2 4-bedroom units. Cable TV, movies; no air conditioning. Heated pool. No pets. AE, CB, DI, MC, VI. Restaurant, 7 am-2 & 5-9 pm; $10-$15; cocktails. Ⓓ ⊘

SILVER SURF MOTEL ⒶⒶ   ♦♦ Motel
3½ miles south on SR 1 at 9390 Castillo Dr (93452).
(805) 927-4661; FAX (805) 927-3225.

5/26-6/29 & 9/4-10/14	1P	...	2P/1B	$ 49- 59	2P/2B	$ 49- 79
6/30-9/3	1P	...	2P/1B	$ 60- 65	2P/2B	$ 60- 85
10/15-5/25	1P...		2P/1B	$ 29- 45	2P/2B	$ 29- 65

XP $5. Credit card guarantee. Senior discount. 2 stories; exterior corridors. 72 rooms; 1 2-bedroom unit; 4 rooms with gas fireplace, $49-$85; some small rooms. Large lawn area. Cable TV; some ocean views and balconies; no air conditioning. Small heated indoor pool, whirlpool. Coin laundry. Pets, $5. AE, CB, DI, DS, MC, VI. Restaurant nearby. Ⓓ ⊘

RESTAURANT

EUROPA RESTAURANT ⒶⒶ   ♦♦ Continental
East side of SR 1 at El Rey Inn, 9240 Castillo Dr (93452).
(805) 927-3087.

$11-20. Open 5:30-9 pm; closed 12/1-12/25. Reservations suggested. American & European food with homemade touch. Fresh seafood, pasta & desserts made on premises. Casual attire. Children's menu. Beer & wine. MC, VI. Smoke-free premises

Santa Barbara

LODGING

AMBASSADOR BY THE SEA MOTEL ⒶⒶ   ♦♦ Motel
3 blocks south of US 101, between Bath & Chapala sts at 202 W Cabrillo Blvd (93101).
(805) 965-4577; FAX (805) 965-9937.

5/1-10/1 [CP]	1P	...	2P/1B	$ 88-178	2P/2B	$ 88-148
10/2-4/30 [CP]	1P	...	2P/1B	$ 68-148	2P/2B	$ 68-118

XP $10. Reservation deposit required; 3-day cancellation notice. Senior discount. 2 stories; exterior corridors. 32 rooms; 4 2-bedroom units. Kitchens, $20 extra. Across from beach. 2 sun decks with beach view. Some refrigerators; no air conditioning. Small heated pool. No pets. AE, DI, DS, MC, VI. Ⓓ

BATH STREET INN ⒶⒶ　　　◆◆ Bed & Breakfast
2½ blocks south of Mission St at 1720 Bath St (93101).
(805) 682-9680.

Sun-Thu 10/1-6/30 [BP]	1P	$ 70-125	2P/1B	$ 75-125	2P/2B	$ 90
Fri-Sat [BP]	1P	$ 90-145	2P/1B	$ 95-150	2P/2B	$115

XP $20. Reservation deposit required; 3-day refund notice. 2-night minimum stay weekends. 3 stories; interior corridors. 10 rooms; 1 unit with fireplace & whirlpool bathtub. 1873 Queen Anne Victorian house in residential area. Refrigerators; some cable TV, air conditioning, phones, whirlpools (fee). Bicycles. No pets. Tea and refreshments served after 4 pm. AE, MC, VI. Ⓓ Smoke-free premises

BAYBERRY INN　　　◆◆ Bed & Breakfast
Corner of Chapala St & 111 W Valerio St (93101).
(805) 682-3199; FAX (805) 962-0103.

All year [BP]	1P	$85 -150	2P/1B	$ 85-150	2P/2B	...

Credit card guarantee; 7-day cancellation notice. 2-night minimum stay weekends. 2 stories; interior corridors. 8 rooms; 4 units with wood-burning fireplace. 1886 Federal-style house in residential area. Attractively landscaped grounds. Some cable TV hookups, phone jacks, whirlpools; no phones, air conditioning. Bicycles. Small pets only with advance notice. AE, CB, DI, DS, MC, VI. Ⓓ Smoke-free premises

BEST WESTERN-BEACHSIDE INN ⒶⒶ　　　◆◆ Motor Inn
4 blocks south of US 101, corner of Cabrillo Blvd and Castillo St at 336 W Cabrillo Blvd (93101).
(805) 965-6556; FAX (805) 966-6626.

Fri-Sat 3/3-10/31	1P	$ 89-145	2P/1B	$ 95-151	2P/2B	$119-151
Fri-Sat 11/1-3/2 & Sun-Thu 5/26-10/31	1P	$ 79-135	2P/1B	$ 85-141	2P/2B	$109-141
Sun-Thu 11/1-5/25	1P	$ 69-125	2P/1B	$ 75-131	2P/2B	$ 99-131

XP $10; children age 12 and under stay free. Reservation deposit required. 3 stories; exterior corridors. 60 rooms; some smaller rooms; 3 2-bedroom units. Across from beach, yacht harbor & city park. Cable TV, movies; some coffee makers, refrigerators. Heated pool. Valet laundry. No pets. AE, CB, DI, DS, JCB, MC, VI. Andria's Harborside Restaurant, see separate listing. Ⓓ ⊘

BEST WESTERN ENCINA LODGE ⒶⒶ　　　◆◆◆ Motor Inn
½ mile north of US 101; exit Mission St, 1 block south of Santa Barbara Cottage Hospital at 2220 Bath St (93105).
(805) 682-7277; FAX (805) 563-9319.

All year	1P	$106-126	2P/1B	$110-148	2P/2B	$110-148

XP $6; children age 3 and under stay free. Reservation deposit required. Weekly & monthly rates. Senior discount. 121 rooms; 33 1- & 2-bedroom kitchen apartments, 3 bi-level. Spacious grounds. Cable TV, movies, coffee makers, refrigerators, safes; some air conditioning, patios & balconies. Heated pool, sauna, whirlpool. Coin laundry. Airport transportation. No pets. AE, CB, DI, DS, JCB, MC, VI. Restaurant, 7:30 am-9:30 pm; $11-19; cocktails. Ⓓ ⊘

BEST WESTERN PEPPER TREE INN ⊛ ♦♦♦ Motor Inn

3½ miles northwest, ½ mile east of junction US 101 at 3850 State St (93105).
(805) 687-5511; FAX (805) 682-2410.

All year	1P $96 -132	2P/2B $108-138	2P/2B $108-138

XP $6; children age 3 and under stay free. Reservation deposit required. Senior discount. 2 stories; exterior corridors. 150 rooms. Attractively decorated rooms with patio or balcony. Located across from large shopping mall. Cable TV, movies, refrigerators, coffee makers, safes. 2 heated pools, sauna, whirlpools. Coin laundry. Airport transportation. No pets. Meeting rooms, data ports. AE, CB, DI, DS, JCB, MC, VI. Restaurant, 6 am-9:30 pm; Fri & Sat to 11 pm; $9-16; cocktails. Ⓓ ⊘

BEST WESTERN SOUTH COAST INN ♦♦♦ Motel

Adjacent to US 101, between Patterson & Fairview aves exits, at 5620 Calle Real (93117).
(805) 967-3200; FAX (805) 683-4466.

All year [CP]	1P $ 89-150	2P/1B $ 94-150	2P/2B $ 94-150

XP $10; children age 18 and under stay free. Senior discount. 2 stories; exterior corridors. 121 rooms. Nicely landscaped. Cable TV, free and pay movies; some microwaves, refrigerators. Heated pool, whirlpool; ping pong table. No pets. Meeting rooms. AE, CB, DI, DS, MC, VI. Complimentary beverages Mon-Thu evenings. Ⓓ Ⓢ ⊘

CATHEDRAL OAKS LODGE ⊛ ♦♦♦ Motel

5 miles northwest on US 101; exit Turnpike Rd, 1 block north at 4770 Calle Real (93110).
(805) 964-3511; FAX (805) 964-0075.

All year [CP]	1P $ 75-115	2P/1B $ 85-115	2P/2B $ 95-115

XP $10; children age 11 and under stay free. Credit card guarantee. Senior discount. 2 stories; interior corridors. 126 rooms; 1 2-bedroom unit; many rooms with balconies or patios. Surrounding garden & lagoon area populated by Koi fish & ducks. Cable TV, movies; some coffee makers, refrigerators. Heated pool, whirlpool. Coin laundry. No pets. Meeting rooms. AE, CB, DI, DS, MC, VI. Restaurant nearby. Ⓓ ⊘

THE CHESHIRE CAT ⊛ ♦♦♦ Bed & Breakfast

Corner Chapala & Valerio sts at 36 W Valerio St (93101).
(805) 569-1610.

Fri-Sun [BP]	1P $119-195	2P/1B $119-249	2P/2B ...
Mon-Thu [BP]	1P $ 75-179	2P/1B $ 79-190	2P/2B ...

XP $25. 2-night minimum stay weekends. Reservation deposit required; 7-day refund notice. Senior discount. 14 rooms; large unit with separate living room, efficiency & large whirlpool tub $190-249. 1800 Queen Anne & Victorian homes located in residential area. 2 efficiencies; 3 fireplaces; some cable TV, radios, refrigerators; whirlpools; no air conditioning. Whirlpool, bicycles. No pets. AE, MC, VI. Ⓓ Smoke-free premises

CIRCLE BAR B GUEST RANCH   ♦♦ Ranch

20 miles north on US 101, exit Refugio Rd, then 3½ miles north on narrow, winding road; 1800 Refugio Canyon Rd (93117).
(805) 968-1113.

All Year [AP]   1P $110-198   2P/1B $186-225   2P/2B $186-225

XP $60-75. Reservation deposit required; 14-day cancellation notice. Weekly rates. 1 story; exterior corridors. 13 rooms; 1 2-bedroom unit. Quiet family atmosphere. Located in a scenic canyon 3½ miles from the ocean. No TVs, air conditioning, phones. Pool, whirlpool, horseshoe pit, table tennis. Hiking trails; fee for horseback riding. No pets. MC, VI. Dinner theater May through Nov. Ⓓ ⊘

COAST VILLAGE INN ⒶⒶ   ♦♦ Motel

In Montecito; adjacent to US 101, exit Olive Mill Rd, then ¼ mile north at 1188 Coast Village Rd (93108).
(805) 969-3266; FAX (805) 969-7117.

Fri-Sat 5/15-9/14 [CP]	1P	$ 89- 99	2P/1B	$ 89- 99	2P/2B	$ 95-105
Sun-Thu 5/15-9/14 &					
Fri-Sat 9/15-5/14 [CP]	1P	$ 80- 95	2P/1B	$ 80- 95	2P/2B	$ 85- 95
Sun-Thu 9/15-5/14 [CP]	1P	$ 70- 85	2P/1B	$ 70- 85	2P/2B	$ 75- 85

XP $5; children age 12 and under stay free. Reservation deposit required. Weekly rates. Senior discount. 2 stories; exterior corridors. 25 rooms. Cable TV; some efficiencies, kitchens; no air conditioning. Heated pool. No pets. AE, MC, VI. Restaurant nearby. Ⓓ Smoke-free premises **(See ad below.)**

COUNTRY INN BY THE SEA ⒶⒶ   ♦♦♦ Motel

1½ blocks south of US 101 at 128 Castillo St (93101).
(805) 963-4471; FAX (805) 962-2633.

5/15-9/30 [CP]	1P ...	2P/1B	$ 95-185	2P/2B	$ 95-185
10/1-5/14 [CP]	1P ...	2P/1B	$ 79-165	2P/2B	$ 79-165

XP $10. Reservation deposit required; 14-day cancellation notice. Weekly rates. 3 stories; interior/exterior corridors. 46 rooms; whirlpool suites $189-229. Many rooms with patio or balcony. 2 blocks from beach across the street from city park. Very attractive European country decor. Cable TV, VCPs, movies; some refrigerators. Heated pool, saunas, whirlpool. No pets. AE, CB, DI, MC, VI. Ⓓ ⊘ **(See ad below.)**

EAGLE INN ⊛   ◆◆ Apartment Motel
3 blocks south of US 101, corner Bath St and 232 Natoma Ave (93101).
(805) 965-3586; FAX (805) 966-1218.

Fri-Sat 5/26-9/30 [CP]	1P ...		2P/1B $110-145	2P/2B	$120-145
Sun-Thu 5/29-9/28 [CP]	1P ...		2P/1B $ 75-110	2P/2B	$ 85-120
Fri-Sat 10/1-5/25 [CP]	1P ...		2P/1B $ 85-120	2P/2B	$ 90-125
Sun-Thu 9/29-5/28	1P ...		2P/1B $ 60- 85	2P/2B	$ 65- 95

XP $5; children age 15 and under stay free. Reservation deposit required; 3-day cancellation notice. Weekly & monthly rates. Senior discount. 2 stories; interior corridors. 18 rooms; most apartments with fully equipped kitchens; 4 smaller units without kitchen have microwave, refrigerator & coffee maker. Very clean. 1½ blocks to beach. Cable TV, movies; coffee makers; some efficiencies; no air conditioning. Coin laundry. No pets. AE, CB, DI, DS. Ⓓ

FESS PARKER'S RED LION RESORT   ◆◆◆ Motor Inn
3 blocks south of US 101 via Milpas St at 633 E Cabrillo Blvd (93103).
(805) 564-4333; FAX (805) 564-4964.

All year	1P $195-295	2P/1B $195-295	2P/2B	$195-295

XP $15; children 17 and under stay free. Reservation deposit required; 3-day cancellation notice. Check in 4 pm. Senior discount. 3 stories; interior/exterior corridors. 360 rooms; balconies or patios. Cable TV, free and pay movies; honor bars; some coffee makers. Across from beach on spacious landscaped grounds. Heated pool, sauna, whirlpool, exercise room, basketball and shuffleboard courts, putting green, rental bicycles; fee for 3 lighted tennis courts. Coin laundry. Airport transportation. Pets. Conference facilities. AE, CB, DI, DS, JCB, MC, VI. Coffee shop 6:30 am-11 pm; $7-12; cocktails; Maxis, see separate listing. Ⓓ Ⓢ ⊘

FOUR SEASONS BILTMORE 🅰️🅰️ ♦♦♦♦ Resort Complex
In Montecito; ¼ mile south of US 101, exit Olive Mill Rd; 1260 Channel Dr (93108). (805) 969-2261; FAX (805) 969-4212.

All year 1P $199-370 2P/1B $199-370 2P/2B $199-370

XP $30; children age 18 and under stay free. Reservation deposit required; 3-day cancellation notice. 2 stories; interior/exterior corridors. 234 rooms. Large, well-appointed rooms in lodge & cottages; garden or ocean views. Impressive oceanfront resort on spacious, beautifully landscaped grounds. Spanish architecture. Cable TV, VCPs, pay movies, honor bar, safe; no air conditioning. 24-hour room service, valet laundry. 2 heated pools, saunas, whirlpools, exercise room, putting green, croquet and shuffleboard courts, bicycles; fee for massage, 3 lighted tennis courts. Beach, Casino Beach & Cabana Club (fee). Children's program. Pay valet parking. Small pets in cottages only. Meeting rooms, secretarial services. AE, CB, DI, JCB, MC, VI. Afternoon tea. Dining room, restaurant, deli, 7 am-10 pm, Fri & Sat to 11 pm; $14-40; cocktails. La Marina, see separate listing. Ⓓ ⊘ **(See ad below.)**

LODGING & RESTAURANTS

FRANCISCAN INN   ♦♦♦ Motel
2½ blocks south of US 101 at 109 Bath St (93101).
(805) 963-8845; FAX (805) 564-3295.

Fri-Sat &					
Sun-Thu 5/15-9/15 [CP]	1P	$ 65- 89	2P/1B	$ 75-115	2P/2B	$ 90-175
Sun-Thu 9/16-5/14 [CP]	1P	$ 55- 85	2P/1B	$ 60- 89	2P/2B	$ 70-175

XP $8; children age 5 and under stay free. Credit card guarantee. Weekly & monthly rates. 1-2 stories; exterior corridors. 53 rooms; 4 2-bedroom units. 1 block to beach. Guest rooms have attractive country decor; very pleasant ambience. Cable TV, movies; rental VCPs; some efficiencies, refrigerators, air conditioning. Heated pool, whirlpool. Coin laundry. No pets. AE, CB, DI, MC, VI. Ⓓ ⊘ **(See ad below.)**

THE GLENBOROUGH INN   ♦♦ Bed & Breakfast
1327 Bath St (93101).
(805) 966-0589; FAX (805) 564-2369.

5/21-9/5 &					
Fri-Sat 9/6-5/20 [BP]	1P	$ 70-180	2P/1B	$ 75-180	2P/2B	...
Sun-Thu 9/6-5/20 [BP]	1P	$ 70-165	2P/1B	$ 70-165	2P/2B	...

XP $25. 2-night minimum stay weekends. Credit card guarantee; 3-day cancellation notice. 2 stories; exterior corridors. 11 rooms; 3 suites with fireplace. 3 houses built in 1880s & early 1900s located in residential area. No TVs, no air conditioning. Whirlpool, bicycles. No pets. AE, DI, DS, MC, VI. Complimentary beverages each evening. Ⓓ Smoke-free premises

HARBOR VIEW INN ⓐⓐ ♦♦♦ Motel
3 blocks south of US 101, ½ block west of State St at 28 W Cabrillo Blvd (93101).
(805) 963-0780; FAX (805) 963-7967.

2/1-5/31 [CP]	1P $120-215	2P/1B $ 120-215	2P/2B $120-160
6/1-1/31 [CP]	1P $150-295	2P/1B $150-295	2P/2B $150-295

XP $5; children age 5 and under stay free. Reservation deposit required. 2-3 stories; interior/exterior corridors. 81 rooms; 6 large ocean-view rooms with balcony, $200-215. Variety of room sizes. Across from beach & Stearn's Wharf. Cable TV, movies, coffee makers, refrigerators, safes. Heated pool, wading pool, whirlpool; rental rollerblades, rollerskates bicyles. Valet laundry. No pets. Data ports. AE, CB, DI, MC, VI. Complimentary beverages each evening. Restaurant, 7:30 am-3 & 6-10 pm; $8-15; cocktails, lounge. Ⓓ Ⓢ ⊘ **(See ad below.)**

HOLIDAY INN-SANTA BARBARA/GOLETA ♦♦ Motor Inn
7 miles northwest adjacent to US 101; between Patterson & Fairview aves, exits at 5650 Calle Real (Goleta 93117).
(805) 964-6241; FAX (805) 964-6241.

All year	1P $ 86-125	2P/1B $ 96-135	2P/2B $ 96-135

XP $10. Reservation deposit required. Senior discount. 2 stories; exterior corridors. 154 rooms. Cable TV, pay movies. Heated pool. Coin laundry. Valet laundry. Airport transportation. No pets. Meeting rooms. AE, CB, DI, DS, JCB, MC, VI. Dining room, 6 am-2 & 5-10 pm; $8-15; cocktails. Ⓓ ⊘

INN BY THE HARBOR ⓐⓐ ♦♦ Motel
2 blocks southwest of US 101, 1 block west of Castillo St at 433 W Montecito St (93101).
(805) 963-7851; FAX (805) 962-9428.

2/1-5/25 [CP]	1P $ 59- 89	2P/1B $ 69- 95	2P/2B $ 69- 95
5/26-9/3 [CP]	1P $ 69- 99	2P/1B $ 79-105	2P/2B $ 79-105
9/4-1/31 [CP]	1P $ 69- 93	2P/1B $ 73- 99	2P/2B $ 73- 99

XP $5. Reservation deposit required. Weekly & monthly rates. 2 stories; exterior corridors. 41 rooms; 22 kitchens, $10 extra. Attractive country decor. 3 blocks to beach; within walking distance of city park. Cable TV; no air conditioning. Heated pool, whirlpool. Coin laundry. No pets. AE, CB, DI, DS, MC, VI. Ⓓ Smoke-free premises

INN ON SUMMER HILL ⊕ ♦♦♦♦ Bed & Breakfast

North side of US 101; northbound exit Evans St; southbound exit Summerland, ½ mile east at 2520 Lillie Ave (Summerland, 93067).
(805) 969-9998; FAX (805) 969-9998.

All year [BP]	1P $160-275	2P/1B $160-275	2P/2B $ 170-195

XP $20. 2-night minimum stay weekends. Reservation deposit required; 5-day cancellation notice. 2 stories; exterior corridors. 16 rooms. Beautifully decorated rooms in an English country motif. Ocean view. Gas fireplaces. Cable TV, VCPs, gas fireplaces, whirlpools, refrigerators. No pets. AE, MC, VI. Complimentary dessert and beverages each evening. Ⓓ Smoke-free premises

THE IVANHOE INN Bed & Breakfast

1406 Castillo St. (93101).
(805) 963-8832, (800) 428-1787; FAX (805) 683-8598.

All year [CP]	1P ...	2P/1B $ 95-195	2P/2B ...

XP $15. Check in 3 pm; check out noon. Lower rates available Dec-Mar and weekdays at other times. 5 guest rooms and suites, 3 with private bath. 2 rooms with fireplace. An 1880s Victorian house and cottage in downtown Santa Barbara are furnished with antiques, wicker, plants and ceiling fans. Pets allowed with restrictions. A basket containing an expanded continental breakfast is delivered to the guest room or may be taken to the garden. Wine and cheese in room upon arrival. Picnic baskets available. MC, VI. Smoking permitted

LEMON TREE INN ⊕ Motel

1½ mile northwest at 2819 State St (93105).
(805) 687-6444; FAX (805) 687-4432.

5/16-10/15 [CP]	1P $ 73-110	2P/1B $ 78-120	2P/2B $ 83-130
10/16-5/15 [CP]	1P $ 63-110	2P/1B $ 68-120	2P/2B $ 73-130

XP $5; children age 16 and under stay free. Reservation deposit required; 7-day cancellation notice. Senior discount. Under major renovation. 2 stories; exterior corridors. 55 rooms; many patios or balconies. Large, brightly landscaped pool area. Cable TV, movies; some air conditioning, refrigerators. Heated pool, whirlpool. Valet laundry. No pets. AE, CB, DI, DS, JCB, MC, VI. Ⓓ ⊗

MARINA BEACH MOTEL ⊕ ♦♦ Motel

21 Bath St (93101).
(805) 963-9311; FAX (805) 564-4102.

Fri-Sat 5/15-9/15 [CP]	1P $ 75-135	2P/1B $ 75-140	2P/2B $ 80-200
Sun-Thu 5/15-9/15 [CP]	1P $ 55- 95	2P/1B $ 55-100	2P/2B $ 60-145
Fri-Sat 9/16-5/14 [CP]	1P $ 55-125	2P/1B $ 55-125	2P/2B $ 55-185
Sun-Thu 9/16-5/14 [CP]	1P $ 43- 85	2P/1B $ 43- 95	2P/2B $ 50-130

2-night minimum stay weekends 5/15-9/15. Credit card guarantee. Weekly & monthly rates. 1 story; exterior corridors. 31 rooms; 1 2-bedroom unit; 3 efficiencies; 15 kitchens. ½ block to beach. Cable TV, coffee makers; some refrigerators, whirlpools; no air conditioning. Bicycles. No pets. AE, CB, DI, DS, MC, VI. Ⓓ ⊗

THE MARY MAY INN   ◆◆◆ Historic Bed & Breakfast
1632 Chapala St (93101).
(805) 569-3398.

All Year [BP]	1P ...	2P/1B $150-160	2P/2B ...

XP $25. 2-night minimum stay weekends. Reservation deposit required; 7-day cancellation notice. 2 stories; exterior corridors. 5 rooms. 1880s Queen Anne Victorian house with gabled roof & porches. Phone available on request; no TVs. AE, MC, VI. ⒟ Designated smoking area

MASON BEACH INN ⊛   ◆◆ Motel
2 blocks south of US 101; southbound exit Castillo St; northbound exit Cabrillo Blvd, then north to Castillo St.; 324 W Mason St (93101).
(805) 962-3203; FAX (805) 962-1056.

2/1-5/14 & 9/5-10/31	1P ...	2P/1B $ 68-125	2P/2B $ 68-125
5/15-9/4	1P ...	2P/1B $ 75-145	2P/2B $ 75-145
11/1-1/31	1P ...	2P/1B $ 65-105	2P/2B $ 65-105

XP $10; children age 6 and under stay free. Reservation deposit required; 7-day cancellation notice. Weekly & monthly rates. 2 rooms; interior corridors. 44 rooms; 3 suites with microwave and refrigerator, $95-145. 1 block from beach. Contemporary decor. Cable TV. Heated pool, whirlpool. No pets. AE, CB, DI, DS, MC, VI. ⒟ Ⓢ ⊘

MONTECITO INN   ◆◆◆ Historic Hotel
In Montecito; adjacent to US 101, exit Olive Mill Rd; 1295 Coast Village Rd (93108).
(805) 969-7854; FAX (805) 969-0623.

All year [CP]	1P $150-165	2P/1B $150-165	2P/2B $195

Reservation deposit required. Senior discount. 4 stories; interior corridors. 52 rooms. Charming historic inn built in 1928. Located in center of town. Cable TV, movies; some refrigerators; no air conditioning. Heated pool, sauna, whirlpool; exercise room. Bicycles. Valet laundry, valet parking. No pets. Meeting rooms. AE, DI, DS, MC, VI. Restaurant, 11:30 am-2:30 & 5:30-10 pm, $7-14; cocktails. ⒟ Ⓢ ⊘

MOUNTAIN VIEW INN ⊛   ◆◆ Motel
1 mile east of US 101, exit Los Positas Rd, corner of State & 3055 De la Vina St (93105).
(805) 687-6636; FAX (805) 569-6809.

Fri-Sat 6/15-9/15 [CP]	1P $ 83	2P/1B $ 85	2P/2B $ 87
Sun-Thu 6/15-9/15 [CP]	1P $ 68	2P/1B $ 70	2P/2B $ 72
Fri-Sat 9/16-6/14 [CP]	1P $ 61	2P/1B $ 67	2P/2B $ 69
Sun-Thu 9/16-6/14 [CP]	1P $ 46	2P/1B $ 52	2P/2B $ 54

XP $5; children age 3 and under stay free. Reservation deposit required; 3-day cancellation notice. 2 stories; exterior corridors. 34 rooms. Adjacent to city park. Friendly atmosphere. Cable TV, movies, refrigerators; no air conditioning. Small heated pool. No pets. AE, DS, MC, VI. ⒟ ⊘

OLD YACHT CLUB INN ⊛   ◆◆ Historic Bed & Breakfast
½ block north of Cabrillo Blvd at 431 Corona del Mar (93103).
(805) 962-1277; FAX (805) 962-3989.

Mon-Thu 6/1-9/30 & Fri-Sun [BP]	1P	$ 85-145	2P/1B	$ 90-150	2P/2B	...
Mon-Thu 10/1-5/31 [BP]	1P	$ 75-120	2P/1B	$ 80-125	2P/2B	...

XP $30. 2-night minimum stay weekends. Reservation deposit required; 3-day refund notice. Package plans. Senior discount. 2 stories; interior/exterior corridors. 9 rooms; 2 rooms with whirlpool tub & semi-private deck, $125-135. 1912 California Craftsman and 1920 Early California houses in a residential area. 2 blocks to beach. No TVs; no air conditioning. Bicycles. No pets. AE, DS, MC, VI. Complimentary beverages each evening. 5-course gourmet dinner served most Saturday evenings; additional charge. Ⓓ Smoke-free premises

THE OLIVE HOUSE   ♦♦♦ Historic Bed & Breakfast

1 mile east of US 101; northbound exit Arrellaga St; southbound exit Mission St; 1604 Olive St (93101).

(805) 962-4902.

Mon-Thu 6/30-9/4 & Fri-Sun [BP]	1P	$105-175	2P/1B	$105-175	2P/2B	...
Mon-Thu 9/5-6/29 [BP]	1P	$ 84-140	2P/1B	$ 84-140	2P/2B	...

2-night minimum stay weekends. Reservation deposit required; 7-day cancellation notice. 2 stories; interior corridors. 6 rooms. 1904 California Craftsman house located in a residential area. Some cable TV; no air conditioning; no phones. No pets. AE, DS, JCB, MC, VI. Ⓓ Smoke-free premises

PACIFICA SUITES ⊛   ♦♦♦ Suites Motel

From US 101, exit Patterson Ave, ½ mile south, then ½ mile west on Hollister Ave; 5490 Hollister Ave (93111).

(805) 683-6722; FAX (805) 683-4121.

All Year [BP]	1P	$120-180	2P/1B	$120-180	2P/2B	$120-180

XP $10; children 12 and under stay free. Reservation deposit required. 2 stories; interior/exterior corridors. 75 rooms; 2-room suites. Situated in a grove of exotic plants & trees, adjacent to the restored Sexton House built in 1880s. Attractively decorated. Cable TV, pay movies, refrigerators, coffee makers, microwaves, refrigerators; some VCPs. Heated pool, whirlpool; rental bicycles. Valet laundry Mon-Sat. Small pets. Meeting rooms, data ports. AE, CB, DI, DS, JCB, MC, VI. Complimentary beverages each evening. ⊘

THE PARSONAGE ⊛   ♦♦♦ Historic Bed & Breakfast

1 mile east of US 101; northbound US 101 exit Arrellaga St; southbound exit Mission St; 1600 Olive St (93101).

(805) 962-9336.

All year [BP]	1P	$ 95-185	2P/1B	$ 95-185	2P/2B	...

XP $25; discount for children age 12 and under. 2-night minimum stay weekends. Reservation deposit required; 7-day cancellation notice. Weekly rates. 2 stories; interior corridors. 6 rooms. 1892 Victorian house in residential area. Some shower baths; no TVs, air conditioning. No pets. AE, MC, VI. Complimentary beverages each evening. Ⓓ Smoke-free premises

RADISSON HOTEL SANTA BARBARA    ◆◆◆ Motor Inn
2 blocks east of Milpas St; southbound US 101 exit Milpas St; northbound exit Cabrillo
Blvd; 1111 E Cabrillo Blvd (93103).
(805) 963-0744; FAX (805) 962-0985.

2/6-5/26 & 10/11-11/20	1P	$195	2P/1B	$120-195	2P/2B	$160-195
5/27-10/10	1P	$140-215	2P/1B	$140-215	2P/2B	$180-215
11/21-2/5	1P	$180	2P/1B	$110-180	2P/2B	$145-180

XP $20. Check in 4 pm. Reservation deposit required; 3-day cancellation notice. 3
stories; interior corridors. 174 rooms; few smaller rooms, 8 efficiencies. Many
ocean or mountain-view rooms. Across from beach. Cable TV, pay movies, honor
bars. Heated pool, exercise room; fee for massage. Valet laundry. No pets.
Meeting rooms, data ports. AE, CB, DI, DS, JCB, MC, VI. Restaurant; 6:30 am-
10:30 pm; $11-20; cocktails. Ⓓ Ⓢ ⊘ **(See ad below.)**

THE SANDMAN INN    ◆◆ Motor Inn
3 miles northwest; ¾ mile east of junction US 101 at 3714 State St (93105).
(805) 687-2468; FAX (805) 687-6581.

2/1-5/25 [CP]	1P	$ 69- 89	2P/1B	$ 69- 89	2P/2B	$ 69- 89
5/26-9/4 [CP]	1P	$ 94-104	2P/1B	$ 94-104	2P/2B	$ 94-104
9/5-1/31 [CP]	1P	$ 79- 99	2P/1B	$ 79- 99	2P/2B	$ 79- 99

XP $10; children age 18 and under stay free. Reservation deposit required; 3-day
cancellation notice. 1-2 stories; exterior corridors. 113 rooms; 7 2-bedroom units;
6 kitchens & 11 efficiencies, $10 extra. Cable TV, movies; rental refrigerators;
some air conditioning. 2 pools (1 heated), whirlpool. Coin laundry. No pets.
Meeting rooms. AE, CB, DI, MC, VI. Kokopelli Grill, see separate listing. Ⓓ ⊘

SANDPIPER LODGE    Motel
3 miles northwest, ¾ mile east of US 101 at 3525 State St (93105).
(805) 687-5326; FAX (805) 687-2271.

5/15-9/30	1P	$ 58- 68	2P/1B	$ 58- 68	2P/2B	$ 58- 68
10/1-5/14	1P	$ 48- 58	2P/1B	$ 48- 58	2P/2B	$ 48- 58

XP $5; children age 5 and under stay free. Under major renovation; rating with-
held pending completion of construction. Reservation deposit required. Weekly
& monthly rates. 2 stories; exterior corridors. 73 rooms; 16 2-bedroom units. 7-

night minimum stay in 3 1-bedroom units. On busy commercial strip. Cable TV, movies; some refrigerators; no air conditioning. Pool (heated 5/16-9/30). No pets. AE, DI, MC, VI. Coffee shop nearby. Ⓓ ⊘ **(See ad below.)**

SANTA BARBARA INN ⒶⒶ　　　　　　　　　　♦♦♦ Motor Inn
3 blocks south of US 101, exit Milpas St; 901 Cabrillo Blvd (93103).
(805) 966-2285; FAX (805) 966-6584.

4/2-10/30	1P	$149-209	2P/1B	$149-209	2P/2B	$149-209
10/31-4/1	1P	$ 99-139	2P/1B	$ 99-139	2P/2B	$ 99-139

XP $15; children 16 and under stay free. Reservation deposit required. Weekly rates. Senior discount. 3 stories; interior/exterior corridors. 71 rooms; 6 rooms with kitchen, $10 extra. Across from beach. Spacious rooms with ocean or mountain views. 3rd-floor sun deck with ocean view. Cable TV, refrigerators; coffee makers; some air conditioning. Heated pool, whirlpool. Valet laundry, pay valet parking. No pets. Meeting rooms. AE, CB, DI, DS, MC, VI. Citronelle Restaurant, see separate listing. Ⓓ Ⓢ ⊘

THE SECRET GARDEN ⒶⒶ　　　　　　　　♦♦♦ Bed & Breakfast
Formerly Blue Quail Inn. From US 101, northbound exit Arrellaga St; southbound exit Mission St; 1908 Bath St (93101).
(805) 687-2300.

Fri-Sun [BP]	1P	...	2P/1B	$ 95-165	2P/2B	...
Mon-Thu 11/1-5/15 [BP]	1P	$ 86-149	2P/1B	$ 86-149	2P/2B	$ 86-149

XP $20; discount for children age 18 and under. 2-night minimum stay weekends. Reservation deposit required; 7-day cancellation notice. Weekly rates. Senior discount. 1 story; interior/exterior corridors. 9 rooms. Attractively furnished rooms in main house & cottages on nicely landscaped grounds. No TV; air conditioning; no phones. Bicycles. No pets. AE, MC, VI. Complimentary beverages each evenings. Ⓓ Smoke-free premises

SIMPSON HOUSE INN　　　　　　♦♦♦♦ Historic Bed & Breakfast
1½ blocks east of State St at 121 E Arrellaga St (93101).
(805) 963-7067; FAX (805) 564-4811.

All Year [BP]	1P	$105-275	2P/1B	$105-275	2P/2B	...

XP $25. Reservation deposit required; 7-day cancellation notice. 2 stories; interior/exterior corridors. 14 rooms; some suites with whirlpool tub & fireplace. Beautifully decorated rooms in 1874 historic Eastlake style Italianate Victorian house or in cottage or barn suites. Located in quiet residential area on tree-shaded grounds. Some cable TV, VCPs, whirlpools, refrigerators; no air conditioning. Bicycles. No pets. AE, DS, MC, VI. Complimentary beverages each evening. Ⓓ ⊘

SUMMERLAND INN ⏺⏺   ◆◆◆ Motel
Adjacent to US 101, northbound exit Evans St, southbound exit Summerland; 2161
Ortega Hill Rd (PO Box 1209, Summerland, 93067).
(805) 969-5225.

Fri-Sat [CP]	1P	$ 90-120	2P/1B	$ 90-140	2P/2B	$ 90-140
Sun-Thu [CP]	1P	$ 55- 90	2P/1B	$ 65- 90	2P/2B	$ 80-100

XP $15; children age 5 and under stay free. 2-night minimum stay weekends.
Reservation deposit required; 3-day cancellation notice. Senior discount. 2 stories;
interior/exterior corridors. 11 rooms; 2 units with gas fireplace. Charming coun-
try-inn decor. Cable TV; some air conditioning. No pets. AE, DI, DS, MC, VI. Ⓓ
Smoke-free premises

TIFFANY INN   ◆◆◆ Historic Bed & Breakfast
1323 De la Vina St (93101).
(805) 963-2283.

Fri-Sat [BP]	1P	...	2P/1B	$ 75-190	2P/2B	...
Sun-Thu 10/1-5/31	1P	...	2P/1B	$ 60-165	2P/2B	...

2-night minimum stay weekends. Reservation deposit required; 7-day cancellation notice. Weekly rates. 3 stories; interior/exterior corridors. 7 rooms; 5 units
with wood-burning fireplace. 1898 Colonial Revival-style house located in residential area. Some cable TV, whirlpools; no air conditioning; no phones. No pets.
AE, MC, VI. Ⓓ Smoke-free premises

TRAVELODGE SANTA BARBARA BEACH ⏺⏺   ◆◆ Motel
3 blocks south of US 101 at 22 Castillo St (93101).
(805) 965-8527; FAX (805) 965-6125.

5/1-9/15	1P	$ 85-150	2P/1B	$ 85-150	2P/2B	$ 95-150
9/16-4/30	1P	$ 60- 95	2P/1B	$ 65- 95	2P/2B	$ 75-125

XP $10; children age 14 and under stay free. Credit card guarantee. Senior dis-
count. Exterior corridors. 19 rooms; 4 rooms with patios. ½ block from beach,
across from city park. Cable TV, movies, coffee makers. No pets. AE, CB, DI, DS,
MC, VI. Restaurant nearby. Ⓓ

TROPICANA INN & SUITES ⏺⏺   ◆◆◆ Motel
Southbound US 101 exit Castillo St; northbound exit Cabrillo Blvd, 3 miles west to
Castillo St, then 2½ blocks north to 223 Castillo St (93101).
(805) 966-2219; FAX (805) 962-9428.

2/1-5/25 [CP]	1P	$ 79-116	2P/1B	$ 86-136	2P/2B	$ 86-136
5/26-9/3 [CP]	1P	$ 89-126	2P/1B	$ 96-146	2P/2B	$ 96-146
9/4-1/31 [CP]	1P	$ 89-122	2P/1B	$ 92-142	2P/2B	$ 92-142

XP $5; children age 3 and under stay free. Reservation deposit required. Weekly
& monthly rates. Senior discount. 1-3 stories. 31 rooms; 1 2-bedroom unit, 1
large 2-bedroom suite with kitchen & dining room, $140-199 for up to 8 persons.
Cozy country decor. 2 blocks to beach & harbor; near city park. Cable TV; some
kitchens, refrigerators; no air conditioning. Heated pool, whirlpool; rental bicycles. 28 covered parking spaces. Valet laundry. No pets. AE, CB, DI, DS, MC, VI.
Ⓓ Smoke-free premises

THE UPHAM ⓐⓐ ◆◆◆ Historic Country Inn
From US 101 exit Mission St, 3 blocks north, then 6 blocks east to 1404 De la Vina St
at Sola St (93101).
(805) 962-0058; FAX (805) 962-0058.

All year [CP]	1P	$110-180	2P/1B	$110-180	2P/2B $160

XP $10; children age 12 and under stay free. Credit card guarantee; 3-day cancellation notice. 2 stories; interior/exterior corridors. 49 rooms. A historic Victorian hotel & cottages established in 1871. Beautifully landscaped garden setting. Cable TV; some radios; no air conditioning. No pets. Meeting rooms. AE, CB, DI, DS, MC, VI. Restaurant, 11:30 am-2 & 6-9 pm; Sat-Sun from 6 pm; $9-19; beer & wine. Ⓓ ⊘

VILLA ROSA ⓐⓐ ◆◆ Bed & Breakfast
15 Chapala St (93101).
(805) 966-0851; FAX (805) 962-7159.

Fri-Sat &						
Sun-Thu 7/1-9/30 [CP]	1P	$ 90-190	2P/1B	$ 90-190	2P/2B	...
Sun-Thu 10/1-6/30 [CP]	1P	$ 80-160	2P/1B	$ 80-160	2P/2B	...

2-night minimum stay weekends. Reservation deposit required; 5-day cancellation notice. 2 stories; interior corridors. 18 rooms; 2 rooms with kitchenette & fireplace, $160-190; without fireplace, $160-165. 1 block from beach. A classic 1930s Spanish-style building. Rooms decorated in attractive southwest theme. Some cable TV, efficiencies, refrigerators; no air conditioning. Small pool, whirlpool. Valet laundry. No pets. Meeting rooms. AE, MC, VI. Complimentary beverages each evening. Ⓓ Designated smoking area

WEST BEACH INN ⓐⓐ ◆◆◆ Motel
4 blocks south of US 101; 306 W Cabrillo Blvd at Bath St (93101).
(805) 963-4277; FAX (805) 564-4210.

2/1-6/8 [CP]	1P	$115-165	2P/1B	$115-165	2P/2B	$135-165
6/9-11/2 [CP]	1P	$120-170	2P/1B	$120-170	2P/2B	$140-170
11/3-1/31 [CP]	1P	$ 86-126	2P/1B	$ 86-126	2P/2B	$106-126

XP $15; children age 18 and under stay free. Check in 4 pm. 2-night minimum stay weekends 3/24-11/25. Reservation deposit required. Weekly & monthly rates. 2-3 stories; exterior corridors. 44 rooms; 2 1-bedroom apartments with kitchen, $147-185 for up to 4 people. 1 2-bedroom unit. 1 2-bedroom apartment with fireplace & refrigerator, $187-235 for up to 6 people. Attractive pool area, large whirlpool area with beach view. Small aviary. Across from yacht harbor & beach. Cable TV, movies, refrigerators; some patios or balconies. Heated pool, whirlpool. Coin laundry. No pets. Data ports. AE, CB, DI, MC, VI. Ⓓ ⊘

RESTAURANTS

ANDRIA'S HARBORSIDE RESTAURANT ◆◆ Seafood
At Best Western-El Patio Beachside Inn, 336 W Cabrillo Bl (93101).
(805) 966-3000.

$11-20. Open 6 am-midnight; Fri & Sat to 1 am. Across from beach & yacht harbor. Nice selection of seafood and limited selection of steaks, chicken & pasta.

Casual attire. Children's menu, oyster bar. Cocktails & lounge; entertainment. AE, DS, MC, VI. ⊘

BEACHSIDE CAFE ◆ Seafood
In Goleta 2 miles south of US 101 on SR 217, then 1 mile east on Sandspit Rd at 5905 Sandspit Rd (93117).
(805) 964-7881.

$11-20. Open 11:30 am-4 & 5-10 pm; Fri to 10:30 pm; Sat 11 am-4 & 5-10:30 pm; Sun 11 am-4 & 5-10 pm; closed Thanksgiving & 12/25. Reservations suggested. Beachfront restaurant located adjacent to Goleta Beach County Park & Pier. Casual attire. Early-bird specials. Cocktails. AE, MC, VI. ⊘

CAFE DEL SOL ◆◆ American
½ block south of US 101, exit Cabrillo Blvd, 1 block south, then 1 block west at 30 Los Patos Way (93103).
(805) 969-0448.

$11-20. Open 11:30 am-3 & 5:30-10 pm; Sun 10 am-2:30 & 5:30-10 pm; closed 1/1, Thanksgiving & 12/25. Located across from Andree Clark Bird Refuge. Nice selection of seafood, chicken, steaks & Mexican specialties. Casual attire. A la carte, Sun brunch. Cocktails & lounge. DS, MC, VI. ⊘

CHAD'S ◆◆ American
1 block west of State St, ½ block north of Cota St at 625 Chapala St (93101).
(805) 568-1876.

$11-20. Open 11:30 am-2:30 & 5:30-10 pm; Fri & Sat to 10:30 pm; closed 12/25. Regional American cuisine served in a charming house built in 1876. Casual attire. A la carte. Cocktails & lounge; entertainment. AE, DS, MC, VI. Smoke-free premises

THE CHART HOUSE ◆◆ Steakhouse
1 block south of State St, across from beach at 101 E Cabrillo Blvd (93101).
(805) 966-2112.

$21-30. Open 5:30-10 pm; Fri & Sat 5 -11 pm; Sun 5-10 pm. Nice selection of steaks, prime rib, rack of lamb & fresh seafood. Casual attire. A la carte. Cocktails & lounge. AE, CB, DI, DS, MC, VI. ⊘

CITRONELLE RESTAURANT ◆◆◆ French
In Santa Barbara Inn, 901 Cabrillo Bl (93103).
(805) 963-0111.

Over $31. Open 7-10 am, noon-2:30 & 6-9:30 pm; Fri to 10 pm; Sat to 10:30 pm; Sun 7-10 am, 11:30-2:30 & 6-9:30 pm. Reservations suggested. Fine dining with a panoramic ocean view. Interesting selection of French & California cuisine. Casual attire. Children's menu, a la carte, Sun brunch. Cocktails & lounge. Valet parking. AE, DI, DS, MC, VI. Smoke-free premises 5:30 pm-10:30 pm

DOWNEY'S ◆◆◆ American
Downtown Santa Barbara at 1305 State St (93101).
(805) 966-5006.

$21-30. Open 11:30 am-1:45 & 5:30-9 pm; Fri to 9:30 pm; Sat 5:30-9:30 pm; Sun 5:30-9 pm; closed Mon, 1/1 & 12/25. Reservations suggested. Small restaurant serving excellently prepared & presented cuisine. Menu changes daily. Casual attire. A la carte. Beer & wine. AE, MC, VI. Smoke-free premises

EL PASEO RESTAURANT   ♦♦ Mexican
800 block of State St in El Paseo at 10 El Paseo.
(805) 962-6050.

$11-20. Open 11:30 am-10 pm, Fri & sat to 11 pm, Sun 10:30 am-10 pm. Dining in flower-filled courtyard setting. Lively atmosphere during Sun brunch. Good selection of seafood, chicken & beef. No air conditioning. Fee for parking. Casual attire. A la carte, buffet, Sun Mariachi Margarita brunch 10:30 am-2:30 pm. Cocktails & lounge; entertainment. AE, MC, VI. ⊘

KOKOPELLI GRILL   ♦ American
At The Sandman Inn, 3744 State St (93105).
(805) 687-2828.

$11-20. Open 11:30 am-4 & 5-10 pm; closed 12/25. Reservations suggested. Beef, seafood & barbecue specialties. Casual attire. Sun brunch. Cocktails & lounge. AE, MC, VI. ⊘

LA MARINA   ♦♦♦ Continental
In Four Season's Biltmore, 1260 Channel Dr (93108).
(805) 969-2261.

Over $31. Open 6 am-10 pm; Sat to 11 pm; Sun 10 am-2 & 6-10 pm. Reservations suggested. Fine dining in beautifully appointed dining room. Semi-formal attire. Children's menu, a la carte, Sun brunch. AE, CB, DI, JCB, MC, VI. ⊘

MAXI'S   ♦♦♦ Continental
In Fess Parker's Red Lion Resort, 633 E Cabrillo Bl (93103).
(805) 564-4333.

$21-30. Open 6-9 pm; closed Mon & Tue. Reservations suggested. Elegant decor. Semi-formal attire. Sun brunch. Cocktails & lounge. Valet parking. AE, DI, DS, MC, VI. ⊘

MOUSSE ODILE ⊛   ♦♦ French
½ block east of State St at 18 E Cota St (93101).
(805) 962-5393.

$11-20. Open 8 am-2:30 & 5:30-9 pm; Fri & Sat to 9:30 pm; closed Sun. Reservations suggested, dinner. No air conditioning. Street parking. Casual attire. A la carte. Cocktails. AE, DI, DS, MC, VI. ⊘

ORIGINAL ENTERPRISE FISH COMPANY   ♦♦ Seafood
1 block south of US 101 at 225 State St (93101).
(805) 962-3313.

$11-20. Open 11:30 am-10 pm; Fri & Sat to 11 pm; Sun 11:30 am-10 pm; closed Thanksgiving & 12/25. Reservations suggested. Nautical decor. High noise level on busy nights. Large selection of mesquite-broiled seafood. Casual attire. Children's menu, a la carte. No air conditioning. Beer & wine. AE, MC, VI. ⊘

THE PALACE CAFE   ◆◆ American
Downtown area, 3 blocks northwest of US 101, ½ block east of State St at 8 E Cota St
(93101).
(805) 966-3133.

$21-30. Open 5:30-10 pm; Fri & Sat to 11 pm; closed Thanksgiving & 12/25. Casual dining in a lively atmosphere. Interesting selection of Cajun, Creole & Caribbean cuisine. Casual attire. A la carte. Beer & wine. AE, MC, VI. Smoke-free premises

PALAZZIO TRATTORIA ITALIANE 🆎   ◆◆ Italian
In Montecito, from US 101 exit Olive Mill Rd, then ¼ mile north; 1151 Coast Village Rd
(93108).
(805) 969-8565.

$11-20. Open 11:30 am-2:30 & 5:30-11 pm, Fri & Sat to midnight, Sun 5:30-11 pm. Reservations accepted. Popular local restaurant with creative dishes in large portions. Casual attire. A la carte, carryout. No air conditioning. Beer & wine. Street parking. AE, MC, VI. ⊘

RISTORANTE PIATTI   ◆◆ Northern Italian
1 mile north of US 101, exit San Ysidro Rd; in Montecito Plaza Del Sol Shopping Center;
516 San Ysidro Rd at E Valley Rd (93108).
(805) 969-7520.

$21-30. Open 11:30 am 10 pm, Fri & Sat to 11 pm; closed 1/1, Thanksgiving & 12/25. Reservations suggested. Indoor & outdoor patio dining. Selection of pasta, pizza, seafood & veal. Casual attire. A la carte. Cocktails & lounge. AE, MC, VI. ⊘

WINE CASK RESTAURANT   ◆◆◆ American
Downtown Santa Barbara in El Paseo area at 813 Anacapa St (93101).
(805) 966-9463.

$21-30. Open 11:30 am-2:30 & 5:30-9 pm; Fri to 10 pm; Sat 5:30-10 pm; Sun 5:30-9 pm; closed some major holidays. Reservations suggested. California cuisine served in an attractive dining room or an outdoor courtyard. Extensive wine list. Pay valet parking. Casual attire. Health conscious menu, a la carte, prix fixe, vegetarian entrees upon request, Sun brunch. Beer & wine. AE, MC, VI. Smoke-free premises

Santa Maria

LODGING

BEST WESTERN BIG AMERICA 🆎   ◆◆◆ Motor Inn
On SR 135, ½ mile southwest of junction US 101, Broadway exit; 1725 N Broadway
(93454).
(805) 922-5200; FAX (805) 922-9865.

All year [CP]	1P $ 55- 90	2P/1B $ 55- 90	2P/2B $ 60- 90

XP $7; children 18 and under stay free. Credit card guarantee. 2 stories; exterior corridors. 104 rooms. Attractively furnished rooms & 1-bedroom suites. Cable TV, movies, refrigerators. Heated pool, whirlpool. No pets. Meeting rooms. AE, CB, DI, DS, MC, VI. Restaurant; 6 am-9 pm; $5-11; cocktails. Ⓓ ⊘

HOWARD JOHNSON LODGE   ♦♦ Motel

1 block east of 101, Main St exit; 210 S Nicholson Ave (93454).
(805) 922-5891; FAX (805) 928-9222.

1/1-4/10	1P $ 39- 49	2P/1B $ 44- 54	2P/2B $ 44- 49
4/11-6/15 & 9/5-12/31	1P $ 44- 54	2P/1B $ 49- 57	2P/2B $ 49- 54
6/16-9/4	1P $ 49- 59	2P/1B $ 54- 64	2P/2B $ 54- 59

XP $8; children 16 and under stay free. Credit card guarantee. Senior discount. 2 stories; interior corridors. 62 rooms. Cable TV, movies; some refrigerators. Heated pool, wading pool, whirlpool. Coin laundry. Pets, $10 deposit. AE, DI, DS, MC, VI. Restaurant nearby. Ⓓ ⊘

HUNTER'S INN 🆐   ♦♦ Motel

1 mile west on Stowell Rd from US 101, then ¼ mile south; 1514 S Broadway (93454).
(805) 922-2123; FAX (805) 925-1523.

All year [CP]	1P $49 - 89	2P/1B $55 - 89	2P/2B $ 58- 95

XP $8; discount for children age 10 and under. Reservation deposit required; 7-day cancellation notice. 2 stories; exterior corridors. 70 rooms; 5 2-bedroom units. Cable TV, movies; some microwaves, refrigerators; no air conditioning. Heated pool, whirlpool. Small pets, $10; $10 deposit. AE, CB, DI, DS, MC, VI. Coffee shop nearby. Ⓓ ⊘

RAMADA SUITES 🆐   ♦♦♦ Suites Motor Inn

Adjacent to US 101, Broadway exit; 2050 N Preisker Ln (93454).
(805) 928-6000; FAX (805) 928-0356.

Fri-Sat	1P $ 65-150	2P/1B $ 65-150	2P/2B $ 65-150
Sun-Thu	1P $ 58- 96	2P/1B $ 58- 96	2P/2B $ 58- 96

XP $10; children age 16 and under stay free. Credit card guarantee. 4 stories; interior corridors. 210 rooms; 4 2-bedroom units. Spacious, comfortably furnished suites with efficiencies. Cable TV, free and pay movies, coffee makers, refrigerators. Heated pool, whirlpool. Coin laundry. Pets, $15. Meeting rooms. AE, CB, DI, DS, JCB, MC, VI. Dining room, 6-11 am & 5-10 pm; Sun 7 am-noon; $8-15; cocktails. Ⓓ Ⓢ ⊘

ROSE GARDEN INN 🆐   ♦♦ Motel

On SR 166; 1 block west of junction US 101, Main St exit; 1007 E Main St (93454).
(805) 922-4505; FAX (805) 922-4505.

All year	1P $ 49	2P/1B $ 69- 79	2P/2B $ 69- 79

XP $10. Reservation deposit required; 3-day cancellation notice. Weekly & monthly rates. Senior discount. 2 stories; exterior corridors. 81 rooms. Cable TV; some refrigerators. Heated pool, whirlpool, 2 tennis courts. Small pets. AE, DI, MC, VI. Restaurant nearby. Ⓓ ⊘

SANTA MARIA AIRPORT HILTON   ♦♦♦ Hotel

From US 101, exit Betteravia Rd, 2¼ miles west, then 1¾ miles south on Skyway Dr; at Santa Maria Airport; 3455 Skyway Dr (93455).
(805) 928-8000; FAX (805) 928-5251.

All year   1P $ 59   2P/1B $ 59   2P/2B $ 59

XP $10; children age 18 and under stay free. Credit card guarantee; 3-day cancellation notice. 4 stories; interior/exterior corridors. 190 rooms. Attractive atrium lobby. Cable TV, free and pay movies. Heated pool, whirlpool. No pets. Meeting rooms. AE, CB, DI, DS, MC, VI. Dining room, 6 am-9 pm; Fri & Sat to 10 pm; $9-20; cocktails. Ⓓ Ⓢ ⊘

SANTA MARIA INN ⒶⒶ   ♦♦♦ Historic Hotel

From US 101, Main St 1 mile west, then ½ mile south on Broadway; 801 S Broadway (93454).

(805) 928-7777; FAX (805) 928-5690.

All year   1P $ 69 - 79   2P/1B $ 69 - 79   2P/2B $ 69 - 79

XP $10; children 12 and under stay free. Credit card guarantee. Senior discount. 2-6 stories; interior corridors. 166 rooms. Old English country motif. Small, charming rooms in the original restored building; very spacious, nicely decorated rooms in new tower section. Cable TV, VCPs, refrigerators, coffee makers; some air conditioning. Heated pool, sauna, whirlpool. Airport transportation. No pets. Meeting rooms. AE, CB, DI, DS, JCB, MC, VI. Dining room; 6:30 am-9 pm; Fri & Sat to 10 pm; wine bar & Cellar; $11-21; cocktails; also Santa Maria Inn Restaurant (see separate listing). Ⓓ Ⓢ ⊘ **(See ad below.)**

RESTAURANTS

CENTRAL CITY BROILER   ♦♦ American

¾ mile west of US 101, exit Donovan Rd; 1520 N Broadway (93454).

(805) 922-3700.

$11-20. Open 11:30 am-2 & 5-9 pm; Fri to 10 pm; Sat 5-10 pm; Sun 5-9 pm; closed 1/1, Thanksgiving, 12/24 & 12/25. Early American decor. Selection of barbecue, steaks, chicken, seafood & prime rib. Children's menu. Cocktails & lounge. AE, MC, VI. ⊘

MARIANNE'S ITALIAN VILLA   ♦♦ Italian

From US 101, Main St west 1 mile, then ½ mile south on Broadway; 800 S Broadway (93455).

(805) 347-2737.

$11-20. Open 11 am-9:30 pm, Fri & Sat to 10:30 pm, Sun 3:30-9:30 pm; closed Thanksgiving & 12/25. Reservations suggested. Large selection of Italian cuisine. Pasta, chicken, veal & pizza. Casual attire. Children's menu. Beer & wine. AE, CB, MC, VI. ⊘

SANTA MARIA INN RESTAURANT ♠♠♠   ♦♦♦ American
In Santa Maria Inn, 801 S Broadway (93454).
(805) 928-7777.
$11-20. Open 11 am-9 pm; Fri & Sat to 10 pm. Reservations suggested. Very attractive dining room. Selection of prime rib, steaks, seafood, chicken & continental entrees. Early bird specials, Sun brunch. Cocktails & lounge; entertainment. AE, DI, DS, JCB, MC, VI. ⊘

Santa Paula

LODGING

THE FERN OAKS INN   ♦♦♦ Bed & Breakfast
1 mile north of SR 126, exit Tenth St; 1025 Ojai Rd (93060).
(805) 525-7747.

Fri-Sun [BP]	1P	$ 90-105	2P/1B	$ 95-110	2P/2B ...
Mon-Thu [BP]	1P	$ 80- 95	2P/1B	$ 95-105	2P/2B ...

Reservation deposit required; 3-day cancellation notice. 2 stories; interior corridors. 4 rooms. An elegantly furnished 1929 Spanish Revival house on more than ½ acre of landscaped grounds with rose gardens, oak and citrus trees. No air conditioning, phones, TVs. Pool. Complimentary beverages each evening. Ⓓ Designated smoking area

SANTA PAULA TRAVELODGE ♠♠♠   ♦♦ Motel
¼ block north of SR 126; exit Peck Rd; 350 S Peck Rd (93060).
(805) 525-1561; FAX (805) 525-4230.

All year [CP]	1P	$ 46	2P/1B	$ 52	2P/2B	$ 62

XP $10; discount for children age 17 and under. Reservation deposit required; 5-day cancellation notice. Weekly rates. 2 stories; interior corridors. 50 rooms; 3 efficiencies, no utensils. Cable TV, movies; rental refrigerators, VCPs; some whirlpools. Small heated pool, whirlpool. No pets. Meeting rooms. AE, DS, MC, VI. Restaurant nearby. Ⓓ Ⓢ ⊘

THE WHITE GABLES INN   ♦♦♦ Historic Bed & Breakfast
From SR 126 exit 10th St (SR 150), ½ mile north, 4 blocks west; 715 E Santa Paula St (93060).
(805) 933-3041.

6/1-8/31 &					
Fri-Sun 9/1-5/31 [BP]	1P ...		2P/1B	$ 85-115	2P/2B ...
Mon-Thu 9/1-5/31 [BP]	1P ...		2P/1B	$ 75-105	2P/2B ...

Reservation deposit required; 3-day cancellation notice. 3 stories; no elevator. 3 rooms; 1 with balcony; spacious 3rd-floor suite with sitting room, bedroom & bath. Historical 1894 Victorian Queen Anne house located in a designated historical district. No air conditioning, phones, TVs. No pets. MC, VI. Ⓓ Designated smoking area

---

Room rates are subject to change.

RESTAURANT

FAMILIA DIAZ ◆ Mexican
Adjacent to north side of SR 126, exit 10th St (SR 150); 245 S 10th St (93060).
(805) 525-2813.

Up to $10. Open 11 am-2:30 & 4:30-9 pm; Sat & Sun 11 am-9 pm; closed major holidays & 8/2-8/13. Casual atmosphere. Children's menu, carryout, a la carte. Cocktails & lounge. DS, MC, VI.

Simi Valley

LODGING

CLARION HOTEL ◆◆◆ Motor Inn
1 mile south of SR 118; exit Madera Rd; 1775 Madera Rd (93065).
(805) 584-6300; FAX (805) 527-9969.

All year [CP]	1P $ 76- 96	2P/1B $ 86-106	2P/2B $ 86-106

XP $10; children 17 and under stay free. Reservation deposit required; 3-day cancellation notice. 2 stories; interior/exterior corridors. 120 rooms; 1 3-bedroom unit. 16 2-bedroom units. Many balconies. 2 miles north of the Ronald Reagan Presidential Library. Cable TV, free and pay movies, honor bars, coffee makers; many balconies; some refrigerators. Heated pool, whirlpool. Coin laundry. No pets. Conference facilities, meeting rooms. AE, CB, DI, DS, JCB, MC, VI. Complimentary beverages each evening. Restaurant; 6:30 am-1 am; $7-12. Ⓓ Ⓢ ⊘

RADISSON-SIMI VALLEY ⬤ ◆◆◆ Hotel
Adjacent to SR 118; exit 1st St; 999 Enchanted Wy (93065).
(805) 583-2000; FAX (805) 583-2779.

All year	1P $ 69	2P/1B $ 69	2P/2B $ 69

XP $10; children 17 and under stay free. Reservation deposit required. Weekly & monthly rates. Senior discount. 2-4 stories; interior corridors. 195 rooms; 6 suites with whirlpool tub, $129-139. Cable TV, free and pay movies, coffee makers; some honor bars, microwaves. Heated pool, whirlpool. Valet laundry. Small pets, $35 cleaning fee. Conference facilities, meeting rooms, data ports, secretarial services, PC. AE, CB, DI, DS, JCB, MC, VI. Restaurant; 6:30 am-11 pm; $9-15; cocktails; entertainment. Ⓓ Ⓢ ⊘

TRAVELODGE ⬤ ◆◆ Motel
Adjacent to south side SR 118, exit Erringer Rd; 2550 Erringer Rd (93065).
(805) 584-6006; FAX (805) 527-5629.

5/15-9/17 [CP]	1P $ 59	2P/1B $ 65	2P/2B $ 55- 65
9/18-5/14 [CP]	1P $ 49	2P/1B $ 55	2P/2B $ 55

XP $6; children 17 and under stay free. Credit card guarantee. Senior discount. 3 stories; exterior corridors. 96 rooms; 6 1-bedroom suites with microwave & refrigerator, $69-75. Movies; some coffee makers, microwaves, refrigerators, whirlpools. Heated pool, sauna, whirlpool, exercise room. Coin laundry. No pets. Meeting rooms. AE, DI, DS, JCB, MC, VI. Restaurant nearby. Ⓓ Ⓢ ⊘

RESTAURANTS

MARIE CALLENDER'S   ♦♦ American
¼ mile south of SR 118, exit Madera R; 20 W Cochran St (93065).
(805) 582-0552.
$11-20. Open 6:30 am-10 pm; Fri to 11 pm; Sat 8 am-11 pm; Sun 8 am-10 pm; closed 12/25. Selection of entrees, salads, sandwiches, pasta. Pies made & baked on premises. Casual attire. Sun brunch, children's menu, senior's menu, salad bar, carryout, a la carte. Beer & wine. AE, DS, MC, VI. ⊘

THE OLIVE GARDEN   ♦♦ Italian
1 block south of SR 118, exit Sycamore Dr; 2410 Sycamore Dr (93065).
(805) 526-0057.
$11-20. Open 11 am-10 pm; Fri & Sat to 11 pm; closed Thanksgiving, 12/25. Pasta, chicken, veal, salads & bread sticks. Casual attire. Children's menu, carry-out. Cocktails & lounge. AE, CB, DI, DS, MC, VI. ⊘

Solvang

LODGING

BEST WESTERN KING FREDERIK MOTEL 🆔   ♦♦♦ Motel
On SR 246 at 1617 Copenhagen Dr (93463).
(805) 688-5515; FAX (805) 688-2067.

All year [CP]	1P $ 55- 80	2P/1B $ 55- 80	2P/2B $ 65- 85

XP $10; children age 12 and under stay free. Reservation deposit required; 3-day cancellation notice. Senior discount. 2 stories; exterior corridors. 45 rooms; few smaller rooms. Cable TV. Heated pool, whirlpool. No pets. AE, DI, DS, MC, VI. ⒟

BEST WESTERN KRONBERG INN 🆔   ♦♦♦ Motel
5 blocks west on SR 246; 1440 Mission Dr (93463).
(805) 688-2383; FAX (805) 688-1821.

6/16-9/15 [CP]	1P $ 65- 85	2P/1B $ 65- 85	2P/2B $ 70- 90
9/16-6/15 [CP]	1P $ 40- 60	2P/1B $ 40- 60	2P/2B $ 45- 65

XP $5; children age 12 and under stay free. Reservation deposit required. Senior discount. 2 stories; exterior corridors. 39 rooms. Attractive country decor. Cable TV, movies, coffee makers, refrigerator; some whirlpools. Heated pool, whirlpool. Pets, with manager's approval. AE, CB, DI, DS, MC, VI. ⒟ ⊘

CHIMNEY SWEEP INN 🆔   ♦♦♦ Motel
1 block south of SR 246 at 1554 Copenhagen Dr (93463).
(805) 688-2111; FAX (805) 688-8824.

All year [CP]	1P $ 70- 95	2P/1B $ 70- 95	2P/2B $ 85-105

XP $10; children age 11 and under stay free. 2-day minimum stay weekends. Reservation deposit required. Senior discount. 2 stories; interior/exterior corridors. 28 rooms; 8 split-level loft rooms, $95-140; 6 cottage units with fireplace, some with private outdoor whirlpool, $145-255. Located in Tivoli Square.

Beautifully landscaped garden area. Cable TV, coffee makers; some refrigerators. Whirlpool. No pets. AE, DS, MC, VI. Ⓓ ⊘

DANISH COUNTRY INN 🏛   ♦♦♦ Motel
3 blocks west on SR 246 at 455 Mission Dr (93463).
(805) 688-2018; FAX (805) 688-1156.

| Fri-Sat [BP] | 1P | $ 78 | 2P/1B | $ 78 | 2P/2B | $ 78 |
| Sun-Thu [BP] | 1P | $ 65 | 2P/1B | $ 65 | 2P/2B | $ 65 |

XP $10; children 12 and under stay free. Credit card guarantee. 3 stories; interior corridors. 82 rooms; 6 split-level loft rooms, $115-150 for 2 persons. Spacious rooms. Cable TV, VCPs, refrigerators. Small heated pool, whirlpool. No pets. Meeting rooms. AE, DI, DS, MC, VI. Complimentary beverages each evening. Ⓓ Ⓢ ⊘ **(See ad below.)**

HAMLET MOTEL 🏛   ♦♦ Motel
1 block west on SR 246 at 1532 Mission Dr (93463).
(805) 688-4413; FAX (805) 686-1301.

| Fri-Sat | 1P | ... | 2P/1B | $ 65- 90 | 2P/2B | $ 65- 95 |
| Sun-Thu | 1P | $ 35- 45 | 2P/1B | $ 40- 60 | 2P/2B | $ 45- 60 |

XP $10 Fri & Sat; XP $5 Sun-Thu. Reservation deposit required; 3-day cancellation notice. 2 stories; exterior corridors. 14 rooms; 1 2-bedroom unit, $85-120 Fri & Sat. Nicely furnished rooms. Cable TV; some refrigerators. No pets. AE, DI, DS, MC, VI. Restaurant nearby. Ⓓ ⊘

PETERSEN VILLAGE INN 🏛   ♦♦♦♦ Motel
On SR 246 at 1576 Mission Dr (93463).
(805) 688-3121; FAX (805) 688-5732.

| All year [CP] | 1P | ... | 2P/1B | $105-170 | 2P/2 B | $130-150 |

XP $10. Credit card guarantee; 3-day refund notice. Package plans, golf. 2 stories; interior/exterior corridors. 40 rooms; 1 smaller unit. Charming, old-world ambiance with large, tastefully decorated rooms. Cable TV. No pets. Meeting rooms, data ports. AE, MC, VI. Complimentary beverages each evening. Restaurant nearby. Ⓓ Ⓢ ⊘ **(See ad below and on back cover.)**

QUALITY INN OF SOLVANG ⓐⓐⓐ   ♦♦♦ Motel
3 blocks west on SR 246 at 1450 Mission Dr (93463).
(805) 688-3210; FAX (805) 688-0026.

Fri-Sat 6/1/-9/30 [CP]	1P ...		2P/1B $ 95		2P/2B $100
Fri-Sat 10/1-5/31 &					
Sun-Thu 6/1-9/30 [CP]	1P ...		2P/1B $ 75		2P/2B $100
Sun-Thu 10/1-5/31 [CP]	1P ...		2P/1B $ 60		2P/2B $ 80

XP $5; children age 18 and under stay free. Reservation deposit required. Senior discount. 2 stories; exterior corridors. 75 rooms; 3 rooms with whirlpool, $95-185. Cable TV, movies, coffee makers; some refrigerators. Heated indoor pool, video games, pinball machines & air hockey games, recreation program. No pets. AE, CB, DI, DS, MC, VI. Ⓓ ⊘

THE ROYAL COPENHAGEN MOTEL ⓐⓐⓐ   ♦♦♦ Motel
On SR 246 at 1579 Mission Dr (93463).
(805) 688-5561; FAX (805) 688-7209.

Fri-Sat	1P $ 60- 80	2P/1B $ 65- 80	2P/2B $ 60- 80
Sun-Thu	1P $ 54- 72	2P/1B $ 49- 72	2P/2B $ 54- 72

XP $6. Reservation deposit required; 3-day cancellation notice. Senior discount. 2 stories; interior/exterior corridors. 48 rooms; 4 split-level loft rooms, $95. Exterior of buildings are replica of Danish village. Large rooms. Cable TV, movies. Heated pool. No pets. AE, DS, MC, VI. Ⓓ ⊘

SOLVANG ROYAL SCANDINAVIAN INN ⓐⓐⓐ   ♦♦♦ Hotel
2 blocks south of SR 246 (Mission Dr) at 400 Alisal Rd (PO Box 30, 93464).
(805) 688-8000; FAX (805) 688-0761.

3/1-5/31 & 10/1-11/30	1P ...		2P/1B $ 85-125		2P/2B $ 85-125
6/1-9/30	1P ...		2P/1B $ 95-135		2P/2B $ 95-135
12/1-2/28	1P ...		2P/1B $ 75-115		2P/2B $ 75-115

XP $10; children 18 and under stay free 3/1-11/30. Check in 4 pm. Credit card guarantee; 3-day cancellation notice. Weekly & monthly rates. Package plans, golf. Senior discount. 3 stories; interior corridors. 133 rooms. Large rooms, some with balconies or patios. Attractive pool area with view of Santa Ynez Mountains and foothills. Cable TV, pay movies; rental refrigerators. Heated pool, whirlpool. Valet laundry. No pets. Meeting rooms. AE, DI, DS, JCB, MC, VI. Restaurant, 7 am-10 pm; $9-16; cocktails; entertainment. Ⓓ Ⓢ ⊘ **(See ad below.)**

STORYBOOK INN ◉   ◆◆◆ Bed & Breakfast

Corner Oak St at 409 1st St (93463).
(805) 688-1703.

Fri-Sat [BP]	1P $ 95-189	2P/1B $ 95-189	2P/2B ...
Sun-Thu [BP]	1P $ 79-145	2P/1B $ 79-145	2P/2B ...

XP $25. Credit card guarantee. 3 stories; interior corridors. 9 rooms, most with fireplace. Newly constructed, tastefully decorated rooms. Most units with fireplace. Some whirlpools; no phones, TVs. No pets. AE, CB, DS, MC, VI. Complimentary beverages each evening. Ⓓ ⊗

SVENDSGAARD'S DANISH LODGE ◉   ◆◆◆ Motel

On SR 246 at Alisal Rd; 1711 Mission Dr (93463).
(805) 688-3277; FAX (805) 688-3997.

6/16-9/17 &

Fri-Sat 9/18-6/15 [CP]	1P $ 57- 88	2P/1B $ 57- 88	2P/2B $ 69- 90
Sun-Thu 9/18-6/15 [CP]	1P $ 44- 75	2P/1B $ 44- 75	2P/2B $ 49- 75

XP $6. Credit card guarantee; 3-day cancellation notice. Weekly & monthly rates. 3 stories; interior/exterior corridors. 48 rooms; many rooms with fireplace; 3 2-bedroom units; 4 kitchen units, $5 extra. Cable TV; refrigerators; some shower baths. Some radios. Pool, whirlpool. No pets. AE, CB, DI, DS, JCB, MC, VI. IMA. Ⓓ ⊗

THREE CROWNS INN ◉   ◆◆ Motel

1½ blocks west of SR 246 at 1518 Mission Dr (93463).
(805) 688-4702.

Fri-Sat	1P $ 50- 75	2P/1B $ 50- 75	2P/2B $ 60- 80
Sun-Thu	1P $ 40	2P/1B $ 40- 45	2P/2B $ 50

XP $5. Reservation deposit required. 1-2 stories; exterior corridors. 31 rooms; 2 2-bedroom units; 1 cottage for 4 persons, $95-195. Various accommodations from economy rooms to large rooms with whirlpool tubs & efficiency units. Charming waterfall & pond with Koi fish. Cable TV; some coffee makers, microwaves, refrigerators, whirlpools. No pets. AE, DS, MC, VI. Restaurant nearby. Ⓓ ⊗

VIKING MOTEL ◉   ◆ Motel

2 blocks west on SR 246 at 1506 Mission Dr (93463).
(805) 688-1337.

Sat	1P $ 52- 78	2P/1B $ 52- 78	2P/2B $ 58- 85
Sun-Fri	1P $ 30- 55	2P/1B $ 34- 55	2P/2B $ 38- 60

XP $6; children age 12 and under stay free. Reservation deposit required; 3-day cancellation notice. 1 story; exterior corridors. 12 rooms. Modest rooms. Located in center of town. Cable TV, movies; some refrigerators. Small pets, $5. AE, DS, MC, VI. Ⓓ ⊗

RESTAURANTS

BIT O' DENMARK RESTAURANT ◉   ◆ American

½ block south of SR 246 at 473 Alisal Rd (93463).
(805) 688-5426.

$11-20. Open 9 am-9 pm; Fri & Sat to 9:30 pm; closed 12/25. Nice selection of Danish & American entrees. Smorgasbord lunch & dinner. Casual attire. Children's menu. Cocktails. AE, CB, DI, MC, VI. ⊘

THE DANISH INN RESTAURANT   ♦♦ Danish
1 block west on SR 246 at 1547 Mission Dr (93463).
(805) 688-4813.

$11-20. Open 11:30 am-10 pm; Sat & Sun 9 am-10 pm. Reservations suggested. Located in center of town. Attractive restaurant featuring Scandinavian & Continental cuisine. Smorgasbord lunch & dinner. Casual attire. Cocktails & lounge. AE, DI, DS, MC, VI. ⊘

MASSIMI RISTORANTE   ♦♦♦ Italian
On SR 246 in Petersen Village Square at 1588 Mission Dr (93463).
(805) 688-0027.

$11-20. Open 5:30-9:30 pm; closed Mon & major holidays. Reservations suggested. A small, charming restaurant with indoor and outdoor patio dining. No air conditioning. Casual attire. A la carte. Beer & wine. AE, MC, VI. Smoke-free premises

Templeton

RESTAURANTS

A J SPURS ⏣   ♦ American
1¼ mile southeast of US 101, exit Main St; 508 Main St (93465).
(805) 434-2700.

$11-20. Open 4-9:30 pm; closed 1/1, 1/23, 12/24 & 12/25. Reservations suggested, not accepted on Sat. Casual western atmosphere. Large selection of steaks, barbecue & seafood. Casual attire. Children's menu, early bird specials. Cocktails & lounge. AE, DI, MC, VI.

MCPHEE'S GRILL   ♦♦♦ American
1¼ mile southeast of US 101, exit Main St; 416 Main St (93465).
(805) 434-3204.

$11-20. Open 11:30 am-2:30 & 5-9:30 pm; closed 12/25. Reservations suggested. Casual attire. Beer & wine. MC, VI. Smoke-free premises

Thousand Oaks

LODGING

BEST WESTERN OAKS LODGE ⏣   ♦♦ Motel
1 block north of US 101, 1 block northwest on Thousand Oaks Blvd; exit Moorpark Rd; 12 Conejo Blvd (91360).
(805) 495-7011; FAX (805) 495-0647.

| All year [CP] | 1P $ 47- 57 | 2P/1B $ 52- 62 | 2P/2B $ 52- 62 |

XP $5; children age 12 and under stay free. Weekly rates. 2 stories; exterior corridors. 76 rooms; 6 efficiencies, $5 extra (7-night minimum stay). Adjacent to shopping plazas. Movies; some refrigerators. Pool, whirlpool. Coin laundry. No pets. AE, CB, DI, DS, JCB, MC, VI. Restaurant nearby. D ⊗

DAYS INN ◆◆ Motor Inn
1 block southeast of US 101, exit Ventu Park Rd; 1320 Newbury Rd (91320).
(805) 499-5910; FAX (805) 498-5783.

| All year | 1P $ 48 | 2P/1B $ 48 | 2P/2B $ 48 |

XP $10; children age 18 and under stay free. Senior discount. 3 stories; exterior corridors. 122 rooms; 2 units with bedroom, living room & 2 bathrooms. Quiet location. Free and pay movies, safes; some coffee makers, refrigerators. Heated pool, whirlpool. Coin laundry. No pets. Meeting rooms, data ports. AE, CB, DI, DS, MC, VI. Restaurant, 6 am-1 & 5-9 pm; $7-12; cocktails. D S ⊗

ECONO LODGE ◉ ◆◆ Motel
3 blocks northeast of US 101, exit Rancho Rd; 1425 Thousand Oaks Blvd (91362).
(805) 496-0102; FAX (805) 494-1295.

| All year [CP] | 1P $40 - 48 | 2P/1B $ 44- 54 | 2P/2B $ 48- 58 |

XP $5. Reservation deposit required. Weekly rates. Senior discount. 2 stories; exterior corridors. 60 rooms. Located off the main street. Cable TV, movies; some microwaves, refrigerators; rental VCPs. Pool. No pets. AE, CB, DI, DS, JCB, MC, VI. D ⊗

HOLIDAY INN ◉ ◆◆ Motor Inn
Adjacent to north side US 101, exit Ventu Park Rd; 495 N Ventu Park Rd (91360).
(805) 498-6733; FAX (805) 498-9789.

| All Year | 1P $ 69- 89 | 2P/1B $ 79- 99 | 2P/2B $ 79- 99 |

XP $10; age 19 and under stay free. Senior discount. 2-3 stories; exterior corridors. 154 rooms. Cable TV; rental microwaves, refrigerators. Heated pool, whirlpool. Guest laundry. No pets. Conference facilities. AE, DI, DS, MC, VI. Dining room, 6 am-10 pm, Sun to 2 pm, $10-16; limited menu in lounge 4-10 pm; cocktail lounge, entertainment. D ⊗ **(See ad below.)**

THOUSAND OAKS INN ◆◆ Motor Inn
Formerly Howard Johnson Hotel. Adjacent to US 101, exit Moorpark Rd, then ¼ mile west; 75 W Thousand Oaks Blvd (91360).
(805) 497-3701; FAX (805) 497-1875.

| All year [CP] | 1P $ 59- 69 | 2P/1B $ 59- 69 | 2P/2B $ 59- 69 |

XP $10; children age 17 and under stay free. Senior discount. 4 stories; exterior corridors 107 rooms. Adjacent to shopping plaza. Free and pay movies; some refrigerators. Small heated pool, whirlpool. Coin laundry. No pets. Conference facilities, meeting rooms. AE, CB, DI, DS, JCB, MC, VI. Restaurant, 6 am-10 pm; $7-12; cocktails. [D] ⊘

RESTAURANTS

BLACK ANGUS ◆◆ American
Adjacent to US 101, exit Moorpark Rd, ½ mile west; 139 W Thousand Oaks Blvd (91360).
(805) 497-0757.

$11-20. Open 11 am-10 pm; Fri & Sat to 11 pm; closed 12/25; reservations suggested. Beef, seafood, chicken, pasta, salads, prime rib, rack of lamb, lobster. Children's menu. Cocktails & lounge. AE, DI, DS, MC, VI. Smoke-free premises

HUNAN CHINESE RESTAURANT ◆ Chinese
Corner of Moorpark Rd & Janss St, south end of shopping plaza at 1352 N Moorpark Rd (91360).
(805) 371-0075.

Up to $10. Open 11:30 am-9:30 pm; Fri & Sat to 10 pm. Authentic Hunan, Cantonese, Mandarin & Szechwan cooking. Casual attire. Carryout. Beer & wine. AE, MC, VI. Smoke-free premises

Ventura

LODGING

BELLA MAGGIORE INN 🆔 ◆◆◆ Historic Bed & Breakfast
¼ mile north of US 101, exit California St; 67 S California St (93001).
(805) 652-0277.

All year [BP]	1P	$ 75-150	2P/1B	$ 75-150	2P/2B	...

XP $10; children age 12 and under stay free. Reservation deposit required. 3 stories; no elevator; interior corridors. 24 rooms. Renovated historic landmark built in 1926. Attractive southern European ambiance. Some shower baths, air conditioning, refrigerators, whirlpools. No pets. Meeting rooms. AE, CB, DI, DS, MC, VI. Complimentary beverages and cheese each evening. Restaurant, 11 am-2:30 pm, Sun brunch 8 am-1 pm; closed Mon; $7-9. [D] ⊘

BEST WESTERN INN OF VENTURA 🆔 ◆◆ Motel
2 blocks east of California St; from US 101, northbound exit California St, southbound exit Ventura Ave; 708 E Thompson Blvd (93001).
(805) 648-3101.

4/1-9/30	1P	$ 52- 62	2P/1B	$ 59- 69	2P/2B	$ 60- 70
10/1-3/31	1P	$ 49- 59	2P/1B	$ 54- 64	2P/2B	$ 56- 66

XP $5. Reservation deposit required in summer. Senior discount. 2 stories; exterior corridors. 75 rooms. Cable TV, movies. Heated pool, whirlpool. No pets. AE, CB, DI, DS, MC, VI. Coffee shop nearby. [D] ⊘

Room rates may increase during special events.

COLONY HARBORTOWN MARINA RESORT ⊕   ♦♦♦ Motor Inn
From US 101, exit Seaward Ave, then 1½ mile south on Harbor Bl at Ventura Harbor;
1050 Schooner Dr (93001).
(805) 658-1212; FAX (805) 658-6347.

5/1-9/30 [BP]	1P $ 79- 99	2P/1B $ 79- 99	2P/2B $ 79- 99
10/1-4/30 [BP]	1P $ 69	2P/1B $ 69	2P/2B $ 69

XP $10; children age 17 and under stay free. Check in 4 pm. Reservation deposit required. 3 stories; exterior corridors. 154 rooms; 4 2-bedroom units; many rooms with marina view & balcony or patio. Cable TV, movies; some coffee makers, refrigerators; no air conditioning. Heated pool, whirlpool; 3 lighted tennis courts. Valet laundry. No pets. Conference facilities, meeting rooms, secretarial services. AE, CB, DI, DS, MC, VI. Complimentary beverages each evening. Restaurant; 6:30 am-10 pm; $12-22; cocktails, entertainment. Ⓓ Ⓢ ⊘

COUNTRY INN AT VENTURA ⊕   ♦♦♦ Motel
1 block east of California St & 1 block south of Thompson Blvd; from US 101, north-
bound exit California St, southbound exit Ventura Ave; 298 Chestnut St (93001).
(805) 653-1434; FAX (805) 648-7126.

All year [BP]	1P $ 69	2P/1B $ 69	2P/2B $ 69

XP $10; children age 12 and under stay free. 3 stories; interior corridors. 120 rooms; some balconies. Ocean or mountain views. Cable TV, refrigerators, microwaves, VCPs. Heated pool, whirlpool. Coin laundry. No pets. AE, CB, DI, DS, JCB, MC, VI. Complimentary beverages each evening. Restaurant nearby. Ⓓ Ⓢ ⊘
(See ad below.)

DOUBLETREE HOTEL AT VENTURA ⊕   ♦♦♦ Motor Inn
Adjacent to west side of US 101, exit Seaward Ave; 2055 Harbor Blvd (93001).
(805) 643-6000; FAX (805) 643-7137.

All year	1P $ 89-119	2P/1B $ 99-129	2P/2B $ 99-129

XP $10; children age 18 and under stay free. Reservation deposit required. 4 stories; interior corridors. 284 rooms. Attractively landscaped courtyard & pool area. 1 block to San Buenaventura State Beach. Free and pay movies; rental refrigerators. Heated pool, saunas, whirlpool. Valet laundry. No pets. Conference facilities, meeting rooms, secretarial services, data ports, PC. AE, CB, DI, DS, MC, VI. Restaurant; 6:30 am-10 pm; Sat & Sun from 7 am; $9-16; cocktails; sports bar 3 pm-midnight; Fri & Sat to 1 am; limited menu. Ⓓ Ⓢ ⊘

HOLIDAY INN BEACH RESORT ⊕   ♦♦♦ Hotel
Adjacent to US 101; northbound exit California St, southbound exit Main St; 450 E
Harbor Blvd (93001).
(805) 648-7731; FAX (805) 653-6202.

4/2-10/31	1P $110	2P/1B $150	2P/2B $150
11/1-4/1	1P $ 79	2P/1B $ 89	2P/2B $ 89

Check-in 4 pm. Reservation deposit required. Monthly rates. Senior discount. 12 stories; interior corridors. 260 rooms. Beachfront hotel with balconies. Cable TV, free and pay movies; some refrigerators. Heated pool, wading pool, playground. Coin laundry. No pets. Conference facilities, secretarial services. AE, CB, DI, DS, MC, VI. Dining room, 6 am-10 pm; $10-16; cocktails, entertainment. Ⓓ ⊘

INN ON THE BEACH ⒶⒶ ◆◆ Motel
½ mile west of US 101; exit Seaward Ave; 1175 S Seaward Ave (93001).
(805) 652-2000; FAX (805) 652-1912.

All year [CP]	1P $ 80-130	2P/1B $ 80-130	2P/2B $100-130

XP $5; children 6 and under stay free. Reservation deposit required. Senior discount. 3 stories; interior corridors. 24 rooms. At the beach; ocean view. Patios or balconies. Cable TV, movies; some refrigerators. No pets. AE, CB, DI, MC, VI. Ⓓ Ⓢ ⊘

LA MER EUROPEAN BED & BREAKFAST ◆◆ Historic Bed & Breakfast
½ mile north of US 101; northbound exit California St, southbound exit Ventura Ave, 1 block west of California St; 411 Poli St (93001).
(805) 643-3600.

All year [BP]	1P $100-150	2P/1B $105-155	2P/2B ...

Check in 4 pm. 2-night minimum stay weekends. Reservation deposit required; 7-day refund notice. 2 stories; interior/exterior corridors. 5 rooms. House built in 1890. Each room furnished in a different European motif. No air conditioning, phones, TV. No pets. MC, VI. Ⓓ ⊘

LA QUINTA INN ◆◆◆ Motel
½ block south of US 101, exit Victoria Ave; 5818 Valentine Rd (93003).
(805) 658-6200; FAX (805) 642-2840.

All year [CP]	1P $ 48- 55	2P/1B $ 53- 60	2P/2B $ 53- 55

XP $6; children age 18 and under stay free. 3 stories; exterior corridors. 142 rooms. Cable TV, free and pay movies; rental refrigerators. Heated pool, whirlpool. Small pets. Meeting rooms. AE, CB, DI, DS, MC, VI. Restaurant nearby. Ⓓ Ⓢ ⊘

PIERPONT INN ⒶⒶ ◆◆ Motor Inn
Adjacent to US 101; northbound exit Sanjon Rd, southbound Seaward Ave exit; 550 Sanjon Rd (93001).
(805) 653-6144; FAX (805) 641-1501.

5/1-10/1	1P $ 68	2P/1B $ 79- 89	2P/2B $ 79- 89
10/2-4/30	1P $ 58	2P/1B $ 69- 79	2P/2B $ 69- 79

XP $10; children age 12 and under stay free. Monthly rates. 2 stories; interior/exterior corridors. 70 rooms; 14 units with fireplace; 8 ocean-view suites with balcony, $129. 2 cottages, $139-159. Rental bicycles. Across freeway from beach. Attractive grounds. Many rooms with ocean views; many with balconies. Cable TV, movies, coffee makers; some refrigerators; no air conditioning. 2 heated pools

(1 indoor); rental bicycles; fee for racquetball, 12 lighted tennis courts, exercise room, massage. No pets. Meeting rooms. AE, CB, DI, DS, MC, VI. ⒟ ⊘

RAMADA CLOCKTOWER INN ⓐⓐ   ♦♦♦ Motor Inn
½ mile northwest of US 101; northbound exit California St, southbound exit Ventura Ave; 181 E Santa Clara St (93001).
(805) 652-0141; FAX (805) 643-1432.
All year [CP]   1P $ 75   2P/1B $ 80   2P/2B $ 80

XP $10; children age 12 and under stay free. Reservation deposit required. 2 stories; interior corridors. 49 rooms; 5 rooms with fireplace & 8 with balcony. Attractive Southwest decor. Adjacent to San Buenaventura Mission & Mission Park. 1½ blocks to beach. Cable TV, movies; some coffee makers, microwaves, refrigerators. Valet laundry. Pets. Meeting rooms. AE, CB, DI, DS, MC, VI. Restaurant; 11 am-2:30 & 5-9 pm; closed Sun; $11-20; cocktails. ⒟ ⓢ ⊘

VAGABOND INN ⓐⓐ   ♦♦ Motor Inn
¼ mile east on US 101 business route; from US 101 northbound exit California St, southbound exit Ventura Ave; 756 E Thompson Bl (93001).
(805) 648-5371; FAX (805) 648-5613.
4/16-9/15 [CP]   1P $ 50- 55   2P/1B $ 55- 60   2P/2B $ 60- 65
9/16-4/15 [CP]   1P $ 44- 48   2P/1B $ 48- 53   2P/2B $ 52- 57

XP $5; children 18 and under stay free. Reservation deposit required; 3-day cancellation notice. 2 stories; exterior corridors. 82 rooms; 2 2-bedroom units. Cable TV, movies, coffee makers; some refrigerators. Heated pool, whirlpool; playground. Small pets, $5. AE, CB, DI, DS, MC, VI. Coffee shop; 24 hrs; $5-10. ⒟ ⊘

RESTAURANTS

THE CHART HOUSE   ♦♦ Steak & Seafood
Adjacent to US 101; northbound exit Sanjon Rd; southbound exit Seaward Ave; 567 Sanjon Rd (93001).
(805) 643-3725.

$11-20. Open 5:30-10 pm; Fri to 10:30 pm; Sat 5-11 pm; Sun 4-10 pm. Reservations suggested. Contemporary-style restaurant overlooking the ocean. Features steak, fresh seafood, chicken & prime rib. Children's menu, a la carte, carryout, salad bar. Cocktails & lounge. AE, DI, DS, MC, VI. ⊘

EL TORITO   ♦♦ Mexican
East side of US 101, exit Seaward Ave; 770 S Seaward Ave (93001).
(805) 648-5219.

$11-20. Open 11 am-10 pm; Fri & Sat to 11 pm; Sun 9 am-1- pm; closed Thanksgiving & 12/25. Sun brunch. Children's menu. Cocktails & lounge. AE, CB, DI, DS, JCB, MC, VI. ⊘

OLD VIENNA RESTAURANT ⓐⓐ   ♦♦ German
1 mile east of Main St; 3845 Telegraph Rd (92003).
(805) 654-1214.

$11-20. Open 11:30 am-2 & 5-9:30 pm; Mon from 5 pm; Fri to 10 pm; Sat 5-10 pm; Sun 11 am-2 & 4:30-9 pm; closed 12/25. Reservations suggested weekends. Large menu selection, including venison & roast goose in season. Children's menu. Cocktails. AE, CB, DI, DS, MC, VI. ⊘

PIERPONT INN   ♦♦ American
In Pierpont Inn, 550 San Jon Rd (93001).
(805) 653-6144.

$11-20. Open 6:30-10:30, 11:30 am-2 & 5:30-9 pm; Sat 6:30-10:30,11:30 am-2:30 & 5:30-10 pm; Sun 8 am-3 & 5:30-9 pm, limited lounge menu noon-9 pm. Reservations suggested. Fine ocean-view dining at inn established in 1928. Entrees include beef, chicken & seafood. Desserts made on premises. Children's menu, early bird specials, carryout. Cocktails & lounge; entertainment. AE, CB, DI, DS, MC, VI. Smoke-free premises

SMOKEY'S DINING HALL & SALOON ⊕   ♦♦ American
½ mile northwest of US 101, northbound exit California St, southbound exit Ventura Ave; 211 E Santa Clara St (93001).
(805) 643-3264.

$11-20. Open 11:30 am-11 pm, Fri & Sat to 1 am; Sun 2-11 pm; closed Thanksgiving & 12/25. Reservations suggested. Historic 1912 Victorian building. Barbecue pit, salads, chicken, pork, beef & baby back ribs, seafood, quail & some Mexican cuisine. Casual attire. Children's menu, early bird specials, carryout. Cocktails & lounge. AE, CB, DI, MC, VI. ⊘

SPINNAKER SEAFOOD BROILER   ♦♦ Seafood
From US 101, exit Seaward Ave, 1¼ mile southwest on Harbor Blvd, ¾ mile west on Spinnaker Dr, Suite 109, in Ventura Harbor Village at 1583 Spinnaker Dr.
(805) 658-6220.

$11-20. Open 11 am-9:30 pm; Fri & Sat to 10:30 pm; closed 12/25. Mesquite grilled seafood, steaks, chicken & ribs. Casual attire. Children's menu, early bird specials, a la carte, carryout. Cocktails & lounge. Dancing Fri & Sat 8 pm-midnight. AE, CB, DI, DS, MC, VI. ⊘

YOLANDA'S MEXICAN CAFE   ♦♦ Mexican
½ mile east of Seaward Ave; 2753 E Main St (93003).
(805) 643-2700.

Up to $10. Open 11 am-10 pm; Fri & Sat to 11 pm; Sun 10 am-9 pm; closed Thanksgiving & 12/25. Reservations suggested. Colorfully decorated restaurant. Southwestern cuisine. Children's menu, carryout. Cocktails & lounge. AE, MC, VI. ⊘

Westlake Village

LODGING

HYATT WESTLAKE PLAZA HOTEL ⊕   ♦♦♦ Hotel
Adjacent to US 101; exit Westlake Blvd; 880 S Westlake Blvd (91361).
(805) 497-9991; FAX (805) 379-9392.

All Year   1P $145-160   2P/1B $160-175   2P/2B $160-175

XP $25; children age 18 and under stay free. Senior discount. 5 stories; interior corridors. 256 rooms; luxury-level rooms. Spacious lobby with a fountain. Cable TV, free and pay movies; some coffee makers, refrigerators; rental VCPs. Heated pool, saunas, whirlpools, exercise room. Rental bicycles. 24-hour room service. Valet laundry. Valet parking. No pets. Conference facilities, secretarial service, data ports, PC. AE, CB, DI, DS, JCB, MC, VI. Restaurant, 6 am-11 pm; $15-25; cocktails, entertainment. [D] [S] ⊘

WESTLAKE INN HOTEL   ♦♦♦ Motor Inn
1¼ mile southeast of US 101, exit Westlake Blvd; 31943 Agoura Rd (91361).
(818) 889-0230; FAX (818) 879-0812.
All Year [CP Mon-Fri]   1P $ 89- 99   2P/1B $110-175   2P/2P $200-350

Senior discount. Credit card guarantee. 2 stories; exterior corridors. 105 rooms; 3 suites with living room, bedroom, fireplace, whirlpool bath & refrigerator. Nicely landscaped grounds. Patio or balcony. Cable TV, movies, honor bars, refrigerators; rental microwaves; some coffee makers. Heated pool, whirlpool, 10 tennis courts (6 lighted), exercise room; fee for 18 holes golf & putting green. No pets. Conference facilities, meeting rooms, data ports. AE, CB, DI, DS, MC, VI. Restaurant, 6 am-10 pm; $7-14; cocktails, entertainment. Westlake Inn Restaurant, see separate listing. [D] ⊘

RESTAURANTS

OTTAVIO'S   ♦♦ Italian
1 block east of Westlake Blvd, ¼ mile southeast of US 101; exit Westlake Blvd; 2799 Townsgate Rd (91361).
(805) 373-1993.

$11-20. Open 11 am-10 pm, Fri & Sat to 11 pm, Sun to 9 pm. Dining on patio, weather permitting. Seafood, pasta, salads, chicken, veal, lamb & steak. Sun brunch, health conscious menu, a la carte, carryout. Cocktails & lounge. AE, CB, DI, MC, VI. ⊘

THE WESTLAKE INN RESTAURANT   ♦♦ Continental
At the Westlake Inn Hotel, 32001 Agoura Rd (91361).
(818) 889-1662.

$21-30. Open 11:30 am-2 & 5-9 pm, Fri & Sat 5-10 pm, Sun 10 am-2 & 5-9 pm; closed Mon. Reservations suggested. Scenic lakeside dining. Casual attire. Fresh seafood, pasta, salad, chicken, steak, lamb & lobster tail. Sun brunch, children's menu, carryout, salad bar. Cocktails & lounge; entertainment. AE, CB, DI, DS, MC, VI. ⊘

Campgrounds & Trailer Parks

An attractive alternative to indoor lodging is tent or RV camp-
ing, and the Central Coast offers campgrounds in terrain that
ranges from oceanside to mountainside. Campgrounds are
generally listed here under the city or large recreation area in
which they are located or to which they are closest. Unless
otherwise noted, campgrounds are open all year.

In the listings that follow, fees shown are for one night's camping, usually for two people and, unless otherwise noted, include a recreational vehicle or automobile (with or without trailer). Electricity, water and sewer hookups are indicated by the letters E, W and S, respectively. Elevations (El) for national forest campgrounds are shown, since most of them are in mountainous areas.

All camping fees are subject to change, unless otherwise noted.

State park campgrounds which use the MISTIX reservation system are indicated by "MISTIX," and reservations are essential during the busy summer months. Charge reservations through MISTIX by phone with MasterCard or VISA by calling (800) 444-7275; the TTD/TTY number for hearing or speech impaired users is (800) 284-7275.

When a campsite can be reserved by telephoning the campground or administering agency directly, the listing simply states "Reservations."

Any other reservation system is outlined; otherwise, it's "first come, first served."

Bringing the family pet? Pets are welcome in most campgrounds. Be aware that some campgrounds do charge a nominal fee for pets (these are noted), and dogs are not allowed in beach campgrounds.

Private campgrounds are so designated, and they have been inspected by an Automobile Club representative and meet current AAA quality standards. The ⏺ symbol in a listing identifies that establishment as a AAA Official Appointment; it indicates that the campground has expressed a particular interest in serving AAA members. For a detailed listing of additional public and private campgrounds, see the Auto Club's *Central and Southern California Camping* map. Automobile Club members can make reservations only for private campgrounds at any Club district office.

Avila Beach

AVILA HOT SPRINGS SPA & RV RESORT (Private)
½ block west of US 101 via Avila Beach Dr; turnoff at 250 Avila Beach Dr (mailing address: 250 Avila Beach Dr, San Luis Obispo 93405).
(805) 595-2359; FAX (805) 595-7914.

$16.50-26 for up to 8 persons. Reservations accepted; deposit required. 25 tent sites, 50 RV spaces. 40 E, 30 WS. Piped water, flush toilets, showers, disposal station. Pool, hot mineral pool, mineral spa and massage (fee). AE, DS, MC, VI.

Buellton

FLYING FLAGS TRAVEL PARK (Private) ⊕
2 blocks southwest of junction US 101 and SR 246 on Avenue of Flags (mailing address: PO Box 1845, Buellton 93427).
(805) 688-3716.

$15-21.50 per night for 2 persons; $2 per night for each additional person. Reservations are accepted, deposit required. 303 tent or RV spaces, 250 EW, 220 S. Sanitary disposal station, piped water, flush toilets, showers, barbecues, tables. Heated pool, indoor spa, playground, video games, cable TV hookups (fee); coin laundry, propane, groceries. Pets are permitted for an additional fee of 50¢ per night.

Cambria

SAN SIMEON STATE PARK
3 miles north of Cambria off SR 1 (mailing address: 750 Hearst Castle Rd, San Simeon 93452).
(805) 927-2068.

San Simeon Creek ³⁄₁₀ *mile off east side of SR 1.*
$14-16. MISTIX. 18 tent sites, 116 tent or RV spaces, 35-foot maximum length. Piped water, flush toilets, showers (fee), disposal station, tables, fire rings, swimming, fishing; propane, groceries, laundry within 5 miles.

Washburn ½ *mile off east side of SR 1.*
$7-9. 68 tent or RV spaces, 35-foot maximum length (trailers 21 feet). Piped water, chemical toilets, tables, fire rings, swimming, fishing; propane, groceries, laundry within 5 miles.

Carpinteria

CARPINTERIA STATE BEACH
Off US 101 via SR 224 (mailing address: 1933 Cliff Dr, Ste 27, Santa Barbara 93109).
(805) 684-2811.

$14-21 without hookups, $18-25 with hookups. MISTIX. 159 tent or RV spaces, 35-ft RV maximum length, 86 EWS. Sanitary disposal station, piped water, flush toilets, pay showers, fire pits, tables, fishing, swimming, propane, groceries, restaurant, coin laundry within ½ mile.

Casitas Springs

FOSTER PARK
2 miles southwest of Casitas Springs off SR 33 on Casitas Vista Rd (mailing address: SLO County Gov't Center, San Luis Obispo 93408).
(805) 654-3951.

$11. 30 tent or RV spaces. Piped water, flush toilets, fire rings, tables; playground; fishing, propane, groceries, coin laundry within 5 miles.

Fillmore

KENNEY GROVE
3 miles northwest of Fillmore via Old Telegraph Rd on Oak Ave (mailing address: SLO County Gov't Center, San Luis Obispo 93408).
(805) 654-3951.
$10. Reservations. 33 tent or RV spaces, 20 E. Piped water, flush toilets, showers, fire rings, tables; playground; fishing, propane, groceries, coin laundry within 5 miles.

Goleta

EL CAPITAN STATE BEACH
12 miles west of Goleta off US 101 (mailing address: 10 Refugio Beach Rd, Goleta 93117).
(805) 968-1033.
$14-16. MISTIX. 140 tent or RV spaces, 3 group tent sites, 30-ft RV maximum length, no hookups. Sanitary disposal station, piped water, flush toilets, showers (fee), fire pits, tables, ocean fishing and swimming; limited groceries within 5 miles.

GAVIOTA STATE PARK
23 miles west of Goleta off US 101 (mailing address: 10 Refugio Beach Rd, Goleta 93117).
(805) 968-1033.
$14-16. 59 tent and RV spaces, no hookups. Flush toilets, showers (fee), fire pits and tables; fishing and swimming.

REFUGIO STATE BEACH
15 miles west of Goleta off US 101 (mailing address: 10 Refugio Beach Rd, Goleta 93117).
(805) 968-1033.
$14-16. MISTIX. 85 tent or RV spaces, 1 group site, 30-ft RV maximum length, no hookups. Piped water, flush toilets, showers (fee), fire pits, tables, ocean fishing and swimming; limited groceries.

El Capitan State Beach offers seaside camping.

It's time to pitch a tent beneath an old oak tree near Lake Cachuma.

Lake Cachuma

LAKE CACHUMA COUNTY PARK

8 miles east of Santa Ynez off SR 154 (mailing address: Star Rte, Santa Barbara 93105). (805) 688-4658.

$13 without hookups; $16 EW, and $18 EWS. Individual campsites on a first-come, first-served basis; group reservations (fee). 125 RV spaces, 500 tent or RV spaces, 25 EW, 100 EWS. Sanitary disposal station, piped water, flush toilets, showers, coin laundry, playground, boat and bicycle rentals, fishing, swimming during summer months, propane and groceries available. Pets $1.

Lake Casitas

LAKE CASITAS RECREATION AREA

5 miles southwest of Ojai off SR 150 (mailing address: 11311 Santa Ana Rd, Ventura 93001).
(805) 649-2233; reservations (805) 649-1122.

$12. Reservations. 750 tent or RV spaces, 141 EW. Sanitary disposal station, piped water, flush toilets, showers, barbecues or fire rings, tables, playground, fishing; propane, groceries, coin laundry within 5 miles.

Lake Piru

LAKE PIRU RECREATION AREA

5 miles north of Piru on west shore of Lake Piru (mailing address: PO Box 202, Piru 93040).
(805) 521-1500.

$12. 247 tent or RV spaces, 106 E, 4 EWS. Sanitary disposal station, piped water, flush toilets, showers, barbecues or fire rings, tables, playground, swimming and fishing; propane, groceries, coin laundry within 5 miles.

Lake San Antonio

LAKE SAN ANTONIO *31 miles northwest of Paso Robles off US 101, via County Rd G14 (mailing address: PO Box 367, Salinas 93906).*
(805) 472-2311.

Harris Creek *On south shore.*
$14-20. Senior discount. 117 tent or RV spaces, 35-ft RV maximum length. 26 EW, 91 W. Piped water, flush toilets, showers, disposal station, tables, stoves, swimming, fishing; propane, groceries, coin laundry within 5 miles.

Lynch *On south shore.*
$14-20. Senior discount. 106 tent or RV spaces, 35-ft maximum length. 54 EW, 52 W. Piped water, flush toilets, showers, disposal stations, tables, stoves, swimming, fishing; propane, groceries, coin laundry within 5 miles.

Pleyto *On north shore.*
$14-20. Senior discount. 346 tent or RV spaces, 35-ft RV maximum length. 96 EW, 276 W, 14 EWS. Piped water, flush toilets, showers, disposal station, tables, stoves, swimming, fishing; propane, groceries, coin laundry within 5 miles.

Redonda Vista *On south shore.*
$14-20. Senior discount. 259 tent or RV spaces, 35-ft RV maximum length. 86 EWS, 173 W. Piped water, flush toilets, showers, disposal station, tables, stoves, swimming, fishing; propane, groceries, coin laundry within 5 miles.

Lompoc

JALAMA BEACH COUNTY PARK
20 miles southwest of Lompoc off SR 1 on Jalama Rd (mailing address: Star Rte, Santa Barbara 93105).
(805) 736-3504, (805) 736-6316 (recording).

$13 without hookups; $16 E. Fee for group reservations; call (805) 934-6211. 100 tent or RV spaces, 15 E. Individual campsites on a first-come, first-served basis; group reservations (fee). Piped water, flush toilets, showers, tables, playground; fishing; groceries; snack bar.

RIVER PARK
SR 246 and Sweeney Rd junction, east side of Santa Ynez River (mailing address: 125 W Walnut Ave, Lompoc 93436).
(805) 736-6565.

$15 RV; $10 tent sites, $4 bicyclist or hiker. 36 tent or RV spaces (EWS). Disposal station $2, flush toilets, showers, tables, playground, fishing pond; propane, groceries, coin laundry within 5 miles. Pets, $1.

Lopez Lake

LOPEZ LAKE RECREATION AREA
12½ miles northeast of Arroyo Grande off US 101 (mailing address: SLO County Gov't Center, San Luis Obispo 93408).
(805) 489-1122; (805) 489-8019.

$12-20. Reservations. 143 tent or RV spaces, 146 tent sites, 60-ft RV maximum length, 66 E, 143 EWS. Flush toilets, piped water.

Los Osos

MONTAÑA DE ORO STATE PARK
6 miles southwest of Los Osos via Pecho Rd (mailing address: 3220 S Higuera St #311, San Luis Obispo 93401).
(805) 528-0513.

$9. MISTIX Memorial Day through Labor Day. 50 tent or RV spaces, 24-ft RV maximum length. Tank water, pit toilets, tables, fire rings.

Los Padres National Forest

HEADQUARTERS *6144 Calle Real, Goleta 93117.*
(805) 683-6711.

Unless noted, Los Padres campgrounds are open all year and are accessible by car. Naturally, special care must be taken when attempting mountain roads in inclement weather.

Each campsite has a table and fire pit, but there are no electric, water or sewer hookups; many campsites are equipped with piped water and are so noted. At some campgrounds, particularly those at higher elevations, water may be turned off during the winter. The majority of Forest Service campgrounds have pit or chemical toilets; those with flush toilets are noted. Pets are allowed at no extra charge but must be kept on a leash or physically controlled at all times. Changes in campground information may occur, depending upon road and weather conditions and campground maintenance. Fishing and swimming are seasonal.

Other than the two exceptions noted, reservations are not accepted. Some campgrounds listed also offer group campsites, for which larger fees may be charged.

Aliso *8 miles southwest of New Cuyama off SR 166.*
No fee. El 3200 ft. 11 tent or RV spaces, 22-ft RV maximum length. No water.

Ballinger *17 miles southeast of New Cuyama off SR 33.*
No fee. El 3000 ft. 20 tent or RV spaces, 32-ft RV maximum length. No water.

Barrel Springs *17 miles northeast of Sisquoc via Tepusquet and Colson Canyon rds.*
No fee. El 1000 ft. 6 tent spaces. Piped water.

Bates Canyon *18 miles west of New Cuyama on Cottonwood Canyon Rd.*
No fee. El 2900 ft. 6 tent spaces, 16-ft RV maximum length. No water.

Beaver *16 miles north of Ojai off SR 33.*
No fee. El 3000 ft. 12 tent or RV spaces, 23-ft RV maximum length. No water.

Caballo *15½ miles west of Lake of the Woods.*
No fee. Open May-Nov. El 5800 ft. 5 tent or RV spaces, 16-ft RV maximum length. No water.

Cachuma *16 miles northeast of Santa Ynez off SR 154 on Happy Canyon Rd.*
No fee. El 2200 ft. 6 tent or RV spaces, 16-ft RV maximum length. No water.

Campo Alto *24½ miles west of Lake of the Woods.*
No fee. Open May-Nov. El 8200 ft. 17 tent or RV spaces, 22-ft RV maximum length. No water.

Cerro Alto *8 miles northeast of Morro Bay off SR 41.*
$10. El 2080 ft. 24 tent spaces. Piped water.

Colson *12 miles northeast of Sisquoc via Tepusquet and Colson Canyon rds.*
No fee. El 2080 ft. 5 tent or RV spaces, 22-ft RV maximum length. Piped water.

Davy Brown *19 miles northeast of Santa Ynez via Happy Canyon Rd.*
$6. El 4000 ft. 13 tent or RV spaces, 22-ft RV maximum length.

Figueroa *2½ miles northeast of Los Olivos on Figueroa Mountain Rd.*
$6. El 4000 ft. 33 tent or RV spaces, 22-ft RV maximum length. Piped water.

Fremont *18 miles northwest of Santa Barbara off SR 154.*
$8. Open Apr-Oct. El 900 ft. 15 tent or RV spaces, 16-ft RV maximum length. Piped water, flush toilets.

Half Moon *20 miles southwest of Lake of the Woods.*
No fee. Open May-Nov. El 4700 ft. 10 tent or RV spaces, 22-ft RV maximum length. No water.

Hi Mountain *4 miles southwest of Pozo.*
No fee. El 2800 ft. 11 tent or RV spaces, 16-ft RV maximum length. Piped water.

Juncal *21 miles northeast of Santa Barbara off SR 154 via E Camino Cielo Rd.*
$5. El 1800 ft. 6 tent spaces. No water.

Kings Camp *13 miles southwest of Gorman off I-5 via Hungry Valley Rd.*
No fee. El 4200 ft. 3 tent spaces, 4 tent or RV spaces, 16-ft RV maximum length. No water.

La Panza *12 miles northeast of Pozo off Pozo Rd.*
No fee. El 2400 ft. 16 tent or RV spaces, 16-ft RV maximum length. No water.

Lion's Canyon *21½ miles northeast of Ojai off SR 33.*
$7. El 3000 ft. 30 tent or RV spaces, 16-ft RV maximum length.

Los Prietos *19 miles northwest of Santa Barbara off SR 154.*
$8. Open Apr-Oct. El 1000 ft. 38 tent or RV spaces, 22-ft RV maximum length. Piped water, flush toilets.

Marian *16½ miles west of Lake of the Woods.*
No fee. Open May-Nov. El 6600 ft. 5 tent or RV spaces, 16-ft RV maximum length. No water.

McGill *10½ miles west of Lake of the Woods on Mt. Pinos Rd.*
$6. Open Jun-Oct. El 7400 ft. 73 tent or RV spaces, 16-ft RV maximum length. Piped water.

Middle Santa Ynez *44 miles northeast of Santa Barbara off SR 154.*
No fee. El 1500 ft. 9 tent spaces. Piped water.

Mil Potrero Park *(Although this campground is within Los Padres National Forest, it is administered by Kern County's Westside Parks & Recreation Department.) 11 miles west of Lake of the Woods via Cuddy Valley Rd (mailing address: PO Box 1406, Taft 93268). (805) 763-4246.*
$15. Reservations. El 5000. 33 tent & RV spaces; 28-ft RV maximum length. Piped water, flush toilets, showers, barbecue pits and fire rings, playground, propane, groceries, coin laundry within 5 miles.

Mono *48 miles north of Santa Barbara off SR 154.*
No fee. El 1500 ft. 7 tent spaces. No water.

Mt. Pinos *12½ miles west of Lake of the Woods on Mt Pinos Rd.*
$6. Open June-Oct. El 7800 ft. 19 tent or RV spaces, 16-ft RV maximum length. Piped water.

Nettle Spring *34 miles southeast of New Cuyama off SR 33 via Apache Canyon Rd.*
No fee. El 4400 ft. 9 tent sites, 9 tent or RV spaces, 22-ft RV maximum length. Piped water.

Nira *22 miles northwest of Santa Ynez off SR 154 via Happy Canyon and Sunset Valley rds.*
No fee. El 2100 ft. 12 tent spaces. No water.

Ozena *25 miles southwest of Lake of the Woods via Lockwood Valley Rd.*
No fee. El 3600 ft. 12 tent or RV spaces, 22-ft RV maximum length. Piped water.

Paradise *18½ miles northwest of Santa Barbara off SR 154.*
$8. National Forest Reservation Center (800) 280-2267; TTD (800) 879-4496. El 1000 ft. 15 tent or RV spaces, 22-ft RV maximum length. Piped water, flush toilets.

P-Bar Flat *45 miles northeast of Santa Barbara off SR 154.*
No fee. El 1800 ft. 4 tent spaces. No water.

Pine Mountain *35 miles north of Ojai off SR 33 on Reyes Peak Rd.*
No fee. Open May-Nov. El 6700 ft. 6 tent spaces. No water.

Pine Springs *14 miles southwest of Lake of the Woods via Lockwood Valley Rd.*
No fee. Open May-Oct. El 5800 ft. 10 tent or RV spaces, 22-ft RV maximum length. No water.

Reyes Creek *25 miles southwest of Lake of the Woods via Lockwood Valley Rd.*
$5. El 4000 ft. 23 tent spaces, 6 tent or RV spaces, 22-ft RV maximum length. Piped water.

Reyes Peak *36 miles north of Ojai off SR 33 on Reyes Peak Rd.*
No fee. Open Apr.-Dec. El 6800 ft. 6 tent spaces. No water.

Rose Valley Falls *21 miles northeast of Ojai off SR 33.*
$7. El 3400 ft. 9 tent or RV spaces, 16-ft RV maximum length.

Stony Creek *23½ miles northeast of Arroyo Grande via Huasna Rd.*
No fee. El 1800 ft. 5 tent spaces.

Toad Spring *15½ miles west of Lake of the Woods.*
No fee. Open May-Nov. El 5700 ft. 4 tent spaces, 3 tent or RV spaces, 16-ft RV maximum length. No water.

Twin Pines *20½ miles southwest of Gorman off I-5.*
No fee. Open May-Oct. El 6600 ft. 5 tent spaces. No water.

Upper Oso *22 miles northwest of Santa Barbara off SR 154.*
$8. El 1100 ft. 27 tent or RV spaces, 22-ft RV maximum length. Piped water, flush toilets.

Wagon Flat *21 miles northeast of Sisquoc via Tepusquet, Colson and La Brea Canyon rds.*
No fee. El 1400 ft. 5 tent or RV spaces, 16-ft RV maximum length. No water.

Wheeler Gorge *9 miles northwest of Ojai on SR 33.*
$10. National Forest Reservation Center (800) 280-2267; TTD (800) 879-4496. El 2000 ft. 73 tent or RV spaces, 30-ft RV maximum length. Piped water.

Morro Bay (See also Los Osos.)

MORRO BAY STATE PARK
Campground at south end of Morro Bay off SR 1 (mailing address: 3220 S Higuera St #311, San Luis Obispo 93401).
(805) 772-2560.

$18. MISTIX. 135 tent and RV spaces; 31-foot maximum length. 20 EW. Piped water, flush toilets, showers, disposal station, tables, barbecue pits and fire rings, fishing; propane, groceries, laundry within 5 miles.

MORRO STRAND STATE BEACH
Campground at north end of Morro Bay off SR 1 (mailing address: 3220 S Higuera St #311, San Luis Obispo 93401).
(805) 772-2560.

$14. MISTIX. 104 tent or RV spaces, 24-ft maximum length. Piped water, flush toilets, tables, barbecue pits and fire rings, fishing; propane, groceries, coin laundry within 5 miles.

Oceano

OCEANO COUNTY CAMPGROUND
In Oceano off US 101, opposite Oceano Memorial County Park on Airpark Dr (mailing address: SLO County Gov't Center, San Luis Obispo 93408).
(805) 781-5219.

$20. 24 tent and RV spaces. 24 EWS. Piped water, flush toilets, showers (fee), tables, fire pits, swimming, fishing; propane, groceries, coin laundry within 5 miles.

Ojai

CAMP COMFORT
2 miles southwest of Ojai on Creek Rd (mailing address: 800 S Victoria Ave, Ventura 93009).
(805) 654-3951.

$11. 43 tent or RV spaces, 34-ft RV maximum length, 16 E. Piped water, flush toilets, showers, fire rings, tables; playground; swimming within 1 mile; fishing, propane, groceries, coin laundry within 5 miles.

Pismo Beach

LE SAGE RIVIERA (Private)
1½ mile south of Pismo Beach at 319 SR 1, Grover Beach 93433.
(805) 489-5506.

$18-30 for 2 persons, $3 for extra person. Reservation deposit required; 3-day refund notice. 60 RV spaces, 60 EWS. 1 block to Pismo State Beach. Piped water, flush toilets, showers; coin laundry, groceries within ¼ mile.

PISMO COAST VILLAGE (Private) ⦿
165 S Dolliver St, Pismo Beach 93449.
(805) 773-1811.

$22-32 for up to 6 persons; extra person, $2. Reservation deposit required; 10-day cancellation notice; cancellation fee. 400 RV spaces. 400 EWS. No tents allowed. Many sites with shade trees. Piped water, flush toilets, showers, heated pool, cable TV hookups, miniature golf, beach, playground, recreation room, restaurant, propane, groceries, coin laundry.

PISMO DUNES STATE VEHICULAR RECREATION AREA
1 mile south of Grover Beach off SR 1 via beach (mailing address: 3220 S Higuera St #311, San Luis Obispo 93401).
(805) 473-7220.

$6. MISTIX. Vehicles will be required to drive on soft beach sand. Camping available for 1000 vehicles. Chemical toilets, swimming, fishing; propane, groceries, coin laundry within 2 miles.

PISMO STATE BEACH
In Pismo Beach, off SR 1 (mailing address: 3220 S Higuera St #311, San Luis Obispo 93401).
(805) 489-2684.

North Beach Campground *1 mile south of Pismo Beach off SR 1.*
$14. MISTIX. 100 tent or RV spaces, 36-foot RV maximum length. Piped water, flush toilets, disposal station, tables, fire rings, swimming, fishing; propane, groceries, coin laundry within 5 miles.

Oceano Campground *1 mile east of Grover City off SR 1.*
$14. MISTIX. 40 tent sites, 40 RV spaces, 31-foot RV maximum length (trailers 18 ft). 42 EW. Piped water, flush toilets, showers, tables, fire rings, swimming, fishing; propane, groceries, coin laundry within 5 miles.

Sand & Surf RV Park (Private)
2 miles south of Pismo Beach on SR 1 (mailing address: Hwy 1, Oceano 93445).
(805) 489-2384.

$16-24 for 2 persons; extra person, $3; extra vehicle, $2. Reservation deposit required; 3-day cancellation notice; cancellation fee. 2-night minimum stay summer weekends. Weekly and monthly rates available. Discount for children under age 17. 232 RV sites, 232 EWS. Many pull-through and some shaded sites. Piped water, flush and pit toilets, showers, phone hook-ups, coin laundry, propane. DS, MC, VI.

Point Mugu State Park

POINT MUGU STATE PARK
15 miles southeast of Oxnard off SR 1 (mailing address: 9000 Pacific Coast Hwy, Malibu 90265).
(818) 880-0350.

Sycamore Canyon *⁹⁄₁₀ mile off north side of SR 1.*
$14-16. MISTIX. 57 tent or RV spaces, 31-ft RV maximum length, sanitary disposal station. Piped water, flush toilets, showers, fire rings, tables, ocean swimming and fishing; groceries within 5 miles.

Thornhill Broome Beach *South side of SR 1.*
$7-9.75. MISTIX. 75 tent or RV spaces, 31-ft RV maximum length. Piped water, chemical toilets, fire rings, tables; ocean swimming and fishing; groceries within 5 miles.

San Luis Obispo

EL CHORRO REGIONAL PARK
5 miles north of San Luis Obispo on SR 1 (mailing address: SLO County Gov't Center, San Luis Obispo 93408).
(805) 781-5219.

$12. 45 tent or RV spaces. Piped water, flush toilets, showers (fee), tables, fire pits; groceries, coin laundry within 5 miles.

San Miguel

RIOS CALEDONIA ADOBE
½ mile south of San Miguel on Mission St (mailing address: SLO County Gov't Center, San Luis Obispo 93408).
(805) 781-5219.

$12. 8 tent or RV spaces. Piped water, flush toilets, tables, barbecues; propane and groceries within 5 miles.

Santa Margarita

SANTA MARGARITA KOA (Private)
1¾ miles southwest of Santa Margarita, 7 miles south on Pozo Rd at 4765 Santa Margarita Lake Rd, Santa Margarita 93453.
(805) 438-5618.

$25.95 for 2 persons; extra person, $2-3; extra charge for electric, water and sewer hookups. Reservation deposit required; 3-day cancellation notice. Weekly rates. 16 tent spaces, 46 RV spaces. 46 EW, 35 S. Electric heaters and air conditioners (fee). Piped water, flush toilets, tables, barbecues, showers; coin laundry, propane within 5 miles. 6 camping cabins, ¼ mile west of Santa Margarita Lake entrance, $30 for up to 2 persons. MC, VI.

Santa Maria

SANTA MARIA PINES CAMPGROUND (Private)
1 block west of US 101, exit Broadway; 2210 Preisker Ln, Santa Maria 93453.
(805) 928-9534.

$25.95 for 2 persons, $4 for each additional person. 43 tent or RV spaces (EWS). Flush toilets, swimming pool (May 15-Oct. 15), coin laundry. Pets $1, 3-day limit. MC, VI.

Santa Paula

STECKEL COUNTY PARK
4 miles north of Santa Paula off SR 150 (mailing address: SLO County Gov't Center, San Luis Obispo 93408).
(805) 654-3951.

$12. 75 tent or RV spaces, 50 E. Piped water, flush toilets, fire rings and barbecues, tables, playground; fishing within 5 miles; propane, groceries, coin laundry within 5 miles.

Simi Valley

OAK COUNTY PARK
Los Angeles Ave exit off SR 118, 1½ miles to Quimesa Dr (mailing address: SLO County Gov't Center, San Luis Obispo 93408).
(805) 654-3951.

$13. 41 tent or RV spaces, 16 E. Piped water, flush toilets, barbecues or fire rings, playground; propane, groceries, coin laundry within 5 miles.

Ventura

EMMA WOOD STATE BEACH
3 miles northwest of Ventura off US 101 on Pacific Coast Hwy (mailing address: 901 S San Pedro St, Ventura 93001).
(805) 654-4936.

$12. 61 tent or RV spaces, 40-ft RV maximum length. Non-piped water, chemical toilets, fire rings, ocean swimming and fishing; propane, groceries, coin laundry within 5 miles.

FARIA COUNTY PARK
7 miles northwest of Ventura off US 101 on Pacific Coast Hwy (mailing address: 800 S Victoria Ave, Ventura 93009).
(805) 654-3951.

$16. Reservations. 42 tent or RV spaces. Piped water, flush toilets, showers, fire rings, tables; playground within ½ mile; swimming and fishing within 1 mile; propane, groceries, coin laundry within 5 miles.

HOBSON PARK
9 miles northwest of Ventura off US 101 on Pacific Coast Hwy (mailing address: 800 S Victoria Ave, Ventura 93009).
(805) 654-3951.

$16. Reservations. 31 tent or RV spaces, 34-ft RV maximum length. Piped water, flush toilets, showers, fire rings, tables, playground, ocean swimming and fishing; propane, groceries, coin laundry within 5 miles.

RINCON PARKWAY
6 miles north of Ventura off US 101 on Pacific Coast Hwy (mailing address: 800 S Victoria Ave, Ventura 93009).
(805) 654-3951.

$11. 112 RV spaces. No water, chemical toilets, ocean swimming and fishing; propane, groceries, coin laundry within 5 miles.

MCGRATH STATE BEACH
3½ miles south of Ventura off US 101 via Harbor Blvd. (mailing address: 1933 Cliff Dr, Ste 27, Santa Barbara 93109).
(805) 654-4744.

$14-16. Entrance gate closes 8 pm Oct-May; 10 pm Jun-Sep. MISTIX. 174 tent or RV spaces, 34-ft RV maximum length. Piped water, flush toilets, showers, fire rings, tables, ocean swimming and fishing; propane, groceries, coin laundry within 5 miles.

VENTURA BEACH RV RESORT (Private) ⚋
Adjacent to US 101, northbound exit California St, right turn to Main St, left on Main St; 800 W Main St.
(805) 643-9137.

$16-26.95 for 4 persons; $3 per night for each additional person. 28-night maximum stay. Reservation deposit requested; cancellation fee. Many pull-through spaces. Walkway to beach. 144 RV spaces, 21 tent or RV spaces, 168 EW, 144 S. Cable TV hookups, flush toilets, disposal station, swimming pool, putting green, recreation room (adults only), coin laundry, groceries and propane. Pets, $1.

Tourist Information Sources

The chambers of commerce and visitors bureaus listed below are resources for obtaining additional information about the Central Coast. Auto Club district offices provide travel services, materials and highway information to AAA members.

Arroyo Grande Chamber of Commerce
800 W. Branch St., Ste. A
Arroyo Grande, CA 93420
(805) 489-1488

Atascadero Chamber of Commerce
6550 El Camino Real
Atascadero, CA 93422
(805) 466-2044

Camarillo Chamber of Commerce
632 Las Posas Rd.
Camarillo, CA 93010
(805) 484-4383

Cambria Chamber of Commerce
767 Main St.
Cambria, CA 93428
(805) 927-3624

Carpinteria Valley Chamber of
Commerce
5320 Carpinteria Ave.
Carpinteria, CA 93014
(805) 684-5479

Cayucos Chamber of Commerce
P.O. Box 503
Cayucos, CA 93430
(805) 995-1200

Conejo Valley Chamber of Commerce
(Thousand Oaks)
625 W. Hillcrest Dr.
Thousand Oaks, CA 91360
(805) 499-1993

Fillmore Chamber of Commerce
344 Central Ave.
Fillmore, CA 93015
(805) 524-0351

Goleta Valley Chamber of Commerce
5730 Hollister Ave.
Goleta, CA 93117
(805) 967-4618

Grover Beach Chamber of Commerce
177 S. 8th St.
Grover Beach, CA 93433
(805) 489-9091

Lompoc Valley Chamber of Commerce
111 S. I St.
Lompoc, CA 93436
(805) 736-4567

Los Osos-Baywood Park Chamber of
Commerce
781 Los Osos Valley Rd.
Los Osos, CA 93412
(805) 528-4884

Morro Bay Chamber of Commerce
895 Napa St., Ste. A-1
Morro Bay, CA 93442
(805) 772-4467

Nipomo Chamber of Commerce
257 W. Tefft St.
Nipomo, CA 93444
(805) 929-1583

Ojai Chamber of Commerce
338 E. Ojai Ave.
Ojai, CA 93023
(805) 646-8126

Oxnard Chamber of Commerce
Heritage Square
711 S. A St.
Oxnard, CA 93030
(805) 385-8860

Paso Robles Chamber of Commerce
1225 Park St.
Paso Robles, CA 93446
(805) 238-0506

Pismo Beach Chamber of Commerce
581 Dolliver St.
Pismo Beach, CA 93449
(805) 773-4382;
(800) 443-7778 in Calif.

Port Hueneme Recreation and
  Community Services
250 N. Ventura Rd.
Port Hueneme, CA 93041
(805) 986-6555

San Luis Obispo Chamber of
  Commerce
1039 Chorro St.
San Luis Obispo, CA 93401
(805) 781-2777

San Luis Obispo County Visitors &
  Conference Bureau
1041 Chorro St., Ste. E
San Luis Obispo, CA 93401
(805) 541-8000 or (800) 634-1414

San Simeon Chamber of Commerce
P.O. Box 1
San Simeon, CA 94583
(805) 927-3500

Santa Barbara Chamber of
  Commerce
504 State St.
Santa Barbara, CA 93102
(805) 965-3023

Santa Barbara Visitor Center
1 Santa Barbara St.
Santa Barbara, CA 93101
(805) 965-3021

Santa Maria Valley Chamber of
  Commerce
614 S. Broadway
Santa Maria, CA 93454
(805) 925-2403

Santa Paula Chamber of Commerce
Old Train Station
Santa Barbara and 10th sts.
Santa Paula, CA 93060
(805) 525-5561

Santa Ynez Chamber of Commerce
1095 Meadowvale Rd.
Santa Ynez, CA 93460
(805) 688-5318

Simi Valley Chamber of Commerce
40 W. Cochran St., Ste. 100
Simi Valley, CA 93065
(805) 526-3900

Solvang Information Center
1511-A Mission Dr.
Solvang, CA 93464
(805) 688-3317, 688-6144

Templeton Community Services
98 Main St., Ste. D
Templeton, CA 93465
(805) 434-4900

Thousand Oaks (see Conejo Valley
Chamber of Commerce)

Ventura Chamber of Commerce
785 S. Seaward Ave.
Ventura, CA 93001
(805) 648-2875

Ventura Visitors & Convention
  Bureau
89-C S. California St.
Ventura, CA 93001
(805) 648-2075

Automobile Club District Offices —Central Coast

Hours at these offices are Monday through Friday 9 a.m. to 5 p.m.

Lompoc
816 E. Ocean Ave.
Lompoc, CA 93436-7017
(805) 735-2731

San Luis Obispo
1445 Calle Joaquin
San Luis Obispo, CA 93405-7203
(805) 543-6454

Santa Barbara
3712 State St.
Santa Barbara, CA 93105-3135
(805) 682-5811

Santa Maria
2033-B S. Broadway
Santa Maria, CA 93454-7809
(805) 922-5731

Simi Valley
2837 Cochran St.
Simi Valley, CA 93065-2766
(805) 522-7330
(also open Sat. 9 a.m. to 1 p.m.)

Thousand Oaks
100 E. Wilbur Rd.
Thousand Oaks, CA 91360-5589
(805) 497-0911

Ventura County
1501 S. Victoria Ave.
Ventura, CA 93003-6583
(805) 644-7171

Automobile Club Services

Automobile Club of Southern
California district offices can help
members in preparing a trip to the
Central Coast by making reservations
for lodging and transportation and
by providing weather, routing and
emergency road service information.

Auto Club maps covering the Central
Coast, available free to members, are
the *Explore!* series, individually covering Ventura, Santa Barbara and San
Luis Obispo counties. *Simi and Conejo
Valleys* street map covers, among other
towns, Camarillo, Moorpark, Simi
Valley and Thousand Oaks, and *Cities
of Ventura County* covers, among other
towns, Fillmore, Ojai and Santa Paula.
Also available are *Cities of Santa Barbara
County* (covering Santa Barbara and
vicinity, Carpinteria, Santa Ynez
Valley, Lompoc and Santa Maria),
and *Cities of San Luis Obispo County*
(covering, among other towns, Arroyo
Grande, Cambria, Morro Bay, Pismo
Beach and San Luis Obispo).

Auto Club members can also take
advantage of AAA discounts on
lodging, as indicated in the *California/
Nevada TourBook*, available free to
members. The Auto Club's *Member
$aver* is a source for seasonal discounts
on events and points of interest for
Auto Club members.

Index

This index contains listings for points of interest and events.

Index to Advertisers

Acknowledgements

Writer...........................Norma E. Palmer

Cartographer ....Susan A. Lewis

Graphic Artist ....Virginia Matijevac

Cover Design..................Michael C. Lee

Editor...............................Kristine Miller

page 2: *San Luis Obispo County coastline*

page 3: *Mission San Miguel*

Photography by Todd Masinter, except as noted:

pages 30, 33 ....Automobile Club of Southern California Archives

page 36..............................Robert Brown

pages 43, 128 ....Norma E. Palmer

pages 154, 174 ....Hearst-San Simeon State Historical Park

page 198 ....Jeffrey Cords, Old Spanish Days Fiesta

page 205 ....Bernadette Di Pietro

Notes